MW01124688

Noticing

AN ESSENTIAL READER, 1973-2023

by Steve Sailer

Copyright © 2024 Steve Sailer

First published 2024 by Passage Publishing

All rights reserved. No part of this book may be used or reproduced in
any manner whatsoever without written permission from the publisher
except in the case of brief quotations embodied in critical articles, reviews,
or academic projects.

For information, contact support@passage.press

Limited Casebound ISBN: 978-1-959403-01-2
Trade Paperback ISBN: 978-1-959403-02-9

Passage Publishing
www.passage.press

Table of Contents

Chapter Five: Human Biodiversity

Chapter Six: The Level Playing Field

Chapter Seven: The Half-Full Glass

Chapter Eight: The Blank Screen

Chapter Nine: World War T

Chapter Ten: Sailer's Law of Female Journalism

Foreword

WHEN I try to trace the roots of my writing career noticing the congruence between daily life and the social sciences, I blame puberty. As a little boy, I'd always been good at remembering dates and data, such as historical events and baseball statistics. But suddenly at age 13, I also enjoyed logically reasoning about them.

Fortuitously, the 1972-73 subject for high school debate was:

> Resolved: That governmental financial support for all public and secondary education in the United States be provided exclusively by the federal government.

Localities differ widely in tax revenue, so a popular proposal then was to federalize public school funding in order to equalize it. But would that do students all that much good?

This was a timely topic because there had been an unexpected revolution in social science regarding school achievement over the previous half-dozen years. It began when Congress allocated the then-immense sum of one million dollars in the famous 1964 Civil Rights Act to scientifically vindicate the Blank Slate conventional wisdom of the era.

But when sociologist James S. Coleman, after surveying the performance of nearly 600,000 students, delivered the ambitious "Equality in Educational Opportunity" study, his answer was unexpected: that while school spending had some impact on student performance, far more important was whatever it is that students bring to school with them from home, whether socio-economic status, culture, values, work ethic, or (*sotto voce*) genes.

The Johnson administration was unenthused by the subversive Coleman Report, minimizing media coverage by releasing it on Saturday, July 2, 1966. But in 1967, Daniel Patrick Moynihan hosted an influential seminar at Harvard digging into Coleman's immense data set. As a Catholic schoolboy, I found Moynihan—data analyst, adviser to three presidents, political operator (a future four-term U.S. Senator from New York), wit, and open-minded man—a figure of considerable glamor.

It was a stimulating time in the human sciences, made possible in part by computers' growing ability to handle far more data. Even as academia as a whole lurched sharply leftward, new studies raised doubts about the postwar liberal social science consensus exemplified, ironically, by Ronald Reagan's character in the surprisingly highbrow 1951 kids' movie *Bedtime for Bonzo*. Reagan plays a progressive behavioral psychology professor engaged to the daughter of his elderly department chairman. That obsolete eugenicist is dismayed to discover that his prospective son-in-law's father is a conman. So Reagan decides to prove the old Galtonian's suspicion about his hereditary tendencies wrong by raising a chimpanzee as if it were a human child to prove that environment is everything and genetics nothing.

Then in 1969, Berkeley psychologist Arthur Jensen published a landmark article in the *Harvard Educational Review* on the troublesome white-black average IQ gap. Richard Nixon tasked the Democrat Moynihan, his chief domestic policy adviser, with keeping him up to date on the controversy, but also instructing him to leave the President's interest in this important field secret.

In 1971, B.F. Skinner's successor at Harvard, Richard Herrnstein, who had become bored with behaviorism, wrote his famous article "I.Q." for the *Atlantic Monthly*.

In 1972, as the high school debate season was getting going, one of the participants in the Moynihan seminar, future Harvard sociologist Christopher Jencks, published *Inequality: A Reassessment of the Effect of Family and Schooling in America*, his data-driven leftist take on the Coleman Report. Jencks concluded that equality of opportunity would do so little to reduce equality of result that what America needed instead was socialism.

In response, in March 1973, I wrote a letter that was published in *National Review*:

> Having read Ernest van den Haag's article on Christopher Jencks, I am reminded of an old psychiatry joke: A psychotic (egalitarian, in this little morality story) says, "All people are equal, and I'll fight anyone who says I'm wrong." A neurotic (Jencks) says, "People aren't equal, and I just can't stand it."

Today, having seen more of life, I'd be more sympathetic to Jencks' point of view. But it's hard to deny that this paragraph from fifty years ago adumbrated my life's work remarkably well. As David Foster Wallace observed, "Although of course you end up becoming yourself."

I've always tended to be a conservative realist, with a penchant for the satirical in the tradition of Jonathan Swift, Evelyn Waugh, and Tom Wolfe. Tory satirists tend to be at their best when the times are most progressive, such as Waugh in the 1930s. Looking back, I'd guess that my career has been as extended as it has been due to the relative sanity of the 1990s giving way to the craziness of the early 2020s. When I started out writing for money in the 1990s, I seemed to strike people as edgy but interesting. Today, I'm the unquotable Lord Voldemort.

The next time I did any writing for publication was as the rock critic for the Rice University student newspaper in 1978-1980. I managed to briefly be hip in Houston via a simple arbitrage opportunity: I'd go home to the San Fernando Valley, listen to *KROQ*, which tended to be a year ahead of the Houston radio stations, and then report in the *Rice Thresher* that, say, The Police were going to be big.

But I found myself homesick in Houston, so I went to UCLA for my MBA. I discovered that what I really liked doing, no surprise, was data analysis.

During the deep 1982 recession I found a job at a Chicago start-up that was revolutionizing marketing research by being the first to fully exploit the potential of the new laser beam checkout scanners. We operated history's most realistic test markets. Having bought scanners for all the grocery stores in a number of towns, we recruited thousands of volunteers to identify themselves to cashiers so their purchases could be recorded. We also talked our panelists into letting us manipulate which commercials they saw on their living room TVs so we could test whether doubling the client's advertising budget would pay off in higher sales in the supermarkets. (Usual result: No.)

In 1984, the vice-chairman bought himself a $9,000 IBM PC XT with a ten megabyte hard disk, but then realized he was too old to learn to type. So he gave it to me. I devoted 1986-88 to introducing the personal computer to our company.

Then I became the Chairman of the Board's VP of Strategy and worked on deals for him, including one in which real life Bond villain Robert Maxwell, the father of Jeffrey Epstein's paramour Ghislaine Maxwell, tried to cheat my boss out of a Dr. Evilesque "one...million dollars!"

Around 1990, I started a hobby of writing 750 word op-eds for newspapers. Back then, you could mail a column off to random newspapers, like the *Cleveland Plain Dealer* or the *Sacramento Bee* and if they liked it, they'd mail you a check for some amount between $50 and $150.

At that point, I considered whether I should make up a pseudonym like "Mark Twain." I thought about spelling "Sailer" backwards: "Relias," which sounded reliable, realistic, and also easy to prove that it was really me, like Vladimir Nabokov's inclusion of a character named Vivian Darkbloom in *Lolita* in case he published it anonymously. But on the other hand, how do you get the bank to cash a $75 check made out to the mysterious Mr. Relias? Nowadays, I could just look up how to do that on the Internet. But not in 1991. So, out of laziness, I went with my real name.

I wish I hadn't. But not for the obvious reason of too much adulation or approbation from random members of the public who recognize my name: having lived since 2000 back home in Los Angeles where they have real celebrities so absolutely nobody cares about Internet nanocelebrities like myself, I've enjoyed peaceful anonymity without a single person I've met at random in daily life ever having recognized my name.

Still, I'd advise against using your real name. Why? Let's just say life is long and it's hard to anticipate all the eventualities. So, pick out a plausible-sounding pseudonym and stick with it.

My role model as a statistics-driven opinion journalist was Daniel Seligman, who more or less invented blogging with his "Keeping Up" column in *Fortune*. Another influence was baseball analyst Bill James.

In 1994, after a few years of op-ed writing, I felt ready to move up to long magazine articles. I started with "Why Lesbians Aren't Gay," in which I pointed out all the differences between homosexual women and homosexual men and what we might learn from these patterns.

If I recall correctly, my first choice of magazine to publish it would have been *The Atlantic*, my favorite at the time, followed by the then-fashionable *New Republic*, edited by Andrew Sullivan, or the *New York Times Magazine*. But they didn't bite. Finally, the urbane John O'Sullivan of *National Review* wrote to say how much he liked it, which began a highly productive editor-writer relationship across three outlets.

In general, I didn't like freelancing, especially not the delay inherent in pitching ideas and waiting for a response from editors. My ideas tended to be so orthogonal that even good editors were often unable to wrap their heads around them. So, when I've found outlets that respect me, I tend to stick with them.

But I was still mostly dedicated to a corporate career, serving as my firm's internal consultant who could take on weird projects. In the mid-1990s, much like in the mid-1980s with the personal computer, my main obsession was promoting the use of the next big thing, the Internet.

In 1996 I had an opportunity to get rich quick off the nascent Internet Bubble. The chief operating officer was negotiating to leave the firm in Chicago to make his fortune in Silicon Valley. As part of his severance package he could take one employee with him and chose me. But he didn't have a business plan. So I told him: A/B testing. Do for webpages what we already do for TV commercials.

Not a bad idea and somebody I knew eventually came up with it on his own and started his own firm.

But just then...I started feeling worse and worse and so passed on this opportunity. On my 38th birthday in 1996, I was diagnosed with non-Hodgkin's lymphoma.

I hired a young general oncologist to serve as my consultant to help me choose among the three lymphatic cancer specialists in Chicago, something I advise everybody to try when they suddenly get a cancer diagnosis dropped on them. Fortunately, a clinical trial in the Chicago suburbs opened up for the world's first commercial monoclonal antibody, Rituxan. My advisor said: This is the one.

And, 26 years later, he appears to have been right.

It's not uncommon for dedicated employees to work through chemotherapy, but I'd advise against it. Instead, in 1997 I slept twelve hours a day, went for long walks, and fiddled with two big articles for *National Review*.

As a Chicago yuppie, I strolled by many hundreds of people daily, which allowed me, much like Francis Galton in Victorian times, to test my social theories by noticing people walking past. For instance, there were more white man-Asian woman couples on the sidewalk than there were Asian man-white woman couples. But for black-white couples, the sex pattern was reversed. And it was even more skewed for black-Asian couples. (I finally saw my first Asian man-black woman couple in 1999, at an office Christmas party. It probably didn't hurt that the Asian guy was 6'5".) This led to my first big article of this period, "Is Love Colorblind?"

Next followed "Track and Battlefield." The mainstream conventional wisdom was highly feminist in the years between the Clarence Thomas-Anita Hill sexual harassment brouhaha of 1991 and organized feminism's embarrassing rescue of Bill Clinton's presidency during the Paula Jones sexual harassment brouhaha of 1998. A poll before the 1996 Olympics found that a majority of the American public back then believed that performance differences between male and female athletes would fade away.

"Track & Battlefield" was my first article wholly made possible by the Internet. I downloaded all the running results in the Olympics and calculated the "gender gap" in male vs. female times. What leapt out from the data was that the celebrated rapid narrowing of the gender gap during the late Cold War had stopped due to stricter steroid testing after 1988.

The impact of steroids on sports statistics had become an interest of mine because a baseball agent friend had told me around 1994 that "Jose Canseco was the Typhoid Mary of steroids." You could track his influence around baseball by observing sudden changes in musculature and home run totals among his teammates. But few others seemed willing to see what was going on.

At the end of 1997, William F. Buckley asked Rich Lowry to replace John as editor of *National Review*. My relationship with *NR* remained fine into the 2000s, with me continuing to review a wide variety of books for them, such as Jared Diamond's *Guns, Germs, and Steel* and Henry Louis Gates' *Norton Anthology of African American Literature*.

O'Sullivan became the opinion editor of Toronto's *National Post* so I wrote columns for them despite knowing little about Canada other than that its culture was intensely Wayne Gretzkycentric.

In 1998 I coined (or so I imagined) a neologism to describe the focus of my interests: "human biodiversity." This is often assumed to be a euphemism for race, but a glance at "Track & Battlefield" shows that it includes, among much else, sex differences as well as the nurture role of synthetic steroids.

The term "biodiversity" had been popularized in the 1990s by biologist Edward O. Wilson's campaign to save the Amazon rain forests in order to preserve their countless varieties of insects. But I'd always been more interested in people than in bugs. I immediately looked up "human biodiversity" in a pre-Google search engine and found that anthropologist Jonathan Marks had published a book under that title in 1995.

In these early days of email before spam, I discovered that you could simply send a message to smart people, such as Dr. Marks, and often they would reply. So, in early 1999 I launched an ambitious private email group to discuss the topic of human biodiversity. Recruiting went extraordinarily well and I soon was running a highly active forum of many distinguished scientists and public intellectuals from whom I learned much.

Not surprisingly, as the Internet made it easier to pursue my intellectual interests, I was finding it harder to revive my interest in my corporate career after my chemotherapy sabbatical. So when John O'Sullivan offered me a full-time job as national correspondent for *United Press International* in 2000 to cover demographic trends, I jumped at it.

And John's friend Peter Brimelow hired me to write a column for his new *VDARE* webzine. My appreciation for this new income source led me to take a knuckle-headed stand on a point of personal loyalty. When I got back the proofs for a *National Review* book review, I noticed that they had edited out my tagline saying I was a columnist for *VDARE*. I objected and *demanded* it be put back. Rich Lowry called to say that he wasn't going to advertise *VDARE* in his magazine because of the bad things Peter was saying about it. I stuck to my guns and the piece wound up not running.

A number of people unfamiliar with the details of what happened have blamed this spat on Lowry, but it was all my fault. Rich was not only within his rights, but he was being reasonable and I was being unreasonable: this wasn't my fight.

The 2003 Iraq War exacerbated and made more permanent the various divides among conservative writers. While I supported a punitive raid against Afghanistan for harboring Al-Qaeda (but not the lengthy nation-building ordeal it turned into), I was always against America invading Iraq, which had had virtually nothing to do with 9/11. My early 2003 *American Conserva-*

FOREWORD

tive article "Cousin Marriage Conundrum" was a high point of this period in my career.

Meanwhile, over the course of the first decade of the 21st century, the limits of acceptable discourse ratcheted tighter.

One learning experience for me was the furious campaign organized by junk mail genius Morris Dees, co-founder of the Southern Poverty Law Center, and a few very high IQ male-to-female transgender academics to cancel anybody who had helped Northwestern U. psychology professor J. Michael Bailey promote his 2003 book *The Man Who Would Be Queen*. Bailey's crime was to spill the beans on what these highly masculine ex-men wanted to keep covered up: that while some male-to-female transgenders really are effeminate boys who always did feel like a girl on the inside, many of the most prominent were actually heterosexuals who had as youths developed an embarrassing fetish known as autogynephilia for dressing up in their mother's lingerie and masturbating in front of the mirror. I had interviewed Bailey about his book, so I was on their hit list.

The ex-men were clever and relentless in their attacks, and of course Dees' insight that somebody someday would make a lot of money off a transgender craze turned out exactly right. But sometimes a fundraising prodigy like Dees can get too far out ahead of his own time. Eventually, the whoop-tee-doo faded out without much attracting the public's attention (only to return in 2013).

But two other incidents suggested that intellectual freedom was falling out of fashion.

In 2005, the economist Larry Summers, former treasury secretary in the Clinton administration and current president of Harvard (in other words, about as well-connected of an insider as you can be) gave an insightful Pinkeresque speech at a conference on the intriguing question of why there are more men than women at the far right edge of various bell curves, such as in the Harvard mathematics department.

To Summers' evident surprise, numerous female academics took his scientific speculations very personally. For instance, MIT biologist Nancy Hopkins fled his heretical talk, explaining that if she had listened any further, "I would've either blacked out or thrown up."

At the time, Hopkins' statement struck me as awkward for her cause. I've always held to a boyish conception of science as working best as a fair fight, like a sport. But by 2005, our institutions had become feminized enough that

xii

Hopkins' admission was widely seen instead as a self-evident knock-out blow against Summers: he suggested theories that made a *woman* feel bad.

Trying to buy forgiveness and support, Summers allocated $50 million to Harvard's head-feminist-in-charge, history professor Drew Gilpin Faust (whose brilliant career hadn't been hurt by divorcing her first husband and marrying her department chairman, which might not seem like highly princi-pled feminist behavior, but nobody cares about principles). When Summers was forced out the next year over this brouhaha (and other scandals), Doctor Faust found herself with lots of friends who supported her successful bid to replace him. (Summers' career eventually rebounded because Barack Obama, whose 150,000 word memoir displays only part of a single sentence devot-ed to endorsing feminism, didn't care about feminists' complaints and made Larry his adviser.)

In 2007, the octogenarian James D. Watson, the co-discoverer of the structure of DNA in 1953 and likely America's most famous man of science, was quoted as noting that he was "inherently gloomy about the prospect of Africa" because "social policies are based on the fact that their intelligence is the same as ours—whereas all the testing says not really."

After such knowledge, what forgiveness?

For the old man, none. Years later, the press periodically announces with glee some new humiliation piled upon the ancient Watson for his blasphemy.

But then the initial years of the first Obama Administration seemed to represent a bit of a lull in the war on science. In my 2008 book on Obama, I had predicted that his first term would be fairly cautious and moderate on racial issues in order to ensure his re-election. And indeed, Obama ran again mostly on popular issues like health insurance and killing Osama. (There were, however, hints in 2012 of the identity politics storm to come, such as Trayvon Martin and the *Life of Julia* campaign ad.)

By early 2013, I was picking up signals that America had entered a new era, one that internet commenter Spotted Toad later named the Great Awokening.

Why did the Great Awokening arrive around 2013?

My best guess is that it could have happened earlier if Obama hadn't slowed the government-media-academia-volunteer auxiliary thought police juggernaut to avoid alerting their intended victims before his re-election. For the self-interested beneficiaries of the Great Awokening, there is simply too much money, sinecures, and attention at stake to restrain themselves for long.

In an age in which your intended prey aren't supposed to hear the facts, how can you resist exploiting them?

Granted, it had long been widely hoped by not unintelligent people that we could slide by without free discussion. Perhaps elites, such as Nixon in 1969 covertly delegating Moynihan to keep him current on developments in IQ research, could quietly maintain the realism about humanity needed to keep the wheels from coming off while simultaneously silencing mention of awkward realities. But what goes unsaid tends to become unthought, and eventually unthinkable.

The Summers and Watson affairs showed that even hyper-elites could be purged for telling unwelcome truths. For the preservation of your career, it was best to become a true believer lest you inadvertently let loose your awareness of reality. What *1984* calls "crimestop," a.k.a. "protective stupidity," became increasingly a career necessity.

Ironically, the clampdown probably helped my career. Looking back over the last decade, the Great Awokening has been bad for America but it has certainly been good for my relevance.

Noticing works as well as it does relative to the competition not because I've invented revolutionary empirical techniques for understanding the world as it is, nor because I am terribly smart, but because I reject the growing bigotry of the 21st century.

The ascendant theory of intersectionality asserts a hierarchy of human value, a division of the world into the Good and the Bad, the Worthy and the Unworthy based on membership in certain categories assumed to have suffered present, past, or ancestral victimization. The current conventional wisdom therefore divides humanity up into (often hereditary) gradations of moral worth that might have struck a Bronze Age Aryan conqueror off the steppe as a little much.

For example, fat women qualify as worthy of society's concern due to discrimination by men against them. Therefore, the culture's beauty standards must be overturned.

In contrast, short men are of no concern despite the discrimination they experience from women. It never occurs to the dominant *zeitgeist* to worry about the widespread bias among women against short men, much less to campaign against this unthinking discrimination.

Why not? Well, as Stalin liked to say, what matters in politics is "Who? Whom?" (Insert your own transitive verb between the pronouns.) Women, by definition, rank among Good and men likewise are Bad, so the fact that some of the Bad suffer from the height prejudice of the Good is of no concern.

Why are you even interested in this? Are you...*short*?

The theory of intersectionality was originally devised to raise black women up above both black men and white women on the pyramid of victimization and thus of compensatory privilege. In statistical reality, of course, black women tend to do better than black men on numerous measures, such as crime, educational attainment, and white collar employment. But who cares about reality? The point of today's worldview is to establish an inegalitarian hierarchy of moral worth in which some humans (e.g., blacks, women, black women especially, and so forth) are more worthy than some others (most obviously, white men). Those defined as less worthy must pay in terms of reparations, lost jobs, and the like.

But even white men can escape some of the opprobrium inherent in white maleness by declaring their allegiance to some additional privileged identity such as homosexuality.

And of course, political views play a role. Justice Clarence Thomas could start wearing a frock and demanding to be known as Clarissa Thomas, but without changing his mind on abortion, he will always be a Bad Guy.

Conversely, President Biden may be the Platonic exemplification of the overly confident mediocre white man, but, at least through the 2024 election, he's above reproach.

The rules of the moral worth game are clear (the fewer tokens of Good identity you can lay claim to, the lower your humanity). Therefore, the Great Awokening largely consists of hate driven by greed, justified on the grounds that historic turnabout is fair play.

But who exactly is on top of the ziggurat of superiority is left conveniently vague. Social entrepreneurs are free to promote their identities as most deserving.

Thus, over the decade of the Great Awokening, we've seen much tumult within the hierarchy, with, for instance, women briefly on top during #MeToo. But then white women were soon demoted to the despised status of Karens. Lesbians were riding high during the gay marriage era, but have since seen their stock plummet during the transgender craze. After George Floyd's demise, blacks made a historic assertion of their supremacy (such as winning reverential capitalization of the word "Black"). But the immediate surge in black bad behavior, as seen in the homicide and car crash statistics, seems to have inclined the Biden Administration to no longer push the pedal to the metal on race quite as hard, at least until after the 2024 election.

In contrast to the new inegalitarianism, I believe in the equality of the moral worth of all individual humans to be the subject of empirical analysis. In my ethical system, everybody counts and thus everybody is fit to be counted.

That's not a popular attitude, to say the least.

When it comes to data analysis, the contemporary rules are also plain to see. You are encouraged to notice some disparities but not others.

For example, over the decades, I have read hundreds of local news articles exposing the shocking revelation that there exists a racial disparity in test scores in the local school district, which can only be due to racism, and something must be done about it, usually involving experts saying to give more money to racial activists.

On the other hand, I've never read an article, other than the ones I've written myself, pointing out that the Stanford researchers who keep track of test scores in each of the several thousand school districts in the country have never found a single one where blacks outscore whites. That's not the right kind of noticing. It raises awkward questions about what's really going on.

This is not to say that beside that Big Picture fact, there aren't also interesting novel lessons to be learned from the Stanford database. For example, I love to sort data and look at the highs and lows, what many would deride as outliers.

For instance, it turns out that the biggest white-black gaps are found in famously liberal school districts such as Berkeley. In part, this is because white liberals really are pretty smart. But the numbers also suggest that progressive methods of education tend to be particularly ill-suited for blacks. Meanwhile the highest black test scores and smallest white-black disparity are found in the Republican-voting, sports-crazed, fast growing exurb of Frisco, north of Dallas.

This would appear to suggest avenues for future research into helping blacks achieve more. Perhaps schools where a large proportion of the teachers are assistant football coaches tend to elicit better performance from black students than schools where teachers tend to be highly progressive? After all, black males do a lot better in football than in many other fields. Perhaps football culture, such as being yelled at when they do wrong, is better for blacks on average than is grievance culture?

But it's hard to think up these kind of potentially constructive approaches under the current mindset in which the only permissible response to pattern recognition is to blame the predefined Bad Guys: straight white men.

Not surprisingly, American intellectual culture has tended to get dumber and duller under the reigning rules.

I hope you find my anthology a refreshing contrast.

Steve Sailer
August 2023

CHAPTER ONE

Citizenism

Americans First

The American Conservative
February 13, 2006

AMERICANS are idealists. This is both one of our glories and curses because it makes us particularly vulnerable to manipulation by self-interested word-spinners. Nowhere is this more evident than in the immigration debate, where the restrictionists have most of the facts and logic on their side, but the beneficiaries of the current system have succeeded in blocking reform largely by defining themselves as the holders of the ethical high ground.

If you want to win at American politics, you need a moral theory. Fortunately, there is a concept that is both more practical and more attractive to American idealism than either liberal "multiculturalism" or neoconservative "propositionism." I call it "citizenism" because it affirms that true patriots and idealists are willing to make sacrifices for the overall good of their fellow American citizens rather than for the advantage of either six billion foreigners or of the special interests within our own country. The notion is sensible, its appeal broad. Yet it has seldom been explicitly articulated.

Polls consistently show that the public is outraged by illegal immigration and uneasy about the high rate of legal immigration. For example, in a *CBS News* poll last October, 75 percent said the government was "not doing enough" to keep out illegal aliens, while 15 percent were satisfied and merely 4 percent thought efforts were too restrictive.

Yet legislative action has been limited to the middle of each decade, when Congress passes immigration "reforms" that ultimately do nothing. The 1986 compromise—an amnesty for current illegal aliens combined with sanctions on lawbreaking employers to prevent future illegal immigration—looked fair on paper, but enforcement quickly evaporated as firms complained to their congressmen. Similarly, the damp squib of 1996 legislation did nothing significant to slow the influx. Now, 2006 may well bring more of the same unless we publicize a counter-philosophy that our laws should be biased toward our own citizenry.

In our supposedly democratic system, the will of the people on immigration has been consistently thwarted because America's elites on both the Left and Right like the current lack of enforcement. A 2002 poll by the Chicago Council on Foreign Relations found that 60 percent of Americans consider the present level of entry to be a "critical threat to the vital interests of the United States," compared with only 14 percent of prominent Americans. Immigration provides corporations with cheap workers, the upper middle class with off-the-books servants, Democratic political machines with votes, and ethnic activists with careers.

How do they keep winning? The articulate and affluent who profit from illegal immigration look down their noses at anyone who wants to reduce it. They don't debate dissenters; they dismiss them. Their most effective ploy has been to insinuate that only shallow people think deeply about immigration. The more profound sort of intellect, the fashionable imply, displays an insouciant heedlessness about the long-term impact of immigration.

Yet the well-educated and well-to-do aren't expected to subject their own children to the realities of living among the diverse. They search out homes removed by distance or doormen from concentrations of illegal aliens—although not so far that the immigrants can't come and clean their houses tax-free. As our Ascendancy of the Sensitive see it, that their views are utterly contradicted by how they order their daily lives is proof not of their hypocrisy but of how elevated their thinking is.

This doesn't mean that the white elites view minorities as their equals. Far from it. Instead, they can't conceive of them as competition. Nobody from Chiapas is going to take my job. Status competition in the upper reaches of American life still largely consists of whites trying to claw their way to the top over other whites, who, as an example, make up 99 percent of the Fortune 500 CEOs.

4

That's why the media treats the outsourcing of hundreds of thousands of white-collar jobs to English-speaking, high-IQ Indians as a respectable cause for alarm, but not the insourcing of tens of millions of immigrants to perform blue-collar and servile jobs.

Immigration policy, by its very nature, is about discriminating, about selecting whom we should admit and whom we should keep out. It is one of the fundamental responsibilities of our elected representatives because if they don't decide, inevitably some private interest is going to decide who gets in.

Of the five billion foreigners who live in countries with average per capita GDPs lower than Mexico's, how many would like to move to a First World country? The Mexican government recently estimated that one-sixth of all Mexicans now live in the United States, and a poll by the Pew Hispanic Center found that over 40 percent of the 106 million Mexicans left in Mexico wish to follow them here. Without government limits on immigration, the population of America would balloon by hundreds of millions, plateauing only when life here became as miserable as in the Third World.

With countless millions hoping to immigrate to America, our policy could be to choose those applicants whose arrival would most benefit existing citizens. One imperfect but obvious way would be to estimate how much more immigrants are likely to pay in taxes than they cost in government spending. A 1997 National Academy of Sciences study found that immigrants with less than a high-school education each cost the taxpayers $90,000 net over their lifetimes and high-school graduates cost $30,000. But immigrants with a college degree or more brought a net benefit to the Treasury of $100,000.

Yet for a couple of decades, the government has been handing out 50,000 green cards annually via its Diversity Visa Lottery, for which it receives up to 10 million applications, and those are just from countries not represented among the top 15 sources of immigrants. You might think this would be a great opportunity to skim the cream off the top. Yet the federal government simply accepts applicants at random, because choosing would be discriminatory.

Of course, our elites aren't against being personally selected themselves for higher-status positions. Indeed, they compete fiercely to have their children admitted to the most exclusive schools. In the bestselling novel *The Nanny Diaries*, the wealthy Manhattan mother hires a developmental consultant to evaluate nanny's prepping of four-year-old Grayer for the grueling preschool application process. The expert grills the servant with questions such as, "How many bilingual meals are you serving him a week? ... And you are attending the Guggenheim on what basis?" Shocked to learn that nanny is letting little Grayer do the kinds of things four-year-olds like to do, the consultant concludes, "I have to question whether you're leveraging your assets to escalate Grayer's performance."

What is left out of the novel might be even funnier: all toddlers aiming for prestigious private nursery schools in New York City must take the 60-75 minute Wechsler IQ test administered by the Educational Records Bureau for $375. Yet their private obsession with their children's IQ hasn't stopped the Manhattan media mafia, ever since the *Bell Curve* brouhaha, from publicly denouncing IQ testing as a racist and discredited concept.

The typical white intellectual considers himself superior to ordinary white folks for two contradictory reasons. First, he constantly proclaims his belief in human equality, but they don't. Second, he has a high IQ, but they don't.

This anti-discrimination ideology does not mean liberals refrain from discriminating among people in private, which would be impossible. Instead, it simply implies that to discuss in public how the choices among individuals should be made and what their consequences might be would be in the worst possible taste.

Decisions over what Stalin aptly described as the key questions of "Who? Whom?" continue to be made, of course, but by special interests in private. Owners of large farms and slaughterhouses, for instance, continue to recruit illegal aliens, recent immigrants bring over in-laws under "family reunification" rules, and foreigners decide for themselves to sneak into America. The outcome is an extreme degree of discrimination in favor of vested interests.

Neoconservatives have long claimed to dissent from this reigning multiculturalist orthodoxy by advocating a philosophy of immigration that observers have dubbed propositionism. The neocons argue that immigrants should be admitted based on their current—or eventual—assent to the propositions underlying the United States government, such as "All men are created equal." But the neocons have failed to answer numerous questions about how their philosophy would work.

If American values are rare, do we really want to deplete the rest of the world of the few people who agree with us? In many Third World countries, a "brain drain" saps medical care and economic progress. Do we want to be also responsible for "proposition attrition?"

On the other hand, what if agreement with American propositions is as common as the neoconservatives have claimed in trying to justify our Mesopotamian misadventure? President Bush has asserted that most Iraqis share our fundamental political values. If that's true of the furious Iraqis, who are notorious even among other Arabs for self-destructive lunacy, then how many billions of other foreigners qualify to move to America? How then does propositionism help us choose among the hundreds of millions who want to immigrate?

And exactly whom would the propositionists keep out, other than the most fanatical Muslim fundamentalists? With the exception of a handful of refugee dissidents, the vast majority of immigrants to America are in it for the money and are willing to mouth whatever platitudes would be required to get in.

Finally, there's an insidiously Jacobin implication to propositionism. If believing in neoconservative theories should make anyone in the world eligible for immigration, what should disbelieving in them make thought criminals like you and me? Candidates for deportation? For the guillotine?

Ultimately, propositionism seems less like a well thought-through philosophy and more like ethnocentric nostalgia, an intellectualized exercise in ancestor-worship. Emotionally, the neocons abhor asking tough questions about today's immigrants because they see that as the equivalent of asking tough questions about their own Ellis Island immigrant forebears and, thus, about themselves.

Fortunately, in America, citizenship is not an ideological category but a legal one. And emphasizing citizenship offers us a functional, yet idealistic, alternative to the special-interest abuses of multiculturalism and the incoherence of propositionism. Citizenism calls upon Americans to favor the welfare, even at some cost to ourselves, of our current fellow citizens over that of foreigners and internal factions.

Nor does citizenism suffer the fatal paradox dooming the white nationalism advocated by Jared Taylor and others who encourage whites to get down and mud-wrestle with the Al Sharptons of the world for control of the racial spoils system. Unfortunately for Taylor's movement, white Americans don't want, as he recommends, to act like the rest of the world; they want to act like white Americans. They believe on the whole in individualism rather than tribalism, national patriotism rather than ethnic loyalty, meritocracy rather than nepotism, nuclear families rather than extended clans, law and fair play rather than privilege, corporations of strangers rather than mafias of relatives, and true love rather than the arranged marriages necessary to keep ethnic categories clear-cut.

Citizenism is patriotism understood not as shouting that America is the best but as wanting the best for Americans.

The pride of Americans in their country is being exploited by those promoting mass immigration, who tell us that having our country fill up with foreigners proves we're the most desirable place to live. In daily life, though, we recognize that the most prestigious places, such as Harvard, are not the most crowded but the ones with the longest lines trying to get in. For instance, the Augusta National Golf Club reaffirmed its status as the top country club by forcing Bill Gates, the nation's richest man, to cool his heels on its waiting list for quite a few years before finally admitting him.

It's important to note that citizenism applies to present citizens, "to ourselves and our Posterity" as the Preamble to the Constitution says. In this, the demands of citizenism are analogous to the fiduciary duty of corporate managers.

When I was getting an MBA many years ago, I was the favorite of an acerbic old finance professor because he could count on me to blurt out all the stupid misconceptions to which overconfident students are prone. One day he asked the class: "If you were running a publicly traded company, would it be acceptable for you to create new stock and sell it for less than it was worth?"

"Sure," I smugly announced. "Our legal duty is to maximize our stockholders' wealth. While selling the stock for less than it's worth would harm our present shareholders, it would benefit our new shareholders who buy the underpriced stock, so it all comes out in the wash. Right?"

"Wrong!" he thundered. "Your obligation is to your current shareholders, not to somebody who might buy the stock in the future."

That same logic applies to the valuable right to live in America. Just as the managers of a public company have a responsibility to the existing stockholders not to diminish the value of their shares by selling new ones too cheaply to outsiders, our politicians have a moral obligation to the current citizens and their descendents to preserve the scarcity value of their right to live in America.

The American people's traditional patrimony of relatively high wages and low land prices, the legacy of a lightly populated landscape, has made this a blessedly middle-class country. Uncontrolled immigration, however, by driving up the supply of labor and the demand for housing is importing

Latin American levels of inequality into immigrant-inundated states such as California.

Unskilled illegal immigrants pound down the wages of those of our fellow American citizens least able to afford the competition. For example, the wages of slaughterhouse workers today are barely half what they were two decades ago, even without adjusting for inflation. By cutting pay for the worst jobs, illegal immigrants have made honest work less appealing to many citizens, especially young African-American males, too many of whom have dropped out of the workforce and into the lumpenproletariat world of crime. That's bad for both black Americans and for our country as a whole.

One subtle advantage of citizenism is there would be less need for the politically correct censorship to "celebrate diversity," which has become such a blight on free speech in America. We would no longer feel so obliged to browbeat each other into claiming that other citizens are exactly the same in their behavior as we are. That constant lying becomes morally irrelevant because under citizenism, the duty toward solidarity means that the old saying "he's a son of a bitch but he's our son of a bitch" turns into a moral precept.

Benjamin Franklin's American Dream

Chronicles
January 2015

TODAY'S preferred way to think about immigration and the nation-state is exemplified by the title of a 1964 pamphlet that the
Anti-Defamation League published posthumously under the name
of John F. Kennedy: *A Nation of Immigrants*. The next year, for instance, the
martyred President's brother Teddy had his name put on the 1965 Immigration Act of such large and unforeseen consequence.

The pages of JFK's little book are seldom read anymore, but its mantra of
a title has proven wildly successful at sacralizing mass immigration as some
kind of hereditary national onus. "My fellow Americans, we are and always
will be a nation of immigrants.... That's the tradition we must uphold. That's
the legacy we must leave for those who are yet to come," orated President
Barack Obama as justification for his November 2014 demand that, when
it comes to immigration, America must have a government of men and not
of laws.

While the Preamble states that the Constitution is ordained so that "We
the People of the United States" can "secure the blessings of liberty to ourselves
and our posterity," the conception of posterity has vanished from respectable
immigration discourse. The Obama amnesty invokes a civil right to be here
that illegal aliens inherit: not from their ancestors, though, but from their
anchor baby children. Like insanity, amnesty is hereditary; you get it from
your children. After all, we live in an age of globalism and minoritarianism:

the 300 million American citizens are the majority, while the seven billion foreigners are the minority.

But, as you see, this slogan of a Nation of Immigrants has not proven terribly productive intellectually, encouraging schmaltzy ancestor worship rather than unsentimental scholarship. For example, when it was revealed in the press last year that Dr. Jason Richwine had earned his Harvard Ph.D. by quantitatively analyzing the achievements of Hispanics over multiple generations, finding that today's illegal alien "Dreamers" and their children were unlikely to live up to the fond hopes so casually invested in them, Richwine was immediately shoved out of his job at a conservative think tank.

In sharp contrast to this dead end for scholarship, Benjamin Franklin's 1751 pamphlet arguing the logic of immigration restrictions, *Observations Concerning the Increase of Mankind*, was influential upon the central avenue of Anglo-American thought in the human sciences. While lacking a high concept title like *A Nation of Immigrants*, Franklin's *Observations* laid some of the groundwork for Charles Darwin's *The Origin of Species* more than a century later.

Franklin had retired in 1748 from his printing business to concentrate upon natural philosophy. Most famously, he worked out the basic physics of electricity, which helped him invent the lightning rod, a fire safety boon that made him world famous. William F. von Valtier writes:

> Franklin virtually singlehandedly placed America on the scientific map.... While his seminal contributions to electrical science are now widely known and extensively chronicled, it is little known that during the same very productive hemi-decade, 1747-1752, Franklin also pursued a parallel interest in the equally new science of population statistics, then called "political arithmetick."

Franklin's densely argued *Observations* offered a workable strategy for America's future. These 24 numbered paragraphs were the cogent cornerstone of Franklin's audacious scientific-strategic theory for the peopling of America, an interlocking series of arguments about how the world would work. Sociologist Dennis Hodgson observes that in *Observations*, "Policy did not flow from theory, theory flowed from policy." But the policy Franklin advocated was so fruitful over the next two centuries that the theory deserves respect.

Hodgson explains Ben Franklin's American Dream:

> Living in the mid-eighteenth century, [Franklin] had a vision of a middle-class society that was necessarily one in which the majority owned and worked their own lands.... His dream was of a prosperous and middle-class America, peopled largely by the English, that spanned a continent and confidently assumed a preeminent place among nations.

In 1964, four decades after mass immigration had been shut down, the nation looked rather like like how Franklin had imagined. Perhaps unsurprisingly, though, the mechanisms Franklin had identified as crucial to American happiness have since been increasingly forgotten during the Nation of Immigrants nostalgia fest.

This Founding Father's insights on population and immigration are so out of fashion as to make his entire perspective almost incomprehensible to mainstream minds. For example, in his bestselling 2003 biography *Benjamin Franklin: An American Life*, the intelligent establishmentarian Walter Isaacson (the authorized biographer of Steve Jobs), issues a few baffled apologies for this epoch-making essay, then quickly moves on to more congenial matters.

Franklin can be a hard figure for 21st Century Americans to appreciate because we like victims and comeback kids, but he always won. And he usually tried to win in the easiest, least traumatic fashion possible because he had something else to win at tomorrow. He was the greatest team player of his age. His allegiances flowed outward in roughly concentric circles, running from his huge extended family (he had 16 siblings), to his adopted city of Philadelphia, to Pennsylvania, America, the British Empire, the West, and the world.

Franklin did not possess the leapfrogging loyalties of a modern liberal. For instance, he became an active abolitionist, but not until after he'd returned from France in his eighties as the diplomatic architect of victory in the War of Independence. He had argued against slavery in *Observations*, but from the standpoint of the opportunity cost to his people, the English. Today, as the beneficiaries of Franklin's grand strategy, we are shocked, shocked by his English chauvinism:

> I could wish their numbers were increased.... But perhaps I am partial to the complexion of my country, for such kind of partiality is natural to mankind.

No doubt, if Franklin, a master publicist, were writing today, he'd play the victim card harder to appeal to current prejudices. In his own day, he didn't see much reason to apologize for wanting his own people to thrive.

Franklin became interested in immigration reduction due to two abuses that may seem familiar today. First, the British government was dumping convicts on the colonies, and these poor quality immigrants raised the crime rate.

The institutional background of the second is more abstruse, but the injustice Franklin perceived is even more familiar at the moment. Just as the current government is attempting to elect a new people, so too were Franklin's political adversaries. By 1751, the Province of Pennsylvania had become an uneasy hybrid of ownership by the absentee landlords resident in England (the heirs of William Penn) and middle class self-government. The hereditary proprietors attempted to tip the balance against Franklin's local rule party by recruiting immigrants in Germany, who upon arrival in Pennsylvania voted as a bloc for the owners.

Franklin found this unfair. He set out to prove to His Majesty's Government in Westminster that it was in their interest to let the English masses populate America without outside assistance. He pointed out that the population of the American colonies was already doubling about every quarter of a century, largely by natural increase. This first-ever estimate of American population growth provided an uncanny forecast, remaining accurate up through the closing of the frontier in 1890.

It also caused a sensation among European intellectuals, who feared a withering away of humans on their own crowded continent. Britain, for instance, had grown only ten percent from 1651 to 1751. As Franklin noted of Europe, the workings of supply and demand suggested that:

> In countries full settled ... all lands being occupied and improved to the height: those who cannot get land must labor for others that have it; when laborers are plenty, their wages will be low; by low wages a family is supported with difficulty; this difficulty deters many from marriage, who therefore long continue servants and single.

On the other hand, lightly populated America was more favorable for human happiness:

> Land being thus plenty in America, and so cheap as that a laboring man that understands husbandry can in a short time save money

enough to purchase a piece of new land sufficient for a plantation whereon he may subsist a family; such are not afraid to marry.... Hence, marriages in America are more general, and more generally early, than in Europe.

The American population explosion documented by Franklin inspired novel notions about competition over resources among British theorists, most notably economist Thomas Malthus and naturalist Charles Darwin (whose father and grandfather had been friends of Franklin).

A half century later, Franklin's growth estimate inspired Malthus's famously gloomy conclusion that population naturally grows to the limits of the land (of course, Malthus published this just as technological progress was making the Malthusian ceiling less ironclad).

Interestingly, Franklin may have had a better grasp than Malthus that Europeans had already long been doing what Malthus would hector them to try: avoid the looming Malthusian trap by delaying or forgoing marriage and children when their prospects were poor. In this manner, England had avoided mass famine for centuries. Franklin began *Observations* in his glass-is-half-full manner: "When families can be easily supported, more persons marry, and earlier in life."

Decades later, Charles Darwin read Malthus's book and was inspired to generalize this "struggle for existence" to all species. In the copy of Malthus's *Essay* in Darwin's personal library, the scientist has underlined the economist's quote from Franklin's Observations:

> There is in short, no bound to the prolific nature of plants or animals, but what is made by their crowding and interfering with each other's means of subsistence. Was the face of the earth vacant ... of other inhabitants, it might in a few ages be replenish'd from one nation only; as, for instance, with Englishmen.

In *The Descent of Man*, Darwin cites America's 25-year period for doubling, and notes:

> The primary or fundamental check to the continued increase of man is the difficulty of gaining subsistence, and of living in comfort. We may infer that this is the case from what we see, for instance, in the United States, where subsistence is easy, and there is plenty of room.

Anticipating the famous logic of Malthus and Darwin, Franklin had hypothesized that eventually:

> The importation of foreigners into a country that has as many inhabitants as the present employments and provisions for subsistence will bear will be in the end no increase of people;... Nor is it necessary to bring in foreigners to fill up any occasional vacancy in a country; for such vacancy ... will soon be filled by natural generation.

Due to immense increases in productivity, we no longer live in a Malthusian era when population growth in a settled country threatens imminent famine. Yet, Franklin's logic that affordability of family formation depends upon the ratio of wages to land prices is still seen today. To be middle class, Americans need to be able to afford a home with a yard in a decent school district. (And, more and more, only the middle class and above marry.) It doesn't sound like too much to ask, but it increasingly is. This is most egregiously noticeable in the state that once was the promised land of the average American, California, but now has the highest percentage of immigrants. Although California's total population grew from 1990 to 2010 by over eight million, the number of non-Hispanic whites fell by two million.

But Franklin's science was less dismal than Malthus's because he looked westward across the Appalachians to a continent only thinly populated with hunters and voyageurs, hopefully exclaiming:

> So vast is the Territory of North America that it will require many ages to settle it fully; and till it is fully settled, labour will never be cheap here....

The problem, though, was that the French claimed the great Ohio river valley and had access to it via the Mississippi and St. Lawrence rivers. With peace reigning, Franklin could only tactfully plead for some sort of diplomatic coup:

> How important an affair then to Britain is the present treaty for settling the bounds between her colonies and the French, and how careful should she be to secure room enough, since on the room depends so much the increase of her people?

In an era when skepticism about immigration is heresy, Franklin's 1751 objections are often excused because, as time went on, he less insistently pointed out the long-term rationale of restrictionism. But there's a disturbing reason for this trend. Franklin's opposition to inviting the world lessened as the opportunities for invading the world increased. Who needs immigration limits when you have military conquest?

In mid-1754, a Virginia militia unit under the command of the 22-year-old George Washington ambushed a French contingent near the headwaters of the Ohio. Eventually, this French and Indian War in North America became the Seven Years War in Europe, Asia, and Africa: a World War Zero that determined that the global language of the 21st Century would be English rather than French.

Late in 1754, Franklin wrote a pamphlet, *A Plan for Settling Two Western Colonies*, beginning:

> Our people, being confined to the country between the sea and the mountains, cannot much more increase in number; people increasing in proportion to their room and means of subsistence.

He called for a demographic surge into French-controlled territory, including building a town where Cleveland now stands.

In 1759 British troops made Franklin's plans militarily possibly by conquering the walled city of Quebec guarding the St. Lawrence river. When a British pundit then suggested trading cold Canada back to the French for a rich Caribbean sugar island, Franklin published his *Canada Pamphlet* (with *Observations* appended for scientific justification). He argued that if the French regained the St. Lawrence, which empties the Great Lakes, they and their Indian allies could plague the Midwest and prevent its settlement, even though the Midwest could ultimately nourish "a hundred millions of souls."

Franklin seemed to assume that whichever country ruled the Midwest would eventually rule the world. But the Midwest was also crucial in consolidating the middle class America of Franklin's plans. Sounding like Dave Brat defeating House majority leader Eric Cantor, Franklin accused those wanting to trade Canada back to the French of being oligarchs hoping to profit from cheap labor and expensive lands in America:

> You want to have the people confined within your present limits, that in a few years the lands you are possessed of may increase tenfold in value! You want to reduce the price of labor by increasing numbers on the same territory....

The 1763 peace treaty was satisfactory to Franklin. Britain kept Canada, took control of the Midwest east of the Mississippi, and saw the less formidable Spanish acquire New Orleans from the French. But His Majesty's Government displeased colonists with its Proclamation of 1763 slowing settlement of the booty, and by insisting upon taxing Americans to pay for the war.

This all eventually led to Franklin's stupendous career in his seventies as his new nation-state's foremost ambassador. He somehow talked the French dynasty into bankrupting itself to win independence for America. He then struck a peace treaty with Britain, acquiring that vast trans-Appalachian territories that he had long lusted after in return for not much more than a no-hard-feelings attitude on the part of the Americans.

In 2014, though, the elder Franklin's political arithmetick seems less relevant: America hasn't conquered any new territory in a long time. Granted, the spread of automobiles in the middle of the 20th Century opened up new suburban lands for settlement within the United States, keeping housing affordable for awhile. But there's no new technological leap forward—no flying cars, no teleporters—in the offing. Twenty years ago, we were assured that the information superhighway meant we could live anywhere and work from home, but the people who get rich off that hope crowd themselves into Silicon Valley.

Perhaps it's time to go back to Franklin's original peaceful conception of 1751: rather than invading the world, let's just stop inviting the world.

Homesickness: An American History

VDARE
October 24, 2011

HOMESICKNESS sounds like the least important topic imaginable. In modern America, a longing for the familiar places and people we are separated from is routinely castigated as an immature character flaw barely tolerable in children at summer camp, much less in adults.

Yet, when studied sympathetically as in Susan J. Matt's insightful and touching new book, *Homesickness: An American History*, the subject turns out to offer deep insights into human nature.

Matt, a historian at Weber State University in remote Ogden, Utah, works in the subfield of "history of emotions."

Human emotions probably don't change much over time, but the words we use to describe them certainly cycle, whipped by fads and social forces. For example, Matt cites a pair of contemporary psychiatrists who note that many of their unhappy patients come to them having already self-diagnosed themselves as "depressed"—a respectable 21st Century malady for which pharmaceutical firms invent and market expensive pills—"but were in fact lonely."

Matt demonstrates that homesickness—whether for distant family, friends, houses, towns, landscapes, or climates—is close to a human universal. What differs is the particular. We each imprint upon different things.

A friend has long argued that the political divide of the future won't be today's outmoded categories of left v. right, but instead universalist v. localist. Of course, the globalists possess a huge competitive advantage in imposing

18

their simple-minded Davos Man cosmopolitanism because the particularists by definition differ and need to agree to disagree.

While Alexis de Tocqueville and Frederick Jackson Turner emphasized the restless spirit that drove Americans to settle an entire continent, Matt quotes from the poignant letters and diaries of pioneers demonstrating the emotional pain they bore. In her retelling of familiar passages in American history, our forefathers seem more heroic because of the sacrifices they made in terms of loneliness and unease. In one incident from Gold Rush California, a minister's daughter recounts how after Thanksgiving dinner in Stockton in 1851, she began playing on that essential fixture of Victorian domesticity, the piano:

> "[Father] looked out, and to his surprise the sidewalks and porch were filled with old and young men. Along the side of the house stood scores of men in the street as far as the eye could see and some were sobbing. On entering the room he said, 'We have an immense congregation outside. Get out your familiar tunes—"Home, Sweet Home," Etc.... Give these homesick sons and fathers a few songs more.'"[1]

Just as grief eventually accompanies love, homesickness is the flip side of attachment. Human beings have a mechanism that propels us toward contentment: we tend to grow attached to the familiar. Be it ever so humble, there's no place like home. But, then, we grow vulnerable to missing it when it's gone. Matt observes:

> In the nineteenth century, many in the nation believed that it was acceptable to talk openly about these costs.... Homesickness was not yet shameful, for love and loyalty toward home were the marks of a virtuous character.

In the warmer-hearted Victorian era, homesickness was treated sympathetically even by such huge and hardheaded institutions as the U.S. Army. Matt writes:

> The phenomenon of homesickness ... received systematic attention during the Civil War.... The term nostalgia was used to describe the acutely homesick.... In fact, during the war, Union doctors diagnosed more than five thousand soldiers as suffering from nostalgia, seventy-four of whom succumbed to the condition.

Over time, however, as America's big institutions—military, corporate, governmental, educational, and sporting—became even bigger, they became increasingly hostile toward Americans expressing their feelings of homesickness:

> Consequently, by the end of the twentieth century, few native-born adults overtly discussed the emotion, although they displayed it in other ways.

Homesickness was castigated as shamefully immature or lower class. Why? Because a longing for a particular setting makes "individuals less interchangeable, less fungible."

Treating people as fungible makes giant institutions more efficient. After WWII, managers of IBM joked that the corporate acronym stood for "I've Been Moved." The Cold War military relocated officers constantly, with notorious effects on the happiness of their Army Brat children, who grew up without ever having a hometown.

Over the last generation, middle managers and their families have, with some success, quietly rebelled against corporate cultures demanding incessant relocation.

On the other hand, some industries, such as academia, have become more nomadic as temporary hiring becomes the dominant employment mode. Dr. Matt, who now has tenure at Weber St., notes in an aside that she and her husband have lived in six states since they met at Cornell in 1990. Because she dedicates *Homesickness* to her parents and sister, I would guess that she found the frequent moves demanded by modern academic life to be wrenching.

She offers a brilliant analysis of the contrasting careers of homesickness and nostalgia in modern America. By the 1970s, the era of *American Graffiti* and *Happy Days*, nostalgia:

> The longtime companion and sometime synonym of homesickness, has become a less troublesome emotion, signifying a diffuse, unthreatening, and painless longing for the past.... As an emotion, nostalgia has come to be widely celebrated, perhaps because it is now seen as harmless. Whereas the homesick may believe they can return home, the nostalgic know that moving backwards in time is impossible.

While you can't buy a time machine, you can buy nostalgia-assuaging retro-junk. In a review of *Homesickness* in *Slate*, Libby Copeland observes:

HOMESICKNESS: AN AMERICAN HISTORY

> These days, while it's not as permissible as it once was for an adult to muse about, say, missing her parents, it is more than permissible to indulge in casual nostalgia for one's childhood. Specifically, we miss the brands of our childhoods.... This type of nostalgia lets us signal cultural hipness instead of the rootlessness and neediness we feel deep down.

Do you miss the neighborhood where you grew up in the 1980s, which has since "tipped" demographically? Well, not much can be done about that. But feel free to relive the good old days back home by buying on DVD all three *Transformers* movies based on the 1980s toy robots that turn into cars (don't ask).

Homesickness is seen as low class and culturally unsophisticated. Our society deplores people emotionally attached to their old neighborhoods. If they are black or Latino, they are laughingly put down as "homeboys." If they are white, they are angrily denounced as "racists" or "nativists." If you are a refugee from demographic change on the West Side of Chicago or in Southern California, well, you better keep your mouth shut.

Yet, you may have noticed that the biggest winners in American society often indulge their attachments to their native soil. Consider the three Americans who over the last 25 years vied for the title of world's richest man. Sam Walton, founder of Walmart, famously kept his main home in tiny Bentonville, Arkansas in the Ozarks. Warren Buffett lives in his native Omaha. And Bill Gates lives in his hometown of Seattle.

Further, homesickness is hardly confined to the unlettered. The supreme English language novelist of the third quarter of the 20th Century, Vladimir Nabokov, made a career out of his carefully nurtured homesickness for pre-Revolutionary Russia. The exiled Nabokov explained, "homesickness has been with me a sensuous and particular matter." During his years teaching at American universities, Nabokov refused to acquire a home, fearing that putting down roots would interfere with his superb memories of his stolen Russian home. Thus, he (and his saintly wife Vera) only house-sat for other professors on one-year sabbaticals.

Matt's book makes clearer some of the emotional dynamics of immigration. We often hear: "All we have to do is get immigrants to assimilate!" But assimilation is emotionally painful. It's more natural to form enclaves with people like yourself. For example, the federal government initially tried to

21

disperse anti-Castro Cuban refugees across the country, but most of them eventually wound up in Miami (which they then took over).

Moreover, it's common for immigrants to alleviate their homesickness by assuming they will someday go home.

This sojourner mentality can make immigrants formidable economic competitors. American workers are always nagged over why they won't work as cheaply as Mexicans. One answer is because the Americans need to be able to afford a permanent home in America. The Mexicans have homes in Mexico, so they can live in America under conditions (e.g., six men in a garage) that nobody would put up with in their native land.

Of course, many supposed sojourners never go home. Matt points out that a traditional way in which lonely immigrant women become reconciled to life in America is by having children, lots of children:

> It was by establishing a new family in America that immigrants frequently overcame their homesickness, abandoned their plans for return, and began to feel at home in their new land.

This helps explain the very high fertility among women newly arrived from Mexico—higher, in fact, than among those remaining in Mexico.[2]

The policy lesson that I draw from *Homesickness*: scattering Americans via demographic change, while it makes a lot of money for various special interests, doesn't make us happier on the whole.

If you want to move because some other place in America has gotten better, that's great. But if you need to move because your hometown has gotten worse (for example, the public schools have been overwhelmed by the children of immigrants), that's bad.

We're often assured that no harm can come from immigration because America has lots of places left to flee to. Yet having to move to Portland or Grand Junction or some other whitopia hurts not just for the obvious objective reasons, but because you and your loved ones will likely suffer some kind of homesickness for years as you all fall out of intimacy with the people and places you care about.

But Matt's most valuable contribution might be this point: that modern institutions try to bully Americans into becoming as fungible as individual humans can be.

This can explain a number of conundrums of contemporary ideology.

We are constantly propagandized about the importance of equality and diversity. Everybody knows that anybody who isn't completely on board with equality and diversity is a Bad Person. We are lectured on the virtues of equality and diversity by the President (whether Obama, Bush, or Clinton), Bill Gates, the Chief of Staff of the U.S. Army, Oprah, Angelo Mozilo, the editors of the *New York Times*, James Cameron, the CEO of Fannie Mae, the President of Harvard, and other powerful and wealthy people.

Yet, aren't equality and diversity antonyms? And why are the lucky few who have clawed their way to the top so insistent that the rest of us worship diversity?

What's really going on here?

Perhaps the people who run the giant organizations don't actually value equality and diversity. Perhaps that's just the cover story and what they want from us is fungibility. They want their employees, customers, and voters to be as atomized as possible, so that they can be as fungible as pork bellies.

Look how much money was made in 2004-2007 by imagining mortgages to be fungible. That's the classic modern case: Scatter the population to distant exurbs by declaring that all mortgage-holders are equal.

What could possibly go wrong?

How to Help the Left Half of the Bell Curve

VDARE
July to September 2000
(Originally a five-part series)

Part I: IQ and Why We're Afraid to Talk About It

THE last twenty years of immigration have thus brought about a redistribution of wealth in America, from less-skilled workers and toward employers. [Harvard economist George] Borjas estimates that one half of the relative fall in the wages of high school dropouts since the 1980s can be traced directly to mass immigration. At some point, this kind of wealth redistribution, from the less well off to the affluent, becomes malignant. In the 1950s and 1960s, Americans with low reading and math scores could aspire to and achieve the American Dream of a middle class lifestyle. That is less realistic today. Americans today who do poorly in high school are increasingly condemned to a low-wage existence; and mass immigration is a major reason why.[3]

This recent statement is one of the most unusual made by any American candidate for public office in many years. Almost all other politicians and pundits have become far more comfortable offering policy prescriptions for Garrison Keillor's Lake Wobegon—"where all the children are above average." In the real world, however, half the school kids are always going to be lower than the median.

Nor has any other candidate mentioned lately that this mathematical fact imposes upon the rest of us ethical obligations—not to use complex laws, like our immigration policies, to exploit our less acute fellow citizens for our own benefit.

Who is this foolhardy politician who talks like an updated version of Harry Truman? Of course, it's the one candidate with the unerring instinct for making himself unpopular: Pat Buchanan.

Of all the forlorn causes Buchanan has backed, the welfare of Not-So-Sharp-Americans might be the most hopeless. America's growing IQ stratification, and the resulting class war that the clever are waging upon the clueless, is one of the great unmentionables. Nobody else in politics is even thinking about the inevitable conflict between the left half and the right half of the IQ Bell Curve. The notion that Americans with double digit IQ's have a moral right to leaders who defend them never seems even to occur to their countrymen with triple digit IQs.

This series will discuss the moral, economic and political challenges posed by inequality in intelligence.

Why is there such an adamant taboo against hard-headed discussions of IQ? Richard J. Herrnstein's and Charles Murray's book *The Bell Curve* was the nonfiction publishing event of Nineties, with an amazing 400,000 copies of a statistics and graphs-crammed social science tome sold. But subsequent books on IQ have experienced endless difficulties merely becoming physically available to readers.

IQ is off-limits today because people who are verbally facile, such as journalists and academics, tend to assume that reality is largely constructed from words. Thus, if we would all just stop writing about unpleasant facts, they would disappear.

Unpleasant Fact #1: Roughly five out of six African-Americans have IQs below the white average. But not talking about this IQ difference has singularly failed to make it go away. The black-white gap has remained roughly one standard deviation for the last 80 years.

What the censorship has accomplished, however, is preventing the emergence of a more a nuanced and optimistic view of black-white differences. Although IQ is, by far, the single most effective measurement known to the social sciences for predicting human outcomes, it's hardly omniscient. Indeed, African-Americans tend to be better than whites at certain mental abilities that IQ tests are bad at gauging, such as the improvisatory creativity that makes them world-beaters in jazz, basketball, rap, running with the football, and preaching.

Unpleasant Fact #2: Far more subtle, although the Great and the Good ceaselessly sermonize us that racial conflicts are caused by the majority feeling superior to the minority, a quick global survey suggests the opposite. The doltish masses have frequently risen up against astute "middle-man minorities" that control trade.

Southeast Asians have repeatedly launched murderous pogroms against the Overseas Chinese who dominate their economies, such as in Indonesia in 1998. African-Americans burned down hundreds of Korean stores in South Central L.A. in 1992. Fijians, Ugandans, and Trinidadians have all tried to oppress the more clever Asian Indians in their midst. The Turks killed huge numbers of Armenians in 1915. And from 1933 to 1945 the Germans eliminated most European Jews, at a time when German Jews were the best-educated ethnic group in the world.

Thus the truly unmentionable Unpleasant Fact today is not that blacks have mean IQs well below the white average. It's that other groups have mean IQs well above it.

This censorship may be prudent. But it is crippling American intellectual discourse.

Unpleasant Fact #3: Honest talk about IQ would expose some deeply personal inconsistencies among our most influential thinkers. Although the typical white intellectual claims he wants to censor discussion of IQ to shield black self-esteem, his sometimes-berserk reactions reveal that he finds it a peril to his own. The typical white intellectual considers himself superior to ordinary white people for two contradictory reasons: a) he constantly proclaims his belief in human equality, but they don't; b) he has a high IQ, but they don't.

Unpleasant Fact #4: Stifling discourse on intelligence differences allows the IQ upper class to quietly push its interests at the expense of the rest of society. Denouncing Arthur Jensen and Charles Murray proclaims your faith in empirical egalitarianism. Then you can ignore the irksome demands of moral egalitarianism.

Consider:

- the inordinate complexity of the tax system, law, government regulation. This allows a high IQ priesthood of lawyers, accountants and consultants to extract handsome sums from the average citizen in return for interpreting these inscrutable instructions.

- the nonstop propagandizing that anyone who doesn't attend college is doomed. Yet there is very little evidence that college education adds much to earning power—other than by using the SAT to sort high school seniors into IQ strata for the convenience of corporations banned by civil rights law from giving IQ-type tests themselves.

- the IQ overclass's promotion of do-it-yourself sexual morality. For a prudent, coolly logical individual, the wisdom of the ages can be rather redundant. But for people whose passions outrun their foresight, it was a godsend. Thus, in the 1960s when American intellectuals imported Swedish sexual morals, along with Swedish-style welfare for unmarried mothers, it had few ill effects in Minnesota (traditionally the highest IQ state). But it proved an instant disaster for African-Americans.

- above all, immigration. According to two separate methodologies employed by Herrnstein and Murray, the average IQ of recent immigrants and their children is somewhere around a mediocre 95. This is high enough to drive huge numbers of African-Americans (average IQ: 85) out of the legitimate workforce. And high enough to drive down the wages of white blue-collar workers. But not high enough to create competition for the jobs of media people and others with high Verbal SAT scores.

Our political discourse is dominated not by a concern for the needs of the American people as a whole, but by the self-interest and unexamined assumptions of the verbally facile.

Down with the Tyranny of the Glib!

Part II: How the Other Half Lives

Why do half our kids score lower on tests than the other half?

The Democrats blame test bias or underfunded schools or racism. The Republicans point to teachers' unions or gangsta rap or parents who don't help their kids with their homework. Everybody seems to think the problem of kids who perform poorly on tests will be solved by giving them even more tests.

Nobody is willing to publicly admit that a whole lot of young people just didn't draw winning hands in the genetic lottery for intelligence. To state this fact is considered insensitive and, horrors, bad for self-esteem. Maybe, but to ignore it is to acquiesce in the IQ elite setting policies that are starkly self-interested and uncharitable.

Several developments in recent decades threaten to undermine America's traditional knack for incorporating the great majority of citizens into the middle class. First, the relative economic value of a strong brain has risen dramatically compared to that of a strong back. Modern computers and telecommunications turbocharge the productive capacity of the intelligent. For example, Charles Murray pointed out in a follow-up to *The Bell Curve*, "In constant dollars, an engineer earned about $30,000 in 1952 compared with $20,000 for a manufacturing worker,[4] which was not much different from the ratio at the beginning of the century. By 1988, the engineer earned almost $75,000 compared with $22,000 for the manufacturing worker."

Second, we've discovered that equality of opportunity can do surprisingly little to insure equality of result. One of the best methods for disentangling the effects of nature and nurture is to look at differences among children raised in the same household. I pointed out in my recent *VDARE* column the frustrations that lesbian celebrities are likely to encounter when their designer babies don't live up to their hand-picked sperm donor dad's accomplishments.

Why not? The genes a child is dealt at conception don't come solely from those visible in his parents. Instead, they are randomly drawn from his entire family tree (weighted by closeness of relationship). Thus, as U. of Texas psychologist John Loehlin recently wrote: "The IQ difference between siblings is only about 30% smaller (on average) than that between any two randomly chosen people."

U. of Delaware psychometrician Linda S. Gottfredson noted in *Society*:

> Those sibling differences [in IQ] are due mostly to the genetic differences among siblings, because their genotypes correlate only 0.5 on average.... [The exceptions are identical twins. Their IQ's are much more similar because their genomes are the same.] Large IQ differences among siblings in turn produce large differences among them in school achievement and life outcomes. Those differences, in fact, are almost as large as those found between strangers whose IQs differ to the same degree.[5]

HOW TO HELP THE LEFT HALF OF THE BELL CURVE

Charles Murray recently quantified this in an ingenious study of pairs of American siblings raised together in non-poor homes. Murray described his findings in the *Sunday Times of London* in 1997:

> Each pair consists of one sibling with an IQ in the normal range of 90-110, a range that includes 50% of the population. I will call this group the normals. The second sibling in each pair had an IQ either higher than 110, putting him in the top quartile of intelligence (the brights) or lower than 90, putting him in the bottom quartile (the dulls). These constraints produced a sample of 710 pairs. How much difference did IQ make? Earned income is a good place to begin. In 1993, when we took our most recent look at them, members of the sample were aged 28-36. That year, the bright siblings earned almost double the average of the dull: £22,400 compared to £11,800. The normals were in the middle, averaging £16,800.[6]

By the way, these earnings gaps are likely to widen with age, as the blue-collar workers' bodies wear out and therefore their incomes stagnate or fall.

Within families, parents do a better job of equalizing children's environments than any government less tyrannical than the Khmer Rouge could accomplish. Yet, even with the same upbringing, IQ differences are both substantial and play a huge role in the kids' prosperity as adults.

The plight of the left half of the Bell Curve is hardly restricted to ghetto blacks. It can afflict any family. Could your children end up with the fuzzy end of the IQ lollipop? Let's work the numbers assuming that you and your spouse are both solidly ensconced in Murray's brights. Let's say you each have an IQ of 119, which puts you each at the 90th percentile. Well, due to regression toward the mean, the chance that your child will join you in the brights is less than fifty-fifty. In fact, more than one fourth of your children would be expected to inherit only double digit IQ's. A sobering 9% of your offspring are forecasted to end up among Murray's dulls with IQ's in the 80's or worse.

And unless your children marry smarter people than themselves, you can expect that fairly close to half of your grandchildren will have below average IQ's. (Of course, if you and your spouse both come from ethnic groups or family trees with an average IQ well above normal, the mean toward which your kids will regress will be higher.)

Of course, marrying a smart spouse is still the best, if not the only, way of smartening up your offspring. The edge you get, while not decisive in individual cases, would still be very well worth playing at the roulette wheel.

But I hope the exercise of contemplating our possible progeny can engender a little of the empathetic identification with the left half of the Bell Curve that is sorely lacking among the IQ overclass today. But whether their problems strike close to home for you or not, please do keep in mind that half of our fellow American citizens belong to this group today. Half of all Americans always will. Including, probably, some of your children or grandchildren.

How can we best help those who didn't roll sevens in the genetic crapshoot? That's what I'll consider in my next column.

Part III: IQ and the Class Struggle

I'm writing something that as far as I know no one has ever attempted before. When *The Bell Curve* hit the bestseller lists, a handful of the more perceptive reviewers mentioned that the highly heritable nature of IQ does not logically absolve people who were born acute of some responsibility for the fate of people born obtuse. Yet few have pursued this line of argument until now.

Two articles posted on *Salon* nicely illustrated the hopelessly contradictory conventional wisdom about IQ. The first[7] routinely denounced IQ tests, claiming they tried to measure the meaningless. The second[8] routinely denounced Texas (and of course its governor) for executing a confessed murderer-rapist named Oliver Cruz. Why? Because he once scored 64 on one of those "meaningless" IQ tests!

This shamelessness is rampant in the mainstream media. The *New York Times*' editorialists are perfectly capable of excoriating the very concept of intelligence one week—and then thundering the next week that lead paint can lower children's IQs by five points.

And yet it's rapidly reaching the end of its rope, as genetic investigators push ahead.

What then?

The American experiment rests in part upon the idea "that all men are created equal," in "that they are endowed by their Creator with certain unalienable Rights, that among these are Life, Liberty and the pursuit of Happiness." Since WWII, however, any emphasis on the spiritual, moral, and legal equality of humans has been shoved aside by the highly risky assertion that we're all empirically equal. This presumption has served many clever people well. Sneering at *The Bell Curve* enables you to ignore just how lucky you were to have been born out on the right tail of the bell curve.

Since factual equality has become the new public shibboleth (not that anybody believes it in private), the professional leaders of organized pressure groups can blame racism, sexism, ableism, etc. for their groups' failure to achieve economic equality. Since everybody assumes equal opportunity guarantees equal results, activists can logically demand affirmative action jobs for people such as, well, such as themselves.

Likewise, the public assumption that all men are created empirically equal allows the business elites to assuage their consciences—on those rare instances when they actually think about the struggles of blue-collar workers. The assumption lets Stanford MBAs blame growing economic inequality on the laziness of the lower orders, although the scientifically accurate response would be: "There, but for the grace of God, go I."

But the death of the empirical equality fantasy logically impels us toward thinking hard about our moral obligations to those less fortunate in the genetic lottery.

We can start by asking: Whatever happened to the Class Struggle? It's not as if earning a decent living suddenly stopped being a struggle for working class families. "Holding buying power constant, the average hourly earnings of production and non-supervisory workers in the U.S. economy fell 9 percent from $14.09 in 1973, to $12.77 in 1998." And their net worth has plummeted relative to white-collar workers with stock options and big portfolios.

But the attention paid to this once-dominant topic has dwindled almost completely. Why? They say, "History is written by victors." What they don't tell you is that "Journalism is written by the high scorers on the SAT-Verbal." (As are screenplays, political oratory, and TV commercials.) In our increasingly stratified society, the reality of life on the left half of the IQ bell curve is more and more invisible to the media elite.

A big problem for modern class warriors like Pat Buchanan on the right or Jim Hightower on the left is that over the years the number of blue collar workers with the verbal talent needed to articulate their class interests has plummeted. Where'd the smart ones go? To college and then into white-collar jobs. In the past, unions and other working class institutions had leaders and spokesmen who were both highly intelligent and authentically representative of the rank and file (i.e., not you, John Sweeney of the AFL-CIO).

31

In previous eras, many routes to success didn't go through college. These days, though, only supersmart technogeeks like Steve Jobs, Bill Gates, or Michael Dell believe they can afford to blow off college in favor of work. At present, two-thirds of high school girls give college a try.

Far fewer graduate, of course, since probably no more than half of that horde have the native wit to get much out of a genuine higher education. But while they dither around before dropping out, they are providing plenty of campus jobs for professors, counselors, diversity sensitivity consultants, and the like. Today, even among siblings brought up in the same household, a kid in the top quartile of the population intellectually is 28 times more likely to obtain a college degree than his or her brother or sister in the bottom quartile. Charles Murray's clever study[9] of 710 pairs of siblings raised together found that "while 56% of the bright [the top quartile with IQs over 110] obtained university degrees, this was achieved by only 21% of the normals [the middle half with IQs from 90 to 110] and a minuscule 2% of the dulls [the bottom quartile with IQ under 90]."

Universities feverishly obfuscate the true nature of the Educational-Testing Complex. But while almost all of America's colleges indulge in orgies of political correctness, barely any forego the utterly anti-egalitarian SAT or ACT standardized entrance exam. That's because nobody evaluates colleges on how well they actually educate their undergraduates. You'll notice that no college gives its seniors "exit exams" to measure how much they've learned since their "entrance exams." Today, an American college's prestige depends not upon the value it adds, but upon the SAT scores its students achieved... while they were in high school!

Why do parents spend $130,000 to send their heirs to elite private colleges? Assume Junior will not study science or engineering (in which fields, I must admit, highly valuable instruction still takes place). Then the main purpose of getting him into a college with a high average SAT score is not to educate him but to mark him as a lifetime member of the IQ Overclass. Corporate recruiters, largely banned from using IQ tests themselves since the Supreme Court's 1972 *Griggs* decision, use a college's average SAT score as a proxy for a job applicant's IQ. A second purpose: to nudge kids toward marrying somebody with a high score, who thus has a major earning potential.

Hence the decline in class conflict—and the rise in ethnic conflict. Ditch diggers, for instance, no longer have any articulate spokesmen. In fact, each year, due to assortative mating (e.g., Yale students are more likely to marry other Yale students than to marry chicken-pluckers), there are a few less high-IQ young people born into blue-collar families. By contrast, every racial group has at least some verbally facile intellectualoids to fill the role of Aggrieved Professional Ethnic.

This growing IQ gap causes all sorts of problems for an extremely high IQ intellectual like Buchanan. His motto seems to be "I'd rather be Provocative than President." He enjoys coming up with new ideas rather than repeating the same handful of old chestnuts over and over again, as professional politicians must. This makes his ability to connect with his target audience distinctly erratic. For example, he launched his current Presidential bid with the curious stratagem of publishing a book deriding American involvement in WWII. While an interesting historical argument, it was not a move focus-tested for its appeal to highly patriotic folk.

But the role Buchanan is trying to fill may eventually be assumed by somebody more naturally suited to it. Successful football coaches are very good at boiling down the complex game plans invented by their high-IQ offensive coordinators and pounding them into the skulls of guys with necks wider than their heads. Former U. of Colorado coach Bill McCartney has had an enormous impact by founding Promise Keepers. These skills could well prove useful in politics.

Part IV: Helping the Left Half of the Bell Curve - the Not So Hot Ideas

What policies would most aid the left half of the Bell Curve? The essential requirement: policies must help people with double-digit IQs help themselves. In this article, I'll consider ideas ranging from bad to only marginally useful. In the next, I'll consider the more promising alternatives.

Welfare? It's not exactly front-page news anymore: welfare for single mothers has proven morally disastrous for them. But why did the two interrelated Big Ideas imported from Sweden in the Sixties: (1) generous welfare for unmarried mothers; (2) no social disapproval of childbirth outside marriage—turn out to be Bad Ideas?

Because people on the left half of the Bell Curve tend to be below-average at prudent long-term decisions. When American intellectuals imported these concepts from the Swedes, they expected Americans to act like Swedes. That was like expecting Jimi Hendrix to sound like ABBA.

The damage done to Swedes by these ideas has been glacially slow. It takes generations of welfare to undermine the remarkable Swedish work ethic. Same with sex: if you make marriage unfashionable, Swedes will still form long-term relationships and act like they're married. They tend to be too shy to be comfortable with practicing promiscuity and too responsible to walk away from their out-of-wedlock offspring. According to Francis Fukuyama, even now 90% of Swedish illegitimate babies are born to co-habitating couples, compared to only 25% in the U.S.

Not surprisingly, in the U.S. the tide has finally turned against high welfare payments to single mothers. More sophisticated redistribution schemes like the Earned Income Tax Credit do less moral damage, but have distinct limits. They do nothing for those who can't find jobs. And they can impose a sizable marginal disincentive that would keep low-wage workers from looking for higher paying jobs.

Racial quotas?—Whites and Asians are almost twice as numerous on the right side of the Bell Curve as blacks and Hispanics. So racial preferences divide the working class rather than deal with its difficulties. Nor do the lower earnings of blacks stem significantly from irrational discrimination. Blacks earn an average of 98% as much as whites with equal IQs. No, their problem is that their IQs tend not to be equal. The median African-American's IQ is only equal to that of a white at the 16th percentile.

But quotas are a near-inevitable political response to the reality of racial differences. They are at least a semi-serious response to a deeply serious situation. In contrast, the standard conservative debating ploy of blustering, "If you support quotas, then you're really saying blacks aren't equal to whites" is just a slick soundbite. It's not a morally serious response to the reality that, on average, blacks are not equal to whites in the ability to make money.

Sure, African Americans could do better if they got their act together. (In fact, they are doing better than in 1990, during their self-inflicted crack epidemic.) Still, the evidence is overwhelming: as a group, the blacks are no more likely to reach economic equality with whites than whites are likely to reach athletic equality with blacks.

This somber fact poses severe moral and practical challenges for America. And for any state comprised of racial groups with unequal productive capacities—witness a coup in Fiji, pogroms in Indonesia, corruption in Malaysia, genocide in Germany.

HOW TO HELP THE LEFT HALF OF THE BELL CURVE

Many establishment conservatives see unskilled mestizo immigrants as our New, Improved Poor People. The Old, Unimproved Poor People: native-born blacks. But this only makes sense if we could somehow exchange blacks for Hispanic immigrants. Without deporting blacks, immigration will only create a second undercompetitive, and thus resentful, racial group.

Mestizo Hispanics tend to suffer (somewhat) less severe problems than African Americans—but their potential numbers are larger. For example, Fox Butterfield reported in the *New York Times* that Hispanics are 1/3rd as likely to go to jail as blacks (Whites? Merely 1/10th). But by the end of the century, Hispanics may be three times as numerous as blacks. We'll enjoy equally large groups of black and Hispanic jailbirds. Quite a legacy to leave our great-grandchildren.

The essential fact about African Americans is that they are Americans. They did not ask to come here. At minimum, our nation's obligation to them is to not worsen their plight by importing competitors that are slightly more competent.

Republicans point to newly-arrived immigrants outcompeting native blacks as proof that blacks shouldn't blame us for their problems. Okay, fine. It's not our fault. But, in what system of ethics is it the average black's fault that his IQ, which is mostly determined genetically, is 85? Is he to blame for failing to choose his parents wisely?

Class Quotas?—Many in the political center now want to reform affirmative action. Replace race with class background, they argue. Under these schemes, you could simultaneously drink yourself out of the middle class and your kid into Harvard!

But, as *The Bell Curve* made clear by looking at a huge sample of whites, class background is a much weaker predictor of what a person will earn when he grows up than his IQ. Class-based quotas simply miss the point about what causes economic inequality. Today, the U.S. probably does a better job of helping high IQ individuals from all segments of society move up the ladder than any country in history. So analysts find huge economic inequality not just within pairs of strangers coming from the same class, but also within pairs of siblings coming from the same home.

IQ Quotas?—No, if you want to focus affirmative action on those who really need it, you'd have to create IQ quotas - the *reductio ad absurdum* of affirmative action. Nobody wants their hospital to turn down smart surgeons and hire more stupid ones. (Of course, discriminating against the cognitively competent in favor of the mentally mediocre is also in effect the essence of race and class quotas.)

Nor is it clear that quotas do their intended beneficiaries much good. Consider a young man with a strong body, nimble hands, and a decent work ethic. Let's also imagine that reading and writing aren't his strong suits. Would a quota that gives him an entry-level office job where he's supposed to read and write memos all day really offer him such a wonderful opportunity? Or are you just wasting his time by starting him off on what will prove to be an unsuitable career?

Unions?—Private sector unions' effectiveness is heavily dependent upon a tight labor market. Cesar Chavez's success at winning higher wages and safer working conditions for stoop-laborers in the 1960s and 1970s was the result of government policies like President Eisenhower's Operation Wetback deportations that dramatically cut the number of Mexican migrant workers in the 1950s and 1960s. But after the floodgates opened up again, millions of Mexican immigrants undermined the United Farm Workers' power.

The AFL-CIO's leadership, which had been losing members for decades, has seized on a brilliant new strategy for benefiting themselves: Betray their traditional base of regular Joes in windbreakers in favor of government employees—and immigrants. Just like the big corporations, John Sweeney's AFL-CIO now wants to import a new, more malleable proletariat to replace the native working class that, ironically, it too finds unsatisfactory.

Sweeney intends to evade the laws of supply and demand that rule the private sector by playing the racial guilt card in the political sector. Since few white Americans apparently feel they owe any loyalty to fellow native-born Americans in unions (that would be the crime of "nativism"), Sweeney wants to bring in brown foreigners. He appears to believe that upper-middle class whites are more likely to favor laws mandating above-market pay for members of immigrant-dominated unions than for members of unions dominated by their fellow native-born Americans. This strategy has already enjoyed success in winning higher wages for the Mexican janitors of Los Angeles, who had earlier pushed native-born blacks out of the field.

Further, all these immigrants with fifth grade educations will need lots more unionized social workers to look after them.

Protectionism?—As a free marketer I always assumed that protectionism was always a terrible idea. For example, I opposed the Reagan Administration's import quotas for the Japanese cars. Yet by encouraging the Japanese to open assembly plants in the U.S., that move worked out spectacularly better than I predicted. Japanese management showed that Americans workers could achieve much higher quality than American management had assumed.

So protectionism may work in practice more often than it works in theory. But still, it typically makes managements lazy by cutting their competition. Further, other nations can retaliate with higher tariffs. This could start a downward spiral in the world economy.

(Retaliation, by the way, is not a risk if we tighten our immigration policy. Few countries could possibly tighten their restrictions on immigrants from America any more than now. Mexico, China, India, all our major immigrant sources, believe that turnabout is not fair play. We opened our borders unilaterally, if selectively, without any attempt to ensure what in trade negotiations is called "reciprocity.")

Part V: Finally! Some Good Ideas for Helping the Left Half of the Bell Curve

In this, the last installment on my series on how to help the left half of the Bell Curve, I finally get around to offering some promising ideas:

Cut Back on Unskilled Immigration: This is the utterly obvious way to help the left half of America's Bell Curve.

Calls for open borders are occasionally heard in the libertarian and neo-conservative fever swamps. But it's just ideological posturing. Border restrictions are plainly necessary to keep Los Angeles from turning into a real-life set from *Blade Runner*. We must have limits on the number of immigrants. So our immigration policy cannot benefit more than a few of the world's 5.7 billion foreigners. What we can do is help our fellow American citizens.

By providing more jobs and higher wages to the less-gifted American workers, immigration restriction would not only make their wallets thicker. Making it easier for a young man to support a wife and kids also inculcates the bourgeois virtues that government doles undermine. Work and marriage are the great civilizers of young men. But it's hard for Americans to afford a wife and family on the wages prevailing in Mexico.

Sure, this would worsen the upper middle class's Servant Problem. But American civilization will not crumble just because we would no longer have the Western world's lowest-paid pool guys.

The rest of the promising ideas are admittedly more speculative and arguable:

Reduce complexity and credentialism: The U.S. military has elicited a high level of achievement from blacks and whites in the 85-100 IQ range. A major reason: the military demands its high-IQ officers search out what legal scholar Richard Epstein calls simple rules for a complex world. In dismal contrast, lawyers, regulators, consultants, academics, and others who profit from abstruseness increasingly dominate the rest of America.

National Health Insurance: Like all software venture capitalists, Jim Woodhill searches obsessively for high IQ talent. And, like an increasing number of people who have gotten rich off brainy programmers, Woodhill has turned toward trying to help America's social problems.

When other Jedi Geeks such as Gates try their hand at philanthropy, they throw money at pre-meritocracy charities suffering from rapidly diminishing returns, such as college scholarships for favored minorities. For example, Microsoft chairman Bill Gates gave $1 billion for "Gates Scholars." Gates, who found college so enormously valuable that he dropped out after a few months, knew perfectly well that there already was too much financial aid chasing too few high IQ black students. But when the Justice Department is breathing down your neck is not the time to try something novel based on your highly realistic worldview. (Fat lot of good this politically-correct donation did him, though.)

In contrast, Woodhill focuses explicitly on helping the left half of the Bell Curve. His "vision is of a society that gives dignity to the work of the average, and, especially, below-average citizen, while at the same time makes life a Living Hell for those who currently have comfortable livings studying/tending social dysfunction while at the same time promoting more of it."

Woodhill argues, among many other interesting ideas, that the average citizen's nagging fear of losing his health insurance is the prime reason so many vote for politicians allied with the social service bureaucracies that have so damaged the morals of the poor. He says government-funded health insurance imposes none of the moral risks associated with welfare. Men quit their jobs because they can sponge off welfare mom girlfriends for food, shelter and cable TV. But no-one would tell his boss to take this job and shove it just because he knew that the government would give him a $150,000 bone marrow transplant—if, God forbid, he ever needed one.

HOW TO HELP THE LEFT HALF OF THE BELL CURVE

I'll be the first to concede that the arguments over health care are extraordinarily complex. Nonetheless, we should keep in mind Woodhill's point: the "moral hazard" of national health insurance would be far less than of many other government programs.

Reduce regressive payroll taxes: Since cutting payroll taxes on lower income workers would probably require income tax hikes on higher-income individuals, I hope this heresy doesn't get Peter Brimelow in trouble at *Forbes*! The federal payroll tax is 15.3% (divided between employee and employer), with most of it going for Social Security. This year, you don't pay any Social Security taxes on earnings over $76,200. This impacts low and middle-income wage earners proportionately more than the wealthy.

Is this a good thing? Reagan's cuts in marginal tax rates for the rich were essential to reviving a battered economy. But supply side economists failed badly by predicting that Clinton's tax hikes on the well-to-do would undermine prosperity. Apparently, when the "animal spirits" are roaring, as they have been since the 1994 Congressional election, the capitalist system is so productive that a little higher marginal tax rates on the rich don't hurt much.

Exploit Diversity of Talents: Harvard's Howard Gardner has become hugely popular with the educational establishment by pooh-poohing IQ in favor of seven or eight "multiple intelligences." They believe Gardner's theory is inherently more egalitarian, more likely to reveal that all groups are the same, than the single-number IQ model behind *The Bell Curve*.

In fact, the opposite is true. Consider sex differences in intelligence. That males and females have the same average single-number IQ was first proposed by Cyril Burt in 1912, and was definitively demonstrated by Arthur Jensen in 1998; two scientists, ironically, who have been savagely attacked by egalitarians for their other findings. Of course, when you break down the overall IQ number into its multiple components, you find sex differences. Men tend to be better at visual-spatial skills (especially at mentally rotating 3d objects) and at mathematical reasoning. Women are generally superior at short-term memory, perceptual speed, and verbal fluency.

It's theoretically possible that social factors account for all of the 15 point advantage in single-number IQ that whites hold over blacks, or the smaller advantage that East Asians hold over whites. But it's extremely unlikely that all racial groups are identical on not just one, but all eight dimensions of multiple intelligence. That would be like expecting to flip a coin and have it end up on its edge eight times in a row.

While that's bad news for the ideologues of empirical egalitarianism, it's good news for moral egalitarians. Why? Because diversity of talents gives different groups different market niches to exploit.

For example, black basketball players tend to be able to not only jump higher than whites, but also outthink them during the flow of the game. As Thomas Sowell notes, "To be an outstanding basketball player means to outthink opponents consistently in these split-second decisions under stress." Beyond basketball, these black cerebral superiorities in "real time" responsiveness also contribute to black dominance in jazz, running with the football, rap, dance, trash talking, preaching, and oratory. Perhaps, blacks could better exploit these skills, along with their masculine charisma, in the corporate arena by focusing on jobs like salesman, motivational speaker, and headhunter.

Master the Fundamentals: The techniques used by less-naturally-gifted athletes like Pete Rose in baseball or Michael Chang in tennis offer clues for how less cognitively gifted workers can still succeed. Work harder than your more gifted rivals do. Master the fundamentals. Nail the easy stuff. (E.g., the only category in which whites are over-represented among NBA leaders is free throw shooting). Don't improvise: listen to your coach's wisdom. (E.g., the decline of traditional sexual morality has not led to a high pregnancy rate among coldly logical Dutch teens. For African-American teens, though, the rise of do-it-yourself morality in the 1960's was a disaster.) Challenge yourself, but realistically. (E.g., I personally need to get in shape, but an affirmative action program for Sedentary-Americans that sets-aside for me an opening in Lennox Lewis' next heavyweight title bout might not be in my best interest. The same goes for quotas at elite colleges.)

Raise IQs: Ever since the Coleman Report of 1965, the evidence has mounted that enriching students' environments does little toward raising their IQ's. Thus, attention has turned toward earlier and earlier interventions such as Head Start and playing Mozart for your nine-month-old. Head Start helps temporarily, but its effects mostly disappear within half-a-decade. And the much-hyped "Mozart Effect" experiment has never been replicated. (So, play your toddler "The Itsy-Bitsy Spider." He'll enjoy it a lot more than the "Symphony in G Minor.")

Nonetheless, the basic concept of focusing on the earliest possible time remains promising. Since IQ is mostly determined by biology, it makes the most since to focus on biological improvements. The single most promising program would be to encourage breastfeeding. The *Associated Press* reported on 9/22/99:

> The survey by University of Kentucky nutritionist James Anderson [which appeared in the October, 1999 edition of the *American Journal of Clinical Nutrition*] looked at 20 different studies comparing the brain development of infants who had been breast-fed with that of infants who had been given formula." Our study confirms that breast-feeding is accompanied by about a five-points higher IQ than in bottle-fed infants," Anderson said.

The crucial question: does this five-point increase endure, or does it fade, like Head Start's advantage? If it were permanent, this would offer the single easiest way to narrow the black-white IQ gap. Only about 30% of African American children are breast-fed versus about like 60% of white children. Thus, raising black breastfeeding rates to the white level could theoretically increase black average IQ by 1.5 points, or 10% of the white-black IQ gap. This may not sound like much, but its effects on the right end of the black Bell Curve would be substantial. It would increase the number of blacks with IQs above 115 by around 20%.

This would dwarf any the benefits of the Gates Scholars program. And it would probably cost less. It's just a marketing problem. Bottle-feeding is prestigious among blacks for the same reason that Cadillacs are: black status symbols lag a few decades behind white fashions. It wouldn't take a huge push to make breast-feeding trendy among blacks.

If, say, the world's 2nd richest man, Larry Ellison of Oracle, is tired of rooting through Microsoft's garbage cans, here's a classier way to stick one in Bill Gates' eye. Ellison could pay for a definitive study of the long-term impact of breastfeeding. If it turns out as hoped, then he could finance a campaign to get new mothers to breastfeed.

In summary, it can be painful to speak honestly about such a sensitive topic as IQ. But only realism will allow us to do anything beneficial about it.

CHAPTER TWO

Invade the World, Invite the World

What Will Happen In Afghanistan?

United Press International
September 26, 2001

NO great adventure movie, not even *Lawrence of Arabia*, offers more insights into the upcoming war in Afghanistan than John Huston's 1975 film *The Man Who Would Be King*. Starring Sean Connery and Michael Caine, the film is based on Rudyard Kipling's 1888 short story set in Afghanistan.

In the two weeks since 9/11, a couple of contradictory assertions about Afghanistan have become commonplace in the press.

The first is that outsiders inevitably face horrifying defeat in Afghanistan.

The second is that the U.S. must not only kill Osama bin Laden and batter the Taliban regime, but should then take up the Imperial Burden in Afghanistan. The U.S., they say, should conquer and pacify the entire Texas-sized country, build a unified nation out of its warring ethnic groups, reconstruct its economy, liberate its women, calm its furious holy men, and make it a middle class democracy.

The Man Who Would Be King reminds us that neither despair nor utopianism is a realistic attitude for anyone contemplating a military incursion into that harsh land.

It may seem strange to look to a Victorian costume drama for perspectives on a 21st Century war, but few movies have benefited more from the energetic inspiration of a young genius and the skeptical wisdom of an old artist who'd been everywhere and done everything.

Rudyard Kipling, the youngest man to win the Nobel Prize for Literature (at age 41 in 1907), was only 22 when he wrote *The Man Who Would Be King*. Yet, he'd already been shot at by a Pathan tribesman in the famous Khyber Pass that links Pakistan and Afghanistan. Although out of fashion for decades, the Bombay-born Kipling is now the literary immortal of the hour as America contemplates the same question that so long plagued the British Empire: What to do about Afghanistan?

Kipling was long despised for his imperialism. Yet, at a time when many, including more than a few anti-Taliban Afghans, want the U.S. to occupy and take responsibility for Afghanistan, Kipling's sharp eye for the rewards and dangers of imperialism is suddenly relevant once again. In the words of critic John Derbyshire, Kipling "was an imperialist utterly without illusions about what being an imperialist actually means. Which, in some ways, means that he was not really an imperialist at all."

Yet, it took 69-year-old John Huston to richly flesh out Kipling's tall tale. Huston gave the story a classic arc. From a slow beginning, it ascends to a peak of cynical yet rousing adventure comedy, then descends into inexorable tragedy. Further, Huston added an astute post-Vietnam moral. While Joseph Conrad's *Heart of Darkness* (the inspiration for *Apocalypse Now*) is the allegory of a good man corrupted by absolute power over natives, Huston's movie is about a rascal ennobled—yet ultimately doomed—by his growing sense of kingly responsibility for the welfare of the natives that he had come to plunder

To film Kipling's story was the obsession of the erratic second half of Huston's long Hollywood career. Having previously written and directed such Humphrey Bogart classics as *The Maltese Falcon*, *The Treasure of the Sierra Madre*, and *The African Queen*, Huston cast Bogey and Clark Gable as Kipling's anti-heroes, Peachey Carnehan and Daniel Dravot.

These charismatic rogues—former British Army sergeants turned gunrunners and conmen—intend to make themselves "Kings of Kafiristan." They plan to become the first Europeans since Alexander the Great to penetrate this isolated region in Northeastern Afghanistan that was the last refuge of Afghanistan's primordial pagan culture. Then, they'll "loot it six ways from Sunday."

But Bogart died in 1957 and Gable in 1960. Over the years, Huston had three screenwriters pen adaptations. Finally, Huston and his long-time secretary Gladys Hill collaborated on a brilliant fourth version. In Huston's proud but accurate words, "We did a lot of invention, and it turned out to be good invention, supportive of the tone, feeling and spirit underlying the original short story…. I like this script as well as any I ever wrote."

In the early 1970's, Paul Newman and Robert Redford were on-board. Then, Newman, always one of Hollywood's least selfish stars, told Huston his script deserved British actors. He exclaimed, "John, get Connery and Caine!"

Sean Connery and Michael Caine went on to make what might be a more delightful buddy movie than even Newman and Redford's *Butch Cassidy and the Sundance Kid.* Connery's performance as the Scotsman Daniel is widely considered the greatest of his majestic career. And Caine's turn as the clever Cockney Peachey might be better.

Early in the movie, Connery's Daniel tells an incredulous Rudyard Kipling (played by Christopher Plummer), "We have been all over India … and we have decided that India isn't big enough for such as us."

Caine's Peachey chimes in, "We are not little men, and there is nothing that we are afraid of except Drink, and we have signed a Contrack on that. Therefore, we are going away to be Kings."

The two reasons they expected success in their audacious project are directly relevant to the question of whether the U.S. can win in Afghanistan.

It is widely remarked these days that no external power has ever permanently dominated Afghanistan. True, but what's forgotten is that no internal power has either, suggesting that the life expectancy of the five-year-old Taliban regime might be limited.

Why?

The severity of the Afghan terrain works against both conquest and unified resistance. As Kipling warns the buccaneers, "It's one mass of mountains and peaks and glaciers."

Connery's Daniel responds, "The more tribes, the more they'll fight, and the better for us." The more broken the ground, the more broken the society, and thus the harder it is to form a cohesive army to resist an invader.

Kafiristan, located in the Hindu Kush mountains northeast of Afghanistan's capital of Kabul, remains even today a scale model of Afghanistan's overall fractiousness. In this region that only covers 2% of the entire country, there are currently fifteen ethnic groups speaking five different languages.

Following his 1896 jihad, Amir Abdur Rahman, Khan of Kabul, changed the name Kafiristan ("land of infidels") to Nuristan ("land of light"). He offered the conquered Kafir pagans the choice of being put to the sword or to the knife. Most of the men chose the latter and were circumcised into Islam, although in that era before anesthetics and antibiotics, the pain couldn't have been all that much less.

Author Jonny Bealby spent four weeks retracing the fictional footprints of Daniel and Peachey in 1997, walking 250 miles across Kafiristan-Nuristan. (Even today, there are no roads.) "On the four week journey, I'd heard of twelve murders and enough tales of thieving and brigandage to fill a small book," Bealby recounted. "When I asked Ismael, our Nuristani translator, why this should be, he simply shrugged, 'It is our culture,' he said." (Nuristan, by the way, was the first place in Afghanistan to rebel against the Soviets.)

Bealby concluded, "If [Daniel and Peachey] were to tumble from the skies once again, more than a hundred years later, the task confronting them would be exactly the same. Kafiristan is now Nuristan; the infidels have been enlightened. But beyond religion, little of their ways seem to have changed."

Today, Afghanistan as a whole remains subdivided into hostile ethnic groups. The Taliban rulers, who control most but not all of the country, are drawn overwhelmingly from the Pashtun (known as the "Pathan" in Kipling's day), but they only make up three-eighths of the population and are concentrated south of the Hindu Kush. They may be the most war-like of the Afghans, but the reason they are experienced at fighting is because they so often try to kill each other.

A 22-year-old Winston Churchill fought them in an 1897 "butcher and bolt" punitive expedition (depicted in the 1972 film *Young Winston*). Churchill observed, "The Pathan tribes are always engaged in private or public war.... The life of the Pathan is thus full of interest."

A second insight into the difficulties faced by the Taliban at waging modern war—beyond their small and rusty arsenal—is implicit in Daniel's explanation to Kipling of their strategy for becoming Kings of Kafiristan. "In any place where they fight, a man who knows how to drill men can always be a King," Connery's character expounds. "We shall go to those parts and say to any King we find—'D'you want to vanquish your foes?' and we will show him how to drill men; for that we know better than anything else. Then we will subvert that King and seize his Throne and establish a Dynasty."

Daniel's confidence in the might of properly drilled men goes to the heart of the difference between irregular and regular armies. For tens of thousands of years, men have been waging irregular war—shoot-from-behind-a-rock style raiding. If you assume, like many Afghans, that war sputters on forever

—that it is the natural state of human relations—then sniping is the sensible fighting method for clans willing to lose some young warriors but not risk everything on one battle. Ambushes allow your men to slip away into wild country if the enemy proves too strong.

But nation-states long ago developed a more formidable style intended to win wars. The ancient Greeks discovered that trained, disciplined armies could maneuver to win decisive battles. Alexander the Great used this Greek breakthrough to conquer Afghanistan, among much else. (Kipling asserted that Alexander then married a Kafir princess named Roxanne and had a son.)

The famed military historian John Keegan wrote in *A History of Warfare*, "It is a general rule that primitives lose to regulars over the long run; harassment is an effective means of waging a defensive war, but wars are ultimately won by offensives...."

Indeed, when Daniel and Peachey arrive at Er-Heb, their first Kafir village, headman Ootah, familiar only with irregular war, offers them two goats for each of his Bashkai neighbors that they will kill for him. Peachey, the embodiment of regular soldiering, replies suavely, "A handsome offer, but rather than knocking them over one at a time, we'll do the whole thing in one fell swoop: storm Bashkai and give you a proper victory."

The next morning drill instructor Daniel starts teaching the men of Er-Heb to march in ordered ranks like British soldiers. "When we're done with you," he roars at the recruits, "You'll be able to stand up and slaughter your enemies like civilized men!"

Daniel explains to his uncomprehending boot privates, "Good soldiers don't think. They just obey. Do you think that if a man thought twice, he'd give his life for Queen and country? Not bloody likely!" Noticing an Er-Heb man with an extremely small head, Daniel remarks, "Him there with the five and a half hat size has the makings of a bloody hero."

Indeed, their drilled army, stiffened by twenty smuggled rifles, quickly goes from victory to victory. And their pinheaded rifleman distinguishes himself for loyalty. By treating newly conquered villages well, Daniel and Peachey recruit their men into the ever-growing army.

In general, regular armies have been able to take from irregular fighters the kind of land that's most worth taking: flat, fertile farmland.

Yet, what's a regular army to do in a place like Afghanistan that's eminently not worth conquering? In 1842, the British lost all but one of 16,000 trying to retreat from the Afghan capital of Kabul. This showed once again that irregulars could destroy a regular army in severe enough terrain.

By 1878, however, the Afghan ruler was again flirting with the expanding Russian Empire. Fearing the Czar's army would soon be pouring through the Khyber Pass and into the lightly defended plains of colonial India, the British set out to take control of Afghanistan's foreign policy.

In his conquest of Kabul and Kandahar, Sir Frederick Roberts solved the problem of how to beat Afghans in their own mountains. "General Bobs" used professionally drilled mountain men as his shock troops. Passes were taken by the Scottish Highlanders (in which Daniel and Peachey fictitiously served) and the Nepalese Gurkha Rifles (like their loyal translator Billy Fish, who is played by the tremendous Indian actor Saeed Jaffrey).

Today, the U.S. has about 30,000 elite Special Forces troops trained in both regular and irregular fighting. America's British allies have superb S.A.S. commandos, as well as 3,400 Gurkha troops.

Yet, was General Bobs' campaign simply another long-term failure? It depends on whether you consider 40 years of success a failure.

The British eventually placed Abdur Rahman on the throne in Kabul. Within Afghanistan's now carefully defined borders, they let him have his way—such as waging jihad against the poor Kafirs—so long as he delegated the conduct of Afghanistan's external relations to London. In the "Great Game" (the subject of Kipling's masterpiece *Kim*), Britain's spies and diplomats used bribes and threats to keep the Afghans from being bought off by the Russians.

This policy worked well enough for four decades. Finally, exhausted by WWI, Britain lost control in 1919, a date now considered by Afghanistan to be the year of its independence. Afghanistan began to slowly tip toward the Soviet Union, which ultimately led to the Soviet invasion of 1979, a full century after General Bobs' invasion.

Yet, if a war in Afghanistan does prove winnable, which it should, ought the U.S. to undertake a long-term benevolent occupation to attempt to turn that desolate land into a peaceful "normal country?" Huston's movie offers a skeptical perspective.

Initially, the two pirates' plan succeeds wildly. The pagans believe Daniel is a god, the son of Alexander. The high priests place the great Greek's crown upon his head and offer him a treasure room full of rubies and gold. All Daniel and Peachey need to do to become the two richest men on Earth is to fill their packs, wait four months for the snows in the Hindu Kush to melt, and then walk out.

While awaiting Spring, Daniel amuses himself by playing at being king. To the applause of his new subjects, he enforces peace, dispenses justice at traditional *durbars*, sets up granaries to insure against famine, and builds bridges to tie the country together.

When the passes finally open, Peachey learns to his horror that Daniel now feels too responsible for his people to grab the loot and run. The grandiose nation-building urge that in the 1990's helped inspire American interventions in Somalia, Haiti, and Bosnia has infected him. "A nation I shall make of it, with an anthem and a flag," King Daniel thunders.

Worse, Daniel has decided to take a Queen. He has picked out a local beauty called Roxanne—the same name as Alexander's wife. The priests demur. Billy Fish tries to explain to the king why his marriage would be an affront to Kafir beliefs. Daniel, blinded by his victories—"Have I not put the shadow of my hand over this country?"—fails to grasp that what seems a quibble to him is of dread import to the Kafirs.

Catastrophe ensues.

Science fiction novelist Orson Scott Card (*Ender's Game*) summed up *The Man Who Would Be King*: "This is the classic tragedy that Aristotle spoke of—so powerful that some of us can only stand to see the ending once."

Those who advocate that we stay in Afghanistan long after Osama bin Laden and the Taliban are dealt with should ponder Kipling and Huston's parable.

Cousin Marriage Conundrum

The American Conservative
January 13, 2003

MANY prominent neoconservatives are calling on America not only to conquer Iraq (and perhaps more Muslim nations after that), but also to rebuild Iraqi society in order to jumpstart the democratization of the Middle East. Yet, Americans know so little about the Middle East that few of us are even aware of one of the building blocks of Arab Muslim cultures: cousin marriage. Not surprisingly, we are almost utterly innocent of how much the high degree of inbreeding in Iraq could interfere with our nation-building ambitions.

In Iraq, as in much of the region, nearly half of all married couples are first or second cousins. A 1986 study of 4,500 married hospital patients and staff in Baghdad found that 46% were wed to a first or second cousin, while a smaller 1989 survey found 53% were "consanguineously" married. The most prominent example of an Iraqi first cousin marriage is that of Saddam Hussein and his first wife Sajida.

By fostering intense family loyalties and strong nepotistic urges, inbreeding makes the development of civil society more difficult. Many Americans have heard by now that Iraq is composed of three ethnic groups—the Kurds of the north, the Sunnis of the center, and the Shi'ites of the south. Clearly, these ethnic rivalries would complicate the task of reforming Iraq. But that is just a top-down summary of Iraq's ethnic make-up. Each of those three ethnic groups is divisible into smaller and smaller tribes, clans, and inbred extended families—each with its own alliances, rivals, and feuds. And the engine at the bottom of these bedeviling social divisions is the oft-ignored institution of cousin marriage.

The fractiousness and tribalism of Middle Eastern countries have frequently been remarked. In 1931, King Feisal of Iraq described his subjects as "devoid of any patriotic idea,... connected by no common tie, giving ear to evil; prone to anarchy, and perpetually ready to rise against any government whatever." The clannishness, corruption, and coups frequently observed in countries such as Iraq appear to be tied to the high rates of inbreeding.

Muslim countries are usually known for warm, devoted extended family relationships but also for weak patriotism. In the U.S., where individualism is so strong, many assume that "family values" and civic virtues such as sacrificing for the good of society always go together. But, in Islamic countries, family loyalty is often at war with national loyalty. Civic virtues, military effectiveness, and economic performance all suffer.

Commentator Randall Parker wrote:

> Consanguinity [cousin marriage] is the biggest underappreciated factor in Western analyses of Middle Eastern politics. Most Western political theorists seem blind to the importance of pre-ideological kinship-based political bonds in large part because those bonds are not derived from abstract Western ideological models of how societies and political systems should be organized.... Extended families that are incredibly tightly bound are really the enemy of civil society because the alliances of family override any consideration of fairness to people in the larger society. Yet, this obvious fact is missing from 99% of the discussions about what is wrong with the Middle East. How can we transform Iraq into a modern liberal democracy if every government worker sees a government job as a route to helping out his clan at the expense of other clans?

U.S. Army Col. Norvell De Atkine (Ret.) spent years trying to train America's Arab allies in modern combat techniques. In an article in *American Diplomacy* titled, "Why Arabs Lose Wars," a frustrated De Atkine explained, "First, the well-known lack of trust among Arabs for anyone outside their own family adversely affects offensive operations.... In a culture in which almost every sphere of human endeavor, including business and social relationships, is based on a family structure, this orientation is also present in the military, particularly in the stress of battle.

53

"Offensive action, basically, consists of fire and maneuver," De Atkine continued. "The maneuver element must be confident that supporting units or arms are providing covering fire. If there is a lack of trust in that support, getting troops moving forward against dug-in defenders is possible only by officers getting out front and leading, something that has not been a characteristic of Arab leadership."

Similarly, as Francis Fukuyama described in his 1995 book, *Trust: The Social Virtues & the Creation of Prosperity*, countries such as Italy with highly loyal extended families can generate dynamic family firms. Yet, their larger corporations tend to be rife with goldbricking, corruption, and nepotism, all because their employees do not trust each other to show their highest loyalty to the firm rather than their own extended families. Arab cultures are more family-focused even than Sicily, and therefore their larger economic enterprises suffer even more.

American society is so biased against inbreeding that many Americans have a hard time even conceiving of marrying a cousin. Yet, arranged matches between first cousins (especially between the children of brothers) are considered the ideal throughout much of a broad expanse from North Africa through West Asia and into Pakistan and India.

Americans have long dismissed cousin marriage as something practiced only among hillbillies. That old stereotype of inbred mountaineers waging decades-long blood feuds had some truth to it. One study of 107 marriages in Beech Creek, Kentucky in 1942 found 19% were consanguineous, although the Kentuckians were more inclined toward second-cousin marriages, while first-cousin couples are more common than second-cousin pairings in the Islamic lands.

Cousin marriage averages not much more than 1% in most European countries and under 10% in the rest of the world outside that Morocco to Southern India corridor. Muslim immigration, however, has been boosting Europe's low level of consanguinity. According to the leading authority on inbreeding, geneticist Alan H. Bittles of Edith Cowan University in Perth, Australia, "In the resident Pakistani community of some 0.5 million [in Britain] an estimated 50% to 60+% of marriages are consanguineous, with evidence that their prevalence is increasing."

European nations have recently become increasingly hostile toward the common practice among their Muslim immigrants of arranging marriages between their children and citizens of their home country, frequently their relatives. One study of Turkish guest-workers in the Danish city of Ishøj found that 98%—1st, 2nd, and 3rd generation—married a spouse from Turkey who then came and lived in Denmark. (Turks, however, are quite a bit less enthusiastic about cousin marriage than are Arabs or Pakistanis, which correlates with the much stronger degree of patriotism found in Turkey.)

European "family reunification" laws present an immigrant with the opportunity to bring in his nephew by marrying his daughter to him. Not surprisingly, "family reunification" almost always works just in one direction—with the new husband moving from the poor Muslim country to the rich European country. If a European-born daughter refused to marry her cousin from the old country just because she does not love him, that would deprive her extended family of the boon of an immigration visa. So, intense family pressure can fall on the daughter to do as she is told. The new Danish right-wing government has introduced legislation to crack down on these kind of marriages arranged to generate visas. British Home Secretary David Blunkett has called for immigrants to arrange more marriages within Britain.

Unlike the Middle East, Europe underwent what Samuel P. Huntington calls the "Romeo and Juliet revolution." Europeans became increasingly sympathetic toward the right of a young woman to marry the man she loves. Setting the stage for this was the Catholic Church's long war against cousin marriage, even out to fourth cousins or higher. This weakened the extended family in Europe, thus lessening the advantages of arranged marriages. It also strengthened broader institutions like the Church and the nation-state.

Islam itself may not be responsible for the high rates of inbreeding in Muslim countries. (Similarly high levels of consanguinity are found among Hindus in Southern India, although there uncle-niece marriages are socially preferred, even though their degree of genetic similarity is twice that of cousin marriages, with worse health consequences for offspring.) Rafat Hussain, a Pakistani-born Senior Lecturer at the University of New England in Australia, told me, "Islam does not specifically encourage cousin marriages and, in fact, in the early days of the spread of Islam, marriages outside the clan were highly desirable to increase cultural and religious influence." She adds, "The practice has little do with Islam (or in fact any religion) and has been a prevalent cultural norm before Islam." Inbreeding (or "endogamy") is also common among Christians in the Middle East, although less so than among Muslims.

The Muslim practice is similar to older Middle Eastern norms, such as those outlined in Leviticus in the Old Testament. The lineage of the Hebrew Patriarchs who founded the Jewish people was highly inbred. Abraham's son Isaac married Rebekah, a cousin once removed. And Isaac's son Jacob wed his two first cousins, Leah and Rachel. Jacob's dozen sons were the famous progenitors of the Twelve Tribes of Israel. Due to inbreeding, Jacob's eight legitimate sons had only six unique great-grandparents instead of the usual eight. That is because the inbred are related to their relatives through multiple paths.

Why do so many people around the world prefer to keep marriage in the family? Rafat Hussain noted, "In patriarchal societies where parents exert considerable influence and gender segregation is followed more strictly, marriage choice is limited to whom you know. While there is some pride in staying within the inner bounds of family for social or economic reasons, the more important issue is: Where will parents find a good match? Often, it boils down to whom you know and can trust."

Another important motivation—one that is particularly important in many herding cultures, such as the ancient ones from which the Jews and Muslims emerged—is to prevent inheritable wealth from being split among too many descendents. This can be especially important when there are economies of scale in the family business.

Just as the inbred have fewer unique ancestors than the outbred, they also have fewer unique heirs, helping keep both the inheritance and the brothers together. When a herd-owning patriarch marries his son off to his younger brother's daughter, he insures that his grandson and his grandnephew will be the same person. Likewise, the younger brother benefits from knowing that his grandson will also be the patriarch's grandson and heir. Thus, by making sibling rivalry over inheritance less relevant, cousin marriage emotionally unites families. The anthropologist Carleton Coon also pointed out that by minimizing the number of relatives a Bedouin Arab nomad has, this system of inbreeding "does not overextend the number of persons whose deaths an honorable man must avenge."

Of course, there are also disadvantages to inbreeding. The best known is medical. Being inbred increases the chance of inheriting genetic syndromes caused by malign recessive genes. Bittles found that, after controlling for socio-economic factors, the babies of first cousins had about a 30% higher chance of dying before their first birthdays.

The biggest disadvantage, however, may be political.

Are Muslims, especially Arabs, so much more loyal to their families than to their nations because, due to countless generations of cousin marriages, they are so much more genealogically related to their families than Westerners are related to theirs? Frank Salter, a political scientist at the Max Planck Institute in Germany, whose new book *Risky Transactions: Trust, Kinship, and Ethnicity* takes a sociobiological look at the reason why Mafia families are indeed families, told me, "That's my hunch; at least it's bound to be a factor."

One of the basic laws of modern biology, quantified by William D. Hamilton in 1964 under the name "kin selection," is that the closer the genetic relationship between two people, the more likely they are to feel loyalty and altruism toward each other. Natural selection has molded us not just to try to propagate our own genes, but to help our relatives, who possess copies of some of our specific genes, to propagate their own.

Nepotism is thus biologically inspired. Hamilton explained that the level of nepotistic feeling generally depends upon the degree of genetic similarity. You share half your personally variable genes with your children and siblings, but one quarter with your nephews/nieces and grandchildren, so your nepotistic urges will tend to be somewhat less toward them. You share one eighth of your genes with your first cousins, and one thirty-second with your second cousin, so your feelings of family loyalty tend to fall off quickly. But not as quickly if you and your relatives are inbred. Then, you will be related to your kin via multiple pathways. You will all be genetically more similar, so your normal family feelings will be multiplied. For example, because your son-in-law might be also be the nephew you have cherished since his childhood, you can lavish all the nepotistic altruism on him that in outbred Western societies would be split between your son-in-law and your nephew.

Unfortunately, as nepotism is usually a zero-sum game, the flip side of being materially nicer toward your relatives would be that you would have fewer resources left with which to be civil, or even just fair, toward non-kin. So nepotistic corruption is rampant in countries such as Iraq, where Saddam has appointed members of his extended family from his hometown of Tikrit to many key positions in the national government.

Similarly, a tendency toward inbreeding can turn an extended family into a miniature racial group with its own partially isolated gene pool. (Dog breeders use extreme forms of inbreeding to create new breeds in a handful of generations.) The ancient Hebrews provide a vivid example of a partly inbred extended family (that of Abraham and his posterity) that evolved into its own ethnic group. This process has been going on for thousands of years in the Middle East, which is why not just the Jews, but also why tiny, ancient inbreeding groups such as the Samaritans and the John-the-Baptist-worshipping Sabeans still survive.

In summary, although neoconservatives constantly point to America's success at reforming Germany and Japan after World War II as evidence that it would be easy to do the same in the Middle East, the deep social structure of Iraq is the complete opposite of those two true nation-states, with their highly patriotic, co-operative, and (not surprisingly) outbred peoples. The Iraqis, in contrast, more closely resemble the Hatfields and the McCoys.

Five Years After 9/11: Why Did Bush Blunder?

VDARE
September 10, 2006

(O)N Sunday, five years less a day after Saudi and Egyptian terrorists killed 3,000 Americans, the *New York Times* reported in "More Muslims Arrive in U.S., After 9/11 Dip:"

> In 2005, more people from Muslim countries became legal permanent United States residents—nearly 96,000—than in any year in the previous two decades.[1]

Of course, no foreign Muslim can hurt us here in America unless *we let him into America*. But the Bush Administration, instead of securing the borders, is ginning up another round of war fever.

Iran in 2006 is being compared to Germany in 1938—although the clearest comparison is to Iraq in 2002.

Of course, the Iranian Shi'ite government's new influence in the Persian Gulf, which we're supposed to worry so much about, is the *result* of the Administration destroying the Iraqi Sunni secular regime that was deterring Iran—and replacing it with a Shi'ite-dominated administration with close ties to Iran.

As I've been pointing out for some time now, rather than doing something simple and sensible such as increasingly disconnecting America from the chaos of the Muslim world, the Grand Strategy of the Bush Administration in the half decade since 9/11 has contradictorily consisted of:

- Invade the world
- Invite the world
- In hock to the world

The prodigious young blogger Daniel Larison similarly sums up the Bush Administration agenda as: "Imperialism, Immigration, and Insolvency."[2]

Websites like *Belmont Club* try to reassure the faithful by offering ever more convoluted explanations of what the Administration's master strategists are actually up to. But the suspicion is growing that, rather than being masterful Machiavels always seeing a half-dozen steps ahead, the White House has simply lacked the competence to judge what its various spasmodic actions will unleash.

Is there an underlying rationale to Invade-Invite-In Hock?

Or has American policy simply been the chaotic outcome of the shifting power struggles of Administration players each in the grip of his own *idée fixe*?

Whether you're a Pollyanna optimist or a paranoid pessimist, it's still an oddly comforting assumption that somewhere, behind all the nonsensical propaganda, there is somebody smart who is secretly pulling the strings to achieve his goals, whatever they may be.

That there's an Inner Circle comprised of profoundly competent men plotting the course of history is one of the most popular staples of science fiction. In *Star Wars*, the Jedi Knights battle each other to determine the fate of the galaxy. In Isaac Asimov's *Foundation* trilogy, psychohistorian Hari Seldon has scientifically grasped what will happen for the next 1,000 years.

The same pattern is found in science fiction by "serious" authors. The climaxes of both famous English mid-century dystopian novels, Aldous Huxley's *Brave New World* and George Orwell's *1984*, are didactic dialogues in which omniscient and omnipotent Inner Circle representatives proudly explain to the idealistic main characters the sinister logic behind the regime's disinformation.

In 1932, Huxley's Mustapha Mond, the brilliant physicist turned global oligarch, details why the government requires everyone to dither away his or her time on hedonism.

Then in 1948, Orwell followed with the horrifying encounter between Outer Party member Winston Smith and O'Brien of the Inner Party:

"How does one man assert his power over another, Winston?"
Winston thought. "By making him suffer," he said.

FIVE YEARS AFTER 9/11: WHY DID BUSH BLUNDER?

"Exactly. By making him suffer. Obedience is not enough. Unless he is suffering, how can you be sure that he is obeying your will and not his own?... If you want a picture of the future, imagine a boot stamping on a human face— for ever."

So—has America's policy since 9/11 been dictated by benevolent Obiwan Kenobis and Hari Seldons or by evil Mustapha Monds and O'Briens?

"Neither," suggests Gregory Cochran, the physicist and geneticist, who correctly pointed out in 2002 that Saddam Hussein was too broke to have a nuclear bomb program. "There is *no* Inner Party in our government. They just don't know what they are talking about."

The reality, in Cochran's view, is more like *Idiocracy*, the funny new movie from the wonderful Mike Judge, creator of *King of the Hill* and *Office Space*. A 100 IQ soldier played by Luke Wilson is accidentally frozen for 500 years. When he awakes, he discovers that everyone he meets is a moron.

Who is behind this horror? The hero is whisked off to the White House. But instead of meeting an all-seeing Mustapha Mond who can reveal the inner workings of the dystopia, the "President of America" turns out to be a professional wrestler as clueless as the voters who elected him, with a cabinet chosen to make him feel intellectually adequate by comparison.

Similarly, consider today's Number Three man in the Pentagon from 2001 to 2005, the civilian neoconservative "intellectual" Douglas Feith. He was notoriously described as "the #$%^&*@ stupidest guy on the face of the earth" by General Tommy Franks, whose own mental acuity reminded few observers of, say, Admiral Raymond A. Spruance, the victor of Midway.

In a memo a few days after 9/11, Feith proposed first attacking South America as "a surprise to the terrorists," which, it indeed would have been, as well as a surprise to the rest of humanity over the age of two.

Feith's reasons for wanting to use American military might to slaughter random Arab merchants who do business on the Paraguay-Argentina-Brazil "Triple Border" (as well as anybody else who happened to be in the vicinity) were no doubt deeply personal. (Feith's longtime law partner in "Feith & Zell" was L. Marc Zell, who is a prominent spokesman for extremist Zionist settlers in the West Bank.)

Still, Feith's plan was also flagrantly ridiculous. As a coherent entity, "the terrorists" exist even less than any Bush Administration "Inner Party". There are no "the terrorists"— just terrorists, many of whom hate each other, and many of whom are no threat to the U.S. (And there were *definitely* no terrorists endangering America in remotest South America.)

Yet, rather than being eased out of his crucial position immediately after so graphically displaying his unfitness, Feith stayed on for another four years to work his *Idiocracy*-style mischief, pipelining convicted conman Ahmad Chalabi's lies about Saddam Hussein's purported WMD programs to Dick Cheney.[3]

Meanwhile, the Number Two man at the Pentagon, Paul Wolfowitz, another neoconservative intellectual, was using the opportunity presented by the mass murder committed by Saudi and Egyptian Islamist fanatics based in Afghanistan to call for conquering the *anti-Islamist* Iraq regime of the secular socialist Sadam Hussein.

While Feith's chief motive appears to have been to kill Arabs, any Arabs, Wolfowitz is widely considered an idealist who actually believed the Administration's flapdoodle about the Arabs being ripe for democracy.

But why would any grown man think such a thing about the Arabs?

We may never know for sure. But private motivations have been known to drive outsiders in the Middle East in the past. For example, on the 684th and last page of T.E. Lawrence's eloquent memoir *Seven Pillars of Wisdom* comes the stunning statement that Lawrence actually had a secret reason for liberating the Arabs in 1917-1918 and he's *not* going to tell us what it was:

> The strongest motive throughout had been a personal one, not mentioned here, but present to me, I think, every hour these two years.

The least vague answer Lawrence ever provided was once, when asked why he had fought for Arab independence, he replied:

> I liked a particular Arab, and I thought that freedom for the race would be an acceptable present.

The most likely candidate for Lawrence's favorite Arab was a teenage waterboy.[4] Similarly, we found out in 2005, when Wolfowitz of Arabia was being kicked upstairs to head the World Bank (just like that other failed Defense Department official Robert McNamara), that Wolfowitz's favorite Arab was Shaha Riza, a middle-aged Arab feminist. According to the *Washington Post*, his girlfriend "shares Wolfowitz's passion for democratizing the Middle East."[5]

I'm sure Ms. Riza, along with all her family and friends that Wolfowitz met, is highly capable of participating in a Jeffersonian democracy.

But one shouldn't help send one's country off to war based on such an unscientific sample.

The least likely candidate for the role of the brilliant Mustapha Mond: the man who actually holds ultimate responsibility—President George W. Bush.

Yet Bush's former ghostwriter persuasively outlined the mixture of cheap politics and oedipal jealousy that inspired Bush's hopes for an Iraq war well before 9/11:

> "He was thinking about invading Iraq in 1999," said author and journalist Mickey Herskowitz. "It was on his mind. He said to me: 'One of the keys to being seen as a great leader is to be seen as a commander-in-chief.' And he said, 'My father had all this political capital built up when he drove the Iraqis out of Kuwait and he wasted it.' He said, 'If I have a chance to invade ... if I had that much capital, I'm not going to waste it....'"
>
> Herskowitz said that Bush expressed frustration at a lifetime as an underachiever in the shadow of an accomplished father. In aggressive military action, he saw the opportunity to emerge from his father's shadow. The moment, Herskowitz said, came in the wake of the September 11 attacks.

Bush's invite-the-world immigration plan makes little sense either as policy or politics. Five years after 9/11, it's becoming obvious that his Administration's invade-the-world strategy reflects mostly the deluded obsessions of a few men of strong passion and weak reason.

The Zeroth Amendment

Taki's
July 19, 2017

A LITTLE-KNOWN survey[6] revealed the single most decisive reason Donald Trump defeated Hillary Clinton: White Democrats have drifted into ideological extremism over not regulating immigration.

By way of background, a general problem in political science with using polls to track ideological trends over the years is that you want to keep asking the same questions to see how voters' responses evolve. But that means that pollsters seldom ask about new beliefs that would have seemed bizarre even in the recent past.

In turn, pundits, lacking polling data to write about, don't even mention historic developments, such as the rise of mainstream antiwhite American hate discourse over the past half decade. For most mainstream journalists to notice their own increasingly vicious racist attitudes would be like a fish noticing it is wet.

Because I have a better-than-average historical sense, I've been pointing out for the past few years that American elites are mindlessly floating toward an unspoken belief in the sacredness of what I call the Zeroth Amendment: that American citizens should get no say in who gets to move to America because huddled masses of non-Americans possess civil rights to immigrate, no questions asked. And this Zeroth Amendment overrides the obsolete First Amendment, so you aren't allowed to question it.

Last December, Professor Eric Kaufmann of the London School of Economics had YouGov ask the kind of question that would have struck pollsters as absurd not long ago:

> "A white American who identifies with her group and its history supports a proposal to reduce immigration. Her motivation is to maintain her group's share of the population for cultural reasons. Is this person a) racist, b) racially self-interested, which is not racist, c) don't know."

These days, of course, "racist" means...hateful...intolerable...unthinkable. Calling someone "racist" is now approaching a blood libel. The word "racist" is increasingly a dog whistle for violence by masked blackshirts against anyone so demeaned.

The differences among white voters were stark: Only 11% of white Trump voters labeled as racist the view that American whites have a moral right to vote that the immigration system not be exploited to drive them into political and cultural impotence.

In contrast, 73% of Hillary's white voters think that it's racist for white Americans to have an opinion on who gets to immigrate.

Strikingly, Hillary's white supporters were more radical in denouncing whites as racists than were her nonwhite backers. Only 58% of Hillary's nonwhite voters labeled Kaufmann's hypothetical white woman as racist. Kaufmann observes:

> Minority voters are slightly more likely to back the "racist" interpretation than whites, 45-36, but this 12-point difference is dwarfed by the 62-point gap within White America between Clinton and Trump voters.

The longer the university indoctrination of the white Hillary voters, the more unhinged they were about this slander. Among white Clinton supporters with a college degree, 84% said it was racist for whites to be allowed to favor whites in immigration policy. Among Hillary's whites with advanced degrees, 91% agreed.

A federal circuit judge has since discovered hidden in the emanations and penumbras of the Constitution the Zeroth Amendment: "The President shall enforce no law respecting an establishment of borders, or prohibiting the free crossing thereof." (The Supreme Court doesn't yet agree, but without any current Republican justices agreeing to retire and be replaced, this non-hallucinatory reading of the Constitution seems doomed.)

I may have first noticed this growing anti-borders zealotry the day before 9/11 when Bill Clinton, huckstering for cash in Australia, commended "the ultimate wisdom of a borderless world." The Clintons shut up about this for a while after getting away with that, but by the 2010s this it's-not-broken-so-break-it worldview was back in force. Granted, nobody except the most Aspergery libertarians argues in favor of a borderless world, but the center-left increasingly assumes its desirability.

To the Clintonites, it's not an argument that needs to be won in fair debate, or even is desirable to discuss as if it's open to argument. To be precise, they assume the deplorability of anybody who doesn't share their assumption.

In contrast, old-time leftists can be wild cards: Bernie Sanders,[7] for example, in 2015 cogently demolished open borders as a Billionaire Liberation Front stalking horse:

> Bernie Sanders: Open borders? No, that's a Koch brothers proposal.
> Ezra Klein: Really?
> Bernie Sanders: Of course. That's a right-wing proposal, which says essentially there is no United States...
> Ezra Klein: But it would make...
> Bernie Sanders: Excuse me...
> Ezra Klein: It would make a lot of global poor richer, wouldn't it?
> Bernie Sanders: It would make everybody in America poorer "you're doing away with the concept of a nation-state, and I don't think there's any country in the world that believes in that.

Unfortunately, Bernie is easy to bully, so by 2016 he sounded just like Hillary on immigration. Sure, massive immigration is bad for Americans, but it's good for Democratic politicians, so whaddaya whaddaya?

As you know and I know, this latest Democratic orthodoxy is innumerate lunacy. There are 21.7 foreigners on Earth for every resident of America. For the American majority to lose our Constitutional right to control the quantity and quality of immigration would be the absolute ruin of the American republic.

In a July 13 article calling for open borders, *The Economist* magazine noted:

> Gallup, a pollster, estimated in 2013 that 630m people, "about 13% of the world's population," would migrate permanently if

they could, and even more would move temporarily.... So the Gallup numbers could just as well be too low. Today there are 1.4bn people in rich countries and 6bn in not-so-rich ones. It is hardly far-fetched to imagine that, over a few decades, a billion or more of those people might emigrate if there were no legal obstacle to doing so.

Amusingly, this article is locked away behind the closed borders of *The Economist's* paywall. Not so amusingly, open borders, combined with the African population explosion, would devastate whichever country was so foolish as to adopt it.

The test case is Puerto Rico, a Third World nation that enjoys open borders with the United States. Despite a per capita GDP almost triple the world average, Puerto Rico is currently depopulating, with about three-fifths of all Puerto Ricans now in the mainland U.S.

Similarly, being able to choose which immigrants to accept is central to national sovereignty. Countless countries enforce discriminatory policies. For example, Israel recruits Jews from around the world and blocks virtually everyone else, building formidable walls along its borders and actively deporting those who got in earlier.

Japan allowed Brazilians who were racially Japanese to immigrate (although Japan has found them less than satisfactory: Nurture matters as well as nature).

Singapore, perhaps the most competently governed state, has a national immigration policy of maintaining racial balance (i.e., a Chinese majority: The ruling Chinese have lower birth rates in Singapore so their co-ethnics back home are allowed to immigrate in larger numbers).

Switzerland, the Singapore of Europe, lets each neighborhood vote on whether to allow individual immigrants to naturalize. For example, in 2015, an outspoken vegan activist who had lived in Switzerland for 34 years was rejected for Swiss citizenship by a 144-62 vote of her annoyed neighbors.[8]

In the 1990s, Germany gave preference to return to the land of their ancestors to tenth-generation Volga Germans, recruited to farm in central Russia by Czarina Catherine the Great.

Spain is legally partial to Latin Americans (although their rapid influx caused massive unemployment after 2008).

I could go on and on with reasonable examples of how racial and cultural preferences in immigration rules are perfectly compatible with high levels of civilization, but that's hardly the point. The reason a substantial number of Americans have been cajoled into believing it's vile for white citizens to have any say in who their future fellow citizens will be is because promiscuous immigration is good for billionaires and Democrats.

In reality, it's corrupting for a country to allow politicians to import ringers to vote for them, and potentially catastrophic when the bosses encourage their new charges to be hostile and demanding toward the natives. But in the U.S., nonwhite politicians are encouraged to import as many co-ethnics to vote for themselves as they can round up. Democratic strategists frequently boast of how they will soon achieve one-party rule in Washington by hauling in nonwhite immigrants. (In contrast, it never occurs to Republicans to ask in white refugees, such as South African farmers.)

Rigging the electoral process is obviously unethical, so Democrats and their PR flacks in the press constantly denounce as the epitome of immorality any stirrings of resistance. Thus, you hear over and over about the plagues of white privilege and racism, while the topic of how the Democrats are trying to steal the country through foreign collusion is left unmentioned. The best defense is a good offense.

Kaufmann notes experimental evidence suggesting that the pro-immigration side doesn't so much try to win democratic debates as to terrify the majority into silence:

> Other work suggests norms not only lead people to frown on voting for the far right, but even prompt them to hide their views on immigration. Using a "list experiment" that measures average sentiment but permits individuals to conceal their answers, Alexander Janus discovered that 60% of White Americans supported cutting immigration to zero when their identities were concealed, compared to 39% when their identities were known to the researcher. Self-censorship was especially pronounced among the university-educated.

Self-censorship is prudent. Violence against immigration skeptics is increasing, as are you'll-never-work-in-this-town-again career consequences. For example, Texas rock band Dream Machine was last month dropped by its label after a legal immigrant member expressed cynicism about illegal immigration.[9]

Recently, Kaufmann's question was repeated in a number of countries around the world. The U.S. came out the most fanatic with 36% denouncing an intelligent immigration policy as racist, versus only 13% in South Africa. Of course, South Africans were not asked about whites, they were asked whether Xhosas should be tarred as racist for preferring Xhosas. The Xhosas' hostile view of black immigrants from the rest of Africa is spelled out in the immigration allegory movie *District 9*, but few American critics even noticed, since the anti-majoritarian conventional wisdom isn't really based on political philosophy, it's based on antiwhite racist animus.

In other words, this question isn't about whether the majority in a particular country has the right to limit immigration, but whether whites should possess democratic rights like everybody else.

The Current Year's short answer: no.

It's the new White Man's Burden. In 1899, it was to invade the world. In 2017, the White Man's Burden is to invite the world.

The Shadowy Imam of the Poconos

Taki's
January 01, 2014

AS 2014 dawns, the world continues to keep me furnished with material. For example, the current political shakeup in Turkey turns out to be a mashup of various obsessions and hobbyhorses of mine, such as byzantine conspiracy theories, test prep, the naiveté of American education reform, immigration fraud, the deep state, and even the Chechen Bomb Brothers' Uncle Ruslan.[10]

This lattice of coincidence begins with Turkey's prime minister Recip Tayyip Erdoğan, who is presently besieged by graft scandals following police raids on his inner circle.[11]

With Turkey's traditional ruling class "the secularist Kemalist generals" finally neutralized by the Ergenekon show trial, the Muslim civilian factions now appear to be plotting against each other. It is widely assumed among Turkish conspiracy theorists (i.e., roughly 98% of all Turks) that the prosecutorial assault on the prime minister was at the behest of Erdoğan's former political ally, Fethullah Gülen, a powerful and mysterious Muslim cult leader holed up since 1999 in, of all places, the Poconos, where he has become America's largest operator of charter schools.

The imam has been preparing for the struggle in Turkey for decades, launching his adherents on a long march through the institutions. The holy man's Turkish enemies leaked a video in 1999 just before he defected to the

US and took up exile in his fortified compound in Saylorsburg, PA. Gülen was shown advising his believers:

> You must move in the arteries of the system without anyone notic-ing your existence until you reach all the power centers.... You must wait until such time as you have gotten all the state power....

Gülenists have since become common within Turkey's police and judicia-ry, playing a lead role in last year's conviction of 254 secularists for alleged-ly conspiring against the Islamic government. According to *Wikileaks*, the American ambassador to Ankara, James Jeffreys, cabled Foggy Bottom:

> Gülenists also reportedly dominate the Turkish National Police, where they serve as the vanguard for the Ergenekon investigation— an extensive probe into an alleged vast underground network that is accused of attempting to encourage a military coup in 2004. The investigation has swept up many secular opponents of the ruling Justice and Development Party (AKP), including Turkish military figures, which has prompted accusations that the Gülenists have as their ultimate goal the undermining of all institutions which dis-approve of Turkey becoming more visibly Islamist. (COMMENT: The assertion that the TNP [Turkish National Police] is controlled by Gülenists is impossible to confirm but we have found no one who disputes it....)[12]

Amusingly, the Gülenists' December attack on Erdoğan's ethics seems to be retaliation for the government's November attack on Gülen's college ad-mission test preparation centers. *The New York Times* reported:

> Relations soured in recent weeks after the government tried to shut down private test preparation centers in Turkey, many of which are run by followers of Mr. Gülen and are important for the movement's recruitment and finances.... "Erdoğan's efforts to shut down the private schools was the last straw for Gülen and the Gülenists," said Steven A. Cook, a Turkey expert at the Council on Foreign Relations.

He who controls test preparation controls the future.

Seriously, if you can get your followers to score higher on the gatekeeper tests, they may become the ruling class of the future—a lesson that American conservatives might ponder. In general, American conservatives have felt that

71

it wouldn't be sporting for them to think in any organized fashioned about how to game tests such as the SAT. But the older civilizations have little patience for such boyish innocence.

I don't know anything about about test prep in Turkey, but I know a lady who was a high-school physics teacher in Iran, where she made herself unpopular by refusing to teach "summer school." In Iran, it's traditional for public school teachers to provide the highest paying upcoming students a private summer preview course in which they are given all the questions and answers for next year's tests. (This Iranian attitude toward physics education may help explain why Iran's nuclear program has been the world's slowest moving crisis.)

Ambassador Jeffreys commented in his secret cable:

> We have heard accounts that TNP [Turkish National Police] applicants who stay at Gülenist pensions are provided the answers in advance to the TNP entrance exam.

The Gülen movement receives hundreds of millions of dollars from American taxpayers to operate approximately 130 charter schools in America. Not surprisingly, they claim excellent test scores.

In defense of Gülen, it might be argued that he's providing the Anatolian heartland with something that was extremely valuable to northern Europe: a business-oriented religious network in the Weberian mode. One reason Mexico is Mexico is because the Counter-Reformation kept Puritanism out of Latin America, and along with it the Protestant work ethic. Turkey, which has long been a sort of Mexico of Europe, could use an Anatolian business class.

On the other hand, the more I look into Gülen, the more he seems characteristically Ottoman. The adjective "byzantine" stems from the labyrinthine and devious politics of the imperial court of the Byzantine Empire, the successor to the Roman Empire. Not everything has changed since 1453.

Of course, the Gülen movement's test prep schools in Turkey aren't just about test prep. In an aggressively laicized state, after-school school is the best chance for indoctrinating youths in Islam and/or Gülen's cult of personality.

> "It's organised like a cult," a French researcher told *FRANCE 24*, speaking on condition of anonymity. "In certain places where they meet in Istanbul, it really feels like you're in a Scientology centre. Leaders make speeches about universal love, and distribute pamphlets with photos of celebrities on them. Private classes are given,

but we don't know if the teachings are religious or not." Most members are not even allowed to talk about the movement," the French researcher explained. "The way it functions is totally opaque, which is reminiscent of Freemasons."[13]

It wouldn't be a coincidence that Gülen's Anatolian Muslims model their secret society upon the Freemasons. The secularist Europeanizers they hate used the security of Masonic lodges to launch their Young Turks revolution a century ago.

To Americans, the notion that the Ottoman Empire's revolution of 1908-1913 was hatched in part in Masonic lodges sounds like Dan Brown crackpottery. But Freemasonry, with its long initiations and complicated handshakes, was useful in impeding the Sultan's secret policemen at infiltrating cells of reformist conspirators.

You may be wondering who Gülen is. The grade-school dropout's website explains:

> Gülen is an authoritative mainstream Turkish Muslim scholar, thinker, author, poet, opinion leader and educational activist who supports interfaith and intercultural dialogue, science, democracy and spirituality and opposes violence and turning religion into a political ideology.

Gülen's English language PR guys have mastered TED Talk, those bits of jargon that reassure human resources departments and excite CEOs. (For example, charter schools are catnip to US-based Davos Men.)

Still, Gülen's L. Ron Hubbard-level megalomania is reminiscent of Philip Seymour Hoffman introducing himself in *The Master* (a fictionalization of Scientology's roots) as, "I am a writer, a doctor, a nuclear physicist, a theoretical philosopher, but above all I am a man."

Cult leaders can't just be one thing, can they?

Recall Werner Erhard, the former car salesman Jack Rosenberg who renamed himself after physicist Werner Heisenberg and West German finance minister Ludwig Erhard. He founded Est, the existentialist cult that swept white-collar America in the 1970s.[14] Est was like a new, improved version of Scientology shorn of space aliens. Est was Jean-Paul Sartre's famous October 1945 lecture to the young intellectuals of Paris telling them that life was meaningless so they had to take responsibility for choosing their own meanings, just remodeled for American regional sales managers.

Here's how Erhard describes himself today:

> Werner Erhard is considered a leading thinker in academic and cor-
> porate communities and is currently engaged in rigorous examina-
> tion and presentation of his ideas. As a creator of models he provides
> new paradigms to thinkers and practitioners in fields as diverse as
> philosophy, business, education, psychotherapy, third world devel-
> opment, medicine, conflict resolution, and community building.[15]

In 2005 the British magazine *Prospect* and the American magazine *Foreign Policy* held an online poll to name the world's top public intellectuals.
Noam Chomsky came in first and Umberto Eco second. In 2006, however,
Muslims swarmed the poll, demoting Chomsky to eleventh place as Muslims
took the top ten spots. Number one was Gülen (which may have amused Eco,
author of byzantine conspiracy novels such as *Foucault's Pendulum*). I suspect
Gülenists saw this poll as their opportunity for vengeance for *TIME*'s late
1990s Person of the Century poll, which was hijacked by Kemalists voting en
masse for Ataturk.

The Gülen cult, which calls itself Hizmet for "The Service," owns the largest newspaper in Turkey, *Zaman*. A *Zaman* columnist recently elucidated:

> Hizmet does not—and more correctly, by its very nature, cannot—
> take on an all-comprehensive physical form or name, other than
> the very abstract nominalization of "Hizmet," which, for the lack
> of a better word, is used to refer to the diverse civic service initia-
> tives its followers are involved in. It is thanks to this very porous,
> fluid and ether-like electromagnetic nature of Hizmet that it can
> manifest itself in 150 different nations, cultures and regimes, and
> welcome devotees and sympathizers from all walks of life.[16]

Well, that clears that up.

Hizmet runs something like 130 charter schools in the US. Why? Because
that's the kind of thing you do in 21st-century America when you have tons
of money and a potential image problem: teach math to black children. Remember when Mark Zuckerberg of Facebook was concerned about the upcoming *Social Network* biopic, so he suddenly gave $100 million to Newark
public schools? Think of the children!

In contrast to the Zuck's donation, however, the Gülenist charters are paid
for by you and me to the tune of many hundreds of millions of dollars annually in American taxpayer money. Charter schools represent a giant opportuni-

ty for anybody skilled at bureaucratic maneuvering. It's common for schools costing $50 to $100 million to be turned over to charter operators claiming to be in it for the children.

It is rumored that Gülen's charters are intimately wrapped up with immigration fraud. The *Philadelphia Inquirer* reported in 2011:

> Fethullah Gülen is a major Islamic political figure in Turkey, but he lives in self-imposed exile in a Poconos enclave and gained his green card by convincing a federal judge in Philadelphia that he was an influential educational figure in the United States. As evidence, his lawyer pointed to the charter schools, now more than 120 in 25 states, that his followers—Turkish scientists, engineers, and businessmen—have opened....[17]

And because there is apparently a shortage of English-speakers in America, Gülen's charters get H-1B visas (684 in 2009 alone) from the federal government to bring in Turkish men to teach American kids.

> Ruth Hocker, former president of the parents' group at the Young Scholars of Central Pennsylvania Charter School in State College, began asking questions when popular, certified American teachers were replaced by uncertified Turkish men who often spoke limited English and were paid higher salaries. Most were placed in math and science classes. "They would tell us they couldn't find qualified American teachers," Hocker said.

The Turkish teachers are said to have to kick back 40% of their salaries to Gülen's movement. Last month, a few days before Gülen's prosecutors raided Erdoğan's cronies, the FBI raided a Gülen school in Baton Rouge and hauled off documents. (The FBI has yet to announce what they found.)

Why is Gülen in Pennsylvania, rather than his own country? When immigration bureaucrats asked that question in 2006, 29 influential Americans wrote in to vindicate Gülen. One of the most outspoken was Graham E. Fuller, the former CIA station chief in Afghanistan.

This intervention on Gülen's behalf by America's own deep state merely encouraged Turkish conspiracy enthusiasts who think the Gülen movement is a front for the CIA, as the former head of Turkish intelligence Osman Nuri Gundes claimed in a 2010 book.[18]

Fuller came to my attention last spring when I wondered how the Tsarnaevs who blew up the Boston Marathon had gotten refugee status in

America despite being Trouble with a Capital T.[19] As I surmised, the Bomb Brothers' uncle Ruslan Tsarni, a murky player in Beltway circles, pulled some strings. Why did some Chechens have strings to pull in America? Beyond all the geopolitical *raison d'etat*, Fuller's daughter Samantha Ankara Fuller used to be married to Uncle Ruslan.

A major problem with America being the imperial capital of the world is that, with some obvious exceptions, Americans aren't all that adept at imperial court maneuverings. We were raised being told that we have a republic, if we can keep it. And that means we aren't prepared to compete with those who represent thousands of years of training in the art and craft of empire.

Our New Planet Is Going to Be Great!

Taki's
July 17, 2019

THE fundamental issue of the 2020 presidential campaign is rapidly becoming whether or not America's whites, as exemplified in the person of Donald Trump, have the right to block the world's blacks and Muslims, as exemplified in the person of Somalia-born Rep. Ilhan Omar (D-MN), from immigrating *en masse* to the United States.

Or is the entire notion of white citizens democratically voting to keep out nonwhites too racistly triggering for more enlightened entities, such as the Ninth Circuit Court of Appeals, to allow?

The United Nations' publication last month of its World Population Prospects 2019 adds important perspective to this question.[20]

For example, in 1991, when Omar's family fled Somalia due to their complicity in the genocidal regime of the dictator Siad Barre, the population of Somalia was only 7 million.[21]

Today, 28 chaotic years later, Somalia has more than doubled in size to 15 million despite immense outflows of emigrants. The U.N. forecasts that Somalia's population will reach 35 million in 2050 and 76 million in 2100.

Alternatively, millions of Somalis (or, quite possibly, tens of millions of Somalis) might prefer to follow Rep. Omar to the Magic Dirt of the first world. According to a Gallup poll, at present one-third of the population of sub-Saharan African wants to migrate, and it's unlikely that additional population growth will make Africa more attractive.[22]

Here's my latest update of what I call The Most Important Graph in the World:

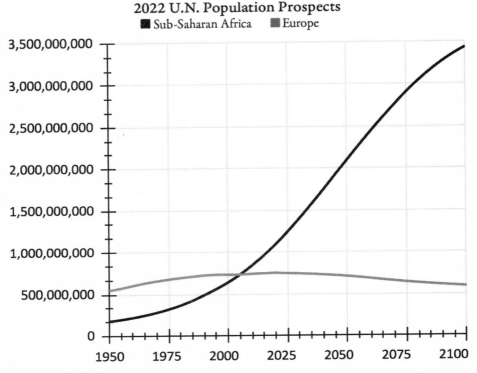

2022 U.N. Population Prospects
■ Sub-Saharan Africa   ■ Europe

The U.N. forecasts that the population of sub-Saharan Africa, which was 504,000,000 in 1991 and is 1,066,000,000 today, will grow to 2,118,000,000 in 2050 and all the way to 3,775,000,000 in 2100.

Do American and European white voters have the right to say no to the hundreds of millions of blacks and Muslims who will want to flee the messes they've made of their own countries?

Or would restricting immigration by nonwhites be "white nationalism" and "white supremacy" and therefore unthinkable?

While this would have seemed like an insane debate as recently as, say, 2011, there is a strategic electoral logic behind the Democrats' Great Awokening that is constantly pushing them in an ever more antiwhite direction. As a Coalition of the Fringes, the only thing that holds together the Democrats is demonizing core Americans. Without ever increasingly whipping up hatred of whites, what is there to keep the Democrats' collection of miscellaneous identity groups from turning on each other?

For example, the current fracas broke out with an intra-Democratic dot vs. feather brawl between two flavors of Indians. The brains behind Rep. Alexandria Ocasio-Cortez's (D-NY) operation, her tech-millionaire chief of staff Saikat Chakrabarti, went on the warpath against fellow Democrats. Chakrabarti denounced as racist those who aren't quite extremist enough on immigration, such as Rep. Sharice Davids (D-KS), who is advertised as "the first openly LGBT Native American elected to the United States Congress."

Unlike Asian Indians, American Indians don't have any relatives abroad to import, so they are increasingly at odds over immigration.

Chakrabarti complained on Twitter:

> I don't believe Sharice is a racist person, but her votes are showing her to enable a racist system.

At that point the House Democratic Caucus, chaired by Nancy Pelosi's ally Rep. Hakeem Jeffries (D-NY), fired back at Chakrabarti and his deficit of Intersectionality:

> Who is this guy and why is he explicitly singling out a Native American woman of color? Her name is Congresswoman Davids, not Sharice. She is a phenomenal new member who flipped a red seat blue.
> Keep Her Name Out Of Your Mouth.

This last line was accompanied by six interspersed emojis representing "clapbacks," which are some kind of hip-hop form of argumentation in which you prove the logic of your point by clapping your hands obnoxiously in your rival's face.

Pelosi is from California, where elderly white Democrats like herself, Dianne Feinstein, Jerry Brown, and Barbara Boxer long held on to power despite decades of demographic change. But that has been due to the political passivity of California's vast Mexican population.

In contrast, this year Pelosi has run into endless trouble with feistier ethnicities such as Palestinian, Puerto Rican, and Somali.

Donald Trump then decided that not enough attention was being paid to him, so he took up a topic that Tucker Carlson has been emphasizing recently: the bizarre spectacle of diverse grifters sermonizing Americans on their sins:

> Nothing they say on the subject of race is sincere. It's all the hustle designed to get them what they want. Omar has made a career of denouncing anyone and anything in her way as racist.[23]

When you stop and think about it, it's kind of nuts that Americans sacralize foreign elites like Omar (her family was high-enough ranking in the old dictatorship that when it fell, her fellow Somalis wanted to kill them as vengeance) from the worst-run countries on Earth and pay them to lecture us on how the only thing that will save us is letting in more of them.

For example, I recently reviewed *This Land Is Our Land: An Immigrant's Manifesto* by the white-hating Calcutta-born NYU professor Suketu Mehta:

> I claim the right to the United States, for myself and my children and my uncles and cousins, by manifest destiny.... It's our country now.

After all, it's a terrible burden that people from Somalia and India take on to move to deplorable America, *but* our sacred newcomers just happen to have a lot more cousins back home who are willing to redeem us with their vibrant diversity. Their relatives are so much more moral than you racists Americans that they will sacrifice themselves by moving here for the good of our souls.

Trump tweeted:

> So interesting to see 'Progressive' Democrat Congresswomen, who originally came from countries whose governments are a complete and total catastrophe, the worst, most corrupt and inept anywhere in the world (if they even have a functioning government at all), now loudly and viciously telling the people of the United States, the greatest and most powerful Nation on earth, how our government is to be run. Why don't they go back and help fix the totally broken and crime infested places from which they came. Then come back and show us how it is done. These places need your help badly, you can't leave fast enough. I'm sure that Nancy Pelosi would be very happy to quickly work out free travel arrangements!

Much like the brouhaha after Trump's January 2018 comments comparing Norway and Haiti, respectable opinion went berserk with rage. You aren't supposed to point out that the conventional wisdom is stupid.[24]

Of course, Pelosi immediately diverted the topic from her squabbles with the diverse Squad to the racist badness of the nondiverse Trump, just as she wound up doing when she tried to discipline Omar last March for pointing out, with her Somali courage (see *Black Hawk Down*), that rich Jewish donors have a lot of influence on American politics. Pelosi instead ended up siding with Omar in blaming white Christian Americans for everything bad that has ever happened in this country, including the Dreyfus Affair in France.

Demonizing old-fashioned Americans is the KKKrazy Glue of the Democrats. But will enough voters catch on to cost them in 2020? Trump isn't terribly adroit at governing, but he's fairly adept at revealing his enemies' hypocrisies and hatreds.

Obviously, Omar isn't going to go back to Somalia to help her people. She's not going to make the mistake made by an immigrant Somali journalist named Hodan Naleyeh who "tried to change the racist media narrative around Somalia and Somalis" by returning home from Canada to report on the good news in Somalia. Just last week, terrorists in Somalia blew the poor woman up.[25]

No, Omar is going to work for the good of her clan by trying to undermine America's borders so more Africans can move here.

There are lots more where she came from.

For example, Tanzania in East Africa had a population of 26 million in 1991, 58 million today, and is on track for 129 million in 2050 and 286 million by the end of the century.

Now, there's nothing inevitable about these forecasts. They depend upon birth, death, and migration rates. In this century, many third-world countries have enjoyed success at moderating their fertility. But Africa has lagged far behind.

The Pew Research Center noted:

> Half of babies born worldwide are expected to be born in Africa by 2100, up from three-in-ten today. Nigeria is expected to have 864 million births between 2020 and 2100, the most of any African country. The number of births in Nigeria is projected to exceed those in China by 2070.[26]

To paraphrase Ann Coulter: Our new planet is going to be great!

The ongoing African population explosion is likely to be at least as globally destabilizing as climate change, yet we seldom hear about it.

Many African leaders continue in thrall to the primal African cult of fertility. Sub-Saharan Africa has traditionally had such high death rates that the culture compensates by trying at all costs to maximize births. For example, just last week, Tanzania's president John Magufuli orated:

When you have a big population you build the economy. That's why China's economy is so huge.... I know that those who like to block ovaries will complain about my remarks. Set your ovaries free, let them block theirs.[27]

We need elites with the courage to make clear to African politicians like Magufuli that their cultural backwardness will not be allowed to swamp the rest of the world. I suspect that many Africans would respond favorably to a Western crusade for more sustainable African fertility levels.

Unfortunately, perhaps the biggest threat facing the world in this century is that contemporary white culture's worship of blacks as holy will keep us from criticizing Africans for their more primitive traits, such as their fertility obsession, and instead indulge them by letting them dispatch their surplus population to our lands.

Maybe that's the explanation for the Fermi Paradox?

In 1950, physicists Edward Teller and Enrico Fermi were discussing UFOs. Suddenly, Fermi pointed out that, considering the vast age of the galaxy, the big question is not if there is evidence for intelligent aliens visiting our planet, but why isn't there *more* evidence that they have already been here.

Perhaps the great filter is that intelligent aliens tend to become obsessed with the Sisyphean task of combating racial inequality, blaming it on their own malevolent bias, and dissipate their energies on that?

CHAPTER THREE

The Sailer Strategy

GOP Future Depends on Winning Larger Share of the White Vote

VDARE
November 28, 2000

THE numbers speak. Their message may be unfashionable, but hardly unpalatable.

Here at *VDARE*, we've discussed repeatedly how dire will be the long-term impact of immigration on the Republican Party. It's crucial to understand, however, that the long-term has not quite arrived. The GOP is not yet held hostage. It still has a window of opportunity—definitely stretching through the next recession but maybe not to the recession after that—to save itself by changing the immigration laws. This can be seen by examining the 2000 election results closely.

The reason George W. Bush struggled so much to eke out a 271-267 win in the Electoral College (assuming that he can hold on to it) is not that he got crushed in the minority vote 77% to 21%. No, it's that he commanded only a measly 54% of the white vote.

To test this theory, I created a huge state-by-state spreadsheet of election results and *Voter News Service* exit poll numbers, which allows me to play what-if games, such as:

What if Bush II had won 57% of the white vote? That's hardly an outlandish figure since Bush I had taken 59% in 1988. If Dubya had garnered 57% instead of just 54% of whites, he would have cruised to an Electoral College landslide of 367 to 171. (Technically, I'm modeling this by raising Bush's share of the white vote by three points in every state.)

Why? Because whites remain by far the dominant bloc in the U.S. They count for 81% of all votes cast. Despite all of Bush's support for diversity, illegal immigrants, bilingualism, "affirmative access," and the like, an overwhelming 92% of his votes came from whites.

What if in upping his share of the white electorate from 54% to 57%, Dubya had alienated more minority voters, causing his share of the nonwhite vote to fall by 8 points from 21% to 13%?

A disaster, right? Wrong. Bush still would have won 310 to 228.

What if in winning those three additional white share points, Dubya had lost every single nonwhite vote in the USA?

Incredibly, he still would have won. Bush would have tied 269-269 in the Electoral College and been elected President by the House of Representatives.

This remarkable finding stems from the sizable advantage the Republicans enjoy in the Electoral College. In this case, Al Gore would have won the popular vote by more than 3 million, but still lost the election because Bush's strength is in small states. Since every state, no matter how small the population, gets three Electoral Votes for having two Senators and a Representative, the Republican dominance of the Great Plains and Great Basin provides a striking advantage.

By the way, this is the flip side of the Republican catastrophe in California. When cultural conservatives flee California for the interior West, the GOP picks up cheap Electoral Votes and Senate seats in small states.

Now, let's turn it around. What if instead of Bush adding 3% of the white vote (for which he would have gained 96 Electoral Votes), he had instead boosted his nonwhite vote by three points, from 21% to 24%?

He would have picked up five more Electoral Votes. Big deal.

If Bush had doubled his share of the nonwhite vote, from 21% to 42% and somehow avoided losing any white votes, he still would have gained only 52 Electoral Votes.

So where could Bush have picked up an additional 3% of the white vote? The most obvious source: white union families. The 26% of the electorate with a union member in their households voted 59% to 37% for Gore. For the time being, most union families are still white. So if Bush could have won enough white labor families to raise his total labor vote from 37% to about 46%, that would have done the trick of lifting his share of the white vote from 54% to 57%.

What could persuade more white union families to vote Republican when the current AFL-CIO leadership is so leftist? Here's a suggestion.

The labor bosses are selling out their old time members' interests in order to try to pad their membership with immigrants, legal and illegal. That's why the AFL-CIO supremos recently called for another amnesty for illegal immigrants.[1] Immigration should be the perfect issue for the GOP to use to split the rank and file from their Democratic bosses.

Since union efforts cost Bush Michigan, Pennsylvania, and Wisconsin (at a minimum), you'd think that the GOP would be hot to win back the Reagan Democrats.

Don't count on it, though. It's just so much more fashionable to continue to chase futilely after Hispanics.

In summary: the GOP could win more elections by raising its fraction of the white vote minimally than by somehow grabbing vastly higher fractions of the minority vote.

I said "could."

"Affordable Family Formation": The Neglected Key To GOP's Future

VDARE
May 8, 2005

N OW that the triumphalism rampant within the GOP after last November's election has died down, and Republicans realize that their current ascendancy is not a historical inevitability but a tenuous margin that needs careful cultivating, it's time to review the fundamental factors making some states red (Republican) and others blue (Democratic).

The key reason why some states vote Republican, I've found, can be summed up in the three-word phrase:

Affordable Family Formation.

In parts of the country where it is economical to buy a house with a yard in a neighborhood with a decent public school, you'll generally find more Republicans.

You'll find fewer in regions where it's expensive.

It's a stereotype that a mortgage, marriage, and babies tend to make people more conservative.

But it's a true stereotype.

That's why it's in the GOP's self-interest to pursue policies that keep demand for housing down (such as limiting immigration) and the quality of public schooling up (such as, well, limiting immigration).

The culture wars between Red States and Blue States (i.e Conservative and Liberal, in the perverse contemporary parlance) are driven in large part by objective differences in how family-friendly they are, financially speaking.

Places that are terribly costly in which to raise children, such as Manhattan and San Francisco, unsurprisingly possess less family-friendly cultures than more reasonably priced locales, such as Nashville and Provo.

According to Google, nobody in the history of the web has ever uttered the phrase "Affordable Family Formation."

So I utter it now:

Affordable Family Formation.

Those three words work both as a hard-headed summary of what drives voting, and as an appealing campaign theme.

The GOP could say to voters:

"We're on the side of making it affordable for you, and your children and grandchildren, to form families. The Democrats are on the side of dying alone."

Of course, Republicans could hardly say that with a straight face as long as their President refuses to repudiate his Open Borders plan. That would allow anyone in the world with a minimum wage job offer from an American employer to move here.

Four interlocking reasons form a chain of causality explaining why Affordable Family Formation paints the electoral map red.

I call them the Four Gaps.

I wrote about each of them in *VDARE* and *The American Conservative* following the election.

But, unfortunately, I discovered them in reverse order of fundamentality.

This time, however, we'll start from the ground up:

1. *The Dirt Gap*:

Blue State metropolises, such as Boston, Chicago, and Los Angeles, tend to be on oceans or Great Lakes. Their suburban expansion is permanently limited to their landward sides. In contrast, Red State metropolises, such as Dallas, Atlanta, and Phoenix, are mostly inland. Thus they tend to be surrounded almost completely by dirt—allowing their suburbs to spread out over virtually 360 degrees. The supply of suburban land available for development is dramatically larger in Red State cities.

2. *The Mortgage Gap*:

The Dirt Gap directly drives the Mortgage Gap. As the Law of Supply and Demand dictates, the limited availability of suburban dirt in most Blue States means housing costs more.

Of course, Blue State cities are also more likely to use environmental and other restrictions on housing to restrict supply artificially. Portland, an inland metropolis, is famous for outlawing development of adjoining land, thereby inflating housing prices and shrinking fertility, as reported in Timothy Egan's March 24, 2005 *New York Times* article on Portland, "Vibrant Cities Find One Thing Missing: Children."

According to the data gathered by the nonprofit organization ACCRA, which measures cost of living so corporations can fairly adjust the salaries of employees they relocate, Bush carried the 20 states with the cheapest housing costs, while Kerry won the 9 states with the most expensive.

(For statheads, the amount of variation "accounted for" by the correlation between housing cheapness and Bush's share of the vote was quite large: the *r*-squared = 46% of the total variation in the data.)

The states with the cheapest housing are Mississippi (where Bush won an extraordinary 85% of the white vote), Arkansas (homestate of Bill Clinton but now solidly Republican) and the GOP's anchor state of Texas.

The most expensive housing is now found in—guess!—California.

California was once the bastion of Phillips-coalition Republicanism; but though GOP Presidential candidates carried California nine out of ten times from 1952 through 1988, they haven't come close since.

Next are Hawaii and the District of Columbia (where Bush won only 9%).

The Mortgage Gap has been growing. Bush was victorious in the 26 states with the least home price inflation since 1980. Kerry triumphed in the 14 states with the most (according to the invaluable *Laboratory of the States* website).

Home prices rose fastest in Kerry's Massachusetts (515%) and second slowest in Bush's Texas (89%). The correlation between low housing inflation and Bush's share was strong: *r*-squared = 52%.

Recently *TaxProfBlog* posted two maps to make the point that "Median Income Data Mirrors Red State-Blue State Divide."[2] These showed that Democratic states generally have higher incomes than Republican states. The negative correlation between Bush's share of the vote and the median income for a four-person family is a moderate *r*-squared = 18%.

That's interesting. But it's more revealing to divide each state's median income by its overall cost-of-living to find its "monetary standard-of-living."

The state with the highest standard of living (at least in the things that money can buy), with a cost-of-living adjusted median income that's 17% above the national average, is Blue Minnesota.

That makes sense. Minnesota is full of hard-working, smart, law-abiding folks who wouldn't mind some monetary compensation for enduring the Gopher State's winters.

And they reside so far from the Mexican border that they haven't been inundated—yet—by wage-depressing illegal immigrants.

Perhaps today's best all-around state is Red Colorado.

The monetary standard-of-living in Colorado is fourth highest—at 9% above average. Plus the scenery is magnificent and the people well-educated and honest.[3]

In contrast, the lowest monetary standard of living, at 40% below the national average, is found in the District of Columbia.

Apparently, DC residents get rewarded in other ways—perhaps by the security of government jobs and the sense of power they enjoy while pushing the rest of us around.

The next worst standard of living is found in Hawaii. Its residents pay high prices and earn low incomes in return for living in paradise.

The third worst monetary standard of living, at 31% below the national average, is California.

The climate isn't as fantastic as Hawaii, but it's a lot better than Minnesota's.

Until about a generation ago, California was probably the all-around champ, a state with great weather, low costs, high wages, and good public schools.

But immigration-driven overcrowding has undermined all that.

There turns out to be only a low (but positive) correlation between Bush's share of the vote and the monetary standard-of-living: r-squared = 3%.

In other words, although Red States tend to have lower nominal incomes, they are ever-so-slightly better off in monetary standard-of-living—due to their much lower cost-of-living indices.

Blue States, though, probably enjoy an advantage in cultural amenities for adults—such as fancy restaurants and quaint neighborhoods.

We can also divide median income by cost of housing to get a standard-of-housing index.

With this, we find a moderate to high correlation with Bush's share of the electorate: r-squared = 28%.

The difference in correlation with voting between this standard-of-housing index and the overall standard-of-living index suggests, once again, that it's housing costs, rather than other costs such as groceries or health care, that are crucial to voting Republican or Democrat.

Despite the explanatory power of the Dirt Gap and the Mortgage Gap, these concepts have not been widely discussed.

The problem limiting their popularity may be that they are too objective, too morally neutral.

What people want to hear instead are explanations for why they, personally, are ethically and culturally better than their enemies.

3. *The Marriage Gap*:

As I first reported in *VDARE* last December, the single best correlation with Bush's share of the vote by state that anybody has yet found is: the average years married by white women between age 18 and 44: an astonishing r-squared = 83%.[4]

(This has to be one of the highest r-squareds for a single factor ever seen in political science.)

Bush carried the top 25 states ranked on "years married."

For example, white women in Utah, where Bush had his best showing with 71% of the total vote, led the nation by being married an average of 17.0 years during those 27 years from age 18 through 44.

In contrast, in Washington D.C., where Bush only took 9%, the average white woman is married only 7.4 years.

In Massachusetts, where Bush won merely 37%, her years married average just 12.2.

Democratic pollster Stanley Greenberg confirmed the partisan power of the Marriage Gap in January, reporting:

> The marriage gap is one of the most important cleavages in electoral politics.... The marriage gap is a defining dynamic in today's politics, eclipsing the gender gap, with marital status a significant predictor of the vote, independent of the effects of age, race, income, education or gender.

According to Greenberg, the exit poll showed Bush carried merely 44% of the single white females but 61% of the married white women—a 17 point difference.

Among white men, Bush won 53% of the singles and 66% of the married—a 13 point difference.

Although there are profound cultural differences among states, the Marriage Gap among whites is driven to a striking extent by the Mortgage Gap.

The cost-of-housing index correlates with "years married" with an r-squared = 53%. Similarly, the housing inflation rate since 1980 and "years married" correlate at r-squared = 48%.

A five-year long study of 162 white, black, and Hispanic single mothers in Philadelphia has put a human face on the relationship between the Mortgage Gap and the Marriage Gap.

Sociologists Kathryn Edin and Maria Kefalas, authors of *Promises I Can Keep: Why Poor Women Put Motherhood Before Marriage*, wrote an essay in the *Washington Post* on May 1, 2005 entitled "Unmarried Because They Value Marriage."

> What we discovered was surprising: Instead of a rejection of marriage, we found a deep respect for it among many young mothers, who told us that getting married was their ultimate life ambition. While they acknowledge that putting children before marriage is not the ideal way of doing things, they're not about to risk going through life childless while waiting for Mr. Right.... Marriage, we heard time and again, ought to be reserved for those couples who've acquired the symbols of working-class respectability—a mortgage on a modest rowhouse, a reliable car, a savings account and enough money left over to host a 'decent' wedding.

Women in higher social classes are more likely to avoid the disasters of giving birth out of wedlock.

But they often postpone marriage and/or children until they can afford the down payment on a house in a neighborhood with good public schools.

And that leads to:

4. *The Baby Gap*:

Bush carried 25 of the top 26 states in white total fertility (number of babies per white woman), while Kerry was victorious in the bottom 16. In Utah, for instance, white women average 2.45 babies. In the District of Columbia, white women average only 1.11 babies.

The correlation between white total fertility and Bush's share produced an impressive r-squared = 74%.

While the Marriage Gap appeared to be somewhat more important than the Baby Gap, together they proved extraordinarily powerful in explaining Bush's performance—their combined r-squared = 88%.[5]

The voting patterns of both blacks and Hispanics are also somewhat affected by these factors. But both groups are shifted toward the Democrats.

This points out a little-understood problem with the much-publicized GOP Establishment hopes of Republicanizing Hispanics while simultaneously keeping the immigration floodgates open.

The contradiction is that immigration increases the population density, which raises land prices, which both makes non-Hispanic whites more Democratic and discourages those Hispanics who successfully assimilate to the norms of local non-Hispanic whites from becoming as Republican.

Formerly Republican California supplies the classic example of both processes at work.

Non-Hispanic whites became sharply less Republican as their marriage and fertility rates plummeted.

Back in 1990, California still had a higher white fertility rate than Texas. But during the Nineties the birthrate for California white women dropped 14% and their years married plummeted to the third lowest in America, behind only ultra-liberal DC and Massachusetts.

In Texas, however, which has much more available dirt and only about half as many immigrants as a percentage of the total population, white fertility rose 4%. Texas, which voted Democratic in four out of five Presidential elections from 1960 through 1976, is now the mainstay of the GOP.

Meanwhile, those California Hispanics who succeed in assimilating fully now find themselves in a state where most role models vote for Democrats for President.

So, Hispanics in California have stayed well to the left of Hispanics in Texas—where the white elite is fervently Republican.

The same thing has happened to Asian-Americans, who tend to cluster in crowded Blue States.

Although the Democrats captured only 30% of their vote in 1992, they've won near landslides in recent elections.

Demographic analyst Arthur Hu suggests that voting patterns show that Asian Americans traditionally vote slightly more conservatively than their neighbors do—exactly as optimistic Republicans assume.[6]

The problem for the GOP, however, is that Asians tend to have highly liberal white neighbors.[7]

In 2000, 45% of all Asian-born immigrants lived in three heavily Democratic metropolitan areas: San Francisco, Los Angeles, and New York City.

Because of the dual effects on the voting of both whites and immigrants, the spread of immigrants into the middle of the country puts once-solid Republican states into play.

Not only Arizona, Nevada, and Colorado are threatened, but, farther down the road, some states in the now seemingly Solid South, such as Georgia and North Carolina, will be up for grabs.

Considering the narrowness of Bush's victory in the Electoral College, this ought to motivate Republicans to drop their invite-the-world delusion and start promoting Affordable Family Formation for American citizens.

But there's no sign of it yet.

Why not?

The Sailer Strategy

Taki's
November 16, 2016

As the Duke of Wellington more or less said after the Battle of Waterloo, it was a damn close-run thing. But the Trump campaign triumphed using what my editor at *VDARE*, Peter Brimelow, likes to call the Sailer Strategy.

As I explained 16 years ago[8] during the Florida recount after the 2000 election, the reason George W. Bush was desperately hoping to win the Electoral College 271-267 was not that he had lost the nonwhite vote 77-21, but that he had won the white vote merely 54-42.

If Bush had earned 57% of whites, he would have captured the Electoral College 371-167.

But what if adding three more points among whites had cost Bush, say, eight points among nonwhites? Bush still would have won 310-228.

I asked in 2000:

> So where could Bush have picked up an additional 3% of the white vote? The most obvious source: white union families.

How?

> Immigration should be the perfect issue for the GOP to use to split the rank and file from their Democratic bosses. Since union efforts cost Bush Michigan, Pennsylvania, and Wisconsin (at a minimum), you'd think that the GOP would be hot to win back

the Reagan Democrats. Don't count on it, though. It's just so much more fashionable to continue to chase futilely after Hispanics.

But my arithmetic was terribly out of fashion in the GOP for most of the 21st century. After all, working-class Americans in the North were the traditional enemy. It was much more appealing to Republican strategists to fantasize about bribing Latino newcomers by letting in more of their relatives than to work out a *modus vivendi* among white-collar and blue-collar Americans.

So the GOP establishment invested immensely in their strategy of converting Hispanics into home-owning Republicans. George W. Bush's 2002-04 push for Minority Homeownership by signaling to subprime lenders that federal regulators would no longer harass them about traditional mortgage credit standards such as down payments and documentation set off the housing bubble in the Sand States of California, Arizona, Nevada, and Florida.

This boosted Bush to a mere 58-40 loss among Hispanics in 2004.[9]

But when the Bush bubble burst in 2008, taking the world economy down with it, Hispanics, who defaulted disproportionately on mortgages, turned against John McCain 67-31, even though he had cosponsored the failed 2006 amnesty bill with Ted Kennedy.

It took only a decade and a half, but Donald Trump won Michigan, Pennsylvania, and Wisconsin, not to mention Ohio, Iowa, and the White House.

Right after the 2012 election, I pointed out that in those five states, plus Minnesota, which Trump narrowly lost, Romney had won only 52% of the white vote. That was six points worse than Romney did nationally.

> Most notably, Romney did terribly among the white working class in these six states. Thus he did only two points worse among whites with college degrees in the Slippery Six than he did nationally. But among the white "some college" component, he came in six points worse than nationally. And among the white "no college" voters, he performed 11 points worse than across the country, finishing tied with Obama.

In contrast, in 2016 Trump won 64% of whites in Ohio (among voters for the two main parties), 61% in Michigan, 58% in Pennsylvania, 57% in Iowa, and 57% in Wisconsin, giving him 70 incremental electoral votes over Romney's performance. (Minnesota slipped through Trump's fingers because he carried only 54% of the two-party vote there.)

Strikingly, Trump was also able to win Florida by winning 67% of whites among Floridians who voted for Clinton or Trump. It turns out that the media's assumption that the Cubans and Puerto Ricans of Florida care passionately about amnesty for Mesoamericans out of ethnic solidarity isn't all that true. Granted, Trump won only 36% of the Hispanic vote in Florida, but Florida Latinos didn't turn out in tidal-wave proportions.

Across the country, Trump didn't pay much of a price for his skepticism about immigration. He did slightly worse than McCain among Hispanics and Asian voters, but slightly better than Romney.

In general, Hispanics and Asians tend to follow their white neighbors, just well to the left. In conservative states, voters who aren't black or white tend to be centrist, while in liberal states they are leftists.

For example, it's widely stated in the press that the reason Republicans do worse among Hispanics in California (where Trump won 25% of the Hispanic vote) than in Texas (36%) is due to the poisonous heritage of Republican California governor Pete Wilson endorsing Proposition 187 in 1994.

In reality, however, the GOP does fairly well among California Latinos relative to how horribly the party does among California whites (47%). In Texas, in contrast, Trump won 73% of the white vote without even trying in a state where, as the ultimate New Yorker, Trump isn't really that personally appealing (to judge from old *King of the Hill* episodes).

Among blacks, Trump did just enough to get by. He got crushed among black women 94-4, but black guys are fond enough of Trump that his 80-13 loss on light turnout could have been worse. For example, guessing from Dave Chappelle's turn hosting *Saturday Night Live* right after the election, the independent-minded comedian may or may not have voted for Trump, but he probably didn't inflict upon himself the humiliation of voting for Hillary.

Nevada, a state where Trump is culturally at home, shows how immigration is slowly poisoning the well for Republicans. The casino master did fairly well among all four races in the home of gambling (including winning 29% of black men). In Nevada, Trump won (relative to Hillary) 60% of whites, 13% of blacks, 33% of Hispanics, and 37% of Asians. But he still lost Nevada because the state is so diverse.

It has become conventional wisdom that Republican candidates lose because their personal bigotry is sniffed out and punished by minority voters. But the truth is that Nevadans rather like Trump. He's their kind of guy. They just have reasons, though, for voting like their co-racials. Nevada is full of spillover from California (my next-door neighbor, for example, retired from Los Angeles to Las Vegas over 40 years ago), so no Republican has won Nevada since the Bush bubble in 2004.

Eventually, immigration will endanger the Republican hold on Arizona, Georgia, and Texas. Yet in the meantime, as Nate Silver points out, the Republicans may pick up liberal but white Minnesota and New Hampshire.[10] (Of course, the likeliest way for Trump in 2020 to earn the electoral votes of those two states known for good government is to be a good president.)

Ultimately, however, it's important to note that strategizing is easy compared with implementing. Complimenting me for conceiving 16 years ago the broad brush strategy that Trump executed is a little bit like praising Muhammad Ali for improvising during his 1975 fight with heavyweight champ George Foreman his rope-a-dope strategy of conserving energy by leaning on the ropes and getting George to tire himself by letting him punch him at will.

Of course, Ali's strategy was dependent upon his being tough enough to withstand getting slugged relentlessly by George Foreman for seven rounds. Similarly, no candidate in history ever withstood more punches, many below the belt, than did Donald Trump in 2016.

CHAPTER FOUR

Villains & Heroes

The Whip Hand

Taki's
September 25, 2019

THE conventional wisdom of the Great Awokening is in sizable part the dumbed-down heritage of the brilliant and sinister French philosopher Michel Foucault (1926-1984), who happened to be a dead ringer for Austin Powers' archenemy Dr. Evil. According to Google Scholar, Foucault is the most cited academic of all time.

When Ta-Nehisi Coates, for instance, talks about people who believe they are white doing violence on black bodies via FDR's redlining, he's artlessly piling up a number of vaguely recalled affectations of Foucault's. (Coates confesses, "I loved Foucault but didn't finish.")[1]

In his ham-handed way, Coates' hilarious tic of refusing to admit that white people are white, but instead only grudgingly allowing that they might "believe they are white," is reminiscent of the hermeneutics of suspicion in Marx, Freud, Nietzsche, and, more recently, Foucault, who never saw a noun he couldn't put scare quotes around. For instance, on one page of his book *Power/Knowledge*, Foucault felt the need to put "body," "children," "childhood," and "phase" within quotation marks.

The antiquarianism that has become so prevalent in recent years, as seen in the constant invocations of Emmett Till, New Deal FHA regulations, and 1619, is in part a nod to Foucault's historicizing flair. The intensely Eurocentric Foucault knew an immense amount about rather dull bureaucratic aspects of 17th- and 18th-century France. He had a knack for disclosing details from dusty royal reports on how to organize hospitals and schools as if they were the smoking-gun evidence in a conspiracy thriller.

African-Americans were once famous for their souls, but now, 35 years after Foucault, they just have black bodies. Foucault loved the term "the body." In fact, Foucault loved bodies, so long as they were male and engaging in violence, either to him or by him.

Sexual torture was Foucault's favorite pastime.[2] He was a homosexual sadomasochism fetishist who habituated the bathhouses of San Francisco and thus died of AIDS in 1984. How many men he killed by infecting them with the HIV virus is unknown.

"Power" was Foucault's favorite word. His woke followers assume that he was of course on the side of the marginalized against the powerful. But if you pay careful attention, you may notice that Foucault saw power less as an illegitimate usurpation than as the capability to get things done.

Foucault was aroused by power, as the title of his book on the history of prisons, *Discipline and Punish*, ought to suggest.

That Foucault was not a good person was obvious to at least a few leftists. After a debate with Foucault in 1971 on whether "there is such a thing as 'innate' human nature," linguist Noam Chomsky, who is a boyish idealist, like a Jimmy Stewart character of the left, said Foucault struck him as "completely amoral."[3]

Foucault is often considered a forefather of postmodern identity politics and social constructionism. But it's not clear that Foucault, who was extremely smart, believed the things his dumber acolytes take for granted.

Note that, considered together, social constructionism and identity politics are fundamentally incoherent. To argue that, say, race does not exist in nature and that black women's hair must be liberated to be natural is clearly contradictory.

Foucault escaped this conundrum by being radically anti-identity. He saw identities as part of a plot by power to impose categories on individuals.

One interesting contribution Foucault made was to point out that the historical record is unclear whether the type of male homosexual that we are familiar with today existed several centuries ago. There was homosexual behavior, but was there homosexual identity? Similarly, it's struck me that of all the characters in Shakespeare's plays, there don't appear to be any who were written so they had to be played like, say, Jack on *Will & Grace*.

Because homosexuality doesn't, so far as we can tell, play an evolutionary role,[4] social constructionist theorizing about homosexuals is less implausible than when discussing basic males and females.

Of course, Foucault's implication that gays were socially constructed contradicts Lady Gaga's dogma that they are born this way, because it implies that they could be socially deconstructed. But that's a forbidden thought these days.

My guess would be that Foucault didn't like the idea that some men are born this way because that would imply that other men aren't born this way, which would suggest that he would never get to have sex with those men, a conclusion he found intolerable.

For Foucault, innate identities got in the way of his ideal of polymorphous perversity. In Foucault's mind, identity was the enemy of anonymous sex and its partner, death. Foucault's biographer James Miller writes:

> In his 1979 essay, he imagines "suicide-festivals" and "suicide-orgies" and also a kind of special retreat where those planning to commit suicide could look "for partners without names for occasions to die liberated from every identity."

Foucault was one sick puppy.

He reminds me of a gay version of France's rightist sci-fi novelist Michel Houellebecq crossed with actor Kevin Spacey. But because Foucault was on the culturally dominant left, he has, so far, been in little danger of being canceled.

Foucault, with his labyrinthine prose style, was adept at crafting his sentences to make it hard to quote any single one that nails down his position. It's hard to imagine that if Foucault had survived to 2019, he would be saying the kind of things his acolytes are declaring along the lines of:

> Race doesn't exist, but Rachel Dolezal can't possibly be black, while Caitlyn Jenner is of course a woman.

Foucault was much slipperier. The *Stanford Encyclopedia of Philosophy* summarizes his ploy on the sexes:

> He critically appraises the idea of a natural, scientifically defined true sex by revealing the historical development of this form of thought. He does not claim that sex, understood as the categories of maleness and femaleness, was invented in a particular historical period. He rather analyses the ways in which these categories were

founded and explained in discourses claiming the status of scientific truth, and how this allegedly "pure" explanation in fact constituted these categories so that they were understood as "natural." This idea has had enormous influence on feminist philosophers and queer theorists.

In other words, Foucault wouldn't let himself get trapped saying anything clearly stupid, such as that maleness and femaleness were socially constructed. But he didn't mind if you assumed that his use of scare quotes meant he believed that, as long as you were on his side.

Foucault was an immensely intelligent man who devoted his cleverness to promoting stupidity among his acolytes by delegitimizing distinctions, such as between adults and "children." Miller writes:

> Through ... an uninhibited exploration of sadomasochistic eroticism, it seemed possible to breach, however briefly, the boundaries separating the conscious and unconscious, reason and unreason, pleasure and pain—and, at the ultimate limit, life and death—thus starkly revealing how distinctions central to the play of true and false are pliable, uncertain, contingent.

It turned out, however, that even for Foucault, death was not pliable, uncertain, contingent.

Foucault was not all that politically active by the *engagé* standards of French intellectuals. The son of a Catholic surgeon, he'd been a member of the French Communist Party when young, but became an anti-Communist Gaullist technocrat in the early 1960s. He missed out on the fun of May 1968 by being out of France in Tunisia, but remade himself as a leftist *soixante-huitard*.

Late in his life, he seemed to be drifting rightward, speaking up for Poland's Solidarity movement and praising the ideas of U. of Chicago free-market economist Gary Becker.[5] As he spent time indulging his proclivities in the prospering San Francisco Bay area, he perhaps came to see that capitalism and his decadent hedonism weren't so averse.

One political issue close to Foucault's heart was American sociologist Erving Goffman's successful crusade to shut down insane asylums, which liberated the poor lunatics to be homeless and sleep on the sidewalks. (Erving's daughter Alice Goffman is now a leading crusader against "mass incarceration," so you know that will turn out equally well.)

Another cause to which Foucault devoted himself was liberating children to have sex with grown men. In France, the age of consent in 1977 was only 15 years old, but Foucault nevertheless signed a petition, along with Jean-Paul Sartre, Simone de Beauvoir, and Jacques Derrida, to decriminalize pedophilia.

Foucault did a 1978 radio interview to promote the abolition of age-of-consent laws in France. It's noteworthy how smoothly Foucault's usual arguments on other topics service this campaign.[6]

For example, Foucault begins with his usual tactic of making the assertion that history shows that something that might seem like common sense (making child molestation illegal) was only recently socially constructed, so therefore it could (and thus should) be deconstructed:

> This regime is not as old as all that, since the penal code of 1810 said very little about sexuality, as if sexuality was not the business of the law....

How do we know, Foucault goes on, that the child didn't want to be the victim of statutory rape?

> It could be that the child, with his own sexuality, may have desired that adult, he may even have consented, he may even have made the first moves. We may even agree that it was he who seduced the adult.

And who is to say who is a child?

> In any case, an age barrier laid down by law does not have much sense.

In arguing for the legalization of boy bothering, Foucault never quite gets around to claiming that age is just a social construct, but that's the mood music.

How much of Foucault's vast intellectual enterprise of denouncing categorization of individuals as possessing distinct identities was intended to undermine the legal category of children too young to consent? Did Foucault happen to dream up his ideas first and only then realize that his logic proved that it should be legal for him to have sex with boys? Or did he want to have sex with boys first and then dreamt up his vast system of justification?

Foucault himself once said:

> In a sense, all the rest of my life I've been trying to do intellectual things that would attract beautiful boys.[7]

Foucault was an evil man.

But he was right about something: that power helps you control discourse and controlling discourse helps you have power.

Today, though, it's Foucault's fans who have the whip hand.

The Vengeance of Edward Said

Taki's
February 15, 2017

I 'VE been thinking about the tendency for white liberalism to encourage nonwhite reactionaries as I've been reading perhaps the most influential left-wing book by a Middle Eastern immigrant in American academic history, Edward Said's 1978 tome *Orientalism*.

Said was a superbly cultured man. But his legacy has been to make Americans dumber—and smugger over being dumber—about the Arab world.

And that was not an unintended consequence.

Born in Jerusalem in 1935, Said was the wealthy son of a Palestinian Christian father with U.S. citizenship and a Lebanese Christian mother. He used the word "Orient" not in the American fashion of referring to the Far East, but in the European manner of referencing the Middle East and North Africa.

Reading *Orientalism* almost four decades later, it's striking how useless it has been for helping anyone understand the Middle East.

That was Said's intention. Knowledge is power, he believed, so he wanted Westerners to be more ignorant about his homeland in order that they would have less power over it.

No one ever expended more brainpower to encourage stupidity than Said did in *Orientalism*. He achieved his goal of increasing obliviousness by promoting anti-intellectual ploys, such as castigating pattern recognition as stereotyping the Other, that are now used by even the dimmest social justice jihadi, but which seemed relatively novel in 1978.

111

What's more interesting than Said's means were his motivations.

He was much celebrated in academia before his death in 2003 as a radical advocate of the Third World (for example, he broke with Yasser Arafat because Said thought the PLO too moderate).

But it's worth attempting to think about Said instead as a conservative with natural, healthy concentric loyalties to his clan and race, a man who successfully did subtle but substantial damage to the traditional enemies of the Arabs by undermining the self-confidence of Western scholars and students and deconstructing our tools for understanding.

It can be helpful to think of Said as one of those "natural aristocrats" that the American founding fathers saw as rightfully destined to rule. He was a brilliant literary critic, a near professional-level classical pianist, and almost movie-star handsome. His many friends considered him a superior individual.

But cruel accidents of history deprived Said of a nation to govern and sent him into exile in the capital of his enemy, New York, where he became a professor of European literature at Columbia.

Said's youth reminds me vaguely of that of another outsider who came to New York to make his name in literature, the conservative satirist Tom Wolfe. Much as Said's Palestinian heritage put him on his guard in WASP and Jewish New York, Wolfe is a proud son of the Confederacy.

The Virginian's protégé Michael Lewis recently read through Wolfe's old letters to his parents and reported that he saw little sign of Wolfe's brilliance while he was a contented undergraduate at traditionalist Washington and Lee University.

But as soon as Wolfe arrived at Yale in the North for his Ph.D. in American studies, his coruscating talent emerged in poking fun at Northern liberals. Of course, almost two-thirds of a century later, Wolfe is still in the Northeast, but his literary career can perhaps be summed up as one Southerner's campaign of revenge upon the Yankees for defeating his ancestors at Gettysburg.

Said's alienation from the power structure began earlier at a British-run boarding school, where a classmate was the future King Hussein of Jordan. Said recalled, "I was an uncomfortably anomalous student all through my early years: a Palestinian going to school in Egypt, with an English first name, an American passport, and no certain identity, at all."

When Said was an adolescent, the new state of Israel expropriated a house in Jerusalem that had been owned by his extended family. The neoconservative magazine *Commentary* devoted much effort in the 1990s to proving that the building hadn't been the property of Said's father.[8] Instead, *Commentary* triumphantly but anticlimactically trumpeted, the house had belonged to...his aunt.

That *Commentary* article was a moment when I began to feel severe doubts about neoconservatism. The story just made me feel sorry for Said. I'd be sore too, I realized, if my aunt had lost a nice house in the 1940s in Southern California to, say, Japanese invaders. Said must have felt toward the Israelis rather like a South Carolinian whose plantation had been burned down by General Sherman felt toward the damn Yankees.

Despite his many talents, Said was not made head boy of his school. In fact, he hated the head boy, future screen idol Omar Sharif. He was eventually booted out for rebellious mischief and his family sent him to a prestigious boarding school in Massachusetts.

But Said was even more homesick and alienated in America, which had backed the Zionists who had dispossessed his family.

Said may have been a Bart Simpson type who battles authority not because he's against authority in general, but because *he* isn't the authority.

In the most notorious incident of Said's last decade, the 64-year-old man of letters was photographed celebrating the Israeli army's withdrawal from Arab Lebanon by heaving a stone across the border at an Israeli guardhouse.[9] Throwing a rock at the rival gang is a classic juvenile-delinquent gesture. But I have to admire the boyish energy that the aged and ailing professor displayed in his lowbrow attack on his people's hereditary enemy.

It didn't help Said become reconciled to Western supremacy that perhaps the greatest movie of his young manhood, *Lawrence of Arabia*, was about how the Arabs had needed a weird gay English Orientalist named T.E. Lawrence to teach them enough about nationalism to throw off the Ottoman Yoke. It especially couldn't have improved Said's mood to watch the famously stunning scene that catapulted his boyhood archenemy Omar Sharif to global stardom, which concludes with Peter O'Toole telling Sharif (and all Arabs):

> So long as the Arabs fight tribe against tribe, so long will they be a little people, a silly people—greedy, barbarous, and cruel, as you are.

For these insults to his Arab pride, Said took his vengeance cold. In 1978 he published *Orientalism*, which launched Post-Colonial Studies.

Said intensely resented that some Western scholars, writers, and artists had devoted so much attention to what he called the "Arab-Muslim world." He pejoratively labeled these Western intellectuals as "Orientalists" and blamed them for assembling the vast amounts of knowledge that made possible the Western political ascendancy over his homeland (which had culminated in the Zionist confiscation of his family's house in Jerusalem).

My suspicion is that, shocking as it may sound to his fans, Said had normal, masculine, conservative affections for his blood and soil.

In particular, Said complained about Western Orientalists depicting the Middle East as feminine and alluring.

This was not just a literary metaphor for Said. For many years, adventurous European artists and writers like Flaubert had engaged in sex tourism in Muslim lands and come back to whip up spicy works for the European market.

Just as the men of Europe are finally starting to object to the sex tourism *hegira* now running from the Middle East to the blonder lands, Said, as a racial loyalist, resented men of a different ancestry defiling his people's womenfolk...and, perhaps especially, his people's boyfolk.

The cover illustration of *Orientalism*, which was chosen to highlight the evils of Westerners taking any interest in the Middle East, is the vaguely sinister 1879 painting *The Snake Charmer* by Jean-Léon Gérôme of a naked boy posing with a snake before a group of staring men in a Muslim palace. The painting is basically high-gloss pedophilic gay porn. It gets across the disgust Said felt for boy-bothering Orientalists.

Ironically, Said had the IQ and cultural sophistication to devise complex-sounding and thus hugely influential justifications for his basically redneck and wholesome emotion: Don't come around here no more.

Waugh & Wilder:
The Dawn of Sunset Boulevard

Taki's
February 20, 2013

BILLY Wilder's *Sunset Boulevard*, with Gloria Swanson as a silent-screen legend plotting a comeback and William Holden as her toy boy, remains one of the most famous movies ever. Yet *Sunset Boulevard's* origins in an Evelyn Waugh novel have been forgotten. This cultural amnesia is curious since the reactionary novelist and the refugee writer-director are still two of the more talked-about figures of the mid-century.

Until recently being surpassed by Woody Allen, Wilder was Hollywood's most honored writer-director, with eight directing and thirteen screenwriting Oscar nominations. Despite not being fluent in English until after arriving in America as a refugee from Hitler in 1934, Wilder quickly became a master of American smart-aleck vernacular. One source of his popularity with Americans was that even though he was an exile from highbrow Europe, he took on a disarming Average Joe air. (For example, to keep Paramount from noticing too early that his new project was going to be a send-up of the movie business itself, Wilder's working title for *Sunset Boulevard* was *Can of Beans*, a self-parody of his blue-collar tough-guy affectations.)

Still, Wilder was less an auteur than Hollywood's leading collaborator. He needed somebody else's initial spark, and Waugh provided much of Wilder's impetus for *Sunset Boulevard*.

Seeing a revival screening of *Sunset Boulevard* at Glendale's Alex Theatre, a 1925 silent-movie palace suitable for Norma Desmond herself, reminded me of how much Wilder's 1950 showbiz horror-comedy is an inversion of Waugh's 1948 satire on Hollywood and Forest Lawn, *The Loved One*. The imprint of Waugh's macabre tale on Wilder's dark comedy is unmistakable, even though Wilder and his colleagues reversed many elements. The transpositions that make Sunset Boulevard the more enduring work illuminate some insights into audience appeal.

That Waugh's *The Loved One* kick-started *Sunset Boulevard* wasn't originally a secret. Although an extensive Google search finds almost no mention of the connection in recent years, *Sunset Boulevard's* cinematographer John Seitz told film historian Kevin Brownlow of Waugh's influence on the movie, saying that Wilder and producer Charles Brackett "had wanted to do *The Loved One*, but couldn't obtain the rights."

And this isn't just hindsight. After playing herself in *Sunset Boulevard's* final scene, gossip columnist Hedda Hopper burbled on June 15, 1949:

> It was mighty grim on the Sunset Boulevard set after Gloria Swanson shot and killed Bill Holden…. Billy Wilder … was crazy about Evelyn Waugh's book *The Loved One*, and wanted the studio to buy it. Thought it would make another *Lost Weekend*. Waugh wrote it while he was here as a guest of Metro. The studio officials were trying to make up their minds if his book, *Brideshead Revisited* could be filmed.

The main characters in both *The Loved One* and *Sunset Boulevard* are young but washed-up screenwriters who live with older Hollywood has-beens from the silent-movie era in their fading houses with empty swimming pools.

The unmistakable giveaway is that Waugh's Dennis Barlow works for a pet cemetery, while Wilder's Joe Gillis is mistaken for the man from the pet cemetery when he first stumbles into Norma's mansion.

Why has awareness of Waugh's influence on Wilder disappeared?

The Loved One is a minor Waugh novel, although not without some spectacularly funny pages. And the ambitious but uneven 1965 movie version is more a curiosity than a success. Most Waugh adaptations tend to be overly faithful to their hallowed sources, but *The Loved One* was directed by Tony Richardson at the nadir of Waugh's reputation and, following his Best Picture Oscar for *Tom Jones*, the brief apex of Richardson's. Thus, the intermittently funny film is stuffed with over-the-top material invented by Terry Southern of *Dr. Strangelove* notoriety.

Perhaps it was in nobody's interest to talk about the relationship. Even after Wilder's death in 2002 at age 95, *Sunset Boulevard* remains a lucrative piece of intellectual property, especially in the Andrew Lloyd Webber musical adaptation. And it wasn't flattering to Waugh's partisans to press a claim, since Wilder and his cowriters had clearly improved upon Waugh's rather half-baked notions.

Moreover, when watching *Sunset Boulevard* through the lens of *The Loved One*, the Wilder film seems even creepier because its gay angle is more overt.

In Waugh's book, the young poet-turned-pet-mortician initially lives with an elderly British man of letters, Sir Francis Hinsley (played hilariously in 1965 by Sir John Gielgud). The writer's relationship with his host is ambiguous enough that even the intentionally offensive 1965 movie changed the pair to uncle-nephew.

Back in the 1920s, Sir Francis had been "chief script-writer of Megalopolitan Pictures," but by now he's barely hanging on in the publicity department. Some of Wilder's description of Norma's estate is a rewrite of Waugh's depiction of Sir Francis's once-fashionable grounds. In his Augustan style, Waugh recalls, "His swimming pool which had once flashed like an aquarium with the limbs of long-departed beauties was empty now and cracked and overgrown with weed." In his Raymond-Chandler-without-the-poetry manner, Wilder has Holden narrate, "And of course she had a pool. Who didn't then? Mabel Norman and John Gilbert must have swum in it ten thousand midnights ago.... It was empty now." (Spoiler alert: Once refilled, the pool plays a major role in *Sunset Boulevard*.)

When Megalopolitan fires Sir Francis, he kills himself. As Sir Francis's only "Loved One" (the term used by the Forest Lawn-like funeral complex), Dennis meets naive and melancholy cosmetician Aimée Thanatogenos. The heartless poet then outmaneuvers head mortician Mr. Joyboy for her hand.

Upon finally wising up to her fiancé's opportunism, she exclaims: "An American would despise himself for living off his wife." Dennis patiently responds, "Yes, but you see, I'm English, and we have none of these prejudices in the older and more developed civilizations."

Wilder and Brackett reversed this, giving Joe, a newspaperman from Dayton, Ohio, a bad case of American self-loathing for allowing himself to be kept by Norma. When Betty Schaefer, a pretty 22-year-old aspiring screenwriter who wants Joe to work with her on a screenplay of one of his ideas, asks, "Where have you been keeping yourself?" he responds, "I haven't been keeping myself at all, lately."

This cynical Bob Hope-style self-contempt worked well for Holden (who looked and sounded like a more strapping version of Hope). It earned Holden the first of his three Oscar nominations. But Hope's shtick was that his comic lack of self-esteem stemmed from his physical cowardice (a highly relevant character trait during World War II).

In contrast, it's not clear why Holden's Joe is so mortified by shame beyond all redemption when young Betty finally discovers his gigolo-like arrangement with Norma.

Is it because he doesn't support himself? But Betty is a true believer in Joe's underappreciated talent, having worked for weeks with him on a promising script.

Is it because Joe's sleeping with an older woman, albeit the most glamorous woman of her time? Perhaps, but a generation later, we saw a test case of this in the extremely well-publicized 1970s relationship of Burt Reynolds with talk-show hostess Dinah Shore, who was two decades older. It didn't seem to slow Reynolds's ascent to superstardom at all. *Wikipedia* explains, "The relationship gave Shore an updated, sexy image, and took some of the pressure off Reynolds in maintaining his image as a ladies' man." (Don't ask me what that clause about Reynolds means.)

What would make some psychological sense out of *Sunset Boulevard's* histrionic conclusion is if Betty discovers that Joe is living not with an older woman, but with an older man, much like Dennis in the opening scenes of *The Loved One.*

This presumption that Wilder at one time conceived of *Sunset Boulevard* as a homosexual relationship isn't wholly implausible. Hollywood's unofficial history is full of young men who accepted a hand up, then switched teams back to their more natural side once established.

Wilder himself was married for all but three years from 1936 to 2002. He took pains to emphasize to Cameron Crowe in a book-length interview in 1996 that his own days as a Weimar gigolo were quite respectable, with him merely serving as a waltz partner for rich fat matrons whose watching husbands no longer cared to dance.[10]

But Wilder's running joke about gay subtexts finally burst through in his most famous line, the last one in 1959's *Some Like It Hot.* Jack Lemmon, having spent the movie in drag to escape from Al Capone's gang, explains

in frustration to ardent yachtsman Joe E. Brown that they can't marry because—ripping off his wig and dropping his falsetto—"I'm a man."

Brown placidly replies, "Well, nobody's perfect."

Indeed, Wilder's tombstone reads:

I'M A WRITER

BUT THEN

NOBODY'S PERFECT

Yet Wilder's essential insight that makes *Sunset Boulevard* more memorable than *The Loved One* (even to *Sunset Boulevard's* huge gay fan base) is
that male and female—Joe and Norma—are just more interesting than Joe
and Norman.

Bedtime for Bonzo's Behaviorist Bent

Taki's
February 07, 2011

TO celebrate Ronald Reagan's 100th birthday, I watched his most de-rided movie, *Bedtime for Bonzo*. We've been hearing wisecracks about it for generations, so it has to be an embarrassment, right?

Bedtime for Bonzo turns out instead to be a small but nifty family come-dy that was a deserved hit in 1951. The writers were disappointed that they couldn't land Cary Grant for the role of a scientist who tries raising a chim-panzee as if it were a human baby. But it was indeed a Cary Grant-worthy idea. The following year, Grant (aided by Marilyn Monroe, director Howard Hawks, screenwriter Ben Hecht, and Esther the Chimp) portrayed a chemist testing youth elixirs on apes in *Monkey Business*.

Still, Reagan was well suited to play an idealistic and impersonal profes-sor in *Bedtime for Bonzo*. But it's funny how liberal Reagan's character is—a progressive psychologist who believes in nurture over nature. Reagan pro-claims that criminals are merely victims of having been "born and raised in a slum environment."

The script has a surprisingly intellectual underpinning because one of *Bonzo*'s writers, Raphael Blau, had been a graduate student in educational psychology and animal behavior under Edward L. Thorndike at Columbia. *Bedtime for Bonzo* sides with behaviorist psychologists such as B. F. Skinner, who were then ascendant over the old-fashioned Darwinian hereditarians.

The premise is clever, especially compared to recent science-based comedies such as *Human Nature*, the incoherent 2001 flop penned by the normally brilliant Charlie Kaufman. *Bedtime for Bonzo* was inspired by the (inevitably comic) experiments of earnest psychologists such as Winthrop Kellogg and Catherine Hayes, who tried in the 1930s and 1940s to raise baby chimps in their homes to see how human they would turn out.

Thus, Reagan is engaged to a lady professor who is the daughter of the college's dean, an old-fogey geneticist who still believes in heredity. When the dean discovers that his prospective son-in-law's estranged father was a habitual conman, he withdraws his daughter's hand and asks: "But what assurance do I have that your children, my grandchildren, won't inherit criminal tendencies?"

Reagan then has a brainstorm: He'll borrow a baby chimp from the college's Viennese animal researcher and raise it like a human child to prove that "environment is all important" and "heredity counts for very little."

The ideological irony is funny enough, but the really funny thing about *Bedtime for Bonzo* is Bonzo. That little monkey is a riot!

There's a standard joke that Reagan gets out-acted by an ape, but there's no shame in underplaying in the presence of such an extraordinary scene-stealer. Screenwriter Ted Berkman explained that Bonzo was trained to respond "promptly to some 502 instructions" or, as a passing director sourly observed, "about 500 more than a lot of human actors." Director Fred de Cordova supposedly stopped giving instructions to Bonzo's trainer and simply explained directly to the ape how to play each scene. The director couldn't afford to use a lot of cuts, which merely makes Bonzo's performance even more amazing as de Cordova just lets the film roll.

Tragically, young Bonzo died in a fire three weeks after his only film's premiere, leaving him the James Dean of monkey movies. (Of course, with chimps, the older they get, the cuter they ain't. One day he's a cuddly ball of fur doing backflips, the next he's ripping your face off.)

In the 1980s, liberals constantly denounced Reagan as a terrible actor who was fooling the public with his acting genius. On the other hand, Reagan often struck his conservative supporters as worrisomely old-looking.

In contrast to the uncannily unchanging Cary Grant, Reagan's most obvious weakness as a leading man was that his rather fleshy face aged at the normal rate for a human being. In *Bonzo*, he looks like what he was, a handsome 40-year-old man, not the perpetual 35-year-old that audiences want as their male stars. Reagan's Hollywood career wound up a little like the short base-ball career of slugger Hank Greenberg, also born in 1911. Both lost crucial years to the Army during WWII.

Johnny Carson made endless *Bedtime for Bonzo* gags, in part because de Cordova, the *Tonight Show*'s legendary producer, had directed it. De Cordova became the inspiration for perhaps the most stupendous supporting character in the annals of sitcoms, Rip Torn's Artie, the producer on *The Larry Sanders Show*. Artie protects his star like a showbiz samurai. But it's fun to wonder who was the top banana on de Cordova's 1951 set—the president or the primate?

Culture's Bell Curve

The American Conservative
November 17, 2003

Review of *Human Accomplishment: The Pursuit of Excellence in the Arts and Sciences, 800 B.C. to 1950,* by Charles Murray (HarperCollins, 2003)

F EW figures in American intellectual life more admirably combine ambition and modesty than data maestro Charles Murray. Every decade or so, Murray delivers a big book full of graphs and tables that audaciously but judiciously illuminates a vital topic.

In 1984, Murray's *Losing Ground* demonstrated the malign effect of Great Society-era programs on the poor, laying the basis for the successful welfare reform act of 1996.

His huge 1994 best-seller, *The Bell Curve*, co-written with the late Richard J. Herrnstein, had the opposite effect. It made such a definitive case for the broad impact of differences in intelligence that the dread letters "IQ" had to be driven out of polite society. For example, the new book *No Excuses: Closing the Racial Gap in Learning* by conservative scholars Abigail and Stephan Thernstrom obsessively avoids even mentioning *The Bell Curve* until the fine print notes at the back. This post-*Bell-Curve* taboo on IQ made possible the recent No Child Left Behind Act mandating that every public school student in America be academically "proficient" by 2014. Even the Thernstroms recognize that this attempt to legislate America into Lake Wobegon, where all the children are above average, is absurd.

In 1997, Murray quietly began a huge project to rank objectively history's most important discoverers and creators so that he could examine the causes and correlates of greatness. The result is his gracefully written and enthralling *Human Accomplishment: The Pursuit of Excellence in the Arts and Sciences, 800 B.C. to 1950.*

For example, to determine the most significant Western visual artists, Murray assembled 14 leading comprehensive works by art historians such as Gombrich and Janson. For each name in each book's index, he typed into his computer basic measures of importance such as the number of pages mentioning the artist. (No surprise: Michelangelo came out on top.)

This sounds simple, perhaps even simple-minded, but these kinds of metrics of eminence have been repeatedly validated during decades of use by social scientists ranging from Charles Darwin's smarter cousin Francis Galton to Murray's mentor, U.C. Davis psychologist Dean Keith Simonton. Still, the process raised many technical problems that could have biased the results, such as which works to rely upon and how many to use. Murray meticulously dealt with each issue using his mastery of statistics.

Once assembled, his "inventory" of 4,002 significant figures in 21 categories allowed him quantitatively to test some Big Questions. For instance, did the pursuit of excellence flourish more in liberal democracies than in non-despotic monarchies? Answer: no.

Having spent 17 years in the marketing-data business, I love pointing out better ways to crunch numbers. I can identify several weaknesses in Murray's methods. For example, since we don't know the names of most of the countless artists who worked on the great medieval cathedrals, Murray can't include them in his tables of great individuals and thus he underrates the artistic accomplishments of the Middle Ages.

Yet, to my surprise, I can't think of a single way to do it better than he did.

His methods and lists should become the standards for future research. There is little need to reinvent his wheels. If you want to rate other types of famous people, such as soldiers, violinists, or chefs, you can just follow his methodology. Conversely, if you want to explore questions Murray skips over, such as the role of social class, educational level, or left-handedness among the accomplished, you can just use his tables of names as your starting points.

Because Murray measures the consensus of the experts, his rankings aren't too surprising. Galileo is at the top in astronomy; Darwin in biology; Newton and Einstein in physics; Pasteur in medicine; Beethoven and Mozart in

Western music; and, of course, Shakespeare in Western literature. Still, anybody who likes baseball statistics will find *Human Accomplishment* great fun.

For example, Thomas Edison is the only American to lead a category (technology, where he shares the top spot with steam engine developer James Watt). In general, Americans didn't do terribly well in any other category, although we can hope that we improved after 1950, when Murray stops in order to prevent ephemeral recent fads from warping the data.

Ben Franklin drubs Thomas Jefferson in the race to be our nation's foremost Renaissance man. Franklin scores as a major figure in both physics and technology, and a significant one in literature. Others who qualified in three categories include Galileo, Leibniz, Huygens, Archimedes, and Rousseau, who was not just a philosopher and novelist but also a successful comic-opera composer. The top polymaths, showing up as significant in four categories, were Descartes and, predictably, Leonardo Da Vinci.

All the rankings will inspire arguments, of course, but that's one of the book's pleasures.

French postmodernists will sneer at the very concept of objectively measuring greatness, but their brittle *amour propre* will be secretly salved by hearing that the most important city in Murray's lists, by far, is Paris. It was the workplace for 12% of the 4,002 significant scientists and artists. Of course, you can't construct interesting new knowledge like this if you actually believe the boring old deconstructionist dogmas.

France is tied with Britain and Germany as the leading nation, with Italy fourth. Interestingly, 80% of the significant Europeans grew up in a rather narrow axis running from Naples up the Rhine to Edinburgh.

Can we trust these data? The scholars upon whom Murray relies have their personal and professional biases, but, ultimately, their need to create coherent narratives explaining who influenced whom means that their books aren't primarily based on their own opinions but rather on those of their subjects. For example, the best single confirmation of Beethoven's greatness might be Brahms's explanation of why he spent decades fussing before finally unveiling his First Symphony: "You have no idea how it feels for someone like me to hear behind him the tramp of a giant like Beethoven."

In Paul Johnson's just-published and immensely readable book *Art: A New History*, you can see how even this most opinionated of historians must adapt himself to the judgments of artists. Much of the book's entertainment value stems from Johnson's heresies, such as his grumpy comment on Michelangelo's Sistine Chapel: "No one ever wished the ceiling larger." Still, Johnson can't really break free from conventional art history because he can't avoid writing about those whom subsequent artists emulated.

For example, Johnson finds Cézanne (who ranks 10th in Murray's table of 479 significant artists) painfully incompetent at the basics of his craft. Yet, Johnson has to grit his teeth and write about Cézanne at length because he "was in some ways the most influential painter of the late nineteenth century because of his powerful (and to many mysterious) appeal to other painters...." In contrast to Johnson, Murray keeps his artistic opinions upbeat or muted because his goals are scientific.

Human Accomplishment sheds fascinating light on identity-politics issues. Women, for instance, account for merely 2% of the 4,002 personages. They are strongest in Japanese literature, with 8% of the significant names, including the third-ranked Japanese writer, Lady Murasaki Shikibu, author of the thousand-year-old proto-novel *The Tale of Genji*. Women are particularly insignificant in composing classical music (0.2%) and inventing technology (0.0%). Is this changing much? Murray unofficially glanced at who "flourished" after 1950 (depressingly to me, he assumes careers peak at age 40) and found female accomplishment to be up sharply only in literature. In fact, the percentage of Nobel Prizes won by women fell from 4% in the first half of the 20th century to 3% in the second.

Still, Murray's rankings may be slightly unfair to female artists because they are less likely to have brilliant followers. My wife, for example, was incensed that Jane Austen finished behind the lumbering Theodore Dreiser and the flashy Ezra Pound. Yet, these men probably did have more influence on other major writers. That's because subsequent famous authors were mostly male and thus less interested than the female half of the human race in Austen's topics, such as finding a husband.

Dead white European males dominate his inventories, despite Murray reserving eight of his 21 categories (including Arabic literature, Indian philosophy, and Chinese visual art) for non-Western arts. Murray, who was a Peace Corp volunteer in Thailand and has half-Asian children, began this project wanting to devote even more attention to Asian accomplishments but found he couldn't justify his predisposition.

In the sciences, 97% of the significant figures and events turned out to be Western. Is this merely Eurocentric bias? Of the 36 science reference books he drew upon, 28 were published after 1980, by which time historians were desperately searching for non-Westerners to praise. Only in this decade has the most advanced non-Western country, Japan, begun to win science Nobels regularly.

Why is the West best? After five years of work, Murray still didn't know. Then, he had an unexpected epiphany: the single biggest reason most of history's highest achievers came from Christendom was...Christianity.

He writes,

> It was a theology that empowered the individual acting as an individual as no other philosophy or religion had ever done before. The potentially revolutionary message was realized more completely in one part of Christendom, the Catholic West, than in the Orthodox East. The crucial difference was that Roman Catholicism developed a philosophical and artistic humanism typified, and to a great degree engendered, by Thomas Aquinas (1226-1274). Aquinas made the case, eventually adopted by the Church, that human intelligence is a gift from God, and that to apply human intelligence to understanding the world is not an affront to God but is pleasing to him.

From 1850 to 1950, per capita accomplishment tended to decline, which is especially striking considering the huge spread of education. Diminishing returns in the sciences seem inevitable because the low-hanging fruit was picked first. In the arts, though, Murray believes that loss of faith in both the purpose of life and the efficacy of the individual retarded greatness, especially in the post-Freudian age.

Murray expects that almost no art from the second half of the 20th century will be remembered in 200 years. Indeed, Europe, homeland of geniuses, has collapsed into a comfortable cultural stasis reminiscent of Rome in the 2nd century A.D. In addition to Murray's philosophical explanations, I'd also point to causes such as the genocide of Europe's highest-achieving ethnic group (Jews were about six times more likely than gentiles to become significant figures from 1870 onward); the rise of anti-elitist ideologies; and the decline of nationalism. From Vergil to Verdi, great men engendered great works to celebrate their nations. Nobody, however, seems likely to create an epic glorifying the European Union.

CHAPTER FIVE

Human Biodiversity

It's All Relative:
Putting Race in Its Proper Perspective

VDARE
August 2, 2002

FOR the last two summers, University of California's Ward Connerly, leader of the successful 1996 Proposition 209 campaign outlawing racial preferences in California and the 2004 Racial Privacy Initiative, has hosted a small but wide-ranging conference at the Ronald Reagan Presidential Library. This year, he asked Boston U. anthropologist Peter Wood, author of the upcoming book *Diversity: A Biography of a Concept*, and I to debate the fundamental question of whether race is a biologically meaningful concept. This provided me with a wonderful opportunity to outline my approach at adequate length before a distinguished audience.

I'm sometimes complimented on being a perceptive observer of the myriad ramifications of race and asked why I notice more than most writers on the subject. I reply that it helps to have a model in your head that corresponds fairly well with how the world works. When you've got the right theory, it's easy to observe more—you can hold more details in your mind because they fit together.

So...does race exist in a biological sense?

Race is hardly the most important thing in life, but it's not so insignificant that we can blithely ignore it. We need to understand why, here and all over the world, racial conflicts keep popping up their ugly heads.

I'm going to outline a framework for thinking about race that I've found extremely useful. And this novel way of thinking about race suggests a few practical things we can do about it to keep conflicts under control.

My concept of race seems to be relatively new—I can't find anything on Google in English matching my definition. Yet I think it will also strike you as immemorially old. I don't think I'm going to tell you much that you didn't already sense intuitively.

The idea that Race Does Not Exist has become quite fashionable in intellectual circles. But its appeal to the public is limited by its difficulty in passing the Richard Pryor Test. To many regular people, the No Race theory's advocates sound like they are asking, "Who are you going to believe? Us college professors or your lying eyes?"

Before I explain my definition of race, though, I'd like everybody to do a few brain-stretching warm-up exercises.

First Exercise—Which of these four conflicts are between different races and which are merely clashes between some other kinds of groups?

1. President Mugabe's black supporters vs. white farm-owners in Zimbabwe
2. Sudan's civil war between the brown people in the North and the black people in the South
3. Rwanda's civil war between the tall black Tutsis and the short black Hutus
4. The Troubles in Northern Ireland between Catholics (often red-headed) and Protestants (often red-headed).

And if you think you know the answer to which of these fights are between races and which are not, please try to explain to yourself why you drew the line where you did.

It's kind of hard, isn't it? I've noticed that traditional defenders of the concept of race tend to get twisted up trying to draw distinctions between what is a race and what is not quite a race. This allows the Race Does Not Exist crowd to score some easy points.

I avoid all that by focusing on the mechanism that creates racial groups— of whatever size or degree of distinctiveness. One of my goals has been to create what the computer guys call a "scaleable solution"—one that will provide insights about what all four of these unhappy situations have in common.

Second exercise—I'm sure you are familiar with a lot of plausible-sounding objections to the very notion that race might be a meaningful concept.

For example, Peter Wood has argued, "If race is obvious, surely it shouldn't be too hard to count them." Or, as many have demanded, "If race exists, how can there be people who belong to more than one race?"

Many of these criticisms are powerful. But they would be equally strong if they were directed toward many other useful but noncontroversial concepts like, say, "region."

So when I read off a standard complaint about race, think along with me about how you can say the same thing about region.

Q. How come you people who think race exists can't even agree on how many races there are in the world?

A. Well, how many regions are there are in the world? Can we even count all the regions we happen to be in right here at the Reagan Library? Let's see, we're in Ventura Country and the Pacific Rim and North America and the West Coast and the Pacific Time Zone and NAFTA and, well, I could go on for a long time without coming close to enumerating all the regions we are in.

Q. If races exist, doesn't that mean one race has to be the supreme Master Race? And that would be awful!

A. Indeed it would, but no race is going to be best at everything—any more than one region could be the supreme master region for all human purposes. For example, this mountaintop is a stirring place to put a Presidential Library. But if you want to break the land speed record in your rocket car, it's definitely inferior to the Bonneville Salt Flats.

Q. If race exists, how can people belong to more than one race? Mustn't the races be mutually exclusive?

A. If "region" exists, how can people be in more than one at a time—just as we are now in the Western Hemisphere and the Northern Hemisphere?

Of course, some kinds of regions are mutually exclusive, typically the ones that are legally defined. Since we are in Ventura County, we can't be in Los Angeles County. Laws often work that way.

But nature, which often glides gradually from one state to another, seldom does. So you often get poor fits when you try to force something natural into sharp-edged artificial categories.

For example, the various so-called "one drop rules" for defining blacks made the black and white races legally mutually exclusive. In contrast, whites did not always demand mutual exclusivity of whites and American Indians. Herbert Hoover's Vice-President Charles Curtis was famously proud of being at least 1/8th American Indian and having spent several years of his child-hood on a reservation.

After political power shifted from white supremacists to the minority groups, black activists still demanded the one drop rule because they wanted as many voters to benefit from racial preferences as possible in order to keep their political support up. This doesn't cost them anything, because the size of the quota pie automatically expands when somebody new decides to iden-tify himself as black.

Meanwhile, Indian tribes generally require a higher fraction (such as 1/4th) of documented tribal ancestry before they'll give you a slice of their casino pie. After all, their casino privileges are assigned to the tribe, not the tribe member, and are finite. Also, because their tribal privileges are guaran-teed by treaty, not by politics, Indians can afford to be snobbish.

These differing attempts to fit legal definitions to the natural phenome-non of ancestry explain otherwise curious scenes like Halle Berry's blonde mom calling her daughter a credit to the black race.[1]

Now, the key point about debating "Does Race Exist" is that it's essentially a *semantic dispute*. If you can find the dumbest definition anybody ever came up with—something like "racial groups are virtually separate species that al-most never interbreed"—then, under that strawman definition, "race" would definitely *not* exist.

Conversely, of course, if you rigorously define "race" to mean something that actually does exist on Earth, then, by definition, race exists.

It's not hard to find ridiculous definitions of race to prove wrong, since lots of dumb stuff has been said about race over the years, even by scientists. Although in the last few decades there has been some good thinking about what race *is not*, there have been very few attempts to come up with a new understanding of what race *is*...because it has become dangerous to scientists' and intellectuals' careers.

I got interested in coming up with a rigorous definition of race a few years ago when I saw that all we had to choose from were

1. the obsolete definitions that largely failed to incorporate sophisticat-ed sociobiological perspectives or
2. the hip nihilism of the Race Does Not Exist crowd.

Early 19th Century credulity and late 20th Century postmodernism ar-en't adequate. We need a working definition for the 21st Century.

Obviously, there's something that our lying eyes see. But what exactly is it?

Up until the 1960's, physical anthropologists tended to conceive of racial classifications as fitting neatly into a taxonomy of the kind invented by the great 18th Century naturalist Carolus Linnaeaus. The top-down Linnaean system describes how the God of Genesis might have gone about efficiently organizing the Creation. It subdivides living things into genuses and then into species, subspecies, races, and presumably into sub-races and so on.

Linnaean taxonomy is still hugely useful. It even works fairly well for humans: see the July 30, 2002 *New York Times* article, "Race Is Seen as Real Guide to Track Roots of Disease" for how Stanford geneticist Neil Risch's crude model of dividing the world up into five continental-scale races for medical purposes can help save lives.

But naturalists now understood, however, that the Linnaean mindset always imposed a little too much order on the messiness of evolution. All of these Linnaean terms, like genus and subspecies, are not absolute but relative designations. Thus, they tend to be unavoidably arbitrary. Paleontologists are always bickering over whether some new hominid skull dug up in Africa is different enough to deserve its own genus or whether it is just a lousy new subspecies.

Even "species" is less written-in-stone than it sounds. Witness the constant debate over whether dogs, wolves, and coyotes are three species or one.[2] Enforcement of the Endangered Species Act is constantly being bogged down in disputes over whether a particular brand of bug or weed is a separate species. Billions of dollars of Southern California property development has been hung up for years over whether the rare California gnatcatcher bird is a different species than the abundant Baja gnatcatcher. The only difference is that the California gnatcatcher tends to a somewhat different color than the Baja gnatcatcher.

(This is also true of humans, of course, but that doesn't make them different species!)

None of this is to say that the concept of species should be discarded; just that, like races, species tend to be fuzzy sets, too.[3]

Race is all relative, in two senses.

First, it's all about who your relatives are.

A modern Darwinian approach to race would start from the bottom up, with the father, mother, and baby. All mammals belong to biological extended families, with a family tree that features all the same kinds of biological relatives as you or I have—grandfathers, nieces, or third cousins and so forth.

And everybody belongs to multiple extended families—your mom's, your dad's, etc.

Which leads to my modern definition of race:

A racial group is an extended family that is inbred to some degree.

That's it—just an "extended family that is somewhat inbred." There's no need to say how big the extended family has to be, or just how inbred.

We know that humans have *not* been mating completely randomly with other humans from all over the globe. Most people, over the last few tens of thousands of years, just couldn't afford the airfare.

If you go back to 1000 AD, you would theoretically have a trillion ancestors alive at that time—that's how many slots you have in your family tree 40 generations ago. Obviously, your family tree has to be a little bit inbred.

That far back, you'd probably find an individual or two from most parts of the world among your ancestors.

But, in anybody's family tree, certain statistical patterns will stand out. Just ask somebody, "What are you?" and they'll tell you about some of the larger clusters in their family tree, such as, "Oh, I'm Irish, Italian, and Cherokee."

So, my definition is close to a tautology. But then so is "survival of the fittest." And that proved to have a bit of predictive power.

This is a scaleable solution. Do you want to know a lot about a few people? Then, the more inbred, the more distinct the racial group. Or, do you want to know a little about a lot of people? The less inbred, the larger the group.

For example, Icelanders are a lot more inbred and thus a lot more distinct than, say, Europeans, who are, though, much more numerous. Which one is the "true race?"

It's a useless question. They are both racial groups. For some questions, "Icelander" is the more useful group to focus upon. For others "European" is the more effective.

Of course, the bottom-up model accounts for everything seen in top-down approaches. Average hereditary differences are—as one might expect—inherited. The bottom-up approach simply eliminates any compulsion to draw arbitrary lines regarding whether a difference is big enough to be racial. With enough inbreeding, hereditary differences will emerge that will first be recognizable to the geneticist, then to the physical anthropologist, and finally to the average person.

Similarly, two separate racial groups can slowly merge into one if barriers to intermarriage come down.

I'm more interested in the reality that there are partly inbred extended families than in what it's called. Unfortunately, I haven't been able to find a better word than "race."

Various euphemisms have been tried without much success. For example, the geneticists, such as the distinguished Luigi Luca Cavalli-Sforza of Stanford, who study what the normal person would call "race," don't call themselves "racial geneticists." Instead, they blandly label themselves "population geneticists."

That allows them at least sometimes to sneak their research projects by under the radar of the politically correct. But it's important to realize that they are not using "population" in the non-racial sense of phrases like "California's population" or "UCLA's student population," but in the specific sense of "hereditary populations" such as the Japanese or the Icelanders or the Navajo.

Among all the different kinds of "populations," the only ones population geneticists study are the ones whose members tend to share genes because they tend to share genealogies.

That's what I'd call a "racial group." But, if you don't like the word "race," well, maybe we should just hire one of those firms that invent snazzy new names like "Exxon" for unfashionable old corporations like Standard Oil, and then hire an ad agency to publicize this new name for "race."

Unfortunately, I'm a little tapped out until the end of the month. But if you have a spare fifty million dollars, that might cover it.

The *second* sense in which Race is all relative: it's pointless to make absolute statements about the significance or insignificance of race. You always have to ask, "Compared to what?"

For instance, I am constantly informed that genetic differences between racial groups are absolutely insignificant because 99.9% of human genes are shared among all people. Yet we share over 98% of our genes with chimpanzees (and, supposedly, 70% with yeast). Does that mean genetic differences between humans and chimps (or yeast) are insignificant?

You have to look at it relatively. If you were planning to climb Mt. Everest and somebody were to say, "The difference between Mt. Everest and sea level is insignificant, it's just a 0.15% difference in the distance from the center of the Earth," you'd roll your eyes. But, when somebody says the same thing about genetics, it's treated as a profundity.

Similarly, we are constantly told, "there are more genetic differences within races than between races." This is, in general, true. But it hardly means that the differences between races therefore don't exist.

For example, a team of geneticists led by Rick Kittles of Howard U. recently documented that race accounts for 20% of the variations seen in the gene that controls the strength of the body's androgen receptors.[4] Men with stronger androgen receptors tend to behave as if they have higher levels of testosterone and other male hormones. For example, those with the versions of the genes that heighten androgen reception are more susceptible on average to prostate cancer. Men of West African ancestry tend to have more of the gene variants conducive to high androgen receptivity than men of European descent (which is one reason they suffer more from prostate cancer). Whites, in turn, tend to have more testosterone receptivity than men of Northeast Asian descent.

Keep in mind that 80% of the variation observed was within racial groups. Which is about what you'd expect from observing the world around you. In every racial group, there exists a wide variety of physical and personality types among men, from the most hyper-masculine to the most gentle.

Still, few who watch sports on television, follow Olympic running results, or examine interracial marriage patterns, will be surprised that blacks on the whole score highest on those androgen receptor gene alleles associated with greater masculinity.

We've seen what's wrong with the old-fashioned Linnaean taxonomists' approach to race and the fecklessness of the postmodernists' denial of race. But what are the strengths and weaknesses of the typical American's concept of race?

The way most Americans currently think about race tends to fall in between rigor and absurdity. The consensus American view is full of contradictions, obsolete ideas, and fantasies. But in a rough way, it does approximate the American reality.

Yet because the American geographic and historical situation is so unusual, we lack a model that would apply well to rest of the world, which is one reason we are finding it difficult to grasp the politics of Afghanistan.

Afghanistan's division into warring extended families is tragic-comically extreme, probably due to the severity of its terrain. But Afghans are like most people in history who have instinctively viewed the world as consisting of concentric circles of blood relations. Race to them is just family writ large. "My brother and I against my cousin. My cousin and us against the world."

America, however, was populated from across the seas. The striking contrasts between blacks, whites, and American Indians—peoples from different continents—overshadowed the normal pattern of extended family blending almost imperceptibly into racial group as it spread geographically.

We Americans tended to forget that race is relative. We became obsessed with big, continental scale racial differences. Thus in recent decades we have decided that smaller racial differences—whether Norwegians vs. Armenians or Pygmies vs. Dinkas—weren't really there. They were just "ethnic," not racial. We may well be better off not noticing, but one problem is that standard American thinking about race doesn't scale up and down well.

That's why Americans have a hard time understanding the rest of the world. Let's come back to those four civil conflicts. Which ones are racial?

- Zimbabwe
- Rwanda
- Sudan
- Northern Ireland

The conventional American response is: "just Zimbabwe." After all, that's the only dispute between whites and blacks, as we think of them.

In reality, all these disputes are fights between relatively distinct extended families. Take Northern Ireland (please). Americans always call it a "religious war." But the hard men on both sides don't care much about theology. No, even though outsiders can't generally tell the two sides apart by looking at them, this is, in essence, a struggle between two large families. One family used to own Northern Ireland until the other family took it away from them. Some members of the first family want it back.

From this perspective, we can see the commonality in all four conflicts— they are all property disputes between extended families that may not share enough recent common ancestry to make compromise possible because no-one has anybody they can trust on the other side.

And once you understand this, it becomes simpler to think of ways to ameliorate these kinds of conflicts.

My definition of race offers that kind of conceptual power for a host of other issues.

What practical steps are implied by this family-based definition of race?

First, if race is a natural, omnipresent potential fault line in human affairs, that suggests to me that we Americans should be extremely wary of using the vast power of the government to exacerbate the natural divisiveness of race by officially classifying people by race.

Second, in the long run, intermarriage is the most fundamental solution for extended families at odds with each other.

The effects of interracial marriage are more complex than Tamar Jacoby or Gregory Rodriguez assume—that's why 500 years of intermarriage haven't made Mexico or Brazil a racial utopia. Indeed, Brazil has just begun to introduce racial preferences.[5]

Still, intermarriage is what turned the Angles and the Saxons into the Anglo-Saxons. And one way to raise the intermarriage rate is to cut back on immigration. Here in California, native-born Americans are something like three times more likely to intermarry than immigrants.

Third, humans just like to belong to a group. Because race is not, at root, a social construct, we need to promote a positive social construct as an alternative for people to organize around.

Perhaps the most beneficial alternative to race is citizenship. But we need to do more than just promote national solidarity as the alternative to racial solidarity. We need to actually do things for our less fortunate fellow citizens—like reducing immigration so that supply and demand will raise their wages.

In summary: I believe that knowing the truth is a lot more beneficial to humanity than ignorance, lies, or wishful thinking.

Arguing Against Reality

Taki's
June 05, 2019

THE term "Gell-Mann Amnesia effect" was coined by the late novelist Michael Crichton (*Jurassic Park*) in honor of the famous physicist who died last month. Murray Gell-Mann had pointed out to Crichton that he had noticed that journalists aren't very accurate at writing about his own specialty, physics, nor about Crichton's, showbiz, so why do we trust them to write reliably about everything else?

I was reminded of the Gell-Mann effect when reading British journalist Angela Saini's much celebrated new book, *Superior: The Return of Race Science*.

In Saini's sprawling conspiracy theory about the malign forces that inspire evil scientists to keep on noticing differences between human groups despite seventy years of politically correct censorship, I am cast as a villain, along with, among others, polymath Francis Galton, psychometrician Arthur Jensen, geneticist James D. Watson, rock singer Morrissey, Harvard geneticist David Reich, and even Albert Einstein. (That lineup makes me feel like the batboy on the 1927 Yankees: honored just to be on the same field.)

Saini gets her story about me so wrong that it's hard to have much confidence in the rest of her book.

Saini, a pleasant-looking lady who is part of a London media "power couple" with her BBC editor husband Mukul Devichand, is a true believer in today's low-to-middlebrow dogma that race-does-not-exist.

Her style of science denialism is a growing force in this century's culture, as the DNA evidence continues to pile up, embarrassing her resentful emotions. For instance, she laments:

> Ancestry testing has taken the work of well-meaning scientists who only tried to do good in the world and inadvertently has helped reinforce the idea that race is real.

Well...yeah. It has.

In her chapter "Human Biodiversity: How race was rebranded for the twenty-first century," Saini reports that I, personally, facilitated the return to influence of nefarious "race science" by starting a sinister email list in 1998. (Actually, it was in 1999.)

Her source is Jonathan Marks, whom she describes as "a genial, generous professor of anthropology at the University of North Carolina, Charlotte." I've been a fan of Jon for over twenty years, but this may be the first time I've heard him described as "genial." In reality, Dr. Marks has the classic Angry Radical Leftist personality of the more famous Dr. Marx (a comparison I suspect he would find pleasing).

Saini's story begins with Marks getting an email from:

> A little-known science journalist and former writer for the conservative '*National Review*,' Steve Sailer. The invitation was for Marks to join a mailing list of people interested in the subject of human variation. "I knew absolutely nothing about him," Marks recalls. "He just seemed to be someone who was organizing something.... It seemed pretty straightforward and harmless." So he signed up.

Saini says, with justification, "By the summer of 1999, Sailer's roster of members was astounding." Like the CIA, I can neither confirm nor deny the membership of any individuals in any email group I've ever organized without their personal consent. That would be in bad taste.

Because Dr. Marks has decided to snitch, however, I shall assume he has consented.

According to Saini's version, like Captain Renault in *Casablanca* discovering that gambling was going on at Rick's, Marks was shocked, shocked to discover that the discussing of race was going on in a Human Biodiversity email group.

> It dawned on Marks that Sailer's seemingly innocent email list was not so much a way to discuss science in an objective way but more

about tying together fresh science and economics with existing racial stereotypes. One debate that sticks in Marks's mind today, for instance, took place between him and a journalist who claimed that black people were genetically endowed to be better at sports. Marks insisted that this was a scientifically shaky argument, not to mention one with dangerous political implications. The two experts clearly disagreed. But rather than help reach a consensus, "Steve Sailer clearly took his side," he tells me. "At which point I realized, 'Ah! This isn't an impartial scholarly discussion.'"

Dr. Marks implies that he didn't become aware of the shocking fact that he and I don't agree all that much on important empirical and epistemological questions until after he'd joined my seemingly "harmless" email group.

But my recollection is that the two of us had carried on a frank and spirited correspondence for quite some time before I started my email group in 1999. As I blogged in 2010, in the later 1990s:

> I came up with the term "human biodiversity" to describe my chief intellectual interest. I modeled the term on Edward O. Wilson's term "biodiversity." I then looked to see in the pre-Google web search engine Alta Vista if the term had ever been used before. I quickly found Marks's 1995 book *Human Biodiversity: Genes, Race, and History*. I bought it and read it and then exchanged several emails with Marks over it. At one point, he and I agreed to approach magazines to see if they would like to publish a debate between Marks and myself over the reality of race, although enthusiasm on the part of editors turned out to be mild, to say the least.

It's unlikely that Dr. Marks was surprised that I didn't agree with him; after all, we'd been emailing each other from well before I formed my email group in early 1999. I see from Amazon.com that I bought his *Human Biodiversity* book on March 7, 1998, so we likely argued one-on-one in the second half of 1998.

What's more likely is that Jon was surprised the distinguished audience didn't much agree with him. It's only natural that Dr. Marks would like to both dish dirt and avoid blame for his membership in an email group that leaned toward the heretical. So it's understandable that he excuses himself as having been duped into participating. Moreover, he reassures his ego that the reason his self-evidently correct arguments about race and sports were not greeted with the universal acclaim they deserved by the impressive audience was that I used reprehensible trickery.

In any case, vastly more important than what happened in private email arguments over race and sports in 1999 is what has happened in public since then.

For example, back then, in the Olympic men's 100-meter dash, the race to determine the World's Fastest Man, in 1999 the last 32 finalists, going back to the 1984 Olympics, had been at least half sub-Saharan black.

Today, however, the last 72 finalists in the 100-meter dash have been at least half black. Five more Olympics have gone by without a single nonblack qualifying for the eight-man finals.

Similarly, in 1999 there were only a few nonblack cornerbacks starting in the NFL, such as Jason Sehorn. Today, all starting corners for the last fifteen NFL seasons have been black.

If science, in the Popperian view, is about making predictions, whose predictions have turned out to be more correct?

Dr. Marks' argument isn't actually with me. It's now with history.

Saini also goes to interview David Reich, who runs the world's most productive lab for sequencing ancient DNA. (Reich's 2018 book *Who We Are and How We Got Here* is so informative that I wrote three reviews of it.)

Initially, Saini is wowed by Reich's prestige and his polished lines about the ubiquity of ancient "migrations" (a euphemism for invasions, conquests, enslavements, epidemics, and slaughters):

> What we think of as "indigenous" Europeans are, Reich and other scientists now understand, the product of a number of migrations over the past fifteen thousand years, including from what is now called the Middle East.

Saini takes everything personally in that girly style that predominates in 2019, gushing:

> This is the book I have wanted to write since I was a child, and I have poured my soul into it.

As a loyal Indian racialist (her first book was *Geek Nation: How Indian Science Is Taking Over the World*), she has an obsession with finding sciencey-sounding arguments that her people have just as much right to move to England as the native English have to live there. Hence, she is much cheered by Reich's finding that the Battle-Axe Culture steppe invaders exterminated most of the population of England about 4,500 years ago:

> When considered from the perspective of the deep past, race, nationality, and ethnicity are not what we imagine them to be. They are ephemeral, real only to the extent that we have made them feel real by living in the cultures we do, with the politics we have.

Saini reflects:

> If skin color and genetic purity can't be a measure of ethnic identity, because Britons have changed on both these counts over the millennia, then there's nothing to prevent anyone from anywhere from earning citizenship and becoming truly British.

Well, there is the law. But the law didn't stop the Proto-Indo-Europeans (i.e., Aryans, more or less) from conquering Western Europe 4,500 years ago, so why should it stop anybody from doing it again today?

But then Reich goes on to blaspheme against her race is just a social construct creed:

> At the same time [Reich] thinks some categories may have more biological meaning to them. Black Americans are mostly West African in ancestry and white Americans tend to be European, both correlating to genuine population groups that were once separated at least partially for seventy thousand years in human history....
>
> He suggests that there may be more than superficial average differences between black and white Americans, possibly even cognitive and psychological ones, because before they arrived in the United States, these population groups had this seventy thousand years apart during which they adapted to their own different environments.
>
> Reich implies that natural selection may have acted on them differently within this timescale to produce changes that go further than skin deep. He adds, judiciously, that he doesn't think these differences will be large—only a fraction as big as the variation between individuals, just as biologist Richard Lewontin estimated in 1972. But he doesn't expect them to be nonexistent either: as individuals we are so very different from one another that even a fraction of a difference between groups is something.

The scientist's sacrilege causes the scandalized journalist to harrumph:

They are words I never expected to hear from a respected mainstream geneticist.

Is Love Colorblind?

National Review
July 14, 1997

WHILE interracial marriage is increasingly accepted by whites, a surprising number of Asian men and black women are bitterly opposed. Why?

Just three decades ago, Thurgood Marshall was only months away from appointment to the Supreme Court when he suffered an indignity that to-day seems not just outrageous but almost incomprehensible. He and his wife had found their dream house in a Virginia suburb of Washington, D.C., but could not lawfully live together in that state: he was black and she was Asian. Fortunately for the Marshalls, in January 1967 the Supreme Court struck down the anti-interracial-marriage laws in Virginia and 18 other states. And in 1967 these laws were not mere leftover scraps from an extinct era. Two years before, at the crest of the civil rights revolution, a Gallup poll found that 72% of Southern whites and 42% of Northern whites still wanted to ban interracial marriage.

Let's fast-forward to the present and another black-Asian couple: retired Green Beret Lieutenant Colonel Eldrick Woods Sr. and his Thai-born wife, Kultida. They are not hounded by the police—just by journalists desperate to write more adulatory articles about how well they raised their son Tiger. The colossal popularity of young Tiger Woods and the homage paid his parents are remarkable evidence of white Americans' change in attitude toward what they formerly denounced as "miscegenation." In fact, Tiger's famously

147

mixed ancestry (besides being black and Thai, he's also Chinese, white, and American Indian) is not merely tolerated by golf fans. More than a few seem to envision Tiger as a shining symbol of what America could become in a post-racial age.

Interracial marriage is growing steadily. From the 1960 to the 1990 Census, white-Asian married couples increased almost tenfold, while black-white couples quadrupled. The reasons are obvious: greater integration and the decline of white racism. More subtly, interracial marriages are increasingly recognized as epitomizing what our society values most in a marriage: the triumph of true love over convenience and prudence. Nor is it surprising that white-Asian marriages outnumber black-white marriages: the social distance between whites and Asians is now far smaller than the distance between blacks and whites. What's fascinating, however, is that in recent years a startling number of nonwhites—especially Asian men and black women—have become bitterly opposed to intermarriage.

This is a painful topic to explore honestly, so nobody does. Still, it's important because interracial marriages are a leading indicator of what life will be like in the even more diverse and integrated twenty-first century. Intermarriages show that integration can churn up unexpected racial conflicts by spotlighting enduring differences between the races.

For example, probably the most disastrous mistake Marcia Clark made in prosecuting O. J. Simpson was to complacently allow Johnny Cochran to pack the jury with black women. As a feminist, Mrs. Clark smugly assumed that all female jurors would identify with Nicole Simpson. She ignored pre-trial research indicating that black women tended to see poor Nicole as The Enemy, one of those beautiful blondes who steal successful black men from their black first wives, and deserve whatever they get.

The heart of the problem for Asian men and black women is that intermarriage does not treat every sex/race combination equally: on average, it has offered black men and Asian women new opportunities for finding mates among whites, while exposing Asian men and black women to new competition from whites. In the 1990 Census, 72% of black-white couples consisted of a black husband and a white wife. In contrast, white-Asian pairs showed the reverse: 72% consisted of a white husband and an Asian wife.

Sexual relations outside of marriage are less fettered by issues of family approval and long-term practicality, and they appear to be even more skewed. The 1992 *Sex in America* study of 3,432 people, as authoritative a work as any in a field where reliable data are scarce, found that ten times more single white women than single white men reported that their most recent sex partner was black.

Few whites comprehend the growing impact on minorities of these interracial husband-wife disparities. One reason is that the effect on whites has been balanced. Although white women hunting for husbands, for example, suffer more competition from Asian women, they also enjoy increased access to black men. Further, the weight of numbers dilutes the effect on whites. In 1990, 1.46 million Asian women were married, compared to only 1.26 million Asian men. This net drain of 0.20 million white husbands into marriages to Asian women is too small to be noticed by the 75 million white women, except in Los Angeles and a few other cities with large Asian populations and high rates of intermarriage. Yet, this 0.20 million shortage of Asian wives leaves a high proportion of frustrated Asian bachelors in its wake.

Black women's resentment of intermarriage is now a staple of daytime talk shows, hit movies like *Waiting to Exhale*, and magazine articles. Black novelist Bebe Moore Campbell described her and her tablemates' reactions upon seeing a black actor enter a restaurant with a blonde: "In unison, we moaned, we groaned, we rolled our eyes heavenward.... Then we all shook our heads as we lamented for the 10,000th time the perfidy of black men, and cursed trespassing white women who dared to 'take our men.'" Like most guys, though, Asian men are reticent about admitting any frustrations in the mating game. But anger over intermarriage is visible on Internet on-line discussion groups for young Asians. The men, featuring an even-greater-than-normal-for-the-Internet concentration of cranky bachelors, accuse the women of racism for dating white guys. For example, "This [dating] disparity is a manifestation of a silent conspiracy by the racist white society and self-hating Asian [nasty word for "women"] to effect the genocide of Asian Americans." The women retort that the men are racist and sexist for getting sore about it. All they can agree upon is that Media Stereotypes and/or Low Self-Esteem must somehow be at fault.

Let's review other facts about intermarriage and how they violate conventional sociological theories.

1. You would normally expect more black women than black men to marry whites because far more black women are in daily contact with whites. First, among blacks aged 20-39, there are about 10% more women than men alive. Another tenth of the black men in these prime marrying years are literally

locked out of the marriage market by being locked up in jail, and maybe twice that number are on probation or parole. So, there may be nearly 14 young black women for every 10 young black men who are alive and unentangled with the law. Further, black women are far more prevalent than black men in universities (by 80% in grad schools), in corporate offices, and in other places where members of the bourgeoisie, black or white, meet their mates.

Despite these opportunities to meet white men, so many middle-class black women have trouble landing satisfactory husbands that they have made Terry (*Waiting to Exhale*) McMillan, author of novels specifically about and for them, into a best-selling brand name. Probably the most popular romance advice regularly offered to affluent black women of a certain age is to find true love in the brawny arms of a younger black man. Both Miss McMillan's 1996 best-seller *How Stella Got Her Groove Back* and the most celebrated of all books by black women, Zora Neale Hurston's 1937 classic *Their Eyes Were Watching God*, are romance novels about well-to-do older women and somewhat dangerous younger men. Of course, as Miss Hurston herself later learned at age 49, when she (briefly) married a 23-year-old gym coach, that seldom works out in real life.

2. Much more practical-sounding advice would be: Since there are so many unmarried Asian men and black women, they should find solace for their loneliness by marrying each other. Yet, when was the last time you saw an Asian man and a black woman together? Black-man/Asian-woman couples are still quite unusual, but Asian-man/black-woman pairings are incomparably more rare.

Similar patterns appear in other contexts:

3a. Within races: Black men tend to most ardently pursue lighter-skinned, longer-haired black women (e.g., Spike Lee's *School Daze*). Yet black women today do not generally prefer fairer men.

3b. In other countries: In Britain, 40% of black men are married to or living with a white woman, versus only 21% of black women married to or living with a white man.

3c. In art: *Madame Butterfly*, a white-man/Asian-woman tragedy, has been packing them in for a century, recently under the name *Miss Saigon*. The greatest black-man/white-woman story, *Othello*, has been an endless hit in both Shakespeare's and Verdi's versions. (To update Karl Marx's dictum: Theater always repeats itself, first as tragedy, then as opera, and finally as farce, as seen in that recent smash, *O.J., The Moor of Brentwood*.) Maybe Shakespeare did know a thing or two about humanity: America's leading portrayer of Othello, James Earl Jones, has twice fallen in love with and married the white actress playing opposite him as Desdemona.

4. The civil rights revolution left husband-wife balances among interracial couples more unequal. Back in 1960 white husbands were seen in 50% of black-white couples (versus only 28% in 1990), and in only 62% of white-Asian couples (versus 72%). Why? Discrimination, against black men and Asian women. In the Jim Crow South black men wishing to date white women faced pressures ranging from raised eyebrows to lynch mobs. In contrast, the relatively high proportion of Asian-man/white-woman couples in 1960 was a holdover caused by anti-Asian immigration laws that had prevented women, most notably Chinese women, from joining the largely male pioneer immigrants. As late as 1930 Chinese-Americans were 80% male. So, the limited number of Chinese men who found wives in the mid twentieth century included a relatively high fraction marrying white women. In other words, as legal and social discrimination have lessened, natural inequalities have asserted themselves.

5. Keeping black men and white women apart was the main purpose of Jim Crow. Gunnar Myrdal's landmark 1944 study found that Southern whites generally grasped that keeping blacks down also retarded their own economic progress, but whites felt that was the price they had to pay to make black men less attractive to white women. To the extent that white racism persists, it should limit the proportion of black-man/white-woman couples.

Since these inequalities in interracial marriage are so contrary to conventional expectations, what causes them? Academia's and the mass media's preferred reaction has been to ignore husband-wife disproportions entirely. When the subject has raised its ugly head, though, they've typically tossed out arbitrary ideas to explain a single piece of the puzzle, rather than address the entire yin and yang of black-white and white-Asian marriages. For example, a Japanese-American poetry professor in Minnesota has written extensively on his sexual troubles with white women. He blames the internment of Japanese Americans during World War II. Presumably, the similarity of frustrations of Chinese-American men is just a coincidence caused by, say, China losing the Opium War. And the problems of Vietnamese men stem from winning the Vietnam War, etc. But piecemeal rationalizations are unappealing compared to a theory which might explain all the evidence.

The general pattern to be explained is: blacks are more in demand as husbands than as wives, and vice-versa for Asians. The question is, what accounts for it?

The usual sociological explanations for who marries whom (e.g., availability, class, and social approval) never work simultaneously for blacks and Asians. This isn't surprising because these social-compatibility factors influence the total number of black-white or white-Asian marriages more than the husband-wife proportions within intermarriages.

By emphasizing how society encourages us to marry people like ourselves, sociologists miss half the picture: by definition, heterosexual attraction thrives on differences. Although Henry Higgins and Colonel Pickering are so compatible that they break into song about it ("Why Can't a Woman Be More like a Man?"), Higgins falls in love with Eliza Doolittle. Opposites attract. And certain race/sex pairings seem to be more opposite than others. The force driving these skewed husband-wife proportions appears to be differences in perceived sexual attractiveness. On average, black men tend to appear slightly more and Asian men slightly less masculine than white men, while Asian women are typically seen as slightly more and black women as slightly less feminine than white women.

Obviously, these are gross generalizations about the races. Nobody believes Michael Jackson could beat up kung-fu star Jackie Chan or that comedienne Margaret Cho is lovelier than *Sports Illustrated* swimsuit covergirl Tyra Banks. But life is a game of probabilities, not of abstract Platonic essences.

So, what makes blacks more masculine-seeming and Asians more feminine-seeming? Media stereotypes are sometimes invoked. TV constantly shows black men slam-dunking, while it seems the only way an Asian man can get some coverage is to discover a cure for AIDS. Yet try channel-surfing for minority women. You'll see black women dancing, singing, joking, and romancing. If, however, you even see an Asian woman, she'll probably be newscasting—not the most alluring of roles.

Conventional wisdom sometimes cites social conditioning as well. But while this is not implausible for American-born blacks, who come from a somewhat homogeneous culture, it's insensitive to the diversity of cultures in which Asians are raised. Contrast Koreans and Filipinos and Cambodian refugees and fifth-generation Japanese-Americans. It's not clear they have much in common culturally other than that in the West their women are more in demand as spouses than their men.

One reasonable cultural explanation for the sexual attractiveness of black men today is the hypermasculinization of black life over the last few decades. To cite a benign aspect of this trend, if you've followed the Olympics on TV since the 1960s you've seen sprinters' victory celebrations evolve from genteel exercises in restraint into orgies of fist-pumping, trash-talking black machismo. This showy masculinization of black behavior may be in part a delayed reaction to the long campaign by Southern white males to portray themselves as "The Man" and the black man as a "boy." But let's not be content to stop our analysis here. Why did Jim Crow whites try so hard to demean black manhood? As we've seen, the chief reason was to prevent black men from impregnating white women.

So, did all racist whites a century ago make keeping minorities away from their women their highest priority? No. As noted earlier, the anti-Asian immigration laws kept Asian women out, forcing many Asian immigrant bachelors to look for white women (with mixed success). While white men were certainly not crazy about this side effect, it seemed an acceptable tradeoff, since they feared Asian immigrants more as economic than as sexual competitors. But why did whites historically dread the masculine charms of blacks more than those of Asians? Merely asking this question points out that social conditioning is ultimately a superficial explanation of the differences among peoples. Yes, society socializes individuals, but what socializes society?

There are only three fundamental causes for the myriad ways groups differ. The first is unsatisfying but no doubt important: random flukes of history. The second, the favorite of Thomas Sowell and Jared Diamond, is differences in geography and climate. The third is human biodiversity. (On further reflection, I realize that human biodiversity is itself fundamentally the product of the first two causes, but it can be worth thinking of a separate cause.) Let's look at three physical differences between the races.

1. Asian men tend to be shorter than white and black men. Does this matter in the mating game? One of America's leading hands-on researchers into this question, 7'1", 280-pound basketball legend Wilt Chamberlain, reports that in his ample experience being tall and strong never hurt. Biological anthropologists confirm this, finding that taller tends to be better in the eyes of most women in just about all cultures. Like most traits, height is determined by the interaction of genetic and social factors (e.g., nutrition). For example, the L.A. Dodgers' flamethrowing pitcher Hideo Nomo is listed as 6'2", an almost unheard-of height for any Japanese man fifty years ago, owing to the

near-starvation diets of the era. While the height gap between Japanese and whites narrowed significantly after World War II, this trend has slowed in recent years as well-fed Japanese began bumping up against genetic limits. Furthermore, it can be rather cold comfort to a 5'7" Asian who is competing for dates with white and black guys averaging 5'11" to hear, "Your sons will grow up on average a couple of inches taller than you, assuming, of course, that you ever meet a girl and have any kids." In contrast, consider a 5'1" Asian coed. Although she'd be happy with a 5'7" boyfriend if she were in an all-Asian school, at UCLA she finds lots of boys temptingly much taller than that, but few are Asian.

2. This general principle—the more racial integration there is, the more important become physical differences among the races—can also be seen with regard to hair length. The ability to grow long hair is a useful indicator of youth and good health. (Ask anybody on chemotherapy.) Since women do not go bald and can generally grow longer hair than men, most cultures associate longer hair with femininity. Although blacks' hair doesn't grow as long as whites' or Asians' hair, that's not a problem for black women in all-black societies. After integration, though, hair often becomes an intense concern for black women competing with longer-haired women of other races. While intellectuals in black-studies departments' ebony towers denounce "Eurocentric standards of beauty," most black women respond more pragmatically. They one-up white women by buying straight from the source of the longest hair: the *Wall Street Journal* recently reported on the booming business in furnishing African-American women with "weaves" and "extensions" harvested from the follicularly gifted women of China.

3. Muscularity may most sharply differentiate the races in terms of sexual attractiveness. Women like men who are stronger than they; men like women who are rounder and softer. The ending of segregation in sports has made racial differences in muscularity harder to ignore. Although the men's 100-meter dash is among the world's most widely contested events, in the last four Olympics all 32 finalists have been blacks of West African descent. Is muscularity quantifiable? PBS fitness expert Covert Bailey finds that he needs to recommend different goals—in terms of percentage of body fat—to his clients of different races. The standard goal for adult black men is 12% body fat, versus 18% for Asian men. The goals for women are 7 points higher than for men of the same race. For interracial couples, their "gender gaps" in body-fat goals correlate uncannily with their husband-wife proportions in

154

the 1990 Census. The goal for black men (12%) is 10 points lower than the goal for white women (22%), while the goal for white men (15%) is only 4 points lower than the goal for black women (19%). This 10:4 ratio is almost identical to the 72:28 ratio seen in the Census. This correlates just as well for white—Asian couples, too. Apparently, men want women who make them feel more like men, and vice versa for women.

Understanding the impact of genetic racial differences on American life is a necessity for anybody who wants to understand our increasingly complex society. For example, the sense of betrayal felt by Asian men certainly makes sense. After all, they tend to surpass the national average in those long-term virtues—industry, self-restraint, law-abidingness—that society used to train young women to look for in a husband. Yet, now that discrimination has finally declined enough for Asian men to expect to reap the rewards for fulfilling traditional American standards of manliness, our culture has largely lost interest in indoctrinating young women to prize those qualities.

The frustrations of Asian men are a warning sign. When, in the names of freedom and feminism, young women listen less to the hard-earned wisdom of older women about how to pick Mr. Right, they listen even more to their hormones. This allows cruder measures of a man's worth—like the size of his muscles—to return to prominence. The result is not a feminist utopia, but a society in which genetically gifted guys can more easily get away with acting like Mr. Wrong.

George Orwell noted, "To see what is in front of one's nose requires a constant struggle." We can no longer afford to have our public policy governed by fashionable philosophies which insist upon ignoring the obvious. The realities of interracial marriage, like those of professional sports, show that diversity and integration turn out in practice to be fatal to the reigning assumption of racial uniformity. The courageous individuals in interracial marriages have moved farthest past old hostilities. Yet, they've discovered not the featureless landscape of utter equality that was predicted by progressive pundits, but a landscape rich with fascinating racial patterns. Intellectuals should stop dreading the ever-increasing evidence of human biodiversity and start delighting in it.

Hormonal Politics

Taki's
November 07, 2012

I T'S worth thinking about sex hormone influences on voting. From a recent *Economist* article, "Political strength: A man's muscle power influences his beliefs":

> Dr. Petersen and Dr. Sznycer found that, regardless of country of origin or apparent ideology, strong men argued for their self interest: the poor for redistribution, the rich against it. No surprises there. Weaklings, however, were far less inclined to make the case that self-interest suggested they would.[6]

The politics of women, on the other hand, were uninfluenced by their muscularity. Sensibly, "Rich women wanted to stay rich; poor women to become so."

This correlation between male muscularity and politics seems plausible to me, especially with the researchers' clever distinction between proclaimed ideology and political self-interest. (I would expect that strength also correlates with solidarity, that team spirit is stronger on the football field than on, say, the tennis team.)

For example, the rare out-of-the-closet Republican in Hollywood is typically an action movie star.

Likewise, the strong right arm of the Democratic Party was long a beefy union guy in a windbreaker. Or, in the case of my late father-in-law, the classical tuba-playing head of the Chicago Federation of Musicians, a beefy union guy in a tuxedo. To weedier musicians, he looked like what he was: a big man who wouldn't back down in negotiations with the bosses.

In contrast, liberal college professors are frequently ectomorphic runners.

This study raises the follow-on question of whether political predilections are in-born, or if changes in exercise routines can influence opinions.

I often read liberals lamenting how much, holding demographics equal, the country has shifted to the right since the good old days of the mid-1970s. (Note: the mid-1970s may not have been that good for you.)

It occurs to me now that 1974, when the Democrats swept Congress, might have been the skinniest year in recent American history. The jogging craze had been kicked off by Frank Shorter's gold medal in the 1972 Olympic marathon. And weightlifting was completely out of fashion, endorsed mostly by weirdoes like that freakish Austrian bodybuilder with all those consonants in his name.

I don't know how to explain to younger people just how absurd the idea that muscle man Arnold Schwarzenegger would someday be elected governor of California would have struck people in 1974. By 1984, however, a profile of Schwarzenegger in *Rolling Stone* wisely devoted a paragraph to explaining that Arnold was Constitutionally ineligible to become President.

Here's an extremely anecdotal Hollywood example of the political correlates of lifting v. running. Consider two television stars of highly rated cop shows: Gary Sinise (*CSI: NY*) and Mark Harmon (*NCIS*). These two actors strike me as reasonably comparable, perhaps because I used to see them around my son's high school, where their children went too. And, I've admired both Sinise and Harmon for their work long before they became television leading men. Sinise was the artistic director in the 1980s of Chicago's great Steppenwolf theater. And Harmon had a 17-5 won-loss record quarterbacking my favorite college football team, UCLA, in 1972-73.

If I'd had to guess their political causes based on their biographies—Sinise the Chicago theater kid whose father was a film editor v. Harmon the Bel-Air jock whose dad, Tom Harmon, won the 1940 Heisman Trophy—I would have bet on Sinise as the liberal activist and Harmon as the conservative.

In reality, their political concerns are closer to the body types they've worked to develop and maintain. Neither is a big man, but Sinise looks like he lifts weights. Even though Harmon is the rare Hollywood star who was a genuine football hero—his slight frame must have taken a tremendous beating as the running QB of the Bruins' wishbone offense—he hasn't been much into putting on muscle since. Instead, he's a distance runner.

Sinise is one of Hollywood's most outspoken activists in a variety of conservative and patriotic causes. More than a few Republican operatives would like Sinise to carry on the Reagan-Schwarzenegger tradition by running for office.

In contrast, Harmon has been a gun control activist since his wife Pam Dawber's costar Rebecca Schaefer was murdered by some stalker with a gun in 1989.

I don't expect anybody to be terribly persuaded by this Sinise-Harmon comparison. My point, though, is that the proposition that different types of exercise could drive political views could be ethically tested on college students by offering free personal trainers. Randomly assign some volunteers to the weightlifting trainer, others to the running trainer, and measure if their attitudes change along with their shapes.

As Obama's calculatedly divisive 2012 campaign demonstrates, the future of politics may look much stranger than what we're familiar with. The parties will likely want to research how they can mold their own voters.

CHAPTER SIX

The Level Playing Field

How Jackie Robinson Desegregated America

National Review
April 8, 1996

IFTY years ago, on April 18, 1946, Jackie Robinson broke organized baseball's color barrier with a characteristic bang, homering and scoring four runs in his historic first game for the Brooklyn Dodgers' top farm team. This anniversary will no doubt unleash a wave of media meditations, since it combines the two national pastimes of the American male intellectual: denouncing racism and waxing nostalgic over the Brooklyn Dodgers. Spike Lee is preparing *The Jackie Robinson Saga*, and I'm sure Stephen Jay Gould will favor us with his thoughts.

Yet, beyond the obvious platitudes, baseball's long struggle over race can yield some surprising perspectives on our national predicament. The Robinson epic is generally lumped in with the 1954 *Brown* decision against segregated public schools and the 1964 Civil Rights Act outlawing job discrimination. Yet two crucial differences stand out. 1) The integration of organized baseball preceded the civil-rights revolution, and in reality baseball helped make later reforms politically feasible by giving white Americans black heroes with whom to identify. 2) Government had almost nothing to do with this triumph of the competitive market. Baseball owners finally realized that the more they cared about the color of people's money, the less they could afford to care about the color of their skin.

It's ironic that the hallowed civil-rights revolution owed so much to something as seemingly trivial as pro sports. Yet, without this business of produc-

163

ing heroes for public consumption, whites might never have cared enough about blacks to be bothered by racial injustice. It's not the most noble trait of human nature, but we tend to be more outraged by minor slights to winners (note the endlessly recounted tales of the indignities Robinson endured) than by mass atrocities against downtrodden losers.

That competitive markets make irrational bigotry expensive—not impossible, but costly—was first formally demonstrated in 1957 by University of Chicago economist Gary Becker (the 1992 Nobel Laureate), and in the four decades since has barely gained a toehold in conventional thinking. Let me be clear: this idea does not pollyannaishly presume that white people (or any other people) are motivated by disinterested good will. It merely assumes that if forced to by competition, people will hire whoever makes them the most money. Don't forget, though, that we humans are always conniving to exempt ourselves from competition. The more we can insulate ourselves from the open market, the more painlessly we can then discriminate for kin and countrymen and against people we don't like. Baseball's often ugly history shows this clearly.

Back in the 1880s, when the term "organized baseball" reflected ambition more than reality, the general anarchy let a few dozen blacks play in integrated leagues. By the turn of the century, however, blacks had been utterly banished. Although liberal demonology would assume that the owners were the villains, the prime agitators for segregation were, as economic theory would predict, the white ballplayers. Cap Anson was the best known of the many white athletes who threatened strikes or violence against black rivals. The banning of blacks came up for a vote only once, in 1887 in the International League. Following many nasty anti-black demonstrations by white players, the owners of the six all-white teams outvoted the owners of the four mixed teams. Elsewhere, blacks were driven out by "gentlemen's agreements."

Why did all the owners, although often after some resistance, ultimately give in to rabble-rousing white players? Easing the slide into segregation was organized baseball's curious status as a sort of Portuguese man-of-war of economic entities—in some ways an industry of independent competitors, in others a single enterprise. Baseball teams must agree upon how they will compete, and, while they're at it, it's always tempting to agree upon how they won't compete. Congress ratified organized baseball's collusive tendency in 1920 by exempting it from the Sherman Antitrust Act.

HOW JACKIE ROBINSON DESEGREGATED AMERICA

The team owners' ill-named "gentlemen's agreement" to discriminate against blacks closely resembles today's unspoken understanding among the presidents of another government-sanctioned cartel, our elite colleges, that they will all discriminate against whites and Asians. Both clubowners and college presidents chose to head off ugly incidents by pre-emptively caving in to racial activists. They then browbeat all their peers into closing ranks, lest a lone dissident spotlight their spinelessness.

When all teams colluded against blacks, each team could assure itself that it was no worse off competitively than if all hired blacks. Cartels often collapse quickly because of cheating, but it was easier to enforce a national ban on black ballplayers than on, say, black factory workers. A ballclub couldn't hide its black workers away inside the mill, but would have had to flaunt them on the road before hostile, even murderous crowds.

Jackie Robinson's vast (and deserved) fame tends to make us assume that blacks and whites never played together before April 1946. In truth, as the supply of black baseball talent exploded after World War I, the demand for it could not be contained either. There were of course the Negro Leagues. By the 1940s they were booming, and their All Star game frequently outdrew the white version. More forgotten are the many venues outside the South where blacks and whites increasingly played together. 1) Collegiate athletics had been haphazardly integrated for decades. At UCLA, for example, Robinson starred in baseball, football, basketball, track, tennis, golf, and swimming. 2) The California winter baseball league was integrated, though not its individual teams. 3) In the Caribbean winter leagues, race meant even less. Many teams had black and white American stars playing in the same lineups, with few problems. 4) In the mid Forties, a Mexican mogul raided both the Negro and the Major Leagues to stock his summer Mexican League's integrated teams. (Among 18 big-leaguers heading south after the 1945 season was Dodger catcher Mickey Owen. Whether this increased competition for whites encouraged the Dodgers' owner, Branch Rickey, to plunder the Negro Leagues is unknown, but it certainly didn't hurt.) 5) Semipro ball, which was hugely popular before TV, was surprisingly integrated. For instance, in 1935, Bismarck, North Dakota, fielded an awesome team, half white, half black, led by the fabled pitcher Satchel Paige. Soon, practically every town in the Dakotas boasted "semipros" lured from the Negro Leagues. 6) Barnstorming was the chaotic epitome of Disorganized Baseball, requiring only two teams willing to play and a crowd willing to pay. In many Midwestern villages, the annual athletic highlight was the arrival of a Negro Leagues squad to play the local semipros. 7) Each October the black Satchel Paige All Stars and the white Dizzy Dean All Stars barnstormed the nation together. (Predictably, the blacks won a sizable majority of these games.) During World War II, Paige could claim to be the highest-paid player in all of baseball.

In the liberal world-view, discrimination stems from prejudice, from ignorance of the actual talents of blacks. In organized baseball, the opposite was true. White Major Leaguers freely admitted that many blacks could have taken white players' jobs. Yet, somehow, this enlightened perception failed to make the white pros into ardent integrationists. Meanwhile, a number of owners and managers tried to cheat on their gentlemen's agreement. For example, many historians claim that the Washington Senators quietly broke the color barrier in the late 1930s by playing Cubans dark enough to have been banned as Negroes if they had spoken English.

There was strikingly little correlation between the rectitude of the man and his urge to integrate baseball. For example, among managers the most creative was the choleric John J. McGraw, a ferocious scrapper who won ten pennants. In 1901 he almost succeeded in smuggling a light-skinned black second baseman onto his team as a full-blooded Cherokee named "Chief Tokohama." During World War II huckster Bill Veeck tried to buy the dreadful Philadelphia Phillies and stock them with Negro Leagues stars. Like all direct challenges, though, this was rebuffed by the autocratic Commissioner of Baseball, Judge Kenesaw Mountain Landis. After the Chicago Black Sox threw the 1919 World Series, the owners had restored faith in the game by appointing Landis, who was famed for his strict moral standards—one of which was Segregation Forever. After the good Judge went to his reward in late 1944, the owners, hoping to lighten up, picked as Commissioner the Southern politician A. B. "Happy" Chandler. When Happy surprisingly indicated that he wouldn't veto black players, Branch Rickey set his plans in motion.

"Mahatma" Rickey was as renowned as Landis for his righteousness (as Rickey tirelessly reminded his players while chiseling down their salaries). No one should look down upon Rickey, however; pursue his self-interest he certainly did, but with infinitely more intelligence and courage than his rival owners. (Today's elite colleges, for example, have yet to produce their own Branch Rickey, a school president brave enough to dump affirmative action.) Rickey chose Robinson because they had so much in common: both were

Methodists who didn't smoke, drink, or chase women, and both were smart enough to know the historic importance of their undertaking. Most importantly, both were too competitive to back down.

Further undermining the naive presumption that breaking the color line was an act of progressive piety was the key role played by Rickey's favorite field manager, the little ferret Leo Durocher. Bonding the Mahatma and Leo the Lip was a shared passion for victory and money. During spring training in 1947, Rickey scheduled a series between the Dodgers and Robinson's minor-league team. He hoped that when the Dodger players saw Robinson's talents, they would demand his promotion. Instead, fearing for their jobs or those of their friends, they said nothing. But when some Dodgers from Dixie actively protested against Robinson, Durocher deflated their mutiny: "I don't care if the guy is yellow or black, or if he has stripes like a f—— zebra. I'm the manager of this team, and I say he plays. What's more, I say he can make us all rich. And if any of you can't use the money, I'll see that you are all traded."

What lessons can we learn from this tangled tale? A few simple ones seem to leap out. The more greed and lust for victory, the less discrimination. The more competition between teams and businesses, the more cooperation between the races. In contrast, the more collusion, centralization, community standards, and concern for the feelings of people you know, the more bias. If we now look at the remarkable impact that the first few dozen blacks had on Major League baseball, we can confirm the Chicago School's theory that competition tends to make irrational discrimination self-defeatingly expensive.

For instance, the 1946 World Series looked as if it would be only the first of many between the Boston Red Sox and the St. Louis Cardinals. Led by Ted Williams, the greatest hitter since Babe Ruth, the 1946 Red Sox had won an exceptional 104 games, losing only 50. The Cardinals, meanwhile, had averaged 104 wins per season during the four seasons that the young Stan Musial had anchored their lineup. Both leftfielders would long remain superlative hitters. As late as 1957 Musial led the National League (NL) with a batting average of .351, while Williams topped even that with .388, the highest average between the Roosevelt and Carter Administrations. Yet neither man ever returned to the World Series. Why not?

Largely because of St. Louis's and Boston's boneheaded bigotry. With Robinson apprenticing in the minors throughout the 1946 season, the Brooklyn Dodgers finished two games behind the Cards. In 1947, Rookie of the Year Robinson made the difference, as the Dodgers edged the Cards for the pennant. Jackie instantly became the league's biggest draw, with the Dodgers setting NL records for both home and away attendance. During each pre-season alone, Robinson earned his annual salary from the huge Southern crowds, black and white, that turned out to cheer and boo him at Dodger exhibitions. (By barnstorming through Dixie, Rickey was exposing Robinson to a real threat of assassination, as well as the insults of Jim Crow, but, hey, the money was too good to pass up.)

Rickey followed up his masterstroke by signing more Negro Leagues stars like Roy Campanella and Don Newcombe. During Robinson's ten-year tenure, Brooklyn's dividends for desegregating first were six NL titles, fueled by black Dodgers' winning five Most Valuable Player awards and four Rookie of the Year awards.

In contrast, St. Louis frittered away the heart of Musial's stupendous career by not obtaining a black regular until Curt Flood in 1958. The Cards paid a brutal price for discriminating. During the first four years they had Stan the Man (up through 1946), the Cards won almost 18 more games per year than the Dodgers. But during the Robinson era, the Cards fell to nearly 13 victories per year fewer than the Dodgers, a monumental swing of over 30 wins per 154-game season. The Cardinals stubbornly ignored blacks until Augie Busch bought the team in 1954. Fearing a black boycott of Budweiser, he immediately ordered his scouts to find black players, but by then the easy pickings were gone. Although too late for Musial, Busch's integration move finally paid off in the 1960s, as blacks like Flood, Lou Brock, and Bob Gibson became the core of great Cardinal teams.

As could be expected, the National League, which had been sorely trailing the American League (AL) in superstars since the days of Ty Cobb, more aggressively pursued black talent. By the mid Fifties all NL teams except the Cardinals and the hapless Phillies featured at least one black headed for the Hall of Fame. Between 1949 and 1962, blacks won 11 of the 14 NL MVP awards, while no black was the AL MVP until Yankee catcher Elston Howard in 1963. And the AL lacked an African-American superstar until Frank Robinson arrived via a 1966 trade and promptly showed the league what it had been missing by capturing the rare Triple Crown for batting.

Integration electrified the NL's style of play, as blacks showed that sluggers didn't have to be sloggers—e.g., Willie Mays led the league four times in home runs and four times in stolen bases. The balance of power shifted away from the slow, complacent American League. The AL had won 12 of the 16

All Star games played in the Thirties and Forties, but could capture only 5 of the 24 held in the Fifties and Sixties.

Where competition is not particularly intense, however, discrimination can linger. In the AL, the New York Yankees ruled, winning 29 of 44 pennants from 1921 to 1964. Not surprisingly, the Yankees saw little need to rush into integrating, especially after they signed Mickey Mantle, a white man even faster and stronger than the NL's black stars. With most of the AL not expecting to dethrone the Yankees (indeed, some forlorn AL franchises subsisted by routinely selling their top prospects to the Yankees), most other AL teams also lagged at integrating.

The main exception was the Cleveland Indians. Under master promoter Bill Veeck, in 1948 the Tribe suddenly overtook the Red Sox as the Yankees' chief challenger. The Indians edged out the Red Sox for the pennant that year by a single game, a difference more than accounted for by their two blacks, outfielder Larry Doby and a 42-year-old rookie phenom named Paige. As the AL's most integrated team, from 1948 to 1956 the Tribe would average 94 wins, peaking with a 111-43 record in 1954, the best anywhere since 1906. In comparison, under the ownership of beloved philanthropist Tom Yawkey, the Red Sox would fade into mediocrity, wasting Williams's bat as they refused to play a black man until 1959. Still, to be fair, the Red Sox did take only seven more years to hire a black than the Braves—the Osaka Braves, that is.

While the complete integration of baseball through competition took longer than we would have liked, it's worth contrasting baseball's record to the civil-rights milestones dependent upon the Federal Government. For example, the vaunted 1954 Brown decision remained mostly a symbol until the Nixon Administration began broadly enforcing it 15 years later. Likewise, although the decline in job discrimination in the South in the 1960s is often attributed to the 1964 Civil Rights Act, little of the now vast array of bureaucratic and legal machinery for enforcing that law existed before the end of that decade. Far more beneficial during the 1960s than pestering private companies was federal intervention freeing up the Southern economy by cracking down on state-authorized discrimination, whether imposed by legislatures or by mobs winked at by local authorities. These gains became permanent under the most wholly successful civil-rights law, the 1965 Voting Rights Act. By finally establishing a competitive market for political power, this law rapidly made hatemongering unprofitable for Southern office-seekers.

Today, conservatives tend to lionize the 1964 Civil Rights Act for embodying color-blindness. In denouncing quotas while supporting anti-discrimination laws, however, the Right shows a surprising faith in the ability of government bureaucrats and judges to decide case by case which private hiring decisions were tainted by bias. In reality, close study of possible instances of discrimination shows why the sainted 1964 act made quotas inevitable. Frequently, no outsider, and sometimes not even those involved, can know which of the many possible reasons for an employment decision was actually conclusive. For example, the Yankees first employed black minor-leaguers in 1949 but didn't promote any to the big club until 1955. Was this long delay caused by discrimination? If you assume that any team in the early 1950s that didn't have a few blacks must have been discriminating, it appears obvious that the Yankees were guilty. But if you reject this kind of statistical or quota-based reasoning, how do you find the smoking gun?

Did the Yankees trade away their top prospect, the black Puerto Rican Vic Power, for his uppitiness (when a Southern waitress once told him, "I'm sorry, but we don't serve Negroes here," he blithely replied, "That's OK, I don't eat them")? Or were they sincere in claiming they'd lost faith in his potential? Or both? Presumably bias played a role, since Power turned out to be a good (though not great) Major Leaguer. But who can say for sure? Ballclubs constantly make honest mistakes about minor-leaguers (in the same period, the integrated Dodgers discarded another young black Puerto Rican, the great Roberto Clemente). Did the Yankees then force their other most promising black minor-leaguer, outfielder Elston Howard, to convert to catcher in order to delay his rise to the big leagues? Possibly, but this time the Yankees proved right, as Howard became an MVP behind the plate.

This ambiguity inherent in so many hiring decisions explains why aggressive anti-discrimination laws always end up impelling employers toward quotas. Unfortunately, racial quotas have numerous side effects. While the overall impact of reverse discrimination remains harshly controversial, we can safely say that year by year quotas' benefits to blacks diminish while quotas' costs to blacks rise. Since strong anti-bias laws make quotas inevitable and quotas are inexorably becoming a net harm to blacks, then logic would imply that we must eventually repeal enforcement of the Civil Rights Act's prohibitions against discrimination by competitive employers.

How, then would we fight racism in hiring? I suggest: in roughly the same way as we now deter its cousin, nepotism. In noncompetitive organizations like government agencies, laws often ban nepotistic hiring. On the other hand, the government allows the market to police competitive firms. If a CEO promotes Junior and he turns out to be inept, well, the firm pays the price in lost profits.

Our country is probably several years away from even beginning to grasp this logic, but in the long run it may prove compelling. Conservatives, however, can't seize the rational high ground until they stop leaping to defend institutions they, especially, should be wary of—e.g., unions, regulated monopolies, and government agencies—against the threat of racial quotas. True, competition does restrain irrational discrimination. But where competition is lacking—such as in government monopolies like police and fire departments, or in labor unions, which exist to negate competition—then quotas can sometimes be necessary to put a price on discrimination.

Track and Battlefield

by Steve Sailer and Dr. Stephen Seiler
National Review
December 31, 1997

EVERYBODY knows that the "gender gap" in physical performance between male and female athletes is rapidly narrowing. Moreover, in an opinion poll just before the 1996 Olympics, 66% claimed "the day is coming when top female athletes will beat top males at the highest competitive levels." The most publicized scientific study supporting this belief appeared in *Nature* in 1992: "Will Women Soon Outrun Men?" Physiologists Susan Ward and Brian Whipp pointed out that since the Twenties, women's world records in running had been falling faster than men's. Assuming these trends continued, men's and women's marathon records would equalize by 1998, and during the early 21st Century for the shorter races.

This is not sports trivia. Whether the gender gap in athletic performance stems from biological differences between men and women, or is simply a social construct imposed by the Male Power Structure, is highly relevant both to fundamental debates about the malleability of human nature, as well as to current political controversies such as the role of women in the military.

When everybody is so sure of something, it's time to update the numbers. So, I began an in-depth study with my research partner, Dr. Stephen Seiler, an American sports physiologist teaching at Agder College in Norway. (Yes, we do have almost identical names, but don't blame him for all the opinions in this article: of the two of us, I am the evil twin).

The conclusion: Although the 1998 outdoor running season isn't even here yet, we can already discard Ward and Whipp's forecast: women will not catch up to men in the marathon this year. The gender gap between the best marathon times remains the equivalent of the woman record holder losing by over 2.6 miles. In fact, we can now be certain that in fair competition the fastest women will never equal the fastest men at any standard length race. Why? Contrary to all expectations, the overall gender gap has been widening throughout the Nineties. While men's times have continued to get faster, world class women are now running noticeably slower than in the Eighties. How come? It's a fascinating tale of sex discrimination, ethnic superiority, hormones, and the fall of the Berlin Wall that reconfirms the unpopular fact that biological differences between the sexes and the races will continue to play a large, perhaps even a growing, role in human affairs.

First, though, why is running the best sport for carefully measuring changes in the gender gap? Obviously, there are different size gender gaps in different sports (and even within a sport: in basketball, for example, the gap in slam dunking is enormously greater than in free throw shooting). Indeed, women do sometimes "beat top males at the highest competitive levels" in equestrian, yachting, drag racing and a few other riding sports, as well as in some stationary events like shooting. One self-propelled sport where women arguably outperform men is ocean swimming, in which they've achieved amazing firsts like paddling from Alaska to Siberia. (This is a rare sport where a higher body fat percentage is a boon.) Two Olympic sports are open only to females: synchronized swimming and rhythmic gymnastics. In America, however, both the male and the feminist sports establishments roundly ridicule these events (undeservedly in the case of rhythmic gymnastics, an enchanting exercise). Similarly, other demanding but female-dominated physical activities like dancing, aerobics, and cheerleading are seldom considered sports at all by Americans.

Thus, the current climate of opinion demands that we analyze a "major" (i.e., traditionally male) sport. In these games, however, women's sports advocates insist on "separate but equal" competition. Separateness, however, badly hinders the equality of measurements. Since they play in what might as well be alternative universes, it's difficult to confidently quantify, for example, precisely how much better the NBA's Michael Jordan is than the WNBA's Sheryl Swoopes.

Fortunately for our analytical purposes, men and women currently compete under identical conditions in ten Olympic running events, making their times directly comparable. In general, track is ideal for statistical study because it's such a simple sport: all that matters are the times. Another advantage to focusing on running is that it's probably the most universal sport. Track medalists in the 1996 Olympics included an Australian aborigine as well as runners from Burundi, Trinidad & Tobago, South Korea, Mozambique, Norway, and Namibia. Running is so fundamental to life and so cheap that most children on Earth compete at it enough to reveal whether they possess any talent for it.

So, Ward & Whipp were certainly correct to concentrate upon running. As they noted, the gender gap did narrow sharply up through the Eighties. Let's focus upon those ten directly comparable races. Way back in 1970, women's world record times averaged 21.3% higher (worse) than men's. But during the Seventies women broke or equaled world records 79 times, compared to only 18 times by men, lowering the average gender gap in world records to 13.3%. In the Eighties, women set 47 records compared to only 23 by men, and the gender gap shrank to just 10.2%. Further narrowing seemed inevitable in the Nineties.

Yet, male runners are now pulling away from female runners. Women's performances have collapsed, with only five record-setting efforts so far in this decade, compared to 30 by men. (The growth of the gender gap has even been accelerating. Men broke or tied records seven times in 1997, the most in any year since 1968.) The average gender gap for WR's has increased from 10.2% to 11.0%. And since four of the five women's "records" set in the Nineties occurred at extremely questionable Chinese meets (as we shall see later), it's probably more accurate to say that for relatively legitimate records in the Nineties, men are ahead of women 30 to 1, and the average world record gender gap has grown from 10.2% to 11.5%.

Despite all the hype about 1996 being the "Women's Olympics," in the Atlanta Games' central events—the footraces—female medalists performed worse relative to male medalists than in any Olympics since 1972. In the 1988 Games the gender gap for medalists was 10.9%, but it grew to 12.2% in 1996. Even stranger is the trend in absolute times. Track fans expect slow but steady progress; thus, nobody is surprised that male medalists became 0.5% faster from the 1988 to the 1996 Olympics. Remarkably, though, women medalists became 0.6% slower over the same period.

Why is the gender gap growing?

1. *In the Longer Races*

From 800m to the marathon, but especially in the 5,000m and 10,000m races, the main reason women are falling further behind men is discrimination, society forcing women to stay home and have six babies. Of course, I'm not talking about the industrialized world, but about a few polygamous, high-birth rate African nations. All 17 male distance record-settings in the Nineties belong to Kenyans (9), Ethiopians (5), Algerians (2), or Moroccans (1). A culture can encourage all women to pursue glory in athletics or to have a half-dozen kids, but not both. Thus, Kenya's high birth rate (not long ago it was more than five times West Germany's) has contributed to an ever-swelling torrent of brilliant male runners, but has kept any Kenyan woman from winning Olympic gold.

These facts, though, raise a disturbing question: Why is women's distance running so debilitated by sexism in these obscure African countries? Because, as bankrobber Willie Sutton might say, that's where the talent is. You can't understand women's running without comparing it to men's running, and that has become incomprehensible unless you grasp how, as equality of opportunity has improved in men's track, ethnic inequality of result has skyrocketed. The African tidal wave culminated on August 13, 1997 when Wilson Kipketer, a Kenyan running for Denmark, broke the great Sebastian Coe's 800m mark, erasing the last major record held by any man not of African descent.

African superiority is now so manifest that even Burundi, a small East African hell-hole, drubbed the U.S. in the men's distance races at our own Atlanta Games.

Yet, there are striking systematic differences between even African ethnic groups. This can best be seen by graphing each population's bell curve for running. The Olympic events from 100 meters to the marathon run along the horizontal axis, and the percentage of the 100 best times in history go along the vertical axis. For Kenyan men, for example, a lovely bell curve appears showing which distances they are best suited for. These East Africans are outclassed in the 100m and 200m, but become competitive in the 400m, then are outstanding from 800m to 10,000m, before tailing off slightly in the marathon (42,000m). Not surprisingly, the Kenyan's peak is in the middle of their range—the 3,000m steeplechase—where Kenyans own the 53 fastest times ever.

Male Running Talent Follows Ethnic Bell Curves

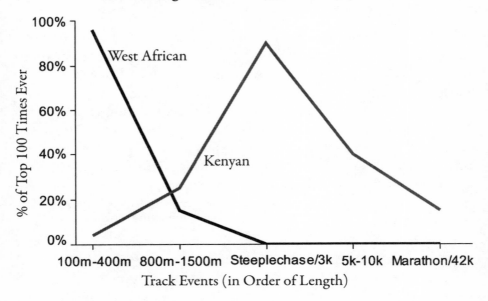

In contrast, for the black men of the West African Diaspora (e.g., U.S., Nigeria, Cuba, Brazil, Canada, Britain, and France), only the right half of their bell curve is visible. They absolutely monopolize the 100m. Men of West African descent have broken the 10 second barrier 134 times; nobody else has ever done it. They remain almost as overwhelming in the 200m and 400m, then drop off to being merely quite competitive in the 800m. They are last sighted in the 1500m, and then are absolutely not a factor in the long distance events.

While there are the usual nature vs. nurture arguments over why African runners win so much, there is no possibility that culture alone can account for how much West African and East African runners differ in power vs. endurance. Track is ultracompetitive: Coaches test all their runners at different distances until they find their best lengths. Even in the unlikely event that Kenya's coaches were too self-defeating to exploit their 100m talent, and Jamaica's leadership was ignoring their 10,000m prodigies, American and European coaches and agents would swoop in and poach them. No, what's infinitely more plausible is that both West Africans and East Africans are performing relatively close to their highly distinct biological limits.

None of this conforms to American obsessions about race. First, we dread empirical studies of human biodiversity, worrying that they will uncover the intolerable reality of racial supremacy. Is this fear realistic? Consider merely running: are West Africans generally better runners than whites? In sprints, absolutely. In distance races, absolutely not. Overall racial supremacy is nonsense; specific ethnic superiorities are a manifold reality.

Second, our crude racial categories blur over many fascinating genetic differences between, for example, groups as similar in color as West and East Africans. And even within the highlands of East Africa there are different track bell curves: Ethiopians, while almost as strong as Kenyans at 5,000m and longer, are not a factor below 3,000m. And the African dominance is not just a black thing. Moroccans and Algerians tend to be more white than black, yet they possess a bell curve similar to, if slightly less impressive than, Kenyans. Further research will uncover many more fascinating patterns: for example, Europeans appear to be consistently mediocre, achieving world class performances primarily at distances like 800m and the marathon that fall outside of the prime ranges for West Africans and Kenyans.

These ethnic patterns among male runners are crucial to understanding the causes of the growth in the gender gap, because it appears that women runners possess the same natural strengths and weaknesses as their menfolk. For example, the bell curves for men and women runners of West African descent are both equally sprint-focused. Therefore, if a nation's women perform very differently than its men, something is peculiar. With high-birthrate African countries like Kenya and Morocco, it's clear the social systems restrain marriage-aged women from competing. This offers hope that the distance gender gap will someday stop widening. Indeed, since the Kenyan birthrate began dropping a few years back, we have begun to see a few outstanding Kenyan women.

2. *In the Shorter Races*

The gender gap is widening not just because men (especially African distance runners) are running faster today, but also because women (especially East European sprinters) are now running slower.

From 1970-1989, white women from communist countries accounted for 71 of the 84 records set at 100m-1500m. In contrast, white men from communist countries accounted for exactly zero of the 23 male records. Those memorable East German frauleins alone set records 49 times in just the sprints and relays (100m-400m). This was especially bizarre because men of West African descent have utterly dominated white men in sprinting. Another oddity of that era is that communist women set only seven (and East Germans none) of the 48 female records in the 5k, 10k, and the marathon.

The crash of women's running was brought about by two seemingly irrelevant events in the late Eighties: Ben Johnson got caught, and the Berlin Wall fell. At the 1988 Olympics, in the most anticipated 100m race of all time, Johnson, the surly Jamaican-Canadian sprinter who could benchpress 396 pounds, demolished Carl Lewis with a jaw-dropping world record of 9.79 seconds. Two days later Johnson was stripped of his medal and record because his urine contained steroids—muscle-building artificial male hormones. Embarrassed that it had let a man called "Benoid" by other runners (because his massively muscled body was so flooded with steroids that his eyeballs had turned yellow) become the biggest star in the sport, track officialdom finally got fairly serious about testing for steroids in 1989.

Then the Berlin Wall fell, and we learned exactly how East German coaches enabled white women to outsprint black women: by chemically masculinizing them. It turns out that masculinity—in its lowest common denominator definition of muscularity and aggressiveness—is not a social construct at all: East German biochemists simply mass-produced masculinity. Obviously, the communists weren't the only dopers, but they were the best organized. *Newsweek* reported, "Under East Germany's notorious State Plan 14.25, more than 1,000 scientists, trainers and physicians spent much of the 1980's developing better ways to drug the nation's athletes." East German coaches are now finally going on trial for forcing enormous doses of steroids on uninformed teenagers. The Soviet Union, although less brilliant in the laboratory, also engaged in cheating on an impressively industrial scale.

Even today, this pattern of women's records coming mostly from communist countries continues: four of this decade's five female marks were set by teenagers at the Chinese National Games, where tough drug testing is politically impossible. (The 1997 Games in Shanghai were such a bacchanal of doping that all 24 women's weightlifting records were broken, but weightlifting's governing officials had the guts to refuse to ratify any of these absurd marks.) In contrast to the astounding accomplishments by China's fuel-injected women, Chinese men's performances remain mediocre.

Exemplifying the differences in drug testing between the Eighties and Nineties are the contrasting fates of two Eastern European women: Jarmila Kratochvílová and Katrin Krabbe. The extremely muscular Miss Kraticholivova, described by *Track & Field News* as a "Mack truck," won the 400m and the 800m at the 1983 World Championships, and her 800m record still stands. Runner Rosalyn Bryant commented, "I'm still not envious of the 'Wonder Woman' of Czechoslovakia. I could have chosen the same way, but I didn't want to change my body, given to me by God, into a new shape.... Five years ago she was a normal woman. Now she is all muscles and runs World Records." Her rival Gaby Bussmann called her, flatly, "a man." Miss K. replied, "One day, if [Ms. Bussman] produces performances like mine, she will have to have sacrificed some of her good looks. In athletics, one has to decide how much to sacrifice. The women of the West don't work as hard as we do." Miss K. was never caught by the drug tests of her day.

In contrast, Katrin Krabbe, a product of the old East German training system, won the 100m and 200m at the 1991 World Championships to rave reviews. *Track & Field News* called her "beautiful" and "sleek," and pointedly contrasted her to the "masculine" Miss Kraticholivova. Even before her victories, young Ms. Krabbe had signed a million dollars in modeling and product endorsement contracts. Although she couldn't have been very heavily doped by Eighties' standards, in 1992 she was disqualified because of tampering with her urine sample. Thus, East German women won eight medals at the 1988 Olympics, but during the 1992 and 1996 Games combined, reunited Germany's women could garner only a single bronze.

The communists were almost completely stumped at producing male champions because the benefits of a given amount of steroids are much greater for women than men. Since men average 10 times more natural testosterone than women, they need dangerously large, Ben Johnson-sized doses to make huge improvements, while women can bulk-up significantly on smaller, less-easily detected amounts. The primitive testing at the 1988 Olympics did succeed in catching Benoid; yet the female star of those Games, America's Florence Griffith-Joyner, passed every urinalysis she ever faced. The naturally lissome Flo-Jo may have been the world's fastest clean 200 meter woman from 1984-1987, but she kept finishing second in big races to suspiciously brawny women.

She then asked Ben Johnson for training advice, and emerged from a winter in the weight room looking like a Saturday morning cartoon superheroine. She made a magnificent joke out of women's track in 1988, setting records in the 100m and 200m that few had expected to see before the middle of the 21st Century. Then, she retired before random drug testing began in 1989, having passed every drug test she ever took.

Why didn't the East German labs synthesize successful women distance runners? Although artificial male hormones are fairly useful to distance runners (in part because they increase the will to win), sprinters get the biggest bang for their steroid buck. The shorter the race, the more it demands anaerobic power (which steroids boost), while the longer the race, the more it tests aerobic and heat dispersal capacities.

Doping has not disappeared from track, but runners have responded to better testing by using fewer steroids, and by trying less potent but harder to detect drugs like Human Growth Hormone. These new drugs affect both sexes much more equally than Old King Steroid. The decline in steroid use has allowed the natural order to reassert itself: before steroids overwhelmed women's track in the Seventies, black women like Wilma Rudolph and Wyomia Tyus dominated sprinting. Today, led by young Marian Jones, who is potentially the Carl Lewis of women's track, black women rule once more. However, white women are still much more heavily represented among the top sprinters than are white men.

This could mean that the "ethnic gap" in natural talent between West Africans and Europeans is smaller among women than men. Or, more likely, doping continues to enhance women's times more than men's. Thus, if testing can continue to improve faster than doping, the gender gap would tend to grow even wider.

In conclusion, studying sports' gender gaps offers new perspectives on a host of contemporary issues seemingly far removed from athletics, such as women in the military. Ironically, feminists in sports have successfully campaigned for the funding of thousands of sexually segregated, female-only teams, while feminists in the media and Congress have compelled the Armed Forces (outside of the defiant Marines) to sexually integrate basic training and many operating units, even including some combat teams.

Who's right? Female college coaches have some powerful reasons for believing that coed competition would badly damage their mission of turning girls into strong, take-charge women. For example, they fear that female athletes would inevitably be sexually harassed.

Even more distracting to their mission than the unwanted sexual advances from male teammates, however, would be the wanted ones. This opinion is based on more than just lesbian jealousy: research on single sex vs. coed schools shows that teenage girls are more likely to develop into leaders in all-female groups, whereas in coed settings young females tend to compete with each other in coyly deferring to good-looking guys. Any hard-headed female basketball coach could tell you that merging her team with the school's men's team would simply turn two dedicated squads now focused on beating their respective opponents into one all-consuming soap opera of lust, betrayal, jealousy, and revenge. (Does this remind you of the current state of any superpower's military?) Yet, feminists utterly forget to apply their own hard-earned wisdom to the armed forces: on the whole, deploying young women in cramped quarters alongside young fighting men does not make the women into better warriors, it make them into moms. For example, the *Washington Times* reports that for every year a coed warship is at sea, the Navy has to airlift out 16% of the female sailors as their pregnancies become advanced.

Reorganizing the military along the lines of the sexually segregated teams characteristic of contemporary college sports will do much both to more fully use the potential of women in uniform and to quell the endless sexual brouhahas currently bedeviling our coed military. Yet, the crucial issue remains: Should women fight? The main justification feminists give for a coed-izing the military is that lack of combat experience unfairly hampers female officers' chances for promotion.

We can again turn for guidance to female coaches. The main reason they favor sexual apartheid on the playing fields is that in open competition males would slaughter females. It seems reasonable to conclude the same would happen on the battlefields. This may sound alarmist. After all, running's gender gap is a rather marginal-sounding 1/8th; surely, many women are faster than the average man, and, by the same logic, many would make better soldiers.

First, though, as economists have long pointed out, competition occurs at the margins: runners don't race against the average Joe, but against other runners. And soldiers fight other soldiers. Second, while the moderate width of track's gender gap is representative of many simple sports that test primarily a single physical skill (the main exceptions are tests of upper body strength like shotputting, where the top men are as much as twice as strong as the top women), in free-flowing multidimensional sports like basketball where many skills must be combined, overall gender gaps tend to be so imposing that after puberty females almost never compete with males. Consider what traits help just in enabling you to dunk a basketball: height, vertical leaping ability, footspeed (to generate horizontal momentum that can be diverted into vertical liftoff), and hand size and hand strength (to dunk one-handed).

THE LEVEL PLAYING FIELD

Not one of these five individual gender gaps is enormous, but they combine to create a huge difference in results: almost everybody in the NBA can dunk compared to almost nobody in the WNBA. Basketball, however, is far more than slam and jam. Throw in the need for massiveness and upper body strength in rebounding and defense, wrist strength in jumpshooting, etc., and multiply all these male advantages together, and the resulting gender gap in basketball ability is so vast that despite the WNBA's state of the art marketing, it's actual product resembles an all white high school boys' game from a few decades ago.

Although the unique ease of our Gulf War victory encouraged the fantasy that technology has made fighting almost effortless, the chaos of combat will continue to demand a wide diversity of both physical aptitudes (like being able to hump a load of depleted-uranium ammunition) and mental attitudes (like the urge to kill) that interact to create a huge gender gap in fighting ability.

While in theory it might be nice if we could accommodate ambitious female officers' need for combat experience by negotiating during wars with our enemies to set up separate all-female battles between our Amazon units and their Amazon units, this is where the analogy with sports finally breaks down: opponents in war don't have to play by the rules...causing our women to be defeated, captured, raped, and killed. Still, if (as, in effect, so many feminists insist) female officers' right to equal promotion opportunities requires that they be furnished with female cannon fodder, there is one proven formula for narrowing the gender gap to give our enlisted women more of a fighting chance. Feminist logic implies that just as our military once imported ex-Nazi German rocket scientists, it should now import ex-Communist German steroid pushers.

From Bauhaus to Golf Course

The American Conservative
April 11, 2005

G OLF course architecture is one of the world's most expansive but least recognized art forms. Yet this curiously obscure profession can help shed light on mainstream art, sociology, and even human nature itself, since the golf designer, more than any other artist, tries to reproduce the primeval human vision of an earthly paradise.

Yet even this most unfashionable of arts was swept in the middle of the last century by the same Bauhaus-derived tastes that made post-WWII modernist buildings so tedious. Only recently has golf course architecture begun to revive the styles and values of its golden age in the 1920s.

Hidden in plain sight, golf courses are among the few works of art readily visible from airliners. (A golf architecture aficionado can often identify a course's designer from 35,000 feet.) Assuming an average of a quarter square mile apiece, America's 15,000 golf courses cover almost as much land as Delaware and Rhode Island combined.

Golf architecture philosophy isn't terribly elaborate compared to the thickets of theory that entangle most museum arts, but one thing all golf designers assert is that their courses look "natural." Growing up in arid Southern California, however, where the indigenous landscape is impenetrable hillsides of gray-brown sagebrush, I never quite understood what was so natural about fairways of verdant, closely-mown grass, but I loved them all the same.

Research since the early 1980s shows that humans tend to have two favorite landscapes. One is wherever they lived during their adolescence, but the nearly universal favorite among children before they imprint upon their local look is grassy parkland, and that fondness survives into adulthood.

Richard Conniff wrote in *Discover*: "In separate surveys, Ulrich, Orians, and others have found that people respond strongly to landscapes with open, grassy vegetation, scattered stands of branchy trees, water, changes in elevation, winding trails, and brightly lit clearings..." In one amusing study, 1001 people from 15 different countries were surveyed about what they'd like to see in a painting. Then the sponsors of the research, conceptual art pranksters Komar and Melamid, painted each country's "Most Wanted Painting."[1] Even though the researchers hadn't mentioned what type of picture it should be, the consensus in 13 of the 15 cultures favored landscapes and 11 of the 15 looked surprisingly like golf courses. All over the world, people want to see grassland, a lake, and some trees, but not a solid forest. And they always want to see it slightly from above. The project was intended to satirize popular taste, but it ended up revealing much about about human desires. For example, Komar and Melamid's rendition of America's Most Wanted Painting is quite similar to the downhill par 3 sixth hole at the Coeur d'Alene golf course in Idaho.

The current theory for why golf courses are so attractive to millions (mostly men), perhaps first put forward in John Strawn's book *Driving the Green: The Making of a Golf Course*, is that they look like happy hunting grounds—a Disney-version of the primordial East African grasslands. Harvard biologist Edward O. Wilson, author of the landmark 1975 book *Sociobiology*, once told me, "I believe that the reason that people find well-landscaped golf courses 'beautiful' is that they look like savannas, down to the scattered trees, copses, and lakes, and most especially if they have vistas of the sea."

Tasty hoofed animals would graze on the savanna's grass, while the nearby woods could provide shade and cover for hunters. Our ancestors would study the direction of the wind and the slopes of the land in order to approach their prey from the best angles. Any resemblance to a rolling golf fairway running between trees is not coincidental.

In 1975, geographer Jay Appleton advanced the similar theory that what people like is a combination of a sense of "refuge," such as the ability to hide in the woods, and of "prospect" across open country.[2] Both theories make the prediction that human beings, especially males, will spend enormous amounts of money to fashion golf courses.

Generally, men (the hunters) tend to prefer sweeping vistas, while women (the gatherers) prefer enclosed verdant refuges. Perhaps it's no accident that a longtime favorite book among little girls is called *The Secret Garden*. Similarly, women make up a sizable majority of gardeners while men often obsess over lawn care.[3]

To create these pleasure grounds, top golf architects typically spend over $10 million per course, and because designers oversee the creation of multiple layouts simultaneously, a "signature" architect like Tom Fazio will end his career with his name on a few billion dollars worth of golf courses.

Famous works of "environmental art," such as Robert Smithson's monumental earthwork "Spiral Jetty" in the Great Salt Lake, are dwarfed by golf courses in extent and thought required.

Among fine artists, only Christo works on a comparable scale, and his projects, such as his recent "Gates" in Central Park, are more repetitious. Nonetheless, Christo's "Gates," which re-emphasized the original landscape architect Frederick Law Olmstead's lovely serpentine pathways, and his 1976 "Running Fence" snaking through the undulating grasslands of Marin County, offer some of the same visual pleasures of following alluring trails as golf architects provide.

The great majority of golfers long thought of courses mostly in terms of length or difficulty rather than of artistry. Even though the taste of golfers has improved in recent decades, many still judge a course more by the manicuring of its grass than by its design. Moreover, in the U.S., relatively few women are interested in golf before menopause, although the game is fairly fashionable among young women in East Asia and Scandinavia.

In recent decades, however, the golf world has come down with a severe case of connoisseurship, publishing hundreds of coffee-table books and calendars, making cult figures of long-forgotten early 20th Century architects like A.W. Tillinghast and Charles Blair Macdonald and brand names out of living designers like Pete Dye and Tom Doak.

Many today truly love good golf design, but until very recently, too few hated poor design enough to name names. Golfers tended to feel that any golf course is nice, so it would be churlish to gripe. It was not until the early Nineties that writing about architecture began to mature when Doak, a young architect, circulated a photocopied samizdat manuscript called the *Confidential Guide to Golf Courses* that lambasted sacred cows.

Today, the gathering ground for architecture aficionados is the web discussion board *www.GolfClubAtlas.com*, where it's common to find, say, 70 messages denouncing the vulgarity of Fazio's redesign of the 7th fairway's bunker on George C. Thomas's classic 1927 Riviera course, where Los Angeles' Nissan Open is played.

This frenzy of art worship among a minority of golfers has gone almost wholly unrecognized in the establishment art world, which otherwise has been so quick to discern artistry in such unlikely forms as graffiti and toilet brushes. Top museums do not stage retrospectives on the Trent Jones family or stock golf course photo books in their gift shops.

The art community would benefit from exposure to golf architecture simply because the best courses, such as Alister MacKenzie's Cypress Point on the Monterey Peninsula, are things of astonishing beauty, comparable in craftsmanship, complexity, and deceptiveness to the finest efforts of 18th-century English landscape artists such as Capability Brown, creator of the majestic grounds for Blenheim Palace.

The first problem limiting the acceptance of golf design as art is that to nongolfers a course can seem as meaningless as a Concerto for Dog Whistle. That a golf course allows people to interact with interesting landscapes without killing wild animals makes sense in the abstract, but not until you've driven a ball over a gaping canyon and onto the smooth safety of the green will the golf course obsession make much sense.

The distinction Edmund Burke made in 1757 between the "sublime" and the "beautiful" applies to golf courses.[4] The beautiful is some pleasing place conducive to human habitat—meadows, valleys, slow moving streams, grassland intermingled with copses of trees, the whole English country estate shtick. The sublime is nature so magnificent that it induces the feeling of terror because it could kill you, such as by you falling off a mountain or into a gorge.

Beautiful landscapes are most suited for building golf courses, since a golf course needs about 100 acres of land level enough for a golf ball to come to rest upon. But golfers get a thrill out of the mock sublime, where you are in danger of losing not your life, but your mis-hit golf ball into a water hazard or ravine. One reason that Pebble Beach on the Monterey Peninsula is so legendary is because it combines sublime sea cliffs with beautiful (and thus functional for golf) rolling plains (My father, though, almost walked off the cliff in the middle of the eighth fairway at Pebble Beach and into the wave-carved chasm, which probably would have satisfied Burke's theoretical rigor.)

Sociology also separates the worlds of art and golf. Conventional artists are urban, golf architects suburban. The art community delights in the venerable game of Shock the Bourgeoisie, while golf courses are too bourgeois to be hip, too elegant to be camp.

Many of the creators, critics, and collectors who have so enriched the arts are male homosexuals, while golf, for whatever reason, has almost no appeal to gay male sensibilities. (On the other hand, the Ladies Professional Golf Association's Nabisco Championship in Palm Springs has become one of the largest annual lesbian get-togethers in the United States, but, as Camille Paglia has noted, lesbians tend not to be as interested in the visual arts as gay men are, and, indeed, are often resentful of the prestige of Dead White European Male artists.)[5]

At a time when art institutions are fixated on celebrating demographic diversity, the golf architecture business remains white (even the golf-mad Japanese frequently import English-speaking designers), male (the woman with the largest influence on architecture has been Pete Dye's wife Alice), and intensely nepotistic (most prominent names in the business today are either champion golfers, such as Jack Nicklaus, Arnold Palmer, and Ben Crenshaw, or the male kin of architects, such as the two sons of Robert Trent Jones, the dominant architect of the postwar modernist era, Rees and RTJ II.). Further, many of the classic courses are owned by exclusive clubs accused of racism, sexism, or anti-Semitism.

Golf architecture might have been the great WASP art form of the 20th century—indeed, it's arguable that the decline of the WASP ascendancy stemmed in part from too much time spent on the golf course. The overwhelming majority of prominent architects have been of British, especially Scottish, descent. Fazio is one of the very few golf architects whose name ends in a vowel. Amusingly, Fazio's detractors often discuss his lovely but not all that strategically interesting courses using much the same terminology as a 19th Century Scotsman might have employed to dismiss an Italian artist: flashy but not fundamentally sound.

Two major novelists, P.G. Wodehouse and John Updike, have written about golf at length, and the golf sportswriter Bernard Darwin was a prose stylist of comparable distinction. But golf doesn't attract as many literary intellectuals as baseball does. Golfers tend to overlap with football fans—prototypically, businessmen with a talent for getting things done but not terribly reflective.

Throughout the history of golf architecture, the genius of a special piece of land has shaped the architect as much as any genius of an architect has shaped the land.

White Men Can't Reach

Taki's
August 28, 2013

STRUCTURED around the dismantling of the profitable notion pushed by self-help seers such as Malcolm Gladwell that 10,000 hours of monomaniacal practice is the secret of success, David Epstein's *The Sports Gene: Inside the Science of Extraordinary Athletic Performance* is one of the best books on human biodiversity in recent years.

Beyond undermining Gladwellian blank-slatism, Epstein extols the sheer pleasure of noticing humanity's variety for its own sake. On his book's penultimate page, he writes:

> Sports will continue to provide a splendid stage for the fantastic menagerie that's human biological diversity. Amid the pageantry of the Opening Ceremony of the 2016 Olympics in Rio de Janeiro, make sure to look for the extremes of the human physique.... It is breathtaking to think that, in the truest genetic sense, we are all a large family, and that the paths of our ancestors have left us wonderfully distinct.

Epstein, a *Sports Illustrated* reporter, builds upon the work of journalists such as Jon Entine (*Taboo*) and me in taking an evenhanded look at the roles of both nature and nurture.

You might think that any sports fan with a television would testify that success in sports depends upon a mélange of genetics, willpower, coaching, character, and opportunity, a mixture that differs from sport to sport and even from competitor to competitor. Much of the fun of watching sports is seeing who will triumph: the gifted goofs or the diligent grinds.

Yet Gladwellian nurturist extremism is the respectable ideology.

Gladwell is annoyed by this new skepticism directed at his massive 2008 bestseller *Outliers*. In response to Epstein's criticism, Gladwell explained at *The New Yorker:*

> In other words, within a group of talented people, what separated the best from the rest was how long and how intently they worked.[6]

No doubt. But what separated the best from the rest within a group of hard-working people was also how talented they were.

Seriously, is it so hard to consider nature and nurture simultaneously? Perhaps F. Scott Fitzgerald was right to observe:

> The test of a first-rate intelligence is the ability to hold two opposed ideas in the mind at the same time, and still retain the ability to function.

Because it's impossible to think comprehensively about sports achievement while flinching from the obvious racial and sexual differences, Epstein bravely goes there. Amusingly, he cites numerous sports scientists who demanded anonymity from him before they'll dare touch the topic.

Epstein, a former college runner, even offers a couple of novel theories of why people of West African descent make the best sprinters. He points out that several of the top Jamaican sprinters, including Usain Bolt (a classic gifted goof), are from Trelawny Parish, historically the home to Jamaica's largest free community of escaped slaves, the Maroons. Perhaps their ancestors were just tougher, and that's why they ran away and stayed free for hundreds of years?

Epstein also speculates that the high fraction of fast-twitch muscle fibers in West Africans might have evolved as a defense against malaria. This is not a *prima facie* ridiculous idea, since *falciparum malaria* is arguably the worst disease on Earth and produces the most Darwinian pressure to evolve defenses. (The sickle cell genetic mutation, which deals out protection from malaria to those who inherit one copy and death to those who inherit two copies, is proof of how far nature will go to slow down malaria.)

My longtime readers will find Epstein's framework and many of his examples (such as his chapters on Kenya's Kalenjin distance runners) familiar. But I learned much from *The Sports Gene*.

For example, the average man has an arm span equal to his height (as in Leonardo da Vinci's famous Vitruvian Man). Yet every NBA player except shooting specialist J. J. Redick has a wingspan greater than his already considerable height. This is especially true of African Americans.

BYU economist Joseph Price provided Epstein with some intriguing data on NBA players:

> The average white American NBA player was 6'7.5" with a wingspan of 6'10." The average African-American NBA player was 6'5.5" with 6'11" wingspan; shorter but longer.

Epstein adds that the average African American in the NBA can jump 29.6" versus 27.3" for whites. Combined with the extra inch of reach, that helps explain the preponderance of blacks in a game where the single most important metric is how high in the air you can get your hand. One scientist told Epstein, "So maybe it's not so much that white men can't jump. White men just can't reach high."

Baseball hitters are generally large men, but in contrast to lanky NBA players, they tend to have physiques less likely to stand out in crowds. What's the ballplayers' physical secret?

Eyesight. The ability to see the rapidly rotating red seams of the baseball as it leaves the pitcher's fingertips is crucial to hitting. The Los Angeles Dodgers employed a team ophthalmologist who had to construct his own ultra-hard eye charts to test hitters' vision because the team was, literally, off the commercial charts. "Half the guys on the Dodgers' major league roster were 20/10 uncorrected."

Finally, if you are a Tiger Father dreaming of your progeny surpassing your sporting achievements, when should you insist your child specialize in one sport?

Not too young. A study of 243 Danish athletes in sports that are measured in "centimeters, grams, or seconds" (such as swimming, weightlifting, or track and field) found that burnout is a sizable threat. The most successful don't start specializing until after age 15. Until their late teens, *contra* the 10,000 Hour Rule, they have fewer cumulative hours of practice than the future also-rans.

In other words, let your kid play normal schoolyard sports such as soccer or basketball for a long time before picking a specialty. The more obscure sports tend to be boring for children, so don't make play an ordeal.

Obviously, this Danish finding, like almost all of Epstein's book, is commonsensical. This lack of counterintuitive Gladwellian advice will no doubt limit the author's success on the public-speaking circuit. But it may prevent a few unhappy childhoods.

One sport that Epstein doesn't tackle in depth is golf. A true believer in Gladwell's 10,000 Hour Rule is a 33-year-old Portland photographer named Dan McLaughlin, who had never played a round of golf in his life before quitting his job in 2010 to put in 10,000 hours of direct golf practice in hopes of becoming a touring pro.[7]

He's now 4,437 hours into his odyssey, most of it spent diligently on the practice tee rather than playing. He first played 18 holes in 2011 and by August 2012, McLaughlin was down to a handicap of only 6.5, which is better than the vast majority of recreational golfers. Unfortunately, diminishing marginal returns have set in, and he's only pared 0.6 strokes off his handicap over the last twelve months.

Waiting until age 30 to start golfing may have thwarted this admirably self-disciplined man's dreams. Numerous outstanding athletes from team sports have retired to the golf course, but only 49er quarterback John Brodie has ever won on the pro senior tour. (Strikingly, washed-up football players have had far more success as actors than as golfers.)

Because it's hard to start golf late, East Asian Tiger Parents have been thrusting their infants onto the practice tee. They've fetishized golf since the half-Asian Tiger Woods became famous as a teen in the 1990s. So far, East Asians have rapidly taken over ladies' professional golf, because golf hasn't been fashionable with Western women, at least not since the Fairway Flappers of *The Great Gatsby* era. But Asians haven't yet stood out on the men's tour.

Among Asian-American golfers, the two most celebrated Tiger Cubs of the last decade, Michelle Wie and Anthony Kim, may have been damaged by their pressurized upbringings. Nine years ago, Wie might have been the best 14-year-old golfer in the world, male or female. But then, apparently, estrogen kicked in. This year, she made only two top tens on the LPGA tour.

Following an intense Korean-American childhood hitting countless golf balls at the driving range down the block from me, Kim was sixth on the

2008 PGA money list at age 22. But now, battling physical and emotional problems, he hasn't been seen on tour since June 2012.

Back in 1850, the French economist Frédéric Bastiat wrote *That Which is Seen, and That Which is Not Seen*. That's a useful title to bear in mind. When Kim was on TV winning golf tournaments, he was living proof of the 10,000 Hour Rule. But out of sight is out of mind.

Some remember him, though. When other Korean parents ask Kim's parents how to raise a golf star, they now reply, "Don't try."

CHAPTER SEVEN

The Half-Full Glass

An IQ FAQ

VDARE
12/03/2007

AFTER the *Washington Post*-owned *Slate* ran a three part series by their human sciences correspondent William Saletan pointing out that the denunciations of James Watson were scientifically illiterate, we were wondering here at *VDARE* if we going to lose our near-monopoly as the professional publication routinely reporting the facts about IQ.

But, then Saletan and his editor Jacob Weisberg apparently lost their nerve and, just like Watson and Larry Summers, violated the cardinal rule: Never apologize for a "gaffe." Showing you're frightened of them just arouses the bloodlust in the jackals.

I figured I'd step back today and answer some common questions about IQ.

Q. Is IQ really all that important in understanding how the world works?

A. In an absolute sense, no. Human behavior is incredibly complicated, and no single factor explains more than a small fraction of it.

In a relative sense, yes. Compared to all the countless other factors that influence the human world, IQ ranks up near the top of the list.

Q. Why do you harp on IQ so much?

A. It's an underexploited market niche. The quantity and quality of writing in the Main Stream Media on IQ and its effects is so abysmal that, simply by being informed and honest about IQ, I can explain how certain important things work that other journalists can't.

Q. What are IQ questions like?

A. They vary wildly. The nonverbal Raven Matrices look like the instruction manual for a DVD player from Mars. Some of the Wechsler questions look like the Word Power vocabulary quiz in the *Reader's Digest*.

Q. How can different questions give similar results?

A. They're validated to make sure they do a good job of predicting real world performance. Obviously, different tests are better at different tasks, such as testing small children, illiterates, or people who speak a different language, but, when used properly, all the major tests present similar results because they are proven predictors of actual behavior.

Q. Aren't IQ tests only good for predicting academic performance?

A. Then why have the U.S. armed forces invested heavily in IQ testing all potential recruits since WWII? Because the military has found, over and over again, that IQ correlates with performance in a huge array of military duties.[1] Over time, a unit with an average IQ of 110 is going to repair jet engines faster and accidentally shoot themselves in the foot less often than a unit with an average IQ of 90.

Q. The military uses IQ tests? I never heard of such a thing!

A. They don't go out of their way to publicize it because it's politically incorrect, but the Armed Forces Qualification Test, which is the central core of the larger ASVAB test, is required of everyone who wants to enlist. It's the equivalent of a highly g-loaded IQ test. During the golden age of recruiting from 1992-2004, only 1% of enlistees got in with scores in the bottom 30% on the test (92 IQ or lower).

Q. Isn't character more important than intelligence?

A. I believe so. Work ethic, honesty, conscientiousness, kindness, together they're more important than intelligence. (Of course, when it comes to making money, less endearing personality traits like aggressiveness also play a big role, but we'll leave that aside for now.)

Can I quantify that? Well, that's where things get tricky...

Q. So why not test for work ethic and the like instead of IQ?

A. We do test for it, in many different ways. Consider the process of applying to college. The two most important elements in the application are high school GPA and the SAT or ACT score. The SAT and ACT are more or less an IQ test, while high school GPA is driven by a combination of IQ and work ethic.

But demonstrating work ethic via GPA is a time-consuming prospect for the applicant...and even for the admissions committee. The student spends four years in high school achieving a GPA, which he presents to the colleges to which he applies. But what does his GPA really say about him? Did he go to an easy school or a hard one? Did he take easy classes or hard ones? Does he have the brainpower to go far beyond high school material? These are complex questions, and it's no wonder that almost every college supplements GPA with the nationally standardized SAT or ACT.

Similarly, how does a would-be employee prove he's honest enough to handle large amounts of money? By slowly working his way up over the years from handling small amounts of money.

In contrast, the SAT takes only a few hours, while the widely used Wonderlic IQ test (mandated by the NFL for all pro football prospects) takes only 12 minutes.

Q. Couldn't somebody invent paper and pencil tests to measure character?
A. They have. They're pretty accurate...overall.

On the other hand, these tests haven't been all that popular, perhaps because they are liable to occasional catastrophic failures. The danger is that somebody with a high IQ but poor character would use his smarts to figure out what answers on the test would make him sound like the second coming of George Washington. And a high-IQ scoundrel is the last person you want to select.

You could call it the Ahmad Chalabi Problem. The Iraqi convicted embezzler with a Ph.D. in math from the U. of Chicago used his enormous brainpower to figure out how to dupe the neocons into believing that he literally was the George Washington of Iraq, so America should invade his homeland to make him president.

In contrast to character tests, the good news about IQ tests is that they are un-outsmartable. If you can use your brain to figure out what answers the test makers want, well, then you have a high IQ.

Q. So, do IQ tests predict an individual's fate?
A. In an absolute sense, not very accurately at all. Indeed, any single person's destiny is beyond the capability of all the tests ever invented to predict with much accuracy.

Q. So, if IQ isn't all that accurate for making predictions about an individual, why even think of using it to compare groups, which are much more complicated?

A. That sounds sensible, but it's exactly backwards. The larger the sample size, the more the statistical noise washes out.

Q. How can that be?

A. If Adam and Zach take an IQ test and Adam outscores Zach by 15 points, it's far from impossible that Zach actually has the higher "true" IQ. A hundred random perturbations could have thrown the results off. Maybe if they took the test a dozen times, Zach just might average higher than Adam.

   But for comparing the averages of large groups of people, the chance of error becomes vanishingly small. For example, the largest meta-analysis of American ethnic differences in IQ, Philip L. Roth's 2001 survey aggregated 105 studies of 6,246,729 individuals.[2] That's what you call a decent sample size.

Q. So, you're saying that IQ testing can tell us more about group differences than about individual differences?

A. If the sample sizes are big enough and all else is equal, a higher IQ group will virtually always outperform a lower IQ group on any behavioral metric.

   One of the very few positive traits not correlated with IQ is musical rhythm—which is a reason high IQ rock stars like Mick Jagger, Pete Townshend, and David Bowie tell Drummer Jokes.

   Of course, everything else is seldom equal. A more conscientious group may well outperform a higher IQ group. On the other hand, conscientiousness, like many virtues, is positively correlated with IQ, so IQ tests work surprisingly well.

Q. Wait a minute, does that mean that maybe some of the predictive power of IQ comes not from intelligence itself, but from virtues associated with it like conscientiousness?

A. Most likely. But perhaps smarter people are more conscientious because they are more likely to foresee the bad consequences of slacking off. It's an interesting philosophical question, but, in a practical sense, so what? We have a test that can predict behavior. That's useful.

Q. Can one number adequately describe a person's intelligence?

A. Sort of.

Q. "Sort of"?!? What the heck kind of answer is that?

A. A realistic one.

Q. How can something be true and not true at the same time?

A. How can the glass be half-full and half-empty at the same time? Most things about IQ testing are partly true and partly false at the same time. That's the nature of anything inherently statistical, which is most of reality.

Humans are used to legalistic reasoning that attempts to draw bright lines between exclusive categories. For example, you are either old enough to vote or you aren't. There's no gray area. But the law is artificial and unlike most of reality. Many people have a hard time dealing with that fact, especially when it comes to thinking about IQ.

Q. Enough epistemology! How can you rationalize summing up something as multifaceted as intelligence in a single number?

A. Think about SAT scores. Your total score says something about you, while breaking out your Math and Verbal scores separately says more. A kid who gets a total of 1400 out of 1600 (Math + Verbal) is definitely college material, while a kid who gets a 600 isn't. That's the big picture. For the fine detail, like which college to apply to, it helps to look at the subscores. A kid with a 1400 who got a 600 Math and an 800 Verbal would be better off at Swarthmore than at CalTech.

A few years ago, the SAT added a third score, Writing, but many colleges aren't sure how useful it is, and there's some sentiment for dropping the Writing test as not worth the extra time or cost. In other words, there are diminishing marginal returns to more detail.

Q. What's this mysterious g Factor that I see lauded and denounced?

A. If Al outscores Bert on the first subtest (say, vocabulary or reaction-times), bet on Al in the next test, no matter how dissimilar (e.g., math, paper-folding, or distinguishing musical pitches). This pervasive correlation is why a crude one-number IQ score is so implausibly useful as a predictor of a host of real world consequences. Lurking behind IQ is a "general factor" or "g" that plays a role (of varying magnitudes) in the accomplishment of any and every mental task, from taking a test to making a living.

Q. Didn't Stephen Jay Gould say, "The chimerical nature of g is the rotten core" of the theory of IQ?

A. That he did. But Gould didn't understand (or chose not to understand) that the usefulness of IQ doesn't depend upon whether or not there is a general factor.[3] Say you work in college admissions on a different planet where applicants' SAT Math and Verbal scores are totally uncorrelated. In this world where there is no *g* factor, somebody who gets an 800 on the SAT Math test would be just as likely to get a 200 as an 800 on the Verbal test. How different would you behave than your colleagues on earth? Not much. You'd still want the applicants who scored the highest on the combined score (Math plus Verbal), because they'd do best in the widest range of college classes.

Of course, back on Earth, there's a rather high degree of correlation between Math and Verbal scores. The only time you see an 800 on the Math test combined with a 200 on the Verbal test is from somebody who just got off the plane from Seoul.

Q. Can you improve your IQ?

A. Maybe. Try exercising your brain. If you spend twice as many hours per day thinking hard, it might improve the quality of your thinking. And even if it doesn't, you've still doubled the quantity of your hard thinking, so what's to lose, other than your TV-watching time?

Q. Is IQ hereditary?

A. At the moment, we only have a vague idea of which genes affect IQ, but the data is pouring in. James Watson figures no more than 15 years until the main genes driving IQ scores are nailed down. It could be faster.[4]

In the meantime, we have a lot of circumstantial evidence, such as twin and adoption studies.[5] Almost all of it points toward IQ having a sizable genetic component.

Q. What does it mean to say IQ has a genetic component?

A. It means that identical twins tend to be more similar in intelligence than fraternal twins, who are more alike than first cousins, and so forth. That appears to be true.

Q. So, everybody in the same family gets the same IQ?

A. No. Think about siblings that you know and you'll likely notice moderate differences in intelligence among them—unless they are identical twins (and thus have identical genes).

Q. Is IQ solely determined by genes?

A. No. Consider, for example, the need for micronutrient supplementation. For example, here in America, manufacturers have been adding iodine to salt and iron to flour since before WWII to combat medical syndromes (such as cretinism) that lower IQ. In poor countries around the world, hundreds of millions of children still suffer cognitively from lack of iodine and iron. Of course, this relatively cheap step for raising the IQs of the poor in Third World countries is rarely discussed, because the whole topic of IQ is so fraught with the chance of getting Watsoned out of your job.

Q. Are there differences in average SAT scores among racial groups?

A. Yes. Ashkenazi (European) Jews appear to average the highest—maybe around 110-112—followed by Northeast Asians (105), and then by gentile white Europeans and North Americans (100). The world mean is around 90, Hispanic-Americans are at 89. African-Americans traditionally average around 85 and Africans in Sub-Saharan Africa around 70.[6]

Q. Aren't all IQ researchers white supremacists who just want to show their race has the highest IQ?

A. If they are, they're doing an awfully lousy job of it. (See above.)

Q. How can anybody talk about race and IQ when race doesn't exist?

A. It's funny how these objections don't come up in regard to affirmative action. Scientists gather race-related data the same way colleges and bureaucrats hand out affirmative action goodies. They let people self-identify.

I spent a lot of time years ago trying to prove that affirmative action is unworkable because there's too much overlap between the races to decide which race somebody belongs to, but I eventually gave up because, at least at present, the situation's good enough for government (and scientific) work.

Q. But what about "black" intellectuals like the identical twins Shelby and Claude Steele? They're likely more than half white, but they are counted as black, so how can you include them as black?

A. If you took out all the self-identified blacks who are over half white by ancestry (people who tend to be above the black average in education and income), the IQ gap would in all likelihood get a little bigger.

Anyway, only about 10% of adults who call themselves black are over half white, so it's not very important.

Q. Are global differences in IQ caused solely by genetics?

A. No. As I wrote in *VDARE* back in 2002:

A clear example of how a bad environment can hurt IQ can be seen in the IQ scores for sub-Saharan African countries. They average only around 70. In contrast, African-Americans average about 85. It appears unlikely that African-Americans' white admixture can account for most of this 15-point gap because they are only around

17%-18% white on average, according to the latest genetic research. (Thus African-Americans' white genes probably couldn't account for more than 3 points of the gap between African-Americans and African-Africans.) This suggests that the harshness of life in Africa might be cutting ten points or more off African IQ scores.[7]

Q. Are IQ tests biased against African-Americans?

A. Not in the most important sense of predictive validity. White and black Army recruits with 100 IQs on the AFQT, for instance, will perform about equally well on the job.

Any kind of non-functional bias against minorities in test design has been radioactive for decades, so all the questions that were "unfair" to minorities were removed long ago.

Q. Isn't there an Ebonics IQ test on which blacks outscore whites?

A. You can make up a test asking, say, "Do you eat, drink, or shoot a '40'?" on which inner city blacks might outscore Korean-Americans. (Such knowledge quickly becomes dated—Jane Elliott is still using the "Chitling Test" from 1971 to humiliate whites, but many blacks couldn't pass it today either.) But it won't have real world predictive validity. The Air Force recruits who know that you drink a 40 won't do a better job of fixing jet engines than the ones who don't. So, it's useless in the real world.

Creating an IQ test on which there's no black-white gap has been the Holy Grail of test designers for 40 years. Any test company that could pull it off would make a fortune, because every school district in the country would dump their current test and switch to the "non-racist" test. It's been attempted repeatedly, but it can't be done without destroying the test's predictive powers.

Q. But I see all these black people on TV being highly entertaining. They look pretty lively upstairs. Could IQ tests be missing something?

A. Yes. IQ test questions, by their nature, must have fixed, objective answers. If African Americans are better at subjective, improvisatory responses than they are at objective problem-solving, then IQ will fail to predict fully their patterns of success in the real world. And, indeed, we see much evidence for that every time we turn on the TV (e.g., Oprah).

Unfortunately, there aren't nearly as many jobs being entertainment or sports superstars as black youths seem to assume, so, overall, IQ remains a quite accurate predictor outside of the tiny sliver of celebrities.

Q. What's the Flynn Effect?

A. All over the world, raw IQ scores have been rising, on average at the rate of about 3 points per decade. Thus, a test performance that a half century ago would have ranked at the 84th percentile (a score of 115) now is only good enough for the 50th percentile (a score of 100).

Q. Will the Flynn Effect bring about racial convergence?

A. Perhaps someday, but the Flynn Effect was first noticed in 1942, and there has been very little narrowing of the various gaps since then.

Q. Enough with the preliminaries! Are racial gaps in average IQ at least partly genetic?

A. Probably some are, but we don't know for sure yet. At this point, we have a lot of data, and Occam's Razor suggests the simplest and thus best explanation is that races differ in average IQ for the same reason that families differ. After all, races are just big extended families.[8]

   But that might turn out to be wrong. We'll know with a high degree of certainty fairly soon. Once we have a quite clear understanding of which genes affect IQ and by how much, it will be relatively trivial to then calculate the "expected IQ" for various racial groups based on their average genetic profiles.

Q. But, but…how can we live in such a world?

A. It appears to be the world we're living in right now.

Q. But only Nazis believe such things. So that means the Nazis are going to be proved right! So the American public will clone Hitler and elect him President!

A. Whatever.

   It just means that you've been a sucker for the smears aimed at outstanding scientists and human beings like Arthur Jensen and Charles Murray.

Q. What's the real story behind the crushing of James Watson?

A. The Establishment knows that evidence is piling up for the Bell Curve theory that they've denounced so vociferously for so long. So they are just trying to postpone the day of reckoning on which it becomes widely understood that they are fools, liars, and smear-artists by silencing anyone like Watson who speaks up.[9] The frenzy will only increase as the genome data comes flooding in.

Q. What can we say for sure about racial gaps?

A. That they'll be around for a long time.

Say it's discovered in 2008 that the entire cause of the black-white IQ gap is some hitherto unknown micronutrient needed by pregnant women that African-Americans don't get enough of, and a crash program is put into place immediately to solve the problem. If that happened, the IQ gap among working-age adults still wouldn't disappear until the 2070s.

So whether the racial IQ gaps are genetic or not, they're going to be around for many decades. And we need to understand them.

Q. Why is all this important? Shouldn't we just think of people as individuals?

A. That sounds good to me, but we don't. We're social and political animals, and many of our government policies are based on group membership: not just explicit affirmative action programs, but most anti-discrimination cases as well are based not on evidence of actual discrimination but on "disparate impact," a legal theory that's built on the big assumption that different groups are identical in IQ and other traits.

Q. How would understanding IQ better help America?

A. It's becoming ever more clear that the combination of racial gaps in IQ and the IQ taboo acts as a black hole that sucks all the intelligence out of an institution. Racial gaps in achievement are the overwhelmingly dominant fact driving school performance, for instance, but nobody is allowed to mention the IQ gap among the races, so misbegotten nonsense rushes in. Last month, the California Superintendent of Schools announced that the cause of low black achievement was "absolutely, positively not genetic."[10] Instead, white teachers imposing too much discipline on black youths "who learn at church that it's good to clap, speak loudly and be a bit raucous" were to blame. Of course, the last thing public schools need is less discipline.

Similarly, in 2001, President Bush and Senator Kennedy got together and passed the No Child Left Behind Act, which is certifiably insane. It mandates eliminating all racial gaps and making every student in America "proficient" (i.e., above average) by 2014.

Q. So what can be done?

A. People who understand reality reasonably well can figure out many small, incremental changes that will make us all better off. In contrast, powerful people who don't know what the hell they are doing will tend to make us all worse off.

Q. What's the initial thing we should do?

A. When you find yourself in a hole, the first thing to do is to stop digging. By letting in so many unskilled (i.e., largely low IQ) immigrants, especially illegal immigrants, we're digging a deeper hole for ourselves.

So let's stop. Now.

The Half-Full Glass

Unpublished
Written June 1998

The following was written at the request of National Review, *but it came out several times longer than they were willing to publish. Further, even at its current 2,700 words, my ideas/words ratio is still far too high for the casual reader. I'm trying to do several things in this, a few of them novel: I recount Arthur Jensen's case for a single-factor model of racial differences in mental ability, then offer the only logical alternative (a multi-factor diversity model), then try to show how they can complement each other.*

Review of *The* g *Factor: the Science of Mental Abilities*, by Arthur R. Jensen (Praeger, 1998)

FOR scientists working in the paradoxical discipline of individual differences in mental abilities, these are the best of times. They've confirmed that performances on all mental tests are positively correlated: If Al outscores Bert on the first assignment (say, vocabulary or reaction-times), bet on Al in the next test, no matter how dissimilar (e.g., math, paper-folding, or distinguishing musical pitches). This pervasive correlation is why a crude one-number IQ score is so implausibly useful, rivaling a "conscientiousness" rating as the best single predictor of a host of real world consequences. Lurking behind IQ is a "general factor" or "*g*" that plays a role (of varying magnitudes) in the accomplishment of any and every mental task, from taking a test to making a living.

Even more strikingly, these "differential" psychologists have finally pushed beyond the social sciences and into the medical laboratory. PET scans and EEG's, which can now roughly estimate IQ's (and thus g's), show that high-g brains work more quickly, economically, and consistently, like well-greased engines. In fact, this analogy could be almost literally true, if Edward M. Miller's hypothesis pans out that one determinant of general mental ability is the thickness of the fatty myelin coating neurons. These physiological studies suggest methods to raise IQ's, such as breastfeeding, the source of the ideal fats for infants' brains. Eventually, this kind of research may lead to higher IQ's through genetic engineering.

Already, better nutrition, better health care, less in-breeding, and other blessings enjoyed by recent generations have helped raise average g's. (For many of the same reasons, average heights have risen comparably.) Sadly, the white-black gap in average IQ's, which has stubbornly hovered around 15 points throughout the last 80 years of extraordinary change, seems likely to linger for at least decades more. Thus, these are the worst of times for g-men to go public with their discoveries. The fulminations against *The Bell Curve* have given way to a quieter, more effective clampdown, which has left missing in action two recent books with the identical title *The g Factor*. In 1996 Chris Brand, an Edinburgh U. psychologist, saw his own publisher yank back the unsold copies of his new book after reporters asked him about the IQ gap. Edinburgh later fired Brand, despite his 27 years of tenure, for expressing "disgraceful" opinions.

Arthur Jensen of Berkeley, the dean of psychometricians with 400 scientific papers published in refereed journals, struggled merely to find a publisher for his version of *The g Factor*, this heroically comprehensive summing up of his life's work. Finally, the small mail order imprint Praeger released Jensen's magnum opus...to shameful neglect. Even today, the only sure source for this fascinating (if dauntingly rigorous) landmark in the science of human nature remains the publisher.

Stephen Jay Gould's *The Mismeasure of Man*, a 1981 book that continues to shape the non-scientific intelligentsia's feelings about IQ, demonized g as the "rotten core" of Prof. Jensen's 1969 article documenting the white-black IQ gap. *The g Factor's* overwhelming vindication of g, drawing on 15 years of new research, might seem likely to end the debate. It won't, of course, for reasons good and bad. The book sheds light on crucial new issues beyond the narrow scope of g (such as racial differences in nerdishness). More depressingly, few will grasp either its strengths or its limitations due to fundamental confusions rampant among American intellectuals about how to think about humanity.

For example, nobody noticed that Gould's assertion that human equality is a factual (rather than a moral, legal, or spiritual) reality centered on denouncing g; yet, g is the only concept that could conceivably make sense of his claim. Ironically, the g-ocentrists are among the last students of human nature making important discoveries within the egalitarian world-view. The one technique capable of uncovering mental equality is Jensen's: minimize the number of data points by measuring only the single most important factor (g) across only a few vast groups. Thus, Jensen, the Great Satan to egalitarian fundamentalists, delivers in Chapter 13 the most important pro-equality finding in recent decades: Men and women really do possess the same average g. Their equal average IQ's scores aren't just an artifact of IQ tests being rigged to produce this result. Jensen's finding is hugely important in itself: it's the best explanation of the splendid performance of women in many white-collar jobs.

Still, this example also shows that g, like any successful reductionist theory, has its limits. Males and females, while similar on mean g (but not on the standard deviation of g: guys predominate among both eggheads and knuckleheads), differ on several specific cognitive talents. Men, Jensen reports in passing, tend to be better at visual-spatial skills (especially at mentally rotating 3-d objects) and at mathematical reasoning. Women are generally superior at short-term memory, perceptual speed, and verbal fluency. Since the male sex is stronger at logically manipulating objects, while the female sex prevails at social awareness, that explains why most nerds are male, while most "berms" (anti-nerds adept at interpersonal skills and fashion) are female. Beyond cognition, there are other profound sex dissimilarities in personality, motivation, and physiology. All this helps explain the sexes' different patterns in career choices.

Because Jensen's simple, single-factor model can detect intellectual equality between men and women, it can also detect intellectual inequality between whites and blacks, if that's what the facts are. Although most responses to Jensen's equality/inequality model haven't risen above name-calling, obfuscation, guilt-by-association, and professional cowardice, there is a logical, fruitful alternative: develop a complex, multi-factor "diversity" model that rather than concentrating upon one difference among a very few groups, focuses on the many differences visible among many groups. Emphasizing the trade-offs necessary for achieving different goals, it makes toting up an over-all winner look a little pointless.

The diversity perspective has much to offer, but only when it's thorough-ly understood that it's inherently less empirically egalitarian than Jensenism. The diversity model's current popularity, however, stems from the wishful thinking that it discredits racial differences, on the assumption that since Di-versity and Equality are both Good Things, they must be synonyms rather than antonyms. One particularly fashionable defense of empirical equali-ty is to combine the doctrine that there "are no such things as races" (just swarms of little ethnic groups) with Harvard professor Howard Gardner's speculations about seven "multiple intelligences." Ergo, all groups must be equal, QED.

Let's do the math: assume, say, 100 ethnic groups and seven "intelligenc-es." That's 700 data points. No way, no how could they all be equal—our uni-verse doesn't work like that. The more complex your model, the less equality and the more diversity you'll perceive in the world.

These kind of wooly-headed delusions that infest contemporary social thought stem fundamentally from the taboo against learning about humani-ty the way we'd learn about anything else: by noticing similarities and differ-ences, which are the raw materials, the warp and woof, of information. The faster and more accurately a computer modem can discriminate the squawks coming down the phone line into 0's and 1's, the more information it can receive. Conversely, the more patterns it can discover among the data it's transmitting, the more it can compress the bits into similar groups, and thus the more information it can send. Disdaining to notice human contrasts isn't Respectable Science; it's intentional ignorance.

Even the 100 ethnic groups / seven intelligences model contains some useful truths. First, in the study of human biodiversity, as in any other sci-ence, there is a constructive tension, ultimately amounting to a symbiosis, between encyclopedically tabulating all genetic differences and devising par-simonious theories to cluster people according to their genetic similarities. The encyclopedist's glass is half full of fascinating ethnic anomalies that don't fit broad-brush racial theories. For example, the average Jewish IQ seems to surpass the average overall white IQ by as much as 17 points. Simultaneously, the theorist can half-fill his glass with sweeping racial patterns. For instance, he can frugally sum up much of the biodiversity that's blatantly obvious in

America with Rushton's Rule: On most physical, cognitive, and behavioral dimensions, the West African and Northeast Asian averages lie at opposite extremes, with the white average in the mediocre middle.

Those who deny the reality of the races rightly point out that nobody agrees exactly on their number, names, or constituents. This is a valid point, but the identical criticism could be made of the reality of "extended families"...precisely because races are extremely extended families. Races differ qualitatively from extended families only in being more coherent and longer lasting, due to greater in-breeding.

Second, are there are lots of mental abilities? Sure. I could rattle off many more than Gardner's seven that I, personally, lack. Like races, nobody can quite agree on precisely what they are. Do we need scores of different cerebral skills, or can we get by with Gardner's seven intelligences? Or is Jensen's g good enough? Since most of the literati still think in terms of Platonic essences, this multiplicity of approaches strikes many as a conceptual scandal, but it's a practical boon: you can pick the optimal trade-off between comprehensiveness and ease-of-use for your particular task.

Isn't there something unscientific about ignoring outlying data that doesn't fit the theory? Interestingly, Jensen and Gardner, despite being so often portrayed as mortal enemies (actually, they are mildly admiring of each other's work), are both reductionists. The highest scientific honors have always gone to the theorists like Newton or Darwin rather than the cataloguers like Tyco Brahe or Linnaeus, because there is simply too much raw data for us to handle. Without scientific hypotheses, rules-of-thumb, prejudices, and gut instincts, we'd be as immobilized as Funes, the Jorge Luis Borges character cursed with infinite powers of perceptual discrimination that cost him his ability to synthesize and abstract meaning out of his oppressively detailed memory-dump.

The narrower the field, the better that simple models like g forecast success. For example, if you look only at major team sports, African-Americans are on average genetically superior at "general athleticism." Thus, race proves useful in predicting success...until you contemplate a broader variety of sports. Then, the greater average muscularity that helps make men of West African descent the kings of football and basketball tends to cause them in, say, marathon-running, dogsled-racing, and English Channel-swimming to (respectively) overheat, freeze, and sink.

Ironically, while diversity models are now popular in the abstract, it's nearly a hanging offense in the current mainstream media climate to actually mention particular talents in which minorities are superior to whites. (Today, "celebrating diversity" is automatically assumed to mean "insisting upon uniformity.") Gardner, for instance, coyly refuses to discuss the obvious racial and sexual disparities implicit in his seven factor model.

In the most publicized recent attempt to honestly flesh out a diversity model, the Reverend Reggie White of the Green Bay Packers asked the Wisconsin legislature, "Why did God make us so different?" He then listed what he saw as the different strengths of America's races, and concluded, "When you put all of that together...it forms a complete image of God." Despite being black, a football hero, an outstanding citizen, obviously well-intended, and in at least some of his examples undeniably right (e.g., Asians are gifted at invention, "they can turn a TV into a watch"), the Rev. White was pilloried by the press: "Stereotypes!"

Of course, none of the tut-tutters asked: Is a diversity model needed to describe specific black mental advantages overlooked by g? As a Reggieist (i.e., one who considers human biodiversity both a reality and a net blessing), I'm pleased to point out that IQ tests can't accurately measure at least one mental faculty in which blacks tend to outperform whites and Asians in real life. Despite lower mean IQ's, African-Americans are not a race of talentless dullards, but are instead the most charismatic contributors to 20th Century popular culture. What mental factor underlies the black revolutions in music, sport, oratory, dance, and slang? Subjective, improvisatory creativity.

For example, like a lot of NBA stars, Scottie Pippen's below-market contract, ill-timed trade demands, team-damaging pouts, and numerous child-support obligations imply that when given time to think, he often chooses unwisely. Yet, in the flow of the game, he's a Talleyrand at real-time decision-making. Leading a fast break, there are no permanent right answers. Even "Pass the ball to Michael Jordan" gets old fast as defenses habituate. Similarly, the NFL running back, the jazz soloist, the preacher, and the rapping DJ all must heed others' expectations and instantly respond with something a little unexpected. IQ tests—by necessity objective and standardized—can never measure this adequately.

Further, despite his data's inevitable shortcomings in this regard, Jensen does report that blacks possess particular mental weaknesses and strengths. Among individuals with equal g's, whites and Asians (like males) are typically stronger in those visual-spatial skills so useful in engineering and many skilled trades. In contrast, blacks (like females) often enjoy better short-term memories and thus can mentally juggle more balls in social situations. (This probably contributes to the black advantage in improvisation). Jensen's findings confirm my intuition that while whites and Asians tend to be less masculine than blacks in physique and personality, they are typically more masculine than blacks in mental abilities. Put bluntly, whites and Asians tend to be nerdier than blacks. How many blacks would sincerely disagree?

Thus, the IQ disparity is less apocalyptic than is generally assumed. In fact, it's not all that unique—diversity is among the oldest and most pervasive problems / opportunities inherent in the human condition. Because everybody is less innately talented than somebody else at something, the human race has worked out some pragmatic ways to deal with this.

Since Adam Smith and David Ricardo, economic theory has recommended specializing in whatever's your greatest comparative advantage. The peculiar problem facing blacks, though, is their specific talents are most valuable in winner-take-all professions like entertainment and sports. Still, the masculine bermishness common among blacks should also be helpful in more broadly remunerative occupations like sales.

Even if blacks had no special skills, just a deficiency of g, methods used by white and Mexican athletes to deal with black superiority in team sports might offer blacks practical hints in partially mitigating the g-gap. Specialization, for instance, is still valuable. (As illustrated by their most famous star Fernando Valenzuela, Mexicans don't tend to be endowed with ideal, Ken Griffey Jr.-style bodies for baseball. Yet, through an intense focus on the game they've built a critical mass of baseball expertise.) Avoid affirmative action programs that prevent critical masses from emerging. Look for fields where the inherent demands are less (e.g., golf rather than football) or competition is lighter (e.g., volleyball instead of basketball).

Work harder than your more gifted rivals. Master the fundamentals. Nail the easy stuff. (E.g., the only category in which whites are over-represented among NBA leaders is free-throw shooting). Don't improvise: listen to your coach's wisdom. (E.g., the decline of traditional sexual morality has not led to a high pregnancy rate among coldly logical Dutch teens. For African-American teens, though, the rise of do-it-yourself morality in the 1960's was a disaster.) Challenge yourself, but realistically. (E.g., I need to get in shape, but an affirmative action program for Sedentary-Americans that sets-aside for me an opening in Evander Holyfield next heavyweight title bout might not be in my best interest. The same goes for racial quotas at elite colleges.)

Finally, the U.S. Army offers the bracing example of an institution that has elicited a high level of black achievement, in part by demanding that those with high-IQ's search out what Richard Epstein calls simple rules for a complex world. In dismal contrast, research universities fail blacks because the publish-or-perish system encourages the high-IQ to wallow in abstruseness. Denouncing Jensen proclaims one's faith in empirical egalitarianism, which serves as the perfect excuse for ignoring the irksome demands of moral egalitarianism. By declaring that everyone could Be Like Me (if only they were properly socialized), the clever can, with clear conscience, continue to surreptitiously wage class war against the clueless.

A Few Thoughts on *IQ and the Wealth of Nations*

VDARE
04/14/2002

THE content of the landmark book *IQ and the Wealth of Nations* by Richard Lynn of the U. of Ulster and Tatu Vanhanen of the U. of Helsinki is irresistible—at its heart is a table of the average IQ scores of 81 different countries, most drawn from studies published in peer-reviewed scientific journals. The national average IQs range from 107 for Hong Kong to 59 for Equatorial Guinea.

Lynn and Vanhanen benchmarked their IQ results so that Britain is 100. America scores 98 on this scale, and the world average is 90. IQ's are assumed to form a normal probability distribution ("bell curve") with the standard deviation set at 15. Here are a few examples (right):

Admit it, you want to know what the rest of the table says! Beyond satisfying sheer curiosity, though, the strong correlation between IQ and the wealth of nations is of world-historical importance. From now on, no public intellectual can seriously claim to be attempting to understand how the world works unless he takes IQ into account.

How much can we trust these IQ results?

As soon as I received the book, I turned to Appendix 1, where Lynn and Vanhanen describe all 168 national IQ studies they've found—an average of just over two per country.

Are the results internally consistent? In other words, when there are multiple studies for a single country, do they tend to give roughly the same answer?

Nation	National Avg. IQ	Percentile of Avg. Person Relative to UK	GDP Per Capita Purchasing Power Parity
Eq. Guinea	59	0.3%	$ 1,817
Nigeria	67	1%	$ 795
Barbados	78	7%	$ 12,001
Guatemala	79	8%	$ 3,505
India	81	10%	$ 2,077
Iraq	87	19%	$ 3,197
Mexico	87	19%	$ 7,704
Argentina	96	39%	$ 12,013
US	98	45%	$ 29,605
China	100	50%	$ 3,105
UK	100	50%	$ 20,336
Italy	102	55%	$ 20,585
Japan	105	63%	$ 23,257
Hong Kong	107	68%	$ 20,763

I expected a sizable amount of internal divergence. I spent 18 years in the marketing research industry, so I know how expensive it is to come up with a nationally representative sample. Further, Lynn and Vanhanen use results from quite different IQ tests. They rely most on the non-verbal Raven's Progressive Matrices, which were designed to be used across cultures, even by illiterates. Yet, they also have a lot of results from the Wechsler exams, which are more culture dependent—the Wechsler include a vocabulary subtest, for example. And they report results from other IQ tests, including a few from the Goodenough-Harris Draw-A-Man test. Also, sample sizes vary dramatically, from a few dozen in some obscure countries to 64,000 for one American study. Finally, some studies were of children, others of adults.

This doesn't sound promising. Nevertheless, the results show a high degree of internal consistency. Here are the first eight countries for which they have multiple scores:

Argentina: 93 and 98
Australia: 97, 98, and 99
Austria: 101, 103
Belgium: 99, 103, 98
Brazil: 88, 84, 90, and 85
Bulgaria: 94, 91
China: 100, 92.5, 103.4
Democratic Republic of Congo: 73, 72

That's not bad at all. In fact, leaving aside China, the results are remarkably consistent. There are, of course, a few countries for which different studies came up with quite divergent results, especially Poland, where the two scores Lynn and Vanhanen found were 92 and 106. Still, the correlation among results when there are two or more studies for a country is a striking 0.94.

You shouldn't take every score on faith. The reported IQ for Israel (only 94????!!!) has elicited much criticism. Lynn has replied that he wanted to publish the data as he found it, even if some of it looked implausible. His hope is to encourage further research to resolve seeming anomalies.

The IQ structures of the two giga-countries, China and India, demand more intense study, in part because the future history of the world will hinge in no small part on their endowments of human capital. The demography of India is especially complex due to its caste system, which resembles Jim Crow on steroids and acid. By discouraging intermarriage, caste has subdivided the Indian people into an incredible number of micro-races. In India, according to the dean of population genetics, L.L. Cavalli-Sforza, "The total number of endogamous communities today is around 43,000...." We know that some of those communities—such as the Zoroastrian Parsis of Bombay —are exceptionally intelligent.

But we can't say with any confidence what is the long run IQ potential of Indians overall. Their current IQ score (81) is low, especially compared to China (100), the other country with hundreds of millions of poor peasants. Yet, keep in mind just how narrow life in rural India was for so long.

It appears likely that some combination of malnutrition, disease, inbreeding, lack of education, lack of mental stimulation, lack of familiarity with abstract reasoning and so forth can keep people from reaching their genetic potential for IQ. Lynn himself did early studies demonstrating that malnutrition drives down IQ. The co-authors conclude their book by recommending that:

> The rich countries' economic aid programs for the poor countries should be continued and some of these should be directed at attempting to increase the intelligence levels of the populations of the poorer countries by improvements in nutrition and the like.

A clear example of how a bad environment can hurt IQ can be seen in the IQ scores for sub-Saharan African countries. They average only around 70. In contrast, African-Americans average about 85. It appears unlikely that African-Americans' white admixture can account for most of this 15-point gap because they are only around 17%-18% white on average, according to the latest genetic research. (Thus African-Americans white genes probably couldn't account for more than 3 points of the gap between African-Americans and African-Africans.) This suggests that the harshness of life in Africa might be cutting ten points or more off African IQ scores.

Similarly, West Africans are significantly shorter in height than their distant cousins in America, most likely due to malnutrition and infections. The two African-born NBA superstars, Hakeem Olajuwon and Dikembe Mutombo, are both from the *wa-benzi* (people of the Mercedes Benz) upper class. Only the elite in Africa gets enough food and health care to grow up to be NBA centers.

This also implies that African-Americans might be able to achieve higher IQs too, although the environmental gap between white Americans and black Americans appears to be much smaller than between black Americans and black Africans.

In fact, we know that IQ is not completely fixed over time because raw test scores have been rising for decades, about 2 to 3 points per decade. To counteract this, the IQ test-making firms periodically make it harder—in absolute terms—to achieve a score of 100. Lynn was possibly the first scientist to make this phenomenon widely known, although New Zealand political scientist James Flynn has gotten more credit for this recently. And, indeed, Lynn and Vanhanen scrupulously adjust the test results in their book to account for when each test was taken.

While the causes of the Lynn-Flynn Effect remain rather mysterious, it does resemble several other ongoing phenomena. For example, human beings are getting taller, living longer, and having fewer of their babies die during infancy.

One might expect IQ scores to converge as the richest nations experience diminishing marginal returns on improvements in nutrition, health, and education. By way of analogy, consider how, after 1950, average height has not grown as fast in already well-fed America as it has in rapidly developing East Asia.

It's unlikely the Japanese will ever be as tall on average as, say, Lithuanians or Croatians or African-Americans. But the gap has closed. This partial convergence in height is why you now see 6'-2" East Asian baseball pitchers like Hideo Nomo and Chan Ho Park starring in the American big leagues. Last year Wang Zhizhi at 7'-1" became the first Asian ever to join the NBA.

Perhaps that kind of convergence will happen with IQ scores someday. But the evidence that it is happening now isn't terribly strong. The odd thing about the Lynn-Flynn Effect is that it doesn't seem to have had much impact on comparative rankings of IQ over time. The smart seem to keep on getting smarter.

For instance, one of the best-documented examples of a country with rising raw IQ scores is the Netherlands (current IQ: 102). But even as far back as the 17th Century, the general opinion of mankind was that the Dutch had a lot on the ball.

One potential explanation for why IQ gaps don't seem to be narrowing (for example, the white-black IQ gap in America has been about 15 points for 80 years or so) was offered by Flynn recently. He argued that smart people, because they find cognitive challenges pleasurable, seek out more mentally stimulating environments, which in turn exercise their brains more, making them even smarter. This suggests, for example, that the Dutch will tend to become, say, Internet addicts demanding constant fixes of new information and argument, and thus continue to grow in mental firepower.

While unproven, Flynn's suggestion seems possible. In absolute terms, it's a virtuous circle. But it seems unlikely to lead to the closing of the relative gap.

Ultimately, though, it is hard to avoid concluding that intellectual and income differences between nations stem to some extent from genetic differences. The results simply cluster too much by race. All the countries populated by Northeast Asians score between 100 and 107. The European-populated lands score between 90 and 102. Southeast Asian nations cluster in the low 90s. The Caucasian countries in North Africa and western Asia score mostly in the 80s. And so forth.

A FEW THOUGHTS ON IQ AND THE WEALTH OF NATIONS

The correlation between national IQ and national income is very high. For the 81 countries, the r is .73 for GDP measured in purchasing power parity terms (which makes poor nations with lots of subsistence farmers look better off than they do in standard measures of just the cash economy). In the social sciences, correlations of 0.2 are said to be "low," 0.4 are "moderate," and 0.6 are "high." So 0.73 is most impressive.

This doesn't mean that a high IQ alone is the cause of a high income. Causation probably runs in both directions, in another virtuous circle. Rich countries tend to produce enough food to stave off malnutrition, for instance, which probably leads to higher IQs, which leads to even higher food production due to more sophisticated farming techniques.

Interestingly, per capita income correlates almost as strongly with a nation's level of economic freedom as it does with its level of intelligence. But that's in large part because economic freedom and IQ correlate with each other—at the high level of 0.63.

Freedom and brains probably contribute to each other. Although there are obvious exceptions, countries with smart workers (and smart leaders) tended to find that the capitalist system generated wealth. So there was less impetus to experiment with command economies than in places where free enterprise wasn't getting the job done.

But it could also be that freedom exercises the brain—West Germans averaged 103 while East Germans scored only 95. My pet theory is that having to make all the choices between products available in a successful capitalist economy stimulates mental development. (I believe this because, as I get older and stupider, I increasingly find shopping to be intellectually exhausting.) But evidence for this is not abundant.

Culture can play a role as well—at the extreme, contrast two countries with almost identical per capita GDPs: Barbados and Argentina (at least before Argentina's recent economic collapse). Don't cry for Argentina, because it is blessed with ample IQ (96). But it's dragged down by a notorious lack of economic and political self-discipline. In contrast, Barbados, despite an average IQ of 78, is one of the most pleasant countries in the 3rd World due to its commitment to maintaining a veddy, veddy English culture.

Still, these two countries are close to being the exceptions that prove the rule. The explanatory power of the "cultural realist" models like Thomas Sowell's are necessarily more limited than those of a "biocultural realist" like Richard Lynn. In general, cultures that emphasize, say, foresight are generally found in countries where people have enough IQ to be foresighted. Maybe people in northern countries tend to have higher IQs because people too unintelligent to effectively prepare for winter tended to get removed from the gene pool.

The IQ-income correlation is not perfect either. But even where it breaks down—most notably with China—IQ helps explain otherwise puzzling developments like the recent headline in the *New York Times* announcing "Globalization Proves Disappointing."

> Globalization, or the fast-paced growth of trade and cross-border investment, has done far less to raise the incomes of the world's poorest people than the leaders had hoped, many officials here say. The vast majority of people living in Africa, Latin America, Central Asia and the Middle East are no better off today than they were in 1989...[11]

On the other hand, hundreds of billions in private investment have poured into China, which, despite its parasitical ruling caste, has enjoyed strong economic growth.

So what's the story behind this story? Apparently, capital flows to where wages are low but IQs are high—pre-eminently China, where the average IQ is two points higher than the U.S. already and likely to go higher as economic development continues.

In contrast, these other regions (with the exception of Argentina) average IQs of 90 or less, sometimes considerably less.

This is not to disparage free markets—there's no alternative. The point is simply that humans differ greatly in productive capacity, so not everyone benefits from economic competition to the same extent.

The implications for immigration policy are clear.

First, any conceivable level of immigration to America is insufficient to make any difference in the welfare of the billions of foreigners living in poverty.

Second, in a world where the average IQ is 90, America's nepotism-driven immigration system (legal and illegal) will continue to import primarily foreigners with two-digit IQs. These immigrants' skills are typically insufficient to compete with our native IQ elite, but are ample for driving down the wages of our fellow American citizens who were not blessed in the IQ lottery.

The morality of such a system I leave to the reader to decide.

Idiocracy

The American Conservative
October 6, 2006

ERHAPS the most gifted populist conservative in the entertainment industry is Mike Judge, creator of the TV animated comedies *Beavis & Butt-Head* and *King of the Hill* (now scheduled for an 11th season on Fox in 2007), as well as the 1999 cult classic film *Office Space*.

Despite Judge's commercial consistency, his clever and frequently hilarious new satire *Idiocracy* has been deep-sixed by his own studio, Rupert Murdoch's 20th Century Fox, with the most hostile passive-aggressive release of any film in memory. Over the Labor Day Weekend *Idiocracy* materialized in 130 theatres in seven cities (but not in New York, so national media coverage was nonexistent) bereft of even a trailer or the smallest newspaper ad. Fox couldn't even be bothered to tell *Moviefone* the name of the film—you had to search for it under "New Mike Judge Comedy."

Judge, who worked for years as an engineer at the kind of manhood-crushing cubicle jobs parodied in *Office Space*, is an intensely intelligent paleoconservative observer of Red State life and its degradation by liberal social mores and commercial vulgarization.

His recurrent themes are masculinity, class, IQ, and character. His hero Hank Hill of *King of the Hill* is the most admirable sit-com father since *The Cosby Show*, and likely the white TV dad most worthy of respect since the 1950s. Although a man of no more than average intelligence, Hank diligently embodies the traditional American manly virtues.

Idiocracy is an updating of C.M. Kornbluth's famous 1951 science fiction story about dysgenic breeding, "The Marching Morons." It opens with a yuppie husband and wife on the left half of the screen (IQs of 138 and 141, respectively) endlessly debating the perfect moment to conceive their one child: "We just can't have a child in this market." Meanwhile, on the right side, Clevon is impregnating every woman in the trailer park.

Unambitious Private Joe Bauers (Luke Wilson of *Old School*) is another of Judge's average man heroes. Because he scored at the median of every bell curve from IQ to blood pressure, Bauers is drafted for a military "human hibernation" experiment, an idea presumably lifted from Robert Heinlein's *The Door into Summer*, in which the Army keeps a few divisions on ice in case of war. Due to a scandal, the private is forgotten and awakes in 500 years. To his horror, he discovers that after 20 generations everyone is a Clevon, and he's now the smartest man in America.

As he showed in *Beavis & Butt-Head*, Judge has a genius for stupidity. The visual details of a Washington D.C. populated solely by morons are memorable: a collapsing skyscraper is held together by wrapping it with oversized twine; the White House has broken cars up on blocks on the dying lawn and the "President of America" is a professional wrestler; and at "St. God's Hospital" the illiterate admitting nurse is equipped with a fast food-style touch-screen menu with diagrams of ailments common in 2505 (such as a stick-figure man with a knife stuck in his head). All clothing is plastered with corporate logos and the Secretary of State is paid to insert the phrase "brought to you by Carl's Jr." into everything he says.

Although we like to think of the unintelligent as sweet Forrest Gumps, in Judge's dystopia everyone is a surly jerk to Pvt. Bauers because he speaks in complete sentences, which the denizens of the 26th century find "faggy."

"Idiocracy" isn't perfect. At only 84 minutes, it looks like it was hacked up in editing. A narrator very slowly explains natural selection and too many of the jokes.

Did Fox murder this film's release as part of a complex metamarketing plot to turn it into a DVD hit? Did the corporations satirized in it threaten to pull advertising from the Fox Network? Or did Fox executives not realize until after Judge had delivered his movie in 2004 that he'd lifted his basic idea from *The Bell Curve*, and that You Just Can't Say That anymore?

That the poor have more children than the rich has been observed at least since Adam Smith in 1776. The long-term effect is much less clear. Yet, can't an artist be allowed to explore the comic possibilities of a logic we've all privately thought about? Isn't this the land of the free and the home of the brave? I guess not.

A Matter of Tone

Taki's
August 25, 2021

AN racial gaps in cognitive skills narrow?

Possibly. After all, we have seen a number of historic examples of ethnicities pulling ahead of their neighbors by doing things smarter after they came to enthusiastically acknowledge the superiority of Western European modes of thought. Two famous examples of colonial collaborators were the Parsis of Bombay and the Igbo of southern Nigeria, who now score vastly higher on Nigerian college admissions tests than do the Muslims of northern Nigeria.[12]

The most famous example is Japan's sudden acquisition of the advantages of Western thinking after 1853. But perhaps the most historically significant is the Ashkenazi enlightenment that began in the second half of the 18th century. After centuries of being richer and more sophisticated than European Christians, Jewish philosophers like Moses Mendelssohn found their people falling behind, and thus advocated imitation of gentile breakthroughs.

On the other hand, despite its proven track record, in 2021 there isn't much momentum toward adopting what once worked for the West. Dogmatism is gaining in favor over empiricism. Great European intellectual accomplishments, such as the bell curve, worked out by geniuses like Laplace, Gauss, and Galton, are in disrepute because of what they can teach us.

Thus we are losing our former ability to grasp that statistical differences are not absolute differences. For instance, about 8 million African-Americans have higher IQs than the average white. But the fact that on average blacks have lower IQs is now considered unspeakable.

For example, in the ten weeks since the publication of Charles Murray's *Facing Reality: Two Truths About Race in America*, the *New York Times* has not deigned to mention its existence, even though it succinctly offers an Occam's Razor explanation of America's main racial disparity: Blacks have higher average levels of violent crime and lower average levels of intelligence.

Those who have responded to Murray's book have typically argued that these gaps couldn't possibly be innate.

Perhaps.

Indeed, *Facing Reality* doesn't take a stand on this question. In determining whether the policies advocated by Black Lives Matter are prudent right now, the academic question of whether, say, narrowing the IQ gap would take a few generations of rigorous training or many generations of evolution is not terribly relevant.

Yet, it's crucial to understand that if these disparities are not due to genes, then American society since 2013 has been going about trying to close them in the dumbest, most self-destructive way possible.

Assume that the problems of African-Americans today are due to blacks having largely missed out on the Western cognitive revolution that historian Alfred W. Crosby traces back to the 1200s.[13] This slowly converted Europeans from peasants to burghers by making them more quantitative, more bourgeois, more thoughtful, and more self-disciplined.

If so, then the purported solutions for black underachievement promoted by elites during the Great Awokening—blacks should be encouraged to resist arrest, to act out in school, to blame their failings on whites, to work less and nap more, and to demand cash without having to labor for it—are 180 degrees off target.

Our Establishment—rather than telling blacks that to avoid disciplining by the law they must self-discipline, that they need to inculcate their Weberian Protestant work ethic—has been egging on blacks' worst *lumpenproletariat* inclinations, with predictable results, such as the black murder rate being up by approaching 50% since Ferguson in 2014.

Indeed, black traffic fatalities soared 36% in the first seven months of the racial reckoning, June to December 2020, compared with the same period in 2019, as exultant blacks celebrated their liberation from the law by driving recklessly (and therefore wreckfully).[14]

On the other hand, the recent creation of spectacularly detailed longitudinal studies that include both cognitive test scores and DNA data for very large samples of individuals has allowed testing of the long-standing question of whether intelligence varies with racial admixture.

In the U.S., race is determined largely by self-identification. You (or your parents if you are a child) choose which boxes to check.

This sounds highly unscientific, so twenty years ago I set out to show how ridiculous the system was. But I eventually concluded that it was good enough for government work. Since then, DNA studies of ancestry have found a reasonable correlation among non-Hispanics between self-identification and racial genetics.

If race were purely a social construct, and the social designation of race is all that drives IQ score gaps, then the IQs of people within one race should be randomly distributed. In other words, among all those who self-identify as black, how much white ancestry they have should have little influence on their IQ scores.

On the other hand, if IQ differences between races are partly genetic, then people with more white genes from more white ancestors should score higher.

The basic logic of this question was laid out in a clever 1977 *Saturday Night Live* skit in which dark-skinned Garrett Morris interviews light-skinned Julian Bond, head of the NAACP (which darker blacks tended to call the National Association for the Advancement of *Certain* People because so many of its leaders from Walter White through Ben Jealous have been surprisingly fair in appearance), about the racial IQ gap:

> *Garrett Morris*: How did the idea of white intellectual superiority originate?
> *Julian Bond*: That's an interesting point. My theory is that it's based on the fact that light-skinned blacks are smarter than dark-skinned blacks.
> *Garrett Morris*: [Not sure he heard that right] Say what?...
> *Julian Bond*: It's got nothing to do with having white blood. It's just that descendants of the lighter-skinned African tribes are more intelligent than the descendants of the darker-skinned tribes. Everybody knows that.

Me being me, I wanted to know if Bond's punchline is factual. Looking at pictures online, I'd say no: The higher-scoring Igbo of southern Nigeria are blacker than the slightly North African-looking Fulani herders of northern Nigeria.

What about Bond's initial assertion that light-skinned blacks are smarter?

My impression is that Americans' perceptions honestly differ on this question.

One complexity that leads to disagreement is that more than a few of the smartest blacks in the U.S. in 2021 are all-black African immigrants selected for their academic potential.

A further complication is that while there are of course strong positive correlations among racial genes, genealogy, and looks, they don't trend together 100%, so there is some randomness. For instance, Barack Obama is half white, but looks more like he's perhaps one-quarter white.

And a major source of complexity that's not well understood is that while virtually all descendants of American slaves have some white ancestors, not many people who have two parents who identify as black trace more than half their family tree from Europe. In most genetic studies of African-Americans, about four-fifths of their ancestry is sub-Saharan, with a fairly narrow variance.

For instance, in the latest admixture study, "Genetic Ancestry and General Cognitive Ability in a Sample of American Youths" by John Fuerst and Gregory Connor, less than 3% of the children in the nationally representative Adolescent Brain Cognitive Development (ABCD) cohort whose parents identify them as black have over 50% white DNA.[15]

(Lavishly funded, the ABCD is a giant study of 11,750 children that has generated 140 terabytes of data. The ABCD includes an elaborate series of cognitive tests from which IQ scores can be calculated, while racial ancestry can be determined from the genome data in the manner of *Ancestry.com*. The findings are available in anonymized form to expert outside researchers for their own analyses.)

Note that the authors break out a separate Other group for non-Hispanic and non-Asian subjects whose parents consider them more than one of the following: white, black, and American Indian. So, the black group in this report consists of kids considered only black by their parents. (The analysts aren't trying to trick anybody by their methodology; they are clarifying their subjects down to the ones whom Americans are most likely to think of when they talk about black and white: e.g., Michael Jordan rather than Tiger Woods.)

In Fuerst and Connor's sample of 1,690 black-only kids ages 9 to 10, the average genetic ancestry is 16% white (a little lower than most such studies) with a standard deviation of 11%. So, the great majority of African-Americans are under, say, 3/8ths white.

In contrast, among the more than 5,000 children whose parents list them as non-Hispanic white-only, their average white ancestry is 98% (e.g., one black and one Native American ancestor seven generations ago), with an even narrower variance.

This means that there is very little overlap in admixture percentage between self-identifying non-Hispanic whites and self-identifying non-Hispanic blacks.

Why? The Anglo-Saxon concept of the "color line" restricting intermarriage between the races meant that part-black lineages tended to regress over the generations toward the black mean for admixture percentage, unless an ancestor made the arduous leap into "passing" as white, after which the lineage would regress toward the white mean. For example, there emerged over time black Hemmings and white Hemmings, but not many distinctly in-between.

Outside of Louisiana—where the Latin concept of the "color continuum" reigned and thus there were born quite a few prominent people who were mostly but not overwhelmingly white, such as pianist Jelly Roll Morton, literary critic Anatole Broyard, and drag racer Don Prudhomme—there just weren't, until recently, all that many Americans who were visibly part-black but less than half-black by DNA.

Within the restricted range of admixture found among self-identified black-only children, the new report found a positive but small correlation between white ancestry percentage and cognitive test scores for the general factor of intelligence of .10 for all blacks and .13 excluding immigrant stock.

An African-American who has 27% white admixture (one standard deviation above the black mean, about the 84th percentile) would average about three IQ points higher than one who is 5% white (one standard deviation below the black mean in admixture, about the 16th percentile).

Three IQ points is not negligible, but neither is it highly noticeable either. I'd say it's around the edge of perceptibility, which is why people tend to honestly disagree on the Bond-Morris question.

But the gap in white admixture between the average self-identifying black (16%) and the average self-identifying white (98%) is over seven standard deviations. And the white-black gap in the g factor of IQ on the ABCD cognitive tests is around a standard deviation of fifteen points.

Fuerst explains:

> In the Lasker paper, we explained a simple way of thinking about this, which [Arthur] Jensen had pointed out in a reply to Sandra Scarr.
>
> Take a look at our Table 1. Black Americans have a mean 16% European ancestry with a standard deviation of 11%, while Whites have 98% European ancestry.
>
> So, a hypothetical Black American with 98% European ancestry (and there actually was one in the sample) would be (98%-16%) / 11% = 7.45 standard deviations above the Black mean in terms of European ancestry. The advantage in g would then be this times the correlation between g and European ancestry among Blacks, which was between .10 and .13, depending on how you wanted to handle recent African immigrants. And so the g advantage would be .75 SD to .97 SD above the Black mean. The latter number is practically the entire difference.

Interestingly, this 2021 analysis of the ABCD database more or less replicates a 2019 study co-authored by Bryan J. Pesta, a professor at Cleveland State, of the Philadelphia Neurodevelopmental Cohort of nearly 10,000 youngsters.[16]

Now, these two papers don't prove that genetics explain a sizable portion of the race gap in intelligence. It could be, for example, that bias against darker African-Americans depresses their IQ scores.

And yet, as a white American, I have a hard time remembering moderate differences in skin tone among black celebrities: Michael Jordan, I recall, is dark, Obama middling, and Beyoncé light. But what about the precise coloration of LeBron, Oprah, O.J., Eddie Murphy, Bill Cosby, Stevie Wonder, Denzel Washington, Will Smith, Prince, Jesse Jackson, and Al Sharpton? (To simplify things, we'll leave Michael Jackson out.)

Truth be told, I have most of them categorized in my mind simply as "black," and I don't devote a lot of brainpower to remembering subtler tonal distinctions than that.

If anybody is discriminating much on degrees of color, it is likely other blacks.

So, while these studies of two extraordinarily sophisticated new databases haven't established definitively that the racial gap in IQ is substantially genetic in origin, they have certainly failed to falsify that theory.

Considering the vast acclaim that would be bestowed upon any researcher who did falsify this most feared and loathed of all scientific hypotheses, it's curious that most pundits assume it has already been utterly disproven...but they just can't quite remember the name of the guy who did it.

CHAPTER EIGHT

The Blank Screen

Excerpt: *America's Half-Blood Prince*

published by the VDare Foundation, 2008

An excerpt from my 2008 book America's Half-Blood Prince: Barack Obama's "Story of Race and Inheritance," *a reader's guide to Obama's memoir* Dreams From My Father.

> I am new enough on the national political scene that I serve as a blank screen on which people of vastly different political stripes project their own views. As such, I am bound to disappoint some, if not all, of them. Which perhaps indicates a second, more intimate theme to this book—namely, how I, or anybody in public office, can avoid the pitfalls of fame, the hunger to please, the fear of loss, and thereby retain that kernel of truth, that singular voice within each of us that reminds us of our deepest commitments.
>
> Barack Obama
The Audacity of Hope, 2006

THE fundamental irony of Sen. Barack Obama's Presidential candidacy is that no nominee in living memory has been so misunderstood by the press and public, and yet no other candidate has ever written so eloquently (or, to be frank, endlessly) about his "deepest commitments."

While journalists have swarmed to Alaska with admirable alacrity to ferret out every detail of Sarah Palin's energetic life, the media have drawn a curtain of admiring incomprehension in front of Obama's own exquisitely written autobiography, *Dreams from My Father*. Because few have taken the trouble to appreciate Obama on his own terms, the politician functions as our national blank slate upon which we sketch out our social fantasies.

In 2000, without much insight into the real George W. Bush, America elected a pig in a poke to be President. How has that worked out for us? Putting partisan divisions aside, wouldn't it seem like a good idea, on general principles, to try to understand clearly what a Presidential nominee has written about his innermost identity?

Obama spent the first four decades of his life trying to prove to blacks that he's black enough. If the public were finally to become well-enough informed about Obama's own autobiography to compel him to spend the four or eight years of his Presidency trying to prove to the nation as a whole that his "deepest commitments" are to his country rather than to his race, America would be better off.

This book serves as a reader's guide to Obama's *Dreams from My Father*. The would-be President has written a long, luxuriant, and almost incomprehensible book, so I have penned a (relatively) short and brusque book that explains who Obama thinks he is.

Many Americans, whether for Obama, McCain, or None of the Above, appreciate the patriotic, anti-racialist sentiment in the most famous sentence of Obama's keynote address to the 2004 Democratic Convention: "There is not a Black America and a White America and Latino America and Asian America—there's the United States of America."

Yet, Obama's white enthusiasts are often excited by the candidate's race, and for diverse motivations. More than a few white people, for instance, wish to demonstrate their moral and cultural superiority over more backward members of their own race. As Christian Lander's popular website *Stuff White People Like* acerbically documents, white people strive endlessly for prestige relative to other whites, scanning constantly for methods to claw their way to the top of the heap. In this status struggle nonwhites seldom register on white people's radar screens as rivals. Instead, white people see minorities more as useful props in the eternal scuffle to gain the upper hand over other whites. High on Lander's list of stuff white people like is:

> #8 Barack Obama
> Because white people are afraid that if they don't like him that they will be called racist.

As one of Hillary Clinton's advisers explained to *The Guardian*:

If you have a social need, you're with Hillary. If you want Obama to be your imaginary hip black friend and you're young and you have no social needs, then he's cool.

White voters are hungry for a well-educated role model for blacks. And blacks hope that his wife Michelle and his long membership in Rev. Dr. Jeremiah A. Wright, Jr.'s Trinity United Church of Christ are evidence that he is, as Michelle says, keeping it real.

Whatever their reasons, conscious or unconscious, white Obama zealots are prone to assume that Obama is the Tiger Woods of politics: as the postracial product of a happy mixed race family, he must be the anti-Jesse Jackson. His election will enable America to put all that tiresome tumult over ethnicity behind us.

Since 2004, Obama has himself stoked the popular hope among whites that his admixture of black and white genes means that "trying to promote mutual understanding" is "in my DNA," as he asserted at the April 29, 2008 press conference in which he finally disowned his longtime pastor.

Obama launched himself on the national stage at the 2004 convention by devoting the first 380 words of his speech to detailing the two stocks, black and white, from which he was crossbred. He implied that, like the mutual heir to a dynastic merger of yore—think of England's King Henry VIII, offspring of the Lancaster-York marriage that ended the War of the Roses—he is the one we've been waiting for to end the War of the Races.

What kind of President would Barack Obama turn out to be?

I don't like to make predictions because I hate being wrong. It's especially hard to be right about the future interplay of personalities and events. In 2000, another under-examined Presidential candidate, George W. Bush, was elected while promising what his chief foreign affairs advisor, Condoleezza Rice, called for a more "modest" foreign policy.

Then, 9/11 happened.

Whether events would constrain or liberate Obama's "deepest commitments" is impossible to say at this point.

A few likelihoods seem apparent, though. In Obama, ambition and caution are yoked. Becoming President is not his ultimate objective. Becoming a two-term President is. Republican Richard Nixon's first Administration was one of the most liberal in American history. There were hints at the beginning of his second term, before Watergate washed every bit of policy coherence away, that Nixon, having safely won re-election, intended to move toward his innate conservatism. That analogy suggests that a second Obama administration might more truly reflect the real Obama.

What we can discuss with more foreknowledge is the subject dearest to his heart, race, since that never goes away. Events may wax and wane, but the black-white racial situation in the U.S. has changed little since it stabilized in the early 1970s.

First, the reason Obama is on the threshold of the White House is that he more or less blundered into the opportunity of a lifetime. His original plan to be a conventional race man collapsed with his defeat by Rep. Bobby Rush in early 2000. Rush's media consultant Eric Adelstein noted:

> "Certain Democrats in Chicago say it's the best thing that ever happened to [Obama], not winning that race—that he couldn't have been positioned to run for the U.S. Senate from that district.... In that district, you get pigeonholed pretty quickly as 'an African-American congressman,' not as a more transcendent congressman."

Due to racial gerrymandering to ensure the existence of "majority-minority" districts, the House of Representatives has become a career dead-end for black politicians. In Rush's district, Obama would have had to act more like Rush.

At some point following that humiliating rebuff by black voters, Obama, with the assistance of campaign strategist David Axelrod, came up with the Half-Blood Prince strategy of running as the man born and bred to unite black and white. The New Obama is the candidate who is half-white when whites think about voting for him. Yet, he remains all-black, and thus off-limits to polite public skepticism, when anyone tries to get up the courage to criticize him more harshly than by merely saying he is inexperienced.

In any case, numerous white moderates are kidding themselves when they make up stories about how Obama will solve race problems.

If elected, this "blank screen" candidate would inevitably disappoint at least some of his enthusiasts. After all, they espouse profoundly contradictory hopes.

Which ones will he disillusion?

Rather than make a prediction, I prefer to take a more Heisenbergian approach. As Barack Obama Sr. no doubt could have pointed out, Marx said, "The philosophers have only interpreted the world, in various ways; the point is to change it."

EXCERPT: AMERICA'S HALF-BLOOD PRINCE

The point of this book is to change a potential Obama Administration for the better by making the public a little less ignorant about Obama. For all his talk of "audacity," Obama is far more cautious than his brash father was. Fortunately, the son remains a work in progress. His opportunism makes him deterrable. The less gullible the American people are about who Obama truly is, the better chance we have of keeping him from trying to fulfill his "deepest commitments."

More broadly, America has had it easy for decades, but the fat years are coming to an end. We aren't so rich anymore that we can continue to get by with a conventional wisdom built on ignorance, lies, and spin.

The widespread assumption that Obama must be our Half-Blood Prince, born and bred to resolve our racial disputes, is symptomatic of American elites' loosening grip on reality regarding anything dealing with "diversity." Recall how the media, both parties, academia, and Wall Street all pushed for 15 years for laxer mortgage lending standards for minorities...with catastrophic results.

Why? Because everyone who was anyone had agreed that only evil people publicly display skepticism about diversity.

Similarly, the American establishment has been so intellectually enfeebled by political correctness that for two years we've all been fed a steady diet of David Axelrod's implausible campaign concoction starring the author of *Dreams from My Father* as the Great Race Transcender. All these months, our elites barely mentioned (or even noticed) the subtitle of the "postracial" candidate's autobiography: *A Story of Race and Inheritance*.

It's time for new elites.

Making Sense of Obama: The Muslimist

Taki's
October 31, 2012

WHO is the real Barack Obama?

It's an odd question to ask about an incumbent president less than a week before he's up for reelection. It's an especially strange inquiry to make of a president as self-obsessed and introspectively voluble as Obama.

Yet Obama has been the subject of so much fantasizing (not least by Obama himself) that the actual man remains occluded.

A simple explanation of Obama's strengths and weaknesses has finally occurred to me.

The first two-dozen years of Obama's life saw him on a path for a professional niche that nobody has quite explicated before. Until he upped stakes and moved to Chicago in 1985 to participate in the Council Wars racial struggle with the implausible goal of becoming mayor of Chicago, Obama was gliding down an unusual path: to become an international interlocutor, a graceful go-between connecting America and the Muslim world.

In the classic 1974 science-fiction novel *The Mote in God's Eye* by Larry Niven and Jerry Pournelle, humanity comes into contact with an alien race whose ambassadors are articulate, elegant, and empathetic. They can listen to a human's stumbling explanation of his wants and repeat it back to him more deftly than he did. Only slowly do the humans grasp that these polite, likable envoys are merely one caste among the aliens, a special breed called the "mediators."

Here on planet Earth, international intermediaries are not yet bred to specification. Still, area experts and emissaries tend to emerge from certain backgrounds, classes, and personality types.

In American history, Foreign Service specialists are often the mild-mannered descendants of adventuresome old Protestants who became bored with their rocky Northeastern farms, such as the Yankee sea captains, merchants, and Protestant missionaries who dominated 19th-century America's contacts with less developed cultures abroad such as the Kingdom of Hawaii.

In 1971, the ten-year-old Barack Obama enrolled in Punahou School, Hawaii's flagship of Yankee culture. Punahou had been founded 130 years before by the Vermont missionary Hiram Bingham I. Upon Bingham, James Michener had modeled his villain, the Rev. Abner Hale, in his 1959 bestseller *Hawaii*.

As Obama notes in his stump speeches, the Dunhams were from Kansas, but from a particularly Yankee-leaning part of the Jayhawk State. For instance, his grandfather's brother Ralph, a Berkeley Ph.D., traced his name back to that ultimate Unitarian, Ralph Waldo Emerson. (The president's grandmother also had a sibling who earned a doctorate.)

In American history, the two most controversial castes of missionary-derived mandarins were the Old China Hands and the Arabists.

The former were typically sons of Protestant missionaries born or raised in China, such as Owen Lattimore, John Paton Davies, Jr., and John S. Service. The left-leaning diplomatic, academic, and journalistic China Hands clashed with the right-leaning China Lobby in the 1940s and 1950s over whether American should back Mao Tse-tung or Chiang Kai-shek. Was Chiang a loser or was Mao a lunatic? (Unfortunately, it turned out that both could be true simultaneously.)

Similarly, as outlined in Robert D. Kaplan's 1995 book *The Arabists: The Romance of an American Elite*, Protestant missionaries from the Atlantic Seaboard voyaged to the Arab world in the 19th century. They didn't have much luck converting the locals to Protestantism. (Obama's Columbia professor Edward Said was a rare Arab Protestant.) But these intermarried families founded influential schools such as the American University of Beirut.

The Arabists played an influential role in American foreign policy until largely being squeezed out by Zionists angered with Arabist sympathy for the Palestinians.

Much of the Muslim world, however, is not Arab—for example, Indonesia, Pakistan, and large parts of black Africa. And that opened up a potential career path not as an Arabist per se, but as a Muslimist. The Muslimist route became especially promising in 1973 with the Muslim-dominated OPEC's emergence as an economic power. The oil cartel included not only Saudi Arabia, the Emirates, Libya, and Iran, but also Indonesia and part-Muslim Nigeria.

And who was better suited by family, friends, and personality to become a professional Muslimist than Barack Obama? As Obama told his biographer David Maraniss, the "obvious path for me given my background" was to get a graduate degree in international relations and wind up "working in the State Department, in the Foreign Service, or working for an international foundation...."[1]

After all, how common is it for an American citizen to be the biological son of an East African government official and a Ford Foundation employee in Jakarta, and the stepson of an Indonesian who works in government relations for an American oil company because his brother-in-law was in charge of mineral rights for the Jakarta regime?

A few of us have pointed out that the young Obama had numerous two-degrees-of-separation connections with the CIA.[2] Obama himself implied in his autobiography that his mother worked at the US Embassy in Jakarta with purported diplomats who were actually Company operatives.

But little evidence has emerged that Obama was ever cut out to be a cut-out. A less glamorous but more plausible notion is that Obama was never suited for being a spy pretending to be a diplomat. A good agent looks boring on the outside, such as Gary Oldman in *Tinker Tailor Soldier Spy*. In contrast, glory-hogging Obama appears exotic on the outside but is boring on the inside.

Instead, he always had the makings of a plain old diplomat.

Obama's elders recognized that this career path made sense for him. Thus, at substantial expense, he attended Occidental, an underachieving but quite WASPy/international liberal-arts college, and then majored in international relations at Columbia.

Most of Obama's male friends from age 18 through 24 were rich Pakistani Marxists, putting him on the fringes of the powerful Bhutto circle. (They all saw Obama as much less African-American than as "international.")

But it's also telling that his best American buddy, Phil Boerner, with whom he transferred from Occidental to Columbia in 1981, was the son of a peripatetic diplomat.

Likewise, Obama's most serious New York girlfriend, Genevieve Cook, was the daughter of a top Australian diplomat/spy in Indonesia who later became Australia's ambassador to America. Genevieve was also the stepdaughter of the chief counsel of the International Nickel Company, which had lucrative mining interests in Indonesia. (Continuing this Muslimist theme, she rebounded from Obama to marry the son of an Egyptian educator.)

Many have invoked Obama's mother's Ph.D. in anthropology as a key to his watchful persona, but academia is not quite the best analogy. His mother frequently abandoned him to his grandparents' care to work on her 1,043-page Ph.D. dissertation on Indonesian blacksmiths. Obama, in contrast, has been remarkably lacking in the urge to do original work, except in writing about himself. He has All-But-Dissertation written all over him.

Obama's dearth of creativity would not be a defect in, say, a Foreign Service lifer, where his job would have been to relay messages from the State Department to the host government and vice-versa. The "blank screen" aspect of Obama's personality would have suited him well for a job as a relay.

Obama's most obvious talent is that he is good at listening to people speak and then repeating it back accurately and elegantly, showing comprehension as well as rote memorization. This is a crucial skill for diplomats—the ability to grasp the implications of what the foreign official is saying and pass it back to Foggy Bottom.

But Obama didn't like the messages coming from Washington in the 1980s, enormously successful as Reagan's foreign policy turned out to be. Reagan's landslide reelection in 1984 was followed by Obama's bizarre turn to insular Chicago politics in 1985.

Besides Obama's leftism in a Republican era, the fundamental problem with a Foreign Service career from his perspective may have been that diplomats are intermediaries. They are supposed to be efficient pipelines for messages between the true seats of power.

And Obama has a hunger for power, which is tied into his fixation of "playing out a superhero life," according to his ex-girlfriend. It's a seeming anomaly in a low-energy person such as Obama, but the word "power" is a mantra throughout *Dreams from My Father*.

This helps explain his otherwise ludicrous obsession with becoming mayor of Chicago, the least likely job in the world for an elegantly mannered International Man of Mystery.

When Harold Washington was elected mayor in 1983 and immediately got into a huge racial struggle with the white majority of the aldermen—the Council Wars—Obama became galvanized by the notion of the mayor of Chicago as a powerful man, somebody with clout. That was a comically juvenile ambition because you can't be mayor of Chicago if you are an outsider. I moved to Chicago a few years before Obama did, and it never occurred to me to go into Chicago politics.

Obama's upbringing to be a Muslimist helps explain something that puzzles all of Washington: What hold does his wife's old boss, Valerie Jarrett, that empty pantsuit, have on him? Jarrett was Obama's door in to Chicago's tiny black upper class, the only African-Americans with whom Obama feels comfortable. More than that, though, Jarrett, like Obama, had lived in a Muslim country (Iran) as a child.

It's hard to imagine Obama going terribly far in Chicago politics as a Muslimist. But since he was a black politician, Jewish liberal real-estate interests in Chicago such as the Pritzkers adopted him. They didn't take his ambition to be mayor seriously; instead, they thought he should be president!

Would they have been as enthusiastic if he was a professional Muslimist? Likely not.

And perhaps that will be history's judgment on Obama's extraordinary career: It was all just sort of a misunderstanding.

Obama the Musical

Taki's
November 5, 2014

NO doubt the results of the midterm election are being interpreted as a referendum on Obama. But who exactly is this curious individual, and why did we make him president? I've long argued that the most interesting thing about Obama is what we can learn from his career as a "blank screen" upon which Americans project all their myths, longings, and inchoate fantasies about race.

After eight years of trying to make sense of Obama's life story, I've stumbled upon a way to put his famous origin story in historical context, to make it not quite so random.

A particularly screwy aspect of the first black president is that he didn't seem to his friends to be black until in 1985 he suddenly turned his back on the first 24 years of his life and asserted a black identity to replace his previous "international" and "multicultural" identities.

Previously, Obama had been guided by his family and friends (none of whom were black) toward a reasonable career working for U.S. institutions in non-Arab Muslim countries in Asia or Africa: a professional "Muslimist."

Central to Obama's life is Hawaii. In almost all discussions of Obama, whether birther or mainstream, Hawaii is treated as essentially irrelevant to Obama's parentage, a run-of-the-mill location. For example, because Obama's autobiography, *Dreams from My Father: A Story of Race and Inheritance*, was written for mainlanders interested only in black and white, it barely touches on Hawaiian society. And that's convenient for Obama, because 1950s Hawaii's extreme racial liberalism (some 30% of marriages were interracial) doesn't fit in well with contemporary prejudices about America's racist past.

Yet when Obama's 17-year-old mother arrived in Hawaii in 1960 and quickly became pregnant by an exotic black man, Hawaii was of obsessive interest to the liberal mainstream imagination as the leading symbol of America's new post-colonial empire.

It turns out that the strange life the President's mother forged for herself by marrying men of other races brought to Hawaii by Cold War initiatives wasn't just driven by this adventuress's own idiosyncratic desires, as an embarrassed and annoyed Obama discussed in *Dreams from My Father*. She was also following (in an extreme fashion) the messages being transmitted in the 1950s by the most respected voices of mainstream culture about what progressive, patriotic Americans should believe—and even do—in order to ensure the triumph of the free world.

Having been born in Southern California a few years before Obama, I can recall Hawaii's outsized role in American popular culture in the 1960s. For example, the number one box office movie of 1966 was the lavish adaptation of James Michener's innovative 1959 novel *Hawaii*, with Julie Andrews playing the wife of a fictionalized version of the New England missionary Hiram Bingham I, who founded the Punahou School in 1841 (from which Obama graduated in 1979).

Michener was a WWII naval officer whose first book, *Tales from the South Pacific*, was adapted into the 1949 Broadway hit *South Pacific*, with music by Richard Rodgers and book and lyrics by Oscar Hammerstein II.

Hawaii was the novel in which Michener introduced his trademark style that made him the middlebrow publishing sensation of his generation. "Middlebrow" is a term of critical abuse for artists who combine information, entertainment, and uplift, but, in truth, those are all good things. And Michener was prodigiously educational. Back then, if you were going somewhere on a vacation, there was likely a 900-page Michener novel covering the entire history of the place from the Ice Age to the Space Age by tracking a few family trees over the centuries.

I recently discovered a 2003 academic book, *Cold War Orientalism: Asia in the Middlebrow Imagination, 1945-1961*, by Christina Klein, a Boston College English professor. It documents that I'm not just hallucinating my childhood memories of Hawaii's cultural centrality, and explains why state-hood for Hawaii in 1959 was seen by Cold War liberals as such a triumph.

The writers Michener and Hammerstein figure largely in Klein's book, and rightly so. The two classy Democratic Protestants embodied postwar liberalism at its expansive and earnest peak as it tried to reengineer Americans to be able to grapple with the global responsibilities Washington took on in the 1940s.

Hammerstein enjoyed a titanic career on Broadway, from *Show Boat* in 1927 through *Oklahoma!, Carousel,* and *The Sound of Music.* The estates of Rodgers and Hammerstein sold the rights to their copyrights for $235 million due to the endless revivals of their shows, including high school productions that continue to engrain Hammerstein's liberal didacticism in today's youth.

Intermarriage was a theme that ran throughout Hammerstein's works, beginning with Show Boat's sympathetic depiction of a black-white marriage.

Michener and Hammerstein worked hard, together on *South Pacific* and apart in other pieces, to rid American society of prejudice against intermarriage. They had personal and professional reasons.

The father of Oscar Greeley Clendenning Hammerstein II (an aggressively non-Jewish set of given names, by the way) was German Jewish and his mother Scottish and English. Michener was adopted, and the third wife he married in 1955 was named Mari Yoriko Sabusawa.

The professional reason is that in English-language literature and theater, nothing appeals more to the sympathies of audiences than lovers separated by social conventions, as demonstrated by the greatest WASP of them all, William Shakespeare, in *Romeo and Juliet.*

Out of Michener's 19 short stories, Hammerstein selected for *South Pacific's* book the two involving some form of miscegenation. Lt. Joe Cable loves a Tonkinese girl, but does he dare bring her home to Philadelphia's Main Line? Nurse Nellie Forbush (whom my wife played in a high school production) falls in love with an older French planter, but is shocked to discover he has two half-Islander children.

South Pacific was the first of Rodgers and Hammerstein's three musicals about Asians and Pacific Islanders. The other two are *The King and I*—which is driven by the unconsummated sexual tension between the Victorian Englishwoman and the King of Siam—and the all-Asian-American *Flower Drum Song.*

America in the 1945-1965 era is stereotyped as insular and "white-bread," but its middlebrow kings, Rodgers and Hammerstein and Michener, were infatuated with the foreign. Today, if white guys like them tried to do anything as exotic and crazy as, say, "The Small House of Uncle Thomas" ballet in *The King and I*—the Burmese slave girl's adaptation of *Uncle Tom's Cabin*—they would be given a long lecture about Edward Said's theory of Orientalism.

Michener's *Hawaii* was published in 1959, the year Hawaii became a state and regular jet airliner service was inaugurated. A year later the President's grandparents and mother arrived from Seattle. Hawaii occupied a strategic spot, both geographically and ideologically. Klein notes:

> Defense dollars poured into the islands and became a pillar of the post-plantation economy, providing a livelihood for fully one-fourth of the islands' population; more than any other state, Hawaii depended financially upon the continuation of the Cold War.

Likely of more interest to the young Stanley Ann Dunham when she arrived was the vanguard cultural role Hawaii had been assigned:

> The U.S. government also treated Hawaii as an important location from which to wage the struggle for the hearts and minds of Asia.

Granting Hawaii statehood was intended to symbolize the new multiracial America that would appeal to the developing countries:

> Hawaii's campaign for statehood, which ran more or less continuously from 1945 to 1959, kept the territory alive in the nation's political culture.... Race was the big issue: people of Asian and Pacific background outnumbered whites three to one.... There was no legal segregation on the islands and intermarriage was common, with about 10% of marriages before World War I and more than 30% in the 1950s taking place between people of different races.

Southern Democrats fought a rearguard action against admitting Hawaii as a state, but were ultimately overwhelmed by the globalist imperatives for which Michener was an able spokesman:

> To Michener, Hawaii's familial and cultural ties to Asia made it worth incorporating into the Union. He saw the people of Hawaii as an exploitable natural resource who could facilitate U.S. global expansion by serving as native informants and guides.... Other statehood advocates shared this view. BusinessWeek in 1950 ex-

plained that "the islands have brought to the U.S. a new national resource—a population that is the logical stepping stone between the U.S. and the Orient—and went on to praise these people as the "logical intermediaries to carry an understanding of U.S. democracy to the Orient." One of the Congressional committees investigating statehood came to a similar conclusion: "Many of her people have their racial background in that Asian area," ... as a result, Hawaii could become a "natural training ground for leaders to administer American interests in this area."

The traditional understanding of America as a country for whites was seen as a detriment in waging the Cold War:

If Hawaiian statehood rendered America a little less white and Western in its national identity, that was apparently fine with many statehood advocates.... *Newsweek* in 1959 similarly noted that ... "no longer would America be known as a 'land of the white man' and 'tarred with the brush of "colonialism."'" *Time* in turn celebrated statehood as an act through which America "leaped over its old, European-rooted consciousness of Caucasian identity."

These Cold War arguments were repeated a half dozen years later in pushing the 1965 Immigration and Nationality Act.

The federally funded flagship for fighting this cultural Cold War was the U. of Hawaii's East-West Center, with which the President's mother would be affiliated for much of her life:

In 1959 Washington launched the East-West Center in Honolulu, which the Saturday Review hailed, in yet another reworking of Kipling, as the place "Where the Twain Will Meet." The East-West Center promoted both cultural policies of integration and military policies of containment. Designed as a counterpart to Moscow's Friendship University, it brought Asian, Pacific, and American students together in one setting; at the same time it coordinated grants for Indonesian military officers who were undergoing small-arms training before the 1965 military coup that, with the goal of eradicating communism, left a half-million Indonesians dead.

In Janny Scott's 2011 biography of the President's mother, *A Singular Woman*, Obama's half-sister Maya jokes:

"We often say that Mom met her husbands at the East-West Center."

Scott goes on to note that this wasn't unusual:

> Students who married after coming to the center had at least a 33% chance of marrying across national or ethnic lines.

Stanley Ann Dunham Obama Soetoro's predilection for marrying natives reflects a female version of an old WASP pattern that goes far back. In the 21st century, American history is increasingly retconned to emphasize how racist the past was. But the reality was that racial barriers were sharp-edged only with blacks. In fact, Yankee adventurers helped spread American power via strategic marriages to targeted native elites.

What the president's mother did in marrying men of different races picked out by the American intelligence apparatus as future leaders in their homelands was novel only in that she was a WASP adventuress rather than a WASP adventurer.

Traditionally, this flexibility in marriage rules gave the English and their American descendants some political and business advantages over more ethnocentric and illiberal rival cultures that practiced arranged marriage until far more recently, such as Jews. This Anglo preference for giving young people the freedom to contract love matches goes back many centuries.[3]

Ruling class Yankees of mixed ancestry have included the legendary head of CIA counterintelligence James Jesus Angleton, whose mother was Mexican. George P. Bush, who appears to be penciled in by the Bushes for the White House some time after his father Jeb is done with it, also has a Mexican mother.

In early 19th-century California, sailors from Boston and New York would jump ship in the sleepy Mexican province. The most enterprising Yankees would convert to Catholicism and marry the daughters of local landowners (who were typically triracial). Then in the 1840s, the Yankees helped subvert Mexican rule and sponsor California's annexation by the U.S.

Similarly, Northeastern merchants arriving in Hawaii married into the native Hawaiian royal family and obtained title to huge expanses of some of the most beautiful land in the world. In Alexander Payne's 2011 movie *The Descendants*, George Clooney plays a 1/32nd native Hawaiian scion of a King Estate that owns 25,000 acres of Hawaii. In reality, the Bishop Estate—which originated in the 1850 marriage of Princess Bernice Pauahi Pākī to merchant Charles Reed Bishop of upstate New York—owns 365,000 acres, or 9% of Hawaii.

Another Hawaiian example was John Palmer Parker of Massachusetts, who married a native chief's daughter in 1816. His descendant Richard Smart (1913-1992) inherited the half-million-acre Parker Ranch on the Big Island. In keeping with this column's song and dance theme, it's worth noting that the one-quarter Polynesian cattle baron was also a musical comedy leading man who was given his big break on Broadway in 1940 by the future director of *South Pacific*, Josh Logan.

Now, it may seem like I'm just cherry-picking examples for this novel category of "not exactly white but very WASP foreign policy guys." But consider the politician who may have been Obama's role model: his rival for the 2008 Democratic nomination, former UN Ambassador Bill Richardson.

The vaguely mestizo-looking Richardson is 3/4ths Hispanic and 1/4th Boston upper crust. Richardson's father broke Dwight Eisenhower's leg in a 1913 college football game between Tufts and Army, then headed what's now Citibank's office in Mexico City, where he married his secretary. Richardson grew up in Mexico City until boarding school in Concord, Massachusetts at 13. After earning an international relations degree at Tufts, he became a staffer for the Senate Foreign Relations Committee.

Much as Obama did seven years later by moving to Chicago to become a community organizer, foreign policy whiz kid Richardson reinvented himself in 1978 as a Hispanic politician by moving to Santa Fe, New Mexico. He won eight terms in the House. His friend Bill Clinton made him UN Ambassador and Energy Secretary and he later won two terms as governor of New Mexico by wide margins.

In other words, going into the 2008 nomination race, Richardson was vastly more experienced than Obama on the national and world stage, much more successful at winning elections, and more Latino than Obama is black. Richardson launched his candidacy in heavily Hispanic Los Angeles with a bilingual speech denouncing immigration control. "No fence ever built has stopped history," he thundered.

Yet, despite his resume and all the theoretical power of the Latino tidal wave we keep hearing about, Richardson's candidacy was an utter flop with Democratic voters.

Why?

For the same reason that Obama changed identities in 1985: because black and white is still what gets people excited.

Obama is now a couple of years away from retiring to play golf and give speeches to Goldman Sachs. Like the Yankee missionaries who went to Hawaii, it will perhaps be said of him that he went to the South Side of Chicago to do good and wound up doing well.

CHAPTER NINE

World War T

Why Lesbians Aren't Gay

National Review
May 30, 1994

A WARM Saturday afternoon in late May brings all of Chicago to the lakefront. In the Wrigleyville section of Lincoln Park, softball teams with names like "We Are Everywhere" and "The 10 Percenters" compete with an intensity that could shame the Cubs. Girded for battle with sliding pads, batting gloves, and taped ankles, the short-haired women slash extra-base hits, turn the double play, and hit the cutoff woman with a practiced efficiency that arouses admiring shouts from the women spectators.

Meanwhile, on a grassy lakeside bluff a few blocks to the south, the men of the New Town neighborhood bask, golden, in the sun. If ever a rogue urge to strike a ball with a stick is felt by any of the elegantly sprawled multitude, it is quickly subdued. This absence of athletic strife is certainly not the result of any lack of muscle tone: many have clearly spent the dark months in thrall to SoloFlex and StairMaster. But now, the sun is shining and the men are content for their sculpted bodies to be rather than to do.

What are we to make of all this? What does it say about human nature that so many enthusiasms of the average lesbian and the average gay man diverge so strikingly? What broader lessons about current social issues can we learn from this contrariness of their tendencies, this dissimilarity of lesbian and gay passions that has been dimly observable in many cultures and ages, but that now in the wide open, self-fulfillment obsessed America of the 1990s is unmistakable? Well, apparently, we'd be best off not thinking too

Personality	Gay Male Tendencies	Lesbian Tendencies	Comments & Examples
Picnic activity	Sunbathe	Play softball	Softball has been the lesbian game since WWII
Bar activity	Dance	Shoot pool	AIDS has decimated choreographers
Opinion of perfume	Enjoy	Resent	"Scent-free zones" at lesbian-feminist venues
Interest in fashion	High	Low	Versace, Perry Ellis, Yves Saint Laurent
Sense of humor	Campy, self-deprecating, waspish	Satirical, political	You don't see many lesbian drag king shows
Fantasy job	Entertainer	Pro athlete	Lesbians about 30% of golf/tennis touring pros
Leadership drive	Low	High	Male vs. female officer corps
Motivated by need for	Attention & adoration	Leadership & domination	Gay figure skaters vs. lesbian army officers
Distinctive trait	Gay	Resentful	"We're not gay, we're angry!"
Sex	Ravaged by AIDS	Untouched by AIDS	But breast cancer hits lesbians hard
	Promiscuity	Monogamy	Lesbian bathouses in S.F. were big flop
	High sexual activity level	Low sexual activity level	"Lesbian Bed Death" syndrome
	Fascinated by beauty	Resent male fascination with beauty	*Death in Venice*, *Billy Budd* and other operas by Britten
	Avid for pornography	Outraged by porn	But verbal erotica popular with some lesbians
	Often have sex in a semi-public spot	Sex at home	It's dangerous to bring many strange men home
	Fantasy & degradation	Less adventurous	Leather/S&M vs. cuddling
	Gays absent from hetero porn	"Lesbians" a staple of hetero porn	See *Penthouse*
Ideal sex partner	Young, thin, handsome	Looks not too important	See newspaper "Personal" ads
	Masculine stranger	Feminine friend	Only narcissists want lovers like themselves

Careers	Gay Male Tendencies	Lesbian Tendencies	Comments & Examples
	Staff	Line	In army, gays go into medical corps
	Frequently serve women	Seldom serve men	Gay hairdressers outnumber lesbian barbers
	Like working w/ women	Dislike working w/ men	Olivia Records boycotted merely for hiring woman who used to be a man
	Upscale, creative	Downscale, blue-collar	AIDS obituaries reveal gay job patterns
	People-oriented jobs	Machine-oriented jobs	Gays big in PR, hiring, church, spying
	Little interest in military	Great interest in military	3x more lesbians than gays expelled
	Gentrify risky districts	Form rural communes	Men can live safely where women can't
Cognition & Culture	Visual	Verbal	Reflects typical orientations of male/female toddlers
Ensuing jobs	Art critic	Literary critic	English Depts., especially 7 Sisters
	Photographer	Journalist	Fashion mags: gays' images, feminists' words
	Antique-store owner	Bookstore owner	Big growth in "women's" bookstores
	Musical	Wordy	In UK "musical" is euphemism for "gay"
Ensuing jobs	Choir director/organist	Folk singer	Womyn's music favors sincere lyrics
	Opera, ballet, B'way, disco	Conciousness raising	
Cultural tastes	Arts	Crafts	Camille Paglia is exception proving rules
	Classical & avant-garde	Folksy, traditional	Winckelmann, Pater, Blunt, Acton
	See humans as art objects	Resent objectification	Greek sculpture, Wilde's *Dorian Grey*
	Snobbish, hierarchizing	Sensitive to lesser talents	Lesbians big on "Expanding the Canon"
	Idolize Classical Greeks	Resent dead white European males	Greeks made gay traits central to Western art
	Music	Lyrics	Lesbians more verbal than musical

Politics	Gay Male Tendencies	Lesbian Tendencies	Comments & Examples
	Unpolitical, hedonistic	Political, activistic	Where is gay MLK Jr. or Malcolm X?
	Don't claim to speak for all men	Claim to speak for all women	Patricia Ireland, lesbian leader of NOW, titled her memoirs *What Women Want*
	"Why I'm gay: Nature"	"Why I'm a lesbian: Nurture"	Feminists see orientation as a political choice
	Frequently persecuted	Frequently ignored	Lesbianism legal in Victorian England & Nazi Germany
	Estimated 1% to 6% of population	Estimated 0.5% to 3% of population	Lesbians maybe half as common

much about this fact. Better yet, we should avoid even noticing any of these curious details.

At least, that's been the implicit message of most of the recent news coverage of homosexuals, an outspilling enormous in extent, but peculiarly limited in analytical depth to endless rehashes of: "Gays: Sinners Against God or Victims of Society?" The ongoing media hubbub may actually be clouding the public's understanding: so many of today's auto-pilot articles and paint-by-the-numbers newscasts depict homosexuals as merely one dimensional martyrs to prejudice. There are of course obvious political advantages to blandly glossing over just how heterogeneous are homosexuals. Yet, this media stereotyping probably stems more from the natural urge of journalists to reduce complex and unsettling questions about human nature to just another fable starring good guys/gals we all can identify with (in this case, "gays"), who are discriminated against by bad guys ("homophobes") we all can feel good about looking down upon. Whether portraying homosexuals as perverts in the past or as victims today, the press has always found it less taxing to preach morality rather than to try to understand reality.

As with any other large collection of people, numerous fault lines divide homosexuals, but the most remarkable is the one separating gay men from lesbians. (I use "gay" to refer only to male homosexuals. The media's habit of applying the word to female homosexuals is male chauvinism at its most blatant: "gay" is just about the last term lesbians would have invented to describe themselves. As one lesbian activist succinctly put it, "We're not gay, we're angry!") The current fashion of lumping together as "gays" everybody from Liberacé to Martina Navratilova does something less than justice to the individuals so categorized, to one's own intellectual curiosity, and to the productiveness of public discourse.

This handy table of tendencies will of course be denounced as reflecting stereotypes. In the through the looking glass world of contemporary social comment, the more true a statement, the more meticulous its delineation, the more people from the more societies who have observed it to be a fact, then the more automatic the cries of "Stereotype!" Many journalists today write as if they are unable to distinguish between perceptive observations about the average traits of a group and blanket assertions about each and every group member. Thus, even carefully worded summations of the obvious like, "Men tend to be more aggressive than women," are triumphantly refuted with, "So, you think Mister Rogers is more aggressive than Mrs. Thatcher? Huh? Huh?"

Conspicuously missing from current debates is that most useful of all conceptual tools for thinking about both the similarity and the diversity of human beings: the probability distribution (more roughly known as the bell-shaped curve). Rather than help educate the public to think in terms of bell-shaped curves and individual variances, the press instead warns us to abstain altogether from noticing average differences between groups. Such knowledge, according to the media's theory, might bias our treatment of individuals. Of course, these proponents of unsullied individualism are so often the same people who, for their own professional or political ends, rhetorically clump humans into the grossest possible stereotypical categories (e.g., Gays, People of Color, Minorities, Third Worlders, Anglos, Homophobes, the Marginalized, the White Male Power Structure, etcetera etcetera). Worse, this taboo endorses ignorance. Now, benightedness certainly makes life more surprising (in the words of Homer Simpson, "Life is just a bunch of things that happen"), but know-nothingness does have its drawbacks, as has been pointed out on various occasions stretching back to the Ice Ages. Of course, few "social critics" actually try to practice this idealistic ignorance in their private lives. They merely publicly urge it on others.

Since the media spend so much time telling us to be oblivious to facts, it's not surprising that they themselves are suckers for frauds, like that long-lasting media cliche, "10% of all men and women are homosexual." This canard has been based on little more than gay erotic daydreams. One defender of the 10% number, the gay critic Bruce Bawer, has written of how he can know from momentary eye contact that a young father pushing a baby carriage past him on the street is "living a lie." If the 10% concoction were true, there would be four to five times as many homosexuals as Jews!

Are homosexuals fairly common, like, say, tax-cheaters, lefthanders, or tithe-givers? Or are they fairly rare, like prison inmates, identical twins, or clergy? This is certainly an interesting topic, but why this purely empirical question is thought to possess such moral consequence that many people feel compelled to lie about it is beyond me. Of course, there is much in modern media morals that I am not sensitive enough to understand. On the other hand, the fact that there are relatively few homosexuals answers a common type of objection to my table of tendencies: e.g., "You claim lesbians like softball, but most of the women softball players I know are straight." In response, let's assume lesbians are, say, ten times as likely as heterosexual women to play in an all-woman adult softball league. If 10% of the population was actually lesbian, then a majority of the players would be lesbians. More realistically, however, if only 2.5% of women were lesbians, then straight softball players would outnumber lesbians about 4 to 1.

One of the cruelest effects of ignorance about homosexuals' propensities is the heartbreak it causes both a homosexual and his or her parents when the adult child finally reveals the Surprising Truth. We are told that if only the parents hadn't been socialized to hold outdated prejudices, the surprise would not be disappointing. Disappointment, however, is inevitable: the desire to pass on your genes to grandchildren is bedrock human nature. What is far more avoidable, though, is the surprise. A more worldly awareness of those enduring likes and dislikes that tend to correlate with sexual orientation, and which so often manifest themselves early in childhood, could quite frequently allow the parents of children who turn out to be homosexual to have already spent years slowly getting used to the likelihood that this child won't ever make them grandparents, but can still make them proud and happy in many other ways.

It's important to note that the different inclinations of gays and lesbians do not follow easily predicted lines. In roughly half the traits, homosexuals tend to more resemble the opposite sex than they do the rest of their own sex. For example, many heterosexual men and lesbian women are enthusiasts for golf, as well as other hit-a-ball-with-a-stick games like softball and pool. Lesbian-feminist sportswriter Mariah Burton Nelson recently estimated, not implausibly, that 30% of the Ladies Professional Golf Association women touring pros were lesbians. While such estimates are hard to verify, it's clear that the marketers at the LPGA desperately wish they had more mothers-of-three like Nancy Lopez, the most popular woman golfer ever: i.e., a victorious yet still feminine champion with whom other heterosexual women enjoy identifying.

In contrast, pre-menopausal straight women and gay men typically find golf pointless. For example, despite incessant socialization toward golf, only one out of nine wives of PGA touring pros plays golf herself! And gay male golf fanatics are so rare that it's difficult to even come up with an exception that proves this rule (which might explain why golfers wear those god-awful pants).

Yet, for many other traits, homosexuals exhibit their own sex's tendencies to a heightened degree. For instance, all great classical composers have been male. At least since Tchaikovsky, though, an impressive number of leading composers have been gay or bisexual (e.g., Britten, Copland, Barber, Poulenc, Corigliano, and Bernstein). In comparison, although "Womyn's Music" festivals play an important role in lesbian culture, their audiences distrust dazzling exhibitions of musical virtuosity, instead preferring simple folk songs with sincere lyrics. Overall, lesbian culture is intensely verbal, a bias that seems to stem from the verbal superiority of women in general, that general feminine superiority with words that is measurable as far back as toddlerhood.

Has anyone yet deciphered a Unified Field Theory that would explain all of these complex patterns? Not that I'm aware of, but we can't begin to look for one without laying out all the facts first.

The best criticism of this article's gay vs. lesbian dichotomy would be that it doesn't go far enough. For example, people raised in Latin countries might think it peculiar that Americans insist on labeling as "gay" both Truman Capote and that exemplar of murderous masculine charisma, Alexander the Great. Latins are inclined to care less than Americans about whom a man goes to bed with and more about what he does there. Although this dominant vs. submissive distinction has evaporated from America's polite discourse, it remains the main theme of our impolite discourse (as any male motorist can testify who has ever triggered the obscene wrath of an NYC cabbie).

Gay vs. lesbian distinctions are also important for thinking about public policies. Homosexual-related issues like gays in the military, AIDS, and same-sex marriages cannot be discussed realistically without acknowledging the wide differences on average between gays and lesbians. For example, the *New York Times*, the *Wall Street Journal*, the *Atlantic*, and the newsweeklies have been trumpeting, despite the highly preliminary nature of the findings, evidence that homosexuality has biological roots. Generally overlooked, however, is that most of the research was performed on gay male subjects by gay male scientists and then hyped by gay male publicists. Going largely unreported is the lesbian population's profound ambivalence about this half-scientific, half-political crusade. (For example, an attack on the theory that lesbianism has biological causes is one of the main themes of Lillian Faderman's fine history of American lesbians, *Odd Girls and Twilight Lovers.*) This media reticence is noteworthy, considering that the press otherwise so assiduously keeps us informed of the views of the lesbian-dominated National Organization for Women's on child-rearing, marriage, beauty, men and, of course, What the Women of America Want—subjects upon which lesbians might be presumed to have rather less expertise to offer than on the question of why they are lesbians.

Many lesbian-feminists deny that their sexual orientation is biologically rooted, attributing it instead to what they perceive as our culture's decision to socialize males to be domineering. They may claim this simply to avoid contradicting feminist theory, which is, well, "biophobic." (Yes, I know that this trendy practice of insinuating that those who disagree with you politically must suffer from a mental disorder is reminiscent of the imprisoning of Soviet dissidents in psychiatric hospitals, but, hey, once you get the hang of it, it's kind of fun.) On the other hand, the lesbian-feminists might be right and the gay researcher/activists wrong about the nature of homosexuality. Or, homosexuality might not have a single nature: at minimum, there could be a fundamental difference between lesbians and gays.

We would all profit from hearing this question openly hashed out. The ensuing brouhaha could help unshackle American intellectual discussion from the polite fictions about human nature that currently suffocate it. Although the prestige press devotes more than a little ink to scientific discoveries about human nature, it carefully avoids mentioning the political implications of these findings (except, of course, in the case of gays). When discussing all other social controversies, the serious media instead pay mindful lip service to the dogma that socialization is the root of all differences between people. (Fortunately, though, the unserious media like the Fox Network, Dave Barry, and stand-up comedians blithely carry on the court jester's job of telling irreverent truths about humanity.)

While emotionally comforting to many, this faith in the omnipotence of nurture remains unproved, to say the least. By now, it seems inevitable that this strict constructionist creed eventually must be washed away by the ever-growing torrent of scientific evidence to the contrary (of which the research on the possible genetic causes of male homosexuality is the merest and least certain rivulet). Yet, the single event most likely to speed the day when it is politically and socially acceptable to openly discuss the broad relevance of this fast-solidifying scientific consensus that biology plays an important role in human behavior would be a public donnybrook between gay men and lesbian-feminists over nature vs. nurture.

Beyond homosexual-related issues, this gay vs. lesbian dichotomy can cast new light on many social questions. Fundamentally, as Thomas Sowell has pointed out, almost all American social controversies rest on conflicting assumptions about human nature. Is it infinitely malleable? If not, what are its constraints? Whatever other purposes there are for our existence, we know evolution has shaped human nature to promote reproduction. To study reproduction is to study sex and sexuality. To understand heterosexual men and women is difficult without studying homosexual men and women as a frame of reference.

For instance, honest discussion of the differences between lesbians and gays would also generate fresh insights into what feminists imperialistically call "women's" issues. While feminist theory is largely immune from radical questioning in most of the prestige media, few people actually take it seriously...especially feminists. They seldom pay their own theory the respect of treating it like a scientific theory and testing it against the evidence. If feminist theory is truly an attempt to make accurate predictions about reality, rather than simply an elaborate rationalization for blaming your troubles on somebody else, then feminists should welcome a frank appraisal of the contrasting longings and ambitions of gays and lesbians, since this offers fascinating new perspectives from which to assay feminist hypotheses.

For example, feminists tirelessly denounce the fashion and beauty industry for brainwashing American men into craving skin-deep feminine beauty. But which is truly the cause and which is the effect? Luckily, the curious analyst can study people who have rejected heterosexual socialization: among homosexuals, the distinctiveness of men's and women's basic sexual urges is especially vivid. Since "Women Seeking Women" don't need to entice men's visually-focused desires, their newspaper personal ads tend toward wistful vagueness: *Attractive SWF, bi, seeking SF, feminine & discreet, any race, for friendship and possible rltnshp.* In contrast, the "Men Seeking Men" classifieds bristle with statistics quantifying appearance: *John Wayne-type (41, 6'3" 210#, C 46" W 35", brn/grn) seeks Steve Garvey-type (muscular, str8-acting, 20-30, under 6' & 185#, blu eyes a +).*

Even more egregiously swept under the rug by feminists like Naomi Wolf (author of *The Beauty Myth*) is the central creative role of gay men in the fashion business. Thus, feminist pundits routinely portray the current fad in haute couture for "waif" models (young girls lacking in the more popular secondary sexual characteristics) as a conspiracy against women hatched by... yes, you guessed it, The Male Power Structure. This accusation always conjures up for me a vision of Alan Greenspan, Bill Gates, and Colin Powell resolving in secret conclave to put uppity women back in their place by ordering *Vogue* to print a lot of pictures of girls who look like boys.

Feminists' widespread (though hushed-up) exasperation with gay men probably originates in the perennial struggle of the "women's movement" to enlist enough Indians for its ample supply of chiefs. In this battle for the hearts and minds of the female masses, it is the gay imagination that so often crystalizes the misty yearnings of femininity into those beguiling baubles and alluring images that help seduce heterosexual women away from the stern precepts of feminism. Would bridal magazines be 800 pages long without the endlessly creative genius of gay men who make their livings subverting and sabotaging feminism's war on femininity?

The second helpful table summarizes the contemporary issues that the media insist on stereotyping in "victim" vs. "oppressor" terms, but where a frank exploration of the differences between gay men and lesbians offers new angles from which to slice through the cant.

We can never eliminate stereotypes. Instead, we should constantly search for more and better stereotypes, ones that more narrowly and accurately describe reality. The alternative is not some utopia without stereotypes, but our current intellectual dystopia, where the broadest, stupidest, and most dishonest stereotypes reign.

WHY LESBIANS AREN'T GAY

	Homosexual Issues	
The Issues	**Victims**	**Oppressors**
Gays in the military	Homosexuals	The military

Controversy is largely over gay men, who aren't all that interested in enlisting, anyway. Lesbians like military more, do well in it, and more accepted (*de facto*) by other soldiers and brass.

Social discrimination	Homosexuals	Homophobes

Straight men often find lesbians erotic in fantasy, but tiresome in reality. They find gays repugnant in concept but often likable in person.

Homosexual marriage	Homosexuals	Heterosexuals

Lesbians more likely to want to be monogamously married. Gays less interested in being married than in getting married ... in a big ceremony. Gays have never devised equivalent of wedding ring, i.e., an insignia that would say, "Don't bother asking, I'm already taken."

Biological origins of homosexuality	Homosexuals	Unscientific traditionalists

Gay men support but many lesbians disapprove of the search for homosexuality's genetic roots.

Homosexuals raising children	Homosexuals	The heartless

1. Overwhelmingly, a lesbian issue.
2. Lesbians claim they can't mold their kids' sex roles, but, if so, that undermines feminist dogma about nurture over nature. Anecdotal evidence about lesbian moms frustrated by gun-loving sons and Barbie-loving daughters supports this.

AIDS	Everybody	1. Society
		2. Ronald Reagan

Media's "We're all at risk" scare campaign covers up acute danger from being sodomized, causing ill-informed women to get HIV that way.

WORLD WAR T

Feminist Issues

The Issues	Victims	Oppressors
Women in combat	Women	The military
	Promotion-focused female officers (significantly lesbian) want combat. Survival-focused enlisted women (highly heterosexual) don't. Family-focused sailors' wives (all heterosexual) hate coed ships, because their husbands father children with female sailors during cruises.	
"Beauty Myth"	Women	Men
	Gay men dominate fashion/beauty industry. Also, gays want beautiful lovers, lesbian don't care as much.	
"Double Standard"	Women	Society
	Gay men are far more promiscuous than lesbian women.	
Pornography	Women	Men
	Gays buy lots of pornographic pictures of men. Lesbians outraged by erotic pictures of women, but some like erotic texts about women.	
"Glass Ceiling"	Women	Men
	Lesbians more competitive (e.g., sports) and often more successful at leadership (e.g., military) than straight women or gay men.	
Diversifying the "Canon"	The Marginalized	Heterosexist WASP's
	Gleaming pantheon of gay Dead White European Males from Plato to Proust.	

World War T

Taki's
January 22, 2014

A S the gay-marriage juggernaut crushes all resistance within America, it's become obvious that the mainstream media doesn't want to declare victory and go home. They want sequels. But what's left to exploit in demonizing average people after the elites have gotten all they demanded?

One obvious strategy is to go global, to turn the domestic gay crusade into World War G.

The problem from a political-correctness standpoint is that the worst abuses of homosexuals in the world today take place in black Africa or the Muslim Middle East. So it would be racist or Islamophobic to go global at the moment.

Fortunately for the American press, the mostly white and ethnically Christian country of Russia recently passed a law against spreading gay propaganda among minors. And since spreading gay propaganda, especially to impressionable young people, is the essence of the American prestige press' gay-marriage campaign, this has been taken very personally. They are looking forward to using the Winter Olympics of 2014, the 100th anniversary of the start of World War I, to stoke hostility against Russia.

Hopefully, this will just turn into another long, expensive Cold War without anybody actually getting it into his head to invade Russia to prevent what *Slate* is calling "a Gay Holocaust."[1] But even stupider things have happened in history. After all, there is much power and money to be harvested from mindless international tensions. Sometimes, as in 1914, however, they slip out of control.

But what's the post-gay-marriage strategy to keep the pot bubbling here in America? Sure, the gay marriage whoop-dee-doo served as a distraction from the major issues America faces (it's not wholly coincidental that Wall Street ponied up much of the money for the campaign), but perhaps the media can double down and find an even smaller group to noisily champion. How about...transsexuals, transvestites, trans-whatevers?

World War T!

Indeed, I started to notice that World War T was the next domestic campaign last spring when *The New York Times* splashed a big story about how a "transgender" mixed martial arts fighter "Fallon Fox, born Boyd Burton" was being discriminated against by not being allowed to beat up women for money.[2]

Ever since, the press has been running similar stories. And the witch-burning fever has been mounting among the Volunteer Auxiliary Thought Police.

Grantland, Bill Simmons's boutique SWPL sports-journalism website within *ESPN*, is now being widely denounced for "transphobia" after running a terrific piece of long-form investigative reporting by a young freelancer named Caleb Hannan: "Dr. V's Magical Putter: The remarkable story behind a mysterious inventor who built a 'scientifically superior' golf club."

You may wonder why World War T seems to have broken out first on the sports page. Yet there's a reason why run-of-the-mill sportswriters have long been among the most dopily politically correct for years. Political correctness is a war on noticing, and it's harder to not notice patterns when watching sports than almost anywhere else in life. If you turn on *ESPN*, you'll notice that on average, blacks can outjump and outsprint whites, that straight men and lesbian women like sports far more than do gay men and straight women, and that men are much better than women at sports. Indeed, the rare transgender sportsman tends to make a farce out of the *Plessy v. Ferguson* world of women's sports. Hence, mediocre sportswriters have often been among the most militant enemies of noticing.

Simmons, though, is perhaps the best sportswriter of the Internet era precisely because he's a terrific pattern recognizer. He doesn't go into locker rooms to ask what pitch the slugger hit. Instead he inhales information from numerous sources and checks the implications against the other sources. But that independence of mind also means that Simmons is always in some danger of being ratted out as a closet crimethinker.

As an editor of *Grantland*, though, well, it's hard to find other Bill Simmonses among today's thoroughly domesticated young writers. Thus, Hannan's long piece on a golf-club inventor was so appealing: It was as if Simmons had finally found a young reporter on his own pro-noticing wavelength.

It's pretty hard for anybody to come up with something interesting to write about putters "the clubs that golfers use to tap the ball the last few yards toward the hole" without being boring, or at least without recounting what Johnny Carson apocryphally said to Mrs. Arnold Palmer. Golf is an inherently anticlimactic undertaking. You start off each hole on the tee trying to whomp the ball a couple of football fields or more "which is actually pretty fun" but you end up on the green delicately nudging the ball three or four times until it finally topples into a small hole in the ground.

But Hannan pulls off this difficult assignment, putting the story in the broad perspective of the things men will do to roll a golf ball more accurately.

Technological improvements in drivers, which now look like toasters at the end of pool cues, have made the game more fun by allowing hackers to swing from their heels with less fear of whiffing. There were striking advances in club technology toward the end of the Cold War as aerospace engineers took their titanium and carbon fiber skills to innovative firms such as Callaway to beat their swords into pitching wedges.

Thus it's always tempting to buy a newer and even more complicated Stealth Fighter-looking putter because, you know, Science. As golf club businessman Barney Adams told Hannan:

> You need a story to sell. A story that can usually be reduced to five simple words: "Mad scientist invents great product."

But in truth, putting remains largely a test of concentration, willpower, and confidence. A competitor once told George Plimpton that Palmer made the most 20-footers in the early 1960s because he deeply felt he deserved to make each one.

Recently, popular mustachioed golf broadcaster Gary McCord became a huge booster of the Yar putter, which looks like an F-35 crossed with a cup holder. As McCord recounts in an interview with fellow pro Steve Elkington, the Yar was invented by the shadowy aerospace genius Dr. V.

This entrepreneur, who went by the curious name of Dr. Essay Anne Vanderbilt, claimed to be a member of the historic New York society family and have a Ph.D. from MIT in aeronautical physics, credentials that helped draw in money from outside investors, such as a Pittsburgh retiree who wound up losing his $60,000.

McCord, worried at one point that he couldn't actually verify Dr. V's claims of a career deep in classified defense efforts such as the Stealth Bomber, phoned a friend:

> Dan Quayle was also an acquaintance. Unable to help himself, McCord once put the former vice-president on the phone with Dr. V and watched as they chatted about old Pentagon projects.

When the Grantland reporter emailed Dr. V, the inventor insisted the focus of the article be on "the science and not the scientist," explaining:

> I have no issues as long as the following protocols are followed because of my association with classified documents.... If the aforementioned is agreeable to you, please respond to this communiqué at your convenience so we can schedule our lively nuncupative off the record collogue.

That's reassuring.

By the way, Dr. V also claimed to be a woman, one in a lesbian relationship with a lady golfer.

This didn't seem to faze the highly Republican golfers. Nor did the golfers, such as veteran David Frost, seem to worry much that Dr. V was 6'3" and had a deep voice.

After all, there must be a lot of women who are almost a foot taller than the national average and have low voices and have MIT engineering doctorates and worked in the weapons industry and tinker with golf clubs. How sexist do you have to be to suggest that a Venn diagram of all the women in America might not show any overlap?

As Hannan investigated his story, he discovered, perhaps unsurprisingly, that the 60-year-old Dr. V wasn't a doctor, wasn't a Vanderbilt, was a high-school dropout and a failed auto mechanic, had declared bankruptcy after several lawsuits, had been accused of sexual harassment three times, had been revived from a suicide attempt, and had married at least two women and fathered at least two children under the name Stephen Krol.

This is not to say that the Yar is worse than other putters, just that the implicit marketing mantra "mad scientist invents great product" requires some science along with the madness.

You've probably heard that male-to-female transgender individuals "always felt like a girl on the inside." So if the promoter was always a woman trapped in a man's body, why were all of Krol-Vanderbilt's avocations—golf, military technology, chasing women, and so forth—stereotypically masculine?

One group of transgender individuals, though, tends to be caricatures of masculine willfulness and egotism. For example, economist Deirdre McCloskey played football at Harvard. In a photo on computer scientist Lynn Conway's University of Michigan website, the professor is in a flight suit towering over former national security adviser Brent Scowcroft.[3]

When the Northwestern U. psychologist J. Michael Bailey pointed out that some transsexuals are less motivated by being "a woman in a man's body" than by a peculiar sexual fetish, McCloskey and Conway attempted to destroy Bailey's career and that of anybody who'd ever mentioned his research in public. They displayed a masculine ferocity that remains the most memorable in my decades watching people try to shut scientists up.

At a lower intellectual level, guys who declare themselves trans so they can hit on lesbians have been making themselves a nuisance at lesbian-feminist venues for decades. For example, the Michigan Womyn's Music Festival has long had a policy of allowing admission only to "womyn-born-womyn" so its attendees can sit in the dirt and listen to the Indigo Girls without having to fend off the transgendered.

In a sad end to a chaotic life, Dr. V committed suicide on October 18, 2013. An ex-brother-in-law called Hannan to break the news, saying unsympathetically, "Well, there's one less con man in the world now."

What Hannan and Simmons didn't realize, however, was that as part of the rapid redeployment of firepower from World War G to World War T, "transgender" individuals have become 2014's hottest privileged class.

The condemnation from the rest of the press was overwhelming. For example, *Slate* ran the headline: "Digging Too Deep: Grantland's exposé of a trans con artist privileged fact-finding over compassion." After all, the self-proclaimed transgendered are, by definition, victims of the white male power structure, even if they are kicking it around with Dan Quayle.

Simmons soon posted a self-emasculating apology[4] and ran a denunciatory piece[5] by Christina Kahrl, one of the few baseball sabermetricians who wears a dress. (Not surprisingly, Christina used to be Chris and was the husband of a woman.)

In 1861, the comparative legal scholar Henry Maine drew a famous generalization from his study of the differences between ancient Roman and Hindu societies versus the direction Victorian Britain was moving: "We may say that the movement of the progressive societies has hitherto been a movement from Status to Contract." In ancient India, for instance, Brahmins were born privileged and stayed privileged, while Dalits were born despised and stayed despised. In contrast, the modern world then seemed to be moving toward a system that respected laws, not men.

The postmodern world, however, seems to be drifting back toward a new regime of privileged categories that are based on complaining your way into becoming unquestioningly assumed to be disprivileged, no matter how much time you spend on the putting green.

As for putters, well, I've given up trying to buy myself a more scientific stroke. I've gone back to using the putter my late mother gave me in 1971, which I believe she bought in a drugstore for about $2.99. It looks like a welding project from a junior-high shop class.

And I'm still awful at putting.

The Flight From White

Taki's
June 17, 2015

A S YOU may have noticed, the more denunciations we hear of Cisgender Straight White Male Privilege, the more the evidence mounts that, all else being equal, the rewards in 2015 tend to lie on the other side.

If you want to know which side is more powerful at present, just observe who is wielding the rhetorical whip hand. It's human nature to fear, respect, and even admire those with the power to harm you. Hence, it's popular to side with the strong to denounce the weak. As Mencius Moldbug observed in 2013:

> The logic of the witch hunter is simple.... The first requirement is to invert the reality of power.... In a country where anyone who speaks out against the witches is soon found dangling by his heels from an oak at midnight with his head shrunk to the size of a baseball, we won't see a lot of witch-hunting and we know there's a serious witch problem. In a country where witch-hunting is a stable and lucrative career, and also an amateur pastime enjoyed by millions of hobbyists on the weekend, we know there are no real witches worth a damn.[6]

Of course, the more our society obsesses over the Looming Witch Menace, the more absurd becomes the daily news, and the harder it is to refrain from breaking out laughing. Perhaps June 2015 will go down in history as the month the reigning pieties jumped the shark.

For example, white male has-been Bruce Jenner is now superstarette Caitlyn Jenner, a Good Witch in the war upon male dignity, whose courage is lauded by both the president and millions of Kardashian fans.

And don't you dare act as if Jenner having threatened to unman himself on the *E!* network might be a little funny. Clint Eastwood, for example, made the slightest verbal gesture that he found something amusing about it all ("Caitlyn somebody") and had his heresy censored by the *Spike* network.

Shortly after Jenner's transubstantiation, we learned that a social-justice warriorette named Rachel Dolezal had moved to the big city of Spokane, Wash., tanned her skin, permed her hair, and built herself a nice little career as a black activist witch-hunting white racists. And when there weren't enough white witches to be found, she would (apparently) gin up a few of the usual Hate Crime Hoaxes. Life was good, until her mother and father pointed out to the press that they were white.

Many media outlets were baffled that anybody in 21st-century America would find it advantageous to give up all that White Privilege to be perceived as black. After all, we know that vicious white racists lie in wait to victimize black bodies by murdering them, raping them, and not letting them use the swimming pool.

But that raised the uncomfortable (or amusing) question: Weren't the liberals denouncing Dolezal being transphobic?

Among non-SJWs, Ms. Dolezal's embarrassment proved a welcome relief to many who had been baffled by how sanctimoniously the dispensers of conventional wisdom had greeted Jenner's transparent ploy to make millions off an upcoming reality TV show about whether or not in the season finale he'd finally have himself castrated.

Wits leapt all over the seemingly bizarre distinction in current discourse between the transgender (and thus angelic) Jenner and the transracial (and thus demonic) Dolezal. Several media outlets, such as the *BBC* and *USA Today*, fell for a meme tweeted by Godfrey Elfwick:

> My name is Godfrey.
> I am WrongSkin.
> You may not have heard of that but it means I was born to white parents and have white skin but I identify as being black.
> It's not a joke.

It's not OK to mock us.
It's not easy to live like this.
Our struggle is your struggle.
#WrongSkin

When challenged, Elfwick (who describes "xirself" as "Genderqueer Muslim atheist. Born white in the #WrongSkin. Itinerant jongleur. Xir, Xirs Xirself. Filters life through the lens of minority issues") triumphantly retorted on Twitter:

Skin color has nothing to do with the color of a person's skin.

Granted, it was embarrassing to *USA Today* when they had to append to their story "People respond to NAACP incident with #wrongskin" the following message:

Corrections & Clarifications: An earlier version of this story misstated the intentions of a tweet by @GodfreyElfwick. He operates a parody account.

But in defense of *USA Today* and the *BBC*, how in tarnation is anybody supposed to know these days how to distinguish between the latest moral mania and satire? For example, the ongoing World War T was launched in May 2013 with a crusading *New York Times* article about how society is oppressing male-born mixed-martial-arts fighter Fallon Fox by not letting him/her beat up women for money.[7] How is anybody supposed to know that Godfrey Elfwick is parody and Fallon Fox isn't?

Indeed, most of the best-known middle-aged male-to-female transgender celebrities are perpetrating, with enthusiastic media cooperation, a hoax on the public by claiming they always felt since early childhood like a little girl on the inside. Yet who hasn't seen Larry/Lana Wachowski's *The Matrix*? Is there anything at all girl-like about that movie? A far more plausible hypothesis is put forward by Northwestern U. professor of psychology J. Michael Bailey: A sizable proportion of the highly masculine men who decide they want everybody to act as if they are female are in the throes of a sexual fetish known as autogynephilia.[8]

Of course, not knowing that transgenderism is to be celebrated as obvious and transracialism is to be scorned as something that can't possibly even exist is no excuse. These days, you are just supposed to know, and if you get the latest orthodoxy wrong, well, too bad for you...

In truth, nobody can change either race or sex. In the ultimate Darwinian sense, transsexuals and transracials are as real as witches.

Please note that I'm defining both race and sex in terms of the most fundamental level of human reality: one's biological family tree.

Philosophers, at least since Descartes' "I think, therefore I am," have tried to figure out how to ground their perceptions of the world in something assuredly factual. But here's what we can say with some confidence about the human race: At this point in time, every mortal human has had one biological father and one biological mother; one biological paternal grandfather, one biological paternal grandmother, one biological maternal grandfather, and one biological maternal grandmother; and so forth. In the future, humans might be cloned and thus have only one biological parent, or might be genetically engineered to have three biological parents. Anything could happen. But so far it hasn't.

The most rigorous definition of a racial group is a partly inbred extended family. Race is about who your ancestors are on your biological family tree. Nothing Rachel Dolezal can do can change her genetic lineage.

(By the way, the U.S. Census Bureau has typically drawn a distinction between race, which it describes as biological, and ethnicity, which it calls cultural. A useful way to think of ethnicity is as those traits such as language, religion, cuisine, names, customs, and so forth that are typically passed down within biological families, but don't, technically, have to be.)

Moreover, we can rigorously define anyone who has fathered a child in anybody's family tree as a man and anyone who has given birth to a child in anybody's family tree as a woman. No ancestor anybody has had has done both. So far, the human species doesn't actually work as assumed in Robert A. Heinlein's 1959 sci-fi story "All You Zombies" in which a sex-change operation and a time machine allow the narrator to be his/her own father/ mother and son/daughter. Maybe someday Heinlein's story will come true, but it hasn't yet.

In other words, both transsexuals like Bruce Jenner and transracials like Rachel Dolezal are merely fooling around with cosmetics. In the central Darwinian sense of biologically propagating human offspring, nobody can change their ancestors or be both father and mother to their descendants.

So nobody is really transsexual or transracial in the crucial family-tree sense.

But it's also not hard to think of transracial (or transethnic) celebrities in the cosmetic sense that leads other people to change their guesses about ancestry, just as Jenner is getting cosmetic surgery to look more feminine, but that doesn't alter the fact that he shows up on each of his six children's family trees as the father.

On a superficial level, however, transracialism is common in the Third World, where most people believe the whiter the better. For example, the current superstar of Brazilian soccer Neymar used to look like an average black youth. But now that he's rich, he's contrived to look much whiter.

In contrast, in America with its "one drop rule," passing from black to white has gotten even rarer over the generations due to shifting cost-benefit analyses.

One of the last well-known examples of black-to-white passing was the acerbic New York man of letters Anatole Broyard (1920-1990). A New Orleans Creole of color, an ethnic group influenced by the French and Spanish view that one drop of white blood makes you not black, Broyard served as an officer in the segregated ranks of World War II by identifying as white. After the war, he didn't see much reason to shift back.

Broyard was generally recognized in Greenwich Village as being of mixed ancestry (novelist Philip Roth recalls being told the day he met him in 1958 that Broyard was an 'octoroon').[9] But he didn't talk about his ancestry one way or another. He likely would have made more money if he had been officially black, but he managed to make a decent living as a self-made literary critic without having to be a credit to his race.

But it was always hard in America to pass persuasively from black to white because that meant publicly cutting yourself off from your black relatives, as Roth made vivid in his novel *The Human Stain*. That's why state-of-the-art DNA studies find that only about 0.05% of the ancestry of self-identified white (non-Hispanic) Americans is from sub-Saharan Africa, in contradiction of the myth of widespread passing from black to white.[10]

An apparent early example of a white-to-black transracial individual was the con man who founded the Black Muslims in the early 1930s, Wallace Fard Muhammad, a.k.a. Wallace D. Fard. Even a Nation of Islam portrait depicts Fard as a fair-skinned man with straight hair.

Wallace D. Fard was likely the same person as the Wallie D. Ford who had earlier been arrested three times in Los Angeles, most strikingly for violation of the California Wolverine Possession Act. Wallie Ford identified himself on the 1920 Census as a white man from New Zealand, while another time he claimed his father was born in Spain. Another theory is that he was an Afghan, while J. Edgar Hoover contended he was a Turk. (By the way, Gore

Vidal alleged that everybody who grew up in Washington knew that Hoover was from an old mulatto family that had passed.)

A common contributor to examples of transracialism is coming from a foreign culture with different racial standards. For example, one of my son's college roommates remarked that in America everybody calls him black, while back home in Jamaica everybody calls him white.

A prominent recent example of refashioning one's racial affect is *New Yorker* journalist Malcolm Gladwell, who was generally perceived as a white conservative when he arrived from Canada and began his career with *The American Spectator*. But after his 2000 best-seller, *The Tipping Point*, he grew a giant Sideshow Bob-like Afro.

Gladwell claims that the 'fro led to his being hassled by The Man,[11] and that inspired his 2005 best-seller, *Blink*. But calling attention to the fact that his mother was from Jamaica's mulatto middle class certainly hasn't hurt his popularity as a sales-conference speaker.

The best-known celebrity to have transformed his ethnic (rather than racial) identity as an adult is the President of the United States. Of course, Barack Obama successfully retconned his identity to be African-American by moving to Chicago, joining Rev. Jeremiah Wright's megachurch, and penning an autobiography entitled *Dreams From My Father: A Story of Race and Inheritance*. But if you have to write 150,000 words about how you're black, maybe you have some nagging reason for trying so hard?

The African-American identity that the Hawaiian cosmopolitan assumed at age 24 has of course proved a wildly successful career strategy. But the handful of African-Americans who knew Obama growing up seldom thought of him as one of their own. *Washington Post* reporter David Maraniss's 2012 exhaustive semiauthorized biography *Barack Obama: The Story* makes clear how tendentious *Dreams From My Father* was in attempting to set Obama up for a political career on the heavily black South Side of Chicago.

Not surprisingly, when Obama ran against a genuine African-American, Bobby Rush, for the Democratic nomination for the House in 2000, he lost badly. This plunged him into depression, from which he revivified himself by giving up his bizarre dream of being elected mayor of Chicago (which is not a job for transplants from Hawaii) and finally admitting that he was the nice white person's vision of a black politician.

Obama's 2000 humiliation shouldn't have come as a surprise to him because Maraniss tracks down repeated examples of authentic African-Americans finding him inauthentic. For example:

> Adam Sherman ... recalled that his two black roommates ... viewed Obama's racial history and experience as vastly different from theirs and did not think of him as black.

Among Obama's friends from age 18 to 24—almost all of whom were either foreigners or the son of a Foreign Service Officer—most viewed him as "multicultural" or "international."

And we may have two transethnic presidents in a row: Jeb Bush, who lives in a Spanish-speaking household, registered to vote in 2009 as a Hispanic.[12]

Gay as a French Horn

Taki's
August 17 & 24, 2011

IT'S not uncommon for me to get into discussions about celebrities that go something like this:

Him: Hey, you've heard of Mr. Big Name [a world-famous icon of masculinity], right?

Me: Sure. Who hasn't?

Him: Well, he's gay.

Me: Really? That's interesting.

Him: Yeah, my buddy Al, who was a stuntman on a bunch of his early movies, told me.

Me: But isn't he married to that supermodel?

Him: It's just a front.

Me: And don't they have several kids who look just like him?

Him: Everybody in Hollywood knew he was gay way back when.

Me: And wasn't his wife threatening to divorce him a couple of years ago because he was sleeping with his leading lady?

Him: His publicist must have made it up.

Me: And didn't his ex-wife sue him to get his child-support payments raised to $100,000 per month? And didn't he almost ruin his career by insisting that his crazy Danish girlfriend be cast opposite him in all his movies? And didn't he hire private eye Anthony

Pellicano to wiretap those script girls who had filed paternity and sexual-harassment suits against him? And doesn't he maintain a secret second family in Bakersfield?

Him: It's all part of the act.

Me: And didn't he buy that expensive golf course? Heck, I saw him hitting golf balls at the local driving range years ago while he was still on that TV show. How many gays play golf? And before you claim that golf is a devious façade, why would anybody devote thousands of hours playing golf just to bamboozle the world into thinking he's straight when nobody except me has ever noticed that gay men almost never play golf? I mean, I once read up on everybody on *Golf Digest*'s lists of the 160 actors and singers who are the best golfers in the entertainment industry, and only one, 1950s great Johnny Mathis, is obviously homosexual. But who else does that? So all I'm saying is, this guy doesn't sound gay.

Him: He's gay as a French horn.

It seems like I've had this conversation at one time or another about most male celebrities other than, maybe, old linebacker Dick Butkus.

Granted, I am as interested as anybody else in gossip about whether or not Mr. Big Name is secretly homosexual. But I'm also interested in the more statistical question: Overall, how many famous male entertainers really are gay?

I don't know. So I've been trying to think through the various possible explanations for the scant data we have. I'll lay out the potential scenarios, all of which are likely true to some extent. I'll conclude with a rather disturbing possibility that doesn't get much press coverage, perhaps because it would violate the media's current Prime Directive of portraying gays solely as powerless martyrs.

First, maybe straight guys just make up rumors about celebrities they envy. Sylvester Stallone acknowledged in 2006 that Richard Gere still blames Sly for making up the popular rumor about Gere and the gerbil. But it's only a rumor about the rumor, Sly said.

We've seen something analogous to this with the bizarre rumors among blacks that white fashion designers such as Gloria Vanderbilt in the 1980s and Tommy Hilfiger in the 1990s and 2000s had gone on television talk shows to proclaim their hatred of black people.

Presumably these allegations start when some black teens are out trying on designer clothes, and one girl who doesn't want to admit she can't afford them makes up an excuse about how she won't buy any Tommy Hilfiger items because she saw him on Oprah talking about how much he loathes blacks.

Or maybe gays like to make up fantasies about handsome straights. Consider baseball players. I've read gay rumors about Sandy Koufax, Mike Piazza, and Keith Hernandez, all of them handsome and none of them—I would bet a sizable amount of money—gay. In contrast, one of Hernandez's teammates on the Mets was a much more plausible candidate for the distinction of best gay ballplayer ever, but he's almost never the subject of rumors, possibly because he's a little pudgy.[13]

Or perhaps all those rumors are always floating around because a lot of stars really are gay. Where there's smoke, there's often fire.

For example, back in 1972, everybody in my 9th-grade class knew that Rock Hudson and Jim Nabors (the flamingly effeminate star of *Gomer Pyle, U.S.M.C.*) had gotten "married." That wasn't exactly true, but it was closer to the truth than outsiders normally get. According to the Standard Narrative, the entire world was amazed in 1985 when Hudson announced he had AIDS. Yet as a former 9th grader, I can't say I was terribly surprised by the news.

Why are there always rumors about male stars being gay?

Maybe they're true. Screenwriter Joe Eszterhas (*Basic Instinct*) claimed in his amusing 2006 book *The Devil's Guide to Hollywood*, "With the exception of Russell Crowe and Mel Gibson, there are few stars able to play supermacho parts today. Many of Hollywood's top male movie stars are either bisexual or gay." Conversely, some actors are so talented that they can expertly play, say, macho soldiers and bank robbers.

It's likely that gay males are quite drawn to acting and other careers where part of the compensation is applause. The competition in acting is more backstage than in, say, sports, where gay men are highly underrepresented.

Of course, being gay could help open doors within the entertainment industry. Evaluating acting talent is inherently subjective, so personal bias can play a large role. Heck, being a Scientologist helps in Hollywood.

In contrast, sports tend to be more objective. Cam Newton, the NFL's top draft choice this year, is a strong-armed 6'5", 248-pound quarterback who can run past, around, or over most defenders. It probably wouldn't help Newton's football career to be a gay Scientologist.

We know that fairly few male professional athletes are homosexual because not many died of AIDS in the 1980s and 1990s. In contrast, AIDS confirmed stereotypes about dancers by killing Rudolf Nureyev, Alvin Ailey, Robert Joffrey, and Michael Bennett of *A Chorus Line* fame.

Yet AIDS's impact on screen acting was surprisingly marginal: Hudson, Anthony Perkins, and then who? Maybe that guy who played the dad on *The Brady Bunch*. It's not obvious from the AIDS records that a huge fraction of famous movie stars were lifelong homosexuals.

Or maybe lots of big stars are innately bisexual. Yet most of the social science evidence suggests that bisexuality is quite rare among men—rarer than homosexuality. Perhaps artists are more likely to be bisexual? I don't know.

Or maybe a lot of big names *used* to be gay but aren't anymore. These days, we're not supposed to believe that *anybody* can change from gay to straight. Yet among one supremely well-documented group—20th-century British writers—it seemed to happen fairly often: e.g., John Maynard Keynes, Evelyn Waugh, and Stephen Spender.

It's not unknown for women to switch teams, but mostly in the opposite direction. The late Susan Sontag didn't like being called a lesbian, even though she was in a relationship with photographer Annie Leibowitz. She would explain that after she turned 40, she simply got better offers from women than from men.

Or maybe, and most disturbingly, the ex-gay stars never really were gay. Perhaps they just let gay sexual predators exploit them physically to help launch their careers. It wouldn't be hard for gay industry insiders to position this as a test of whether an ambitious young man wants a career badly enough to earn it the hard way.

Many young actresses are exploited by heterosexual power brokers in exactly this fashion. So why would it be different for young actors?

This is a possibility we are really not supposed to discuss, because, as everybody knows these days, all gay men just wanted to get married to other gay men and settle down to utter monogamy.

Thus, when 1980s teen idol Corey Feldman spoke up this month to accuse an unnamed Hollywood mogul of causing the recent drug death of the other 1980s teen idol Corey, Corey Haim, the controversy had to be framed for the press as being about a pedophile predator. Yet "pedophilia" is defined as an interest in prepubescent children. Similarly, the Catholic-priest scandals are spun as being about pedophilia, despite obvious homosexual aspects.

Lou Pearlman, who looks like a more obese Karl Rove, is a gay white-collar criminal who concocted two giant 1990s boy bands, the Backstreet Boys and 'N Sync. The latter featured Justin Timberlake, who is now becoming better known as a golfing movie star in films such as *The Social Network*.

We now know a fair amount about Pearlman because his decades-long career was so out of control that much of it ended in legal disputes. For instance, his first marketing venture involved renting advertising blimps to big companies, but four of his blimps crashed. Pearlman is currently serving a 25-year sentence for running a $300-million Ponzi scheme.

In 2007, while under arrest, Pearlman was accused by the mother of Nick Carter, a lead singer for the Backstreet Boys, of sexual abuse. "Certain things happened and it almost destroyed our family. I tried to warn everyone. I tried to warn all the mothers."

How common is the Pearlman scenario? Nobody knows and nobody seems to want to know.

Maybe the straight guys who wind up world-famous tend to be the ones so ambitious that, when they were young and pretty, they'd put up with the Pearlman types.

CHAPTER TEN

Sailer's Law of Female Journalism

The most heartfelt articles by female journalists tend to be demands that social values be overturned in order that, Come the Revolution, the journalist herself will be considered hotter-looking.

A Specter Is Haunting the Clinton Administration

Unpublished
December 3, 1992

SPECTER is haunting the Clinton Presidency, one that the President-Elect needs to defuse immediately.

The move to drive liberal, pro-feminist Republican Senator Robert Packwood from office as retribution for his quarter century of goatish solicitations of female employees and lobbyists would appear to only solidify the Democratic domination of Washington, but a precedent is being established that could eventually shake the Democratic establishment. Many Democrats luminaries are in danger, not because they are Packwood-style mashers, but because the definition of sexual harassment being wielded against Packwood—"making unwanted sexual advances toward those working for him or with him"—is so broad that a substantial fraction of all men would be implicated, assuming the office Christmas parties I've attended are representative.

Now, most Americans' attitude toward sexual harassment is that they know it when they see it. Everybody would include the quid pro quo, "Sleep with me or lose your job," whether spoken or unspoken. Many would target physical advances, especially Packwood's pawing, slobbering, chase 'em around the desk style reminiscent of a 1950s sex comedy's Dirty Old Boss. Many Americans would also be hard on adulterous advances, although journalists have been reticent on this aspect of Packwood's delinquencies.

Yet none of these characteristics are necessary under the modern strict constructionist formulation of the crime. For example, Anita Hill never alleged any quid pro quo, physical contact, or adulterous intent.

Further, most Americans would probably censure the industrial scale lecher. Some might distinguish between sexual and romantic advances, although others might find that naive, requiring Godlike insight into the human soul. A more workable distinction might be between flirtation and indecent proposals, although once again the line would be hard to draw. Likewise, some would castigate boorish, Marlon Brandoish advances, but exempt debonair Cary Grantish passes. Others might find this distinction a matter of taste. Many would single out recurrent advances, although others would have a hard time distinguishing between the chronic harasser and the lovelorn swain. Yet, none of these exacerbating factors, subjective as they are, are required under the fundamentalist proscription. A further oddity is that no advance no matter how obnoxious is prohibited as long as it ultimately turns out to be wanted.

The word in the orthodox description that especially troubles Americans (and baffles Europeans) is "unwanted." Logically speaking, we could, like the Khmer Rouge in the Year Zero, try to abolish all sexual advances, unwanted and wanted. Given enough secret policemen, it might almost be doable. But to try to eliminate just the advances that turn out to be "unwanted" while preserving the "wanted" ones, requires not just a police state but a time machine. (Possibly, some of the formulators understood this, and simply intended to discourage all male advances. For example, the pioneering theorist, Professor Catharine MacKinnon, has avowed that she thinks all heterosexual intercourse is either rape or prostitution.)

Trust me, few guys like getting rejected. It's just that no advance is wanted or unwanted until it's made. Unwanted sexual advances are the price we all pay for the survival of the species. Maybe I'm just biased; see, my all time personal favorite office sexual advance was the one my Dad made on my Mom in 1946. Still, I suspect that women today are probably more dependent on meeting men at work than in 1946, and thus are even less interested in outlawing wanted advances

Surveys report that a large minority of American women say they have been sexually harassed. What these confirm is that the majority of women don't take the fundamentalist definition seriously, otherwise the surveys would find not 30% or 40% agreement, but virtually 100%. What self respecting woman would admit that no man had ever made an unwanted sexual advance toward her? She'd be admitting either that no man's ever made her a sexual advance or that she's never met a sexual advance she didn't like.

Unfortunately for the honchos of the Democratic party, the truest believers in the nefariousness of unwanted sexual advances are politicized liberal career women in the media, the law, academia, government work, and politics; in other words, exactly those women toward whom so many liberal politicians have made so many on-the-job passes, wanted and unwanted, over the decades. Democrats have made much political hay out of sexual harassment since Anita Hill, but the old boys are about to be hoisted by their own petard.

Senator Kennedy, of course, has dug himself into a hole so deep over the years that there is almost a Falstaffian grandeur to his predicament. A far more intriguing potential target, though, is Bill Clinton.

I know of no evidence whatsoever that Clinton has ever made "unwanted sexual advances to women who worked for him or with him." Yet, if I were an investigative reporter wishing to make a name for myself as the Woodward/Bernstein of the 90's, I'd be highly intrigued by these facts: Governor Clinton has for many years presided over thousands of female state employees. By his own testimony, he has not always paid strict attention to his marriage vows. Finally, he is widely reputed to be a man like any other man, only more so.

On the other hand, Mr. Clinton is younger and more Kennedyesque than the hapless Mr. Packwood, so a higher proportion of any propositions he might have made would have ultimately proven to be "wanted," thus letting him off the hook, according to the fascinating logic of current harassment theory. Yet, not even Warren Beatty has a career batting average of 1.000. So, all in all, it seems likely that some enterprising reporter is going to think it worth his while to go Pulitzer hunting among the secretarial pools and law offices of Little Rock. I'm sure they've been raked over before by journalists, but they were looking for the wrong kind of woman. Far more scandalous in today's environment would be the story of the woman who didn't commit adultery with Bill Clinton.

Most likely, the reporter won't find anybody who'll say anything. Quite possibly, there is nothing to be said. But if there is, at any moment over the next four years a vast brouhaha may erupt. While initially amusing to contemplate, the thought of a Watergate-like paralysis of the executive branch, followed by an Al Gore Presidency and a retributive Democratic attack on every Republican who has ever winked at a pretty girl, is not.

If Mr. Clinton has any secret worries on this score, he should act now. A vague confession and apology would cause a short flurry of tsk-tsking, but the ultimate loser would not be the President but the expansive definition of sexual harassment.

As a parallel, consider how the short-lived marijuana witch hunt of 1987 was declawed. When Judge Douglas Ginsburg's nomination to the Supreme Court was deep-sixed by his admitting to having smoked the demon weed, it briefly seemed likely that by the logic of the scandal much of an entire generation would be permanently disqualified from high office. Fortunately, due to the immediate 'fessing-up of younger Presidential candidates like Al Gore and Bruce Babbitt, this potential inquisition sputtered out. Of course, it flared up again farcically in 1992 when Governor Bill confessed that he had toked, but never inhaled.

Which is another reason why I'd like to see Mr. Clinton address the subject of any past indiscretions: not only would it be good for the country, but judging from his previous equivocations, we can expect another doozy.

A Rape Hoax for Book Lovers

Taki's
December 3, 2014

NUMEROUS identity politics uproars, such as Ferguson, Trayvon, and Duke Lacrosse, have turned out to be humiliating fiascos for the national press when all the facts are finally toted up. Note that these were the mainstream media's wars of choice, battlegrounds chosen to teach the public lessons.

What can we expect from the next crisis in the press's pipeline, the purported fraternity initiation gang rape?

Even as the Ferguson narrative exploded, both metaphorically and literally, in an orgy of media-encouraged looting and arson, vanguard elements were moving on to the upcoming obsession. A long article in *Rolling Stone* by Sabrina Rubin Erdely, entitled "A Rape on Campus: A Brutal Assault and Struggle for Justice at UVA," appeared on November 19th:

> Jackie was just starting her freshman year at the University of Virginia when she was brutally assaulted by seven men at a frat party. When she tried to hold them accountable, a whole new kind of abuse began.

Here's the tale that has been acclaimed across the country with barely any journalistic skepticism for the first 10 days:

A stone-cold sober coed named Jackie is lured by her date "Drew" to an upstairs room at the fraternity house. She is immediately tackled by one of the eight men waiting in the pitch darkness. Their toppling bodies crash through a glass table unaccountably left out in the middle of the rape room. Amidst the shattered glass, the young men beat her and hold her down on the floor. The shards grind into her bleeding back as she is methodically raped in the dark for three hours by seven young men, while her upperclassman date and another man coach them.

The frat boys egg on one reluctant pledge: "Don't you want to be a brother?"

"We all had to do it, so you do, too."

In other words, this is supposed to be some sort of fraternity initiation rite. (That fraternities at UVA hold their initiations in the spring, not in September, isn't mentioned in the article.)

The last lad, whom Jackie somehow recognizes in the dark as a boy in her anthropology class, rapes her with a glass bottle.

What should we make of Erdely's "brutal tableau" of beer bottle rape amidst the shattered glass?

As a work of journalism, it's most interesting for what it inadvertently reveals about the bizarre legends that seem plausible to American media consumers in 2014.

As a creative work of art, however, drawing (consciously or unconsciously) upon multiple influences such as the blockbuster *Girl with the Dragon Tattoo* hate porn franchise and the *Shattered Glass* biopic of magazine article fabricator Stephen Glass, it is more impressive.[1] It's first-rate propaganda, and Erdely's adroit techniques should be studied by those concerned about how gullible Americans are.

Some of the literary power of Erdely's nightmarish retelling of poor Jackie's saga stems from the writer's use of glass, both broken and bottle, as an ominous multipurpose metaphor. Throughout "A Rape on Campus," glass stands for fragility, bloodshed, loss of virginity, alcohol, littering, male brutishness, danger, violence, even a literal phallic symbol. Glass represents not the calm transparency of a window pane, but the occluded viciousness of the white conservative Southern male power structure.

For example:

> The first weeks of freshman year are when students are most vulnerable to sexual assault.... Hundreds of women in crop tops and men in khaki shorts stagger between handsome fraternity houses, against a call-and-response soundtrack of "Whoo!" and breaking

glass. "Do you know where Delta Sig is?" a girl slurs, sloshed. Behind her, one of her dozen or so friends stumbles into the street, sending a beer bottle shattering.

Strangely, just about the only people in America who don't seem to have accepted at face value Jackie's theory of a nine-man conspiracy to rape her are those portrayed in the *Rolling Stone* article as knowing the poor young woman well.

Much of this immense article is devoted to puzzling scenes in which Jackie's friends and female mentors tell her to cheer up and get over it. If you read the article carefully, you'll notice that almost everybody who knows Jackie closely treats her about the way you'd treat a friend who starts talking about having been abducted by aliens. You would try to find out what the real actual thing that happened to her was. But if she kept talking about alien rectal probing, you'd try to change the subject.

Morally, Sabrina Rubin Erdely and *Rolling Stone* should not have exploited an unsettled young woman.

Late in her first year at UVA, depressed and in danger of flunking out, Jackie talks to Dean Nicole Eramo, Chair of the Sexual Misconduct Board. This dean patiently explains to Jackie the three ways she can file charges, but Jackie can't make up her mind. Eventually, Dean Eramo suggests she join a campus rape survivors's support group. There, Jackie makes new friends who appreciate her story (even though it's more violent than their own).

In Erdely's telling, Dean Eramo, a middle-aged lady, is a sinister figure, a *sonderkommando* who shields the rape culture by getting students to confide in her instead of exposing the vileness all about. But there's a problem with the author's interpretation: Jackie and numerous other young women *love* Dean Eramo. She listens. Jackie and others responded to the *Rolling Stone* hit piece against Eramo by writing a long letter to the college newspaper praising the dean.

My vague impression is that Jackie seems like a troubled soul who drew needed comfort from talking to listeners who were sympathetic. She doesn't appear to have been in any hurry over the last couple of years to talk to people who might ask her tough questions about the validity of her allegations, such as police detectives or defense attorneys. That appears to have been prudent on her part.

Unfortunately, *Rolling Stone* was eager to use her for its own commercial and political purposes.

And so her story is now our latest national media crisis.

During her sophomore year, Jackie became prominent in the struggle on campus against rape culture. But the patriarchy struck back brutally last spring, using its favorite tool of violence, the glass bottle. Outside a bar at the Corner:

> One man flung a bottle at Jackie that broke on the side of her face, leaving a blood-red bruise around her eye.

That's horrifying...assuming it happened. Or are we deep into *Gone Girl* territory now? (There's nothing in the article about anybody calling the police over this presumably open-and-shut case.) Erdely continues:

> She e-mailed Eramo so they could discuss the attack—and discuss another matter, too, which was troubling Jackie a great deal. Through her ever expanding network, Jackie had come across something deeply disturbing: two other young women who, she says, confided that they, too, had recently been Phi Kappa Psi gang-rape victims.
>
> A bruise still mottling her face, Jackie sat in Eramo's office in May 2014 and told her about the two others.... (Neither woman was willing to talk to *RS*.)

Eramo had been listening to Jackie's stories for a year at this point:

> As Jackie wrapped up her story, she was disappointed by Eramo's nonreaction. She'd expected shock, disgust, horror.

Erdely attributes this widespread ho-hum reaction among Jackie's old friends and confidantes to a second massive conspiracy, this one to cover up the first conspiracy in order to protect that bastion of the right, UVA.

Erdely's explanation for why those who know Jackie best didn't rush her to the hospital or call 911 or even pay much attention to her claims over the next two years is that the University of Virginia is an alien, hostile, conservative country club with an...

> aura of preppy success, where throngs of toned, tanned and overwhelmingly blond students fanned across a landscape of neoclassical brick buildings.

The *Rolling Stone* writer is bothered by how UVA students look up to founder Thomas Jefferson (a notorious rapist of a black body, I might add).

Erdely finds offense in the campus honor code, by which students promise not to cheat on papers.

By the way, how conservative is UVA? In 2008, Barack Obama carried Charlottesville, home of UVA, by a sizable 11,600 votes. But Charlottesville is probably less extremely liberal than, say, Penn. So to Erdely, UVA is, basically, the Other.

I suppose that Erdely's positing two conspiracy theories is logically consistent. But Occam's razor suggests that the real campus conspiracy may have been to gently humor the unhappy girl.

Perhaps the first person of any prominence in the media to read the *Rolling Stone* article skeptically was Richard Bradley, a veteran author and magazine editor (who used to be named Richard Blow). Bradley asked on his personal blog on November 24th, five days after publication, the simple question: "Is the *Rolling Stone* Story True?"[2]

Bradley began:

> Some years ago, when I was an editor at *George* magazine, I was unfortunate enough to work with the writer Stephen Glass on a number of articles. They proved to be fake, filled with fabrications, as was pretty much all of his work. The experience was painful but educational; it forced me to examine how easily I had been duped.... The answer, I had to admit, was because they corroborated my pre-existing biases.

The career of Stephen Glass at *The New Republic* was made into a decent little movie called *Shattered Glass*, with the fellow who played young Darth Vader in the *Star Wars* prequels as Glass and the always good Peter Sarsgaard as Chuck Lane, the new *TNR* editor who was the first to figure out Glass was just making up all his fabulous stories. The title card to the movie explained one major reason for *TNR's* naïveté: the median age of *New Republic* staffers was 26.

By the way, Erdely said in 1998 that she "adored" Stephen Glass when they were colleagues on a student publication at Penn.[3]

Bradley went on:

> So when, say, the Duke lacrosse scandal erupted, I applied that lesson. The story was so sensational! Believing it required indulging one's biases: A southern school ... rich white preppy boys ... a priv-

ileged sports team ... lower class African-American women ... rape.
It read like a Tom Wolfe novel.

Except the Duke lacrosse team gang rape never happened.

Like most 21st-century brouhahas, "A Rape on Campus" recapitulates many themes of Wolfe's novels. For example, in *A Man in Full*, Atlanta's establishment mobilizes to make go away a Georgia Tech coed's allegation that she was raped by the school's Heisman Trophy winner, Fareek Fanon.

Moreover, Jackie is portrayed as similar to the title character in Wolfe's *I Am Charlotte Simmons*, in which a first-year coed at a prestigious university is plunged into suicidal depression after she semi-consensually loses her virginity to a handsome but callous fraternity boy. Something deeply upsetting likely happened to Jackie, too, but exactly what is a mystery.

The fraternity rape story serves as a welcome distraction from the October arrest of black cabdriver Jesse Matthew for the September murder of white UVA coed Hannah Graham.[4]

A timeline of how Richard Bradley's critique finally made its way to the general public may be of interest.

A reader kindly alerted me to Bradley's post on November 24th. I made four scattershot comments on it on November 25th, beginning with my question:

> Wouldn't the rapists get cut by the broken glass all over the floor, too? I guess they were such sex-crazed animals that they didn't notice the glass cutting their hands and knees for the first three hours.

I continued to mull over the issues that had been raised. (I hate being publicly wrong, so I'm cautious.) On the 27th I returned to Bradley's blog to find I was still the only commenter, and added a fifth:

> Sorry to keep coming back to this, but I've done some more thinking and here's where the story falls apart: pitch darkness *and* broken glass on the floor. The glass table is smashed, but nobody turns on the light to see what happened or where the broken glass is? Instead, each man, having heard the glass table get smashed, still gets down on the floor covered with shards of broken glass, risking not only his hands and knees, but also pulling out an even more personal part of his anatomy, one that he only has one of.
> *Really?*

By the 29th I was still the only commenter, but I finally felt confident enough that there were major problems with the *Rolling Stone* account to link to Bradley's critique from my *iSteve* blog at the *Unz Review*.

That opened the floodgates. Comments finally poured in to Bradley's blog. And on the first two days of December, numerous well-known publications weighed in with skeptical assessments based on Bradley's analysis: Robby Soave at *Reason*, Glenn Reynolds at *Instapundit*, Megan McArdle at *Bloomberg*, Ashe Schow at the *Washington Examiner*, Bret Stephens at the *Wall Street Journal*, Judith Shulevitz at *The New Republic*, Jonah Goldberg at the *Los Angeles Times*, and Erik Wemple at the *Washington Post*.

I remain struck by the literary aspect of the article. This is not crude agitprop, but a polished performance by somebody who has at least thought about how famous journalists negotiate the sometimes blurry line between fact and fiction.

For example, studded throughout Erdely's text is evidence (for instance, her phrase "brutal tableau") of the influence of Wolfe's rival as the greatest comic journalist/novelist of their era, Hunter S. Thompson. The summit of *Rolling Stone's* literary history was the 1971 publication of *Fear and Loathing in Las Vegas: A Savage Journey to the Heart of the American Dream*, a book that has long been subject to debate over whether it should be called New Journalism or a novel. It's full of paranoid fantasies about violence, but also very little action.

The subtitle of Erdely's article, "A Brutal Assault and Struggle for Justice at UVA," sounds like a parody of a Thompson subtitle. Indeed, in his self-parodying old age, Thompson published *Fear and Loathing in America: The Brutal Odyssey of an Outlaw Journalist*.

This is not to assert that Erdely inserted some coded message into her text. I merely observe that the allusions to famous figures like Glass, Wolfe, and Thompson—who fell on various sides of the divide between journalism and novels—reflects a formidable level of literary contrivance on Erdely's part. It's like a serious anti-parody of old parodies. This may help explain why so many readers assumed it to be a trustworthy work of high quality.

Toward the end of *Fear and Loathing*, shattered glass starts becoming a repeated element within narrator Raoul Duke's paranoid skull:

> The [hotel] room looked like the site of some disastrous zoological experiment involving whiskey and gorillas. The ten-foot mirror was shattered, but still hanging together—bad evidence of that af-

ternoon when my attorney ran amok with the coconut hammer, smashing the mirror and all the light bulbs....

The bathroom floor was about six inches deep with soap bars, vomit, and grapefruit rinds, mixed with broken glass. I had to put my boots on every time I went in there to piss....

But then why all this booze? And these crude pornographic photos ... that were plastered on the broken mirror ... and all these signs of violence, these strange red and blue bulbs and shards of broken glass embedded in the wall plaster....

The penultimate joke in *Fear and Loathing* is that almost all the brutal and bizarre violence in the book never actually happens outside of Duke's head.

The ultimate joke in *Fear and Loathing* is that few readers ever got the penultimate joke.

Thanks to Richard Bradley, more people have an opportunity to appreciate this new joke.

Epilogue:

Well, I got that one mostly right. It turned into a huge scandal and Rolling Stone *wound up paying out millions to the libeled fraternity, which, in a literal* Kristallnacht, *had its windows smashed by a campus mob, and Dean Eramo.*

My main mistake was my chivalric sympathy for Jackie Coakley. When a tape of their conversation was played in court, it turned out Jackie was the dominant personality of the pair, making up nonsense about Haven Monahan's depredations out of whole cloth (much of her story borrowed from an old episode of Dawson's Creek), *while the nerdy Erdely chipped in statistics garnered from the Obama Administration's "Dear Colleague" letter and subsequent* New York Times *hysteria about* The Campus Rape Crisis.

Hair Hysteria

Taki's
October 2, 2019

L AST week, the prestige press decided that it was National News that a 12-year-old black girl in the D.C. suburbs had come home with some of her rather unflattering dreadlocks cut off.[5] When her grandmother asked what had happened to her hair, the tween refused to answer. But later she told Grandma that it wasn't her fault her hair was cut because, see, three white boys in her class, you know, had held her down on the school playground, called her hair "nappy," and pulled out scissors.

Granted, this story sounds to you and me like something Jussie Smollett, Tawana Brawley, Crystal Mangum, Jackie Coakley, and Tribal Elder Nathan Phillips would concoct while getting high together on nitrous oxide from whipped cream cans.

After all, few white males younger than 79-year-old Don Imus use the word "nappy." And do roving gangs of male juveniles actually carry scissors for impromptu hairstyling?

But to the national news media, the little girl's tall tale was exactly the kind of thing they imagine is happening everywhere, due to Trump and 1619 and Toxic Masculinity and, most of all, White People Wanting to Touch Black Hair.

Therefore, this ludicrous hate hoax was seized upon by the *Washington Post* and the *New York Times*. The latter darkly noted about the girl's private school:

Immanuel Christian's website ... says that it does not accept gay students and that it requires employees to affirm that marriage should be between one man and one woman.[6]

That just proves that the Good People, such as blacks and gays and the rest of the Democrats' Coalition of the Fringes, are all on the same side against the Bad People (i.e., straight white males).

The fact that Mike Pence's wife, Karen, is a part-time art teacher at this school was gleefully mentioned. Perhaps the thinking was that when Trump is impeached and convicted, and meanwhile the vice president has to resign over this Dreadlockgate, then Speaker of the House Nancy Pelosi would become president! Or something like that...

But on Monday all the fun ended abruptly when the girl's family issued a statement apologizing for her having made the whole hair hoax up.

In the real world, of course, 12-year-old girls do silly stuff to their hair all the time, and then they sometimes make up implausible excuses for what happened to it.

Dreadlocks, by the way, are not a good look on a girl. They are associated with the patriarchal Rastafarians, like the late Bob Marley, who wore dreadlocks to resemble the Lion of Judah with a massive head. As of 2012, about 180 NFL players wore dreadlocks.

So it would hardly be surprising if a sixth-grade girl, or one of her friends, started trying to modify her hairdo, then discovered that cutting your own hair is typically not a good idea, especially in case, if I might speculate, your grandparents might have paid for an expensive dreadlocks weave.

I don't know that that is exactly what happened, but something like it was always far more plausible than the nonsense the media played up.

You might think that national news organs would be aware enough to decide not to run with this trivial matter in case it blew up humiliatingly in their faces. But they are now beyond embarrassment.

To understand why, you have to look into the evolution of extraordinary media delusions and the madness of elites. Why are we currently undergoing World War Hair?

One of the funnier hallucinations is that white people older than first graders go around demanding to touch the hair of blacks, and that the victims are traumatized for life by it. Barack Obama's *Dreams From My Father* seems to have seeded this trope with his claim that "a redheaded girl asked to touch my hair."

Hair-touching has become the go-to anecdote for privileged blacks—like our preppy-from-paradise president—who want to prove that they are still the victims of white racism despite all the evidence to the contrary.

The reigning Theory of Intersectionality was made up thirty years ago by a black woman law professor named Kimberlé Crenshaw (whose Twitter handle is @sandylocks in reference to how she colors her hair) to demand that black women like herself deserve to be more privileged than black men or white women (and, of course, white men).

With Intersectionality ascending to an unquestionable dogma lately, the establishment press has come to believe that it is immensely important to find out what young women of color have on their minds. They must have come up with some incredibly great ideas during their 400 years of marginalization.

So, the media have increasingly turned over their platforms to young women of color.

And what messages do they have for us?

After having read hundreds of their op-eds and the like over the past few years, I've discovered that the No. 1 topic young woman-of-color journalists want us to listen to them talk about is...their hair.

They definitely have a lot to say about their hair.[7]

Why?

Well, first of all, because they are young women. Looking nice is very important to young ladies and it takes up a lot of space in their brains.

Second, due to the decline in prestige of white men, with their tiresome science and rationality, older ways of thinking are growing in influence. And hair plays an important role in Haitian voodoo and Southern hoodoo magic. A guide to voodoo explains:

> Using human hair and/or the finger nails of the intended love interest aids in the creation of a powerful love spell. With such objects voodoo dolls can be created to help one fall in love with another.

Third, although we are constantly lectured that race does not exist, that race is a social construct rather than a biological fact, in truth, race is as visible as the hair on your head.

Racial integration exposes black women to competition in the sexual marketplace with women from races with longer, silkier hair that tends to be more attractive to men.

Why do men generally prefer longer hair on women? Whether or not women can naturally grow their hair longer than men on average seems to be a question in dispute. The only hair-growing experiment I've ever seen refer-enced found that women, on average, could grow hair twelve inches longer than men could before it started to fall out. So perhaps long hair is a second-ary sex characteristic? But the facts remain murky and little-studied.

Anyway, very few cultures in the world encourage their men to grow their hair longer than their women. The only two I can think of offhand are the Rastafarians of Jamaica and the Maasai of Kenya, both of whom favor dread-locks, thick for Rasta men, thin for Maasai warriors.

Not surprisingly, this racial difference in hair is difficult for African-Amer-ican females to deal with, both pragmatically and psychologically. For an insightful, sympathetic introduction to what black women put themselves through to socially construct more attractive hair for themselves, see comedi-an Chris Rock's documentary *Good Hair*.

Fourth, young woman-of-color journalists have been to college, where they are lectured that, as the late Michel Foucault is assumed to have proved, everything is a social construct. If you control the discourse, you have power, and if you have power, you will naturally want to control the discourse.

Why not, then, use power to "change the conversation" to propagandize people into finding black women's hair better-looking than that of their racial rivals?

After all, the fashion-industrial complex is constantly socially engineering changes in what women think they need to look like. With enough power, woman-of-color journalists reason, we can change the discourse enough that men will truly feel that black women's hair is best.

Over the past few years, mighty efforts have been expended by the media to brainwash people into preferring black women's looks. This crusade has done wonders for the careers of a handful of beautiful black models, actress-es, and singers. But whether it has done black women as a whole much good is uncertain.

In any case, the media will keep on trying, in accordance with Sailer's Law of Female Journalism:

> The most heartfelt articles by female journalists tend to be demands
> that social values be overturned in order that, Come the Revolu-
> tion, the journalist herself will be considered hotter-looking.

CHAPTER ELEVEN

Jews and Gentiles

Counting Jewish Achievement

VDARE
11/02/2011

MY favorite *Sesame Street* character is Count von Count, an amiable vampire who always refers to himself in the third person in his thick Transylvanian accent—"The Count loves counting!"—as he enumerates everything in sight.

I love counting, too, which is why I find Richard Lynn's books, such as 2002's *IQ and the Wealth of Nations*, irresistible: Lynn is another countaholic.[1]

Lynn's latest, *The Chosen People: A Study of Jewish Intelligence and Achievement*, tabulates the consistently impressive performance of Northern European Jews—known as "Ashkenazi" Jews, as opposed to the Sephardic Jews from Spanish or Portuguese backgrounds, such as Benjamin Disraeli—across many fields in 17 different countries. Lynn, a psychology professor emeritus at the University of Ulster, calculates "Achievement Quotients" of how heavily Jews are represented in a broad range of desirable categories, from the professions to bridge champions.

To summarize Lynn's findings: Ashkenazi Jews do well in every country they inhabit, and in most every field in which they compete.

Jewish organizations devote much energy to counting the number of high-achieving Jews, as the many Jewish websites devoted to listing famous Jews attest. (For example, do an online search for "Jewish baseball players").

So this information is available to anyone with an internet connection. But it is presently considered Just Not Done for gentiles like Lynn to take a scientific interest in such matters—no matter how appreciative their attitude.

In contrast, the federal government spends huge sums counting blacks, Hispanics, and whites for the purpose of rectifying white "overrepresentation" through quotas and lawsuits.

Lynn, however, blithely plunges ahead with his task. And he is quite right to do so. The impact of Jewish intelligence in the modern world could hardly be more important—or less studied.

For example, the Jewish record in winning Nobel Prizes is extraordinary. Lynn cites Nobel laureate data compiled by the Israel Science and Technology Homepage,[2] a website run by biochemist Israel Hanukoglu, who was the chief science advisor to Benjamin Netanyahu during his first term as prime minister. Updating Lynn's Nobel numbers to include the recently announced 2011 prizes, we find:

Medicine or Physiology: Jews have comprised 51 of the 199 laureates, or 26%

>Physics: 47 of 191, or 25%
>Chemistry 30 out of 160, or 19%
>Literature: 12 out of 108, or 11%
>Peace: 9 out of 101, or 9%
>Economics: 24 out of 69, or 35%

Of course, the latter three prizes are all dubious. The Literature Prize depends upon vagaries of taste and translation (there are likely more famous authors who didn't win the Nobel than ones who did). The Peace Prize is inherently political. And Economics is more ideological than scientific. While there are Republican and Democratic economists, nobody talks about Republican and Democratic chemists.

This is not to say there are no controversies about the hard science Nobels. For example, the only Nobel laureate I've had dinner with is among the most frequently cited as undeserving. When I was a student at Rice University in 1978, the new physics laureate Robert Wilson, a Rice alumnus, came to his alma mater to give a speech. A modest man, he pointed out that it was ironic that he and Arno Penzias had won the Nobel Prize for proving the Big Bang Theory, even though they had to have the cosmic importance of their discovery of microwave background radiation explained to them by astrophysical theorists at Princeton. And the Princetonians, as many other Princetonians have complained, didn't win the Nobel.

But when I mentioned this anecdote about Wilson to an astronomy professor last year, he replied: "Do you think it was a coincidence that they gave the Nobel to the best experimental astronomer of his generation, the guy whose technique was so good that he found what nobody else could find?" So even this notoriously controversial hard science Nobel turns out to be quite legit.

And winning a science Nobel should not be thought of as solely an individual achievement. To earn the chemistry prize, for instance, you need a good laboratory. Thus, it took the U.S. a long time to get started at winning Nobels. From 1901 through 1929, a period in which 30 people born in Germany won Nobels, only one native-born American was a laureate. There was plenty of talent born in America in the 19th Century. But America back then trailed Europe at the highest levels of technical and theoretical sophistication.

Still, if you keep all that in mind, the Nobels are a good data source for Lynn to mine.

Jews have won 23% of the Medicine, Physics, and Chemistry Nobels. This is tremendously impressive because Jews have always comprised a small fraction of the world's population. Before the Holocaust, Jews might have made up about 2.5% of the population of Europe, North America, and Australasia. Today, they make up roughly 0.2% of the world's population.

It has long been predicted that Jewish achievement in science will slow down, as affluent younger Jews turn to more lucrative or fun careers, such as Wall Street and Hollywood. But we don't see that in the Nobel Prize data. In the 21st century so far, Jews have won 24 of the 91 science Nobels, or 26%, which is even higher than their 20th Century rate.

Of course, that doesn't tell us what is actually happening in the last decade. The awarding of hard science Nobels typically lag their discovery by at least a decade, as the Swedish Royal Academy of Sciences has grown cautious about either rewarding work that might not bear the test of time or overlooking the greats of the past before they die. The 2011 winners were recognized for work first published between 1973 and 1998.

Inevitably, all this data raises the inevitable question: Who is a Jew? This is both a fascinating question and the kind of quibble frequently used to intellectually intimidate curious gentiles with the message: Move along, nothing to notice here.

Netanyahu's friend Hanukoglu offers one definition:

> This list includes only Nobel laureates who are Jewish by the strict definition of Halacha (interpretation of the laws of the Hebrew Scriptures) that requires being born to a Jewish mother or formal conversion to Judaism. Definition of being Jewish is similar to nationality and is independent of personal beliefs.

On the other hand, the *JInfo* website, building upon the 1997 *Encyclopedia Judaica*, uses a more inclusive definition, counting anybody who is at least half Jewish, whether upon his mother's or father's side.[3] *JInfo* writes: "Approximately 15% of those [laureates] listed (and about 10% of the Americans listed) are, or were, of half-Jewish descent."

Including everybody who is at least half-Jewish bumps up the percentage of laureates by one to six points: medicine goes up from 26% Jewish to 27%, physics from 24% to 25%, chemistry from 19% to 20%, while economics jumps from 35% to 41%.

Lynn would prefer to take a more precise approach than either website does because he's interested in the genetics of Jewish intelligence. Consider the Bohr family. The great Danish physicist Niels Bohr won the 1922 Nobel in physics. His mother Ellen Adler Bohr was Jewish, while his father Christian Bohr was Christian.

In turn, Niels's son Aage Bohr won the Nobel in physics in 1975. By both Hanukoglu's rabbinical standards and *JInfo*'s ethnic ones, that makes Niels Bohr Jewish but Aage Bohr gentile. Lynn, however, feels it would make the most sense to count Niels as half Jewish and Aage as one quarter Jewish.

And there are always the ambiguous nature-nurture cases. For example, how many Jewish baseball players are in the Hall of Fame? Hank Greenberg and Sandy Koufax are famous as Hall of Famers who are Jewish. But what about Lou Boudreau, the Cleveland Indians shortstop who became a player-manager at 25? Apparently, he had a Jewish biological mother, but was adopted by Catholics.[4]

Statistically speaking, however, these sort of quibbles probably don't make much difference. If laureates who are half Jewish are evenly divided between those with Jewish mothers and those with Jewish fathers, both the rabbinic method and the genetic will produce the same overall percentage results.

COUNTING JEWISH ACHIEVEMENT

By any means of counting, there are quite a number of countries where Jews make up a remarkable percentage of native-born Nobel laureates. For example, among American natives, Lynn counts 200 prizewinners through 2009 (leaving aside the peace prize as non-intellectual). Jews made up 62, or 31%. Since Jews comprised about 3% of the adult population in the U.S. in the middle of the last century, this gives American Jews an Achievement Quotient for Nobel laureates of just over ten.

And the American AQ is fairly low by international standards. In places with very few Jews, AQs can be stratospheric, such as Switzerland (3 Jewish laureates out of 17 total laureates for an AQ of 60), Latin America (2 out of 8 for an AQ of 220) and Italy (4 out of 17 for a 320).

After awhile, *The Chosen People* becomes slightly repetitious as evidence for consistently high levels of Jewish accomplishment pile up.[5] For variety's sake, I started looking for exceptions to prove the rule.

I found a few. British gentiles are pretty good at winning Nobels. They've won 76 while British-born Jews have won only three, for an Achievement Quota of six. This low AQ does not appear to stem from British Jews being untalented or terribly discriminated against, but instead because British gentiles are unusually good at doing Nobel-worthy work.

Similarly, as Lynn documents, Jews do very well in Australia, but gentiles have won all ten Nobels awarded to natives of Australia.

Lynn's data suggests that Jews have their very highest Achievement Quotas in the more abstract fields such as philosophy and mathematics. Lynn notes that IQ tests suggest Jews tend to be strongest at logic involving words and numbers and weakest at visuo-spatial reasoning. In the professions, Jews might be least distinguished as engineers. Yet Jewish engineers still have AQs well above 1.0 in most countries.

One creative career where Jews appear to be less heavily represented than you'd expect: cinematography (although the best-known Mexican cameraman, Emmanuel Lubezki, who works on Terence Malick's movies like *The Tree of Life*, is Jewish). Why? My guess is that Jews in Hollywood who have outstanding visual talent will tend to become directors rather than just be cinematographers.

Perhaps the artistic field where Jewish influence is least powerful is golf course architecture. I've devoted absurd amounts of time over the last 40 years to studying the history of golf course design, but I'm not familiar with any major golf course architect who was Jewish. This is not for lack of opportunity. There are scores of historically-Jewish country clubs in America. But they tend to have better clubhouses and cuisine than golf courses.

There are social reasons for this. Golf is a Scottish game, and the classic courses tend to belong to private clubs dominated by Protestants. Therefore, those who move in old-money circles get more chances to see great golf design. And there are likely also cognitive reasons: the ability to imagine three-dimensionally is crucial to success in golf architecture.

In summary: the sheer comprehensiveness of Lynn's data collection, stretching across many fields and many countries, allows him to consider judiciously the various ad hoc theories that have been proposed to explain specific instances of high Jewish achievement.

His conclusion: we don't need all of the theories, but we do need at least two factors to account for this hugely important pattern.

One reason seems overwhelmingly obvious to Lynn, although apparently not to most of those who have advanced theories (at least in print) for Jewish achievement: higher average IQ.

Lynn digs up 32 IQ studies of American Jews and seven of British Jews. He concludes that Ashkenazi Jews (ones with Yiddish-speaking ancestors) average about ten points higher than non-Hispanic white gentiles, or 110 on a scale where white Americans and Brits average 100. That would put the median Ashkenazi Jew at about the 75th percentile among whites.

IQ testing in Israel suggests that the other Jewish communities trail the Ashkenazi. Lynn estimates that Sephardim score about two points less than white gentiles, or 98. The Mizrahim (Jews from the Arab world) average around 91.

That ten-point gap between Ashkenazi and gentile whites is substantial, but not enormous. The proportion of individuals with IQs of 115 or above is about twice as great among Jews as among white gentiles. But the absolute number of gentiles is much larger.

Jews are, per capita, twice as common relative to American gentile whites over the 115 IQ level that Lynn sees as the bottom threshold for the professions, but are about 5 times more common per capita among doctors and lawyers. And in many other developed countries, these ratios are even higher.

Lynn's significant (and subtle) conclusion: superior Jewish IQ isn't everything. He writes:

This suggests that the success of the Ashkenazim is attributable to more than just their high IQs and that they also possess strong motivational and work-ethic qualities.

This profound subject has only just begun to be explored.

Jews and *Noblesse Oblige*

VDARE
March 8, 2010

The theory behind the dusty old concept of *noblesse oblige* is that a powerful class that thinks of itself as being in the game for the very long run will tend to behave in a more responsible fashion than one that doesn't. As they say, nobody ever washed a rental car.

In the early 20th Century, for example, leadership caste WASPs played a major role in setting aside National Parks and in limiting immigration.

Even more fundamentally, they tolerated criticism of themselves by others. Criticism encourages you to behave better.

Of course, the moribund WASP Establishment's increasing fair-mindedness had its downsides. One problem with letting other people have their say about you is that they may undermine your power. David Samuels writes of

> ...my own personal sorrow about the fate of the Harvard-educated Brahmins I admired in my youth, who cherished their belief in liberal openness while licking at the bleached bones of their family romances. Their mansions are threadbare and drafty, and stickers on their salt-eaten Volvos advertise the cause of zero population growth.[6]

But, shouldn't new elites be held to the same standards of criticism that helped them displace the old elites? Why is it considered admirable for the new establishment to try to destroy the careers of their critics?

For noblesse oblige to work, privileged and influential groups have to be publicly acknowledged to be privileged and influential. If, on the other hand, their main sense of collective identity is that of marginal members of society endangered by the might of the current majority, then the system doesn't operate.

In 2006, blogger Noah Millman was surprised by a rabbi's Purim sermon.[7] Not by the message—Write your Congressman about Darfur!—but by the unusual explanation the rabbi offered: *noblesse oblige*.

> He compared the position of the Jewish community in America today with Queen Esther's position in King Ahashuerus's [Xerxes's] Persia: that is to say, a position of power or, more precisely, profound influence on those who wield power. And, he said, that power implies responsibility.

Millman noted:

> "But you (or at least I) rarely hear a Jewish leader saying, in so many words, that Jews must act to prevent this or that injustice because we are powerful, and power implies responsibility."

Instead, Jewish leaders typically exhort Jews with one of three arguments, all based around feelings of communal self-pity. Millman enumerates them:

1. "We Jews have suffered, so we should be acutely sensitive to others' suffering...";
2. "As God liberated the Jews from captivity in Egypt, ... we have a religious obligation as Jews to help the oppressed";
3. "Jews should be aware of our collective vulnerability, historical and continuing, and therefore for our own good always take the other side of the kinds of groups, movements and individuals who have victimized us in the past, and who could threaten us again in the future."

And yet that plain fact is that in modern America, Jews are the biggest winner among ethnic groups. Although only 2% of the American population, Jews make up about 35% of the *Forbes 400* wealthiest individuals. (That percentage is from after the financial bubble burst in 2007-2008, so it likely reflects a long-run baseline.)

By way of comparison, consider Italian-Americans, who arrived in America at roughly the same time as Jewish-Americans and tend to live in similar parts of the country. Today, Italians are fairly well represented in most aspects of American life: movie stars, the Democratic Speaker of the House, two Republican Supreme Court Justices, and so forth. Indeed, Italians make up 5.4% of the gentile members of the *Forbes 400* and 5.7% of the gentile population. For Italian-Americans, on average, life isn't bad.

Yet, Italians are only 1/30th as likely per capita as Jews to be billionaires.

Thirty to one is a big difference.

This ratio isn't proof of conspiracy or even simple discrimination. It is merely proof of Disparate Impact. Federal law makes a very big deal out of Disparate Impact when it involves "Hispanic" ethnicity. If ethnic Hispanics are less than four-fifths as successful as white non-Hispanics, a longstanding EEOC regulation puts the burden of disproving discrimination on employers.[8]

One-thirtieth is a lot smaller than four-fifths. Yet the law doesn't mention any other kind of ethnicity besides Hispanic.

You really can't understand modern America without thinking about these sorts of numbers. But, do Americans really want to understand America?

On the rare occasions when the topic of Jewish influence surfaces in the Main Stream Media, attempts to confuse are trotted out over and over—such as theological hair-splitting over Who Is a Jew? and reminders that Not All Jews Agree.

Of course, the exact same points could have been made about the old Protestant elites. Indeed, their disagreements are the stuff of American history, for example the Civil War. For that matter, Henry Ford and George S. Patton believed in reincarnation, but nobody claims they therefore weren't ethnically Protestant.

Just as it was worth understanding the Protestant Establishment, its strengths and weaknesses, it is now worth understanding the Jewish elite.

Yet in the Main Stream Media, mentioning the kind of numbers I just cited is mostly just not done.

One possible reason: almost 50% of the *Atlantic 50* list of the most important pundits are Jewish.[9]

Similarly, with the Oscars just selected, it's worth recalling Abe Foxman of the Anti-Defamation League noting in 2008 that "all eight major film studios are run by men who happen to be Jewish."[10]

Samuels contends "New York Jews circa 2008 are wealthy white people whose protestations of outsiderness inspire blank stares or impatient eye rolling."

But is that really true? Or has the public increasingly internalized Politically Correct ignorance?

The ADL has polled Americans four times on whether or not they agree with the proposition "The movie and television industries are pretty much run by Jews". In 1964, 47% agreed versus 21% who disagreed. By 2008, amazingly, only 22% of the public agreed and 63% disagreed.

Columnist Joel Stein laughed: "Actually, it just shows how dumb America has gotten. Jews totally run Hollywood."[11]

In contrast to the Main Stream Media, the Jewish press, such as *The Forward* and the *Jewish Telegraph Agency* (which first compiled an estimate of the Jewishness of the 2009 *Forbes 400*), is usually much more informative on the subject of Jewish influence.

Conclusion: American Jews should start thinking of themselves less as oppressed outcasts who need to go for whatever they can get while the getting is good, and start more accurately thinking of themselves as belonging to the best-connected inner circle of the contemporary American Establishment.

Thus, American Jews should realize that, like the Protestant elite of yore, their privileged position as a de facto leadership caste bestows upon themselves corresponding duties to conserve the long-term well-being of the United States—rather than to indulge in personal and ethnic profit and power maximization.

But that's unlikely to happen until the Jewish elite begin to tolerate non-Jewish criticism, rather than to continue to try to destroy the careers of critics[12]—or even just honest observers—in what seems to be an instinctive reaction intended to encourage the others.

A group self-image of victimization, combined with a penchant for ideological intensity and powerful ethnocentric lobbies, can lead to bizarre political manifestations—such as the dominant Jewish assumption that proper veneration of their Ellis Island ancestors requires opposition to immigration restriction today.

In contrast, Italian-Americans, who lack institutions such as the ADL, appear to feel themselves freer to make up their own minds about what immigration policy will be best for their American posterity.

Stranger in a WASP Land: *The Graduate*

Taki's
September 25, 2013

T HE *Graduate*, the December 1967 box-office smash starring new-comer Dustin Hoffman as Benjamin Braddock and Anne Bancroft as Mrs. Robinson, is often recounted as a major volley in the history of the Generation Gap. Made on a $3-million budget, it took in over $100 million domestically, which would be around $700 million in 2013 dollars. (In this century, only *Avatar* has earned more.)

Continuing my intermittent series reinterpreting American history, it's worth reconsidering what *The Graduate* was actually about.[13] Looking back from nearly a half-century later, the film seems less like a landmark in the short-lived Generation Gap and more of a milestone in the long-lasting Ethnic Gap.

There's very little in the film to situate it in the 1960s hippie/protest/drug era. Young Benjamin, for example, wears a coat and tie throughout. Much of the popular image of *The Graduate* appears to be a projection of Baby Boomers who were then hungry for any kind of cinematic affirmation.

Hollywood seldom adapts nimbly to youth trends because they don't put young people in charge of making movies, which are costly and easily botched. Thus, *The Graduate*'s main contributors were untrustworthy thirtysomethings: Director Mike Nichols was sometimes referred to as a boy genius and the second coming of Orson Welles due to his precocious success directing on Broadway. But he was 36 by the time *The Graduate* was finished.

Similarly, screenwriter Buck Henry was 37. Producer Lawrence Turman, who had discovered the novel by Charles Webb, was now 41. Bancroft's character was supposed to be in her mid-1940s, but the actress was 36.

And while Hoffman, making his movie debut, could effectively portray a socially maladroit 21-year-old, he was 30. Hoffman had been an Off-Broadway actor for a decade and his milieu had hardly been Haight-Ashbury. He'd shared apartments with two other future stars, neither of whom was ever thought of as the face of the counterculture: Gene Hackman and Robert Duvall.

Katharine Ross, 27, played Mrs. Robinson's ingénue daughter. And the 26-year-old musicians Paul Simon and Art Garfunkel added much to *The Graduate's* hepness quotient. Still, Simon and Garfunkel weren't exactly Frank Zappa in terms of alienating the old folks. Their "Mrs. Robinson" was a huge hit on the middle-of-the-road radio station my middle-aged parents listened to in 1968.

The only true 1960s person involved was the eccentric novelist Webb. He had published *The Graduate* in 1963 at age 24 based on his growing up a wealthy WASP in old-money Pasadena. A committed anti-materialist, he'd already turned down a large inheritance and has spent much of his life since his moment of fame in principled poverty.

The Graduate famously failed to impress the Hollywood old guard when previewed for them. Less well known is that a publicity tour of college campuses that Nichols and Hoffman undertook was not a success, either. Nichols recalls:

> In college after college, there was one question: Why isn't the movie about Vietnam?... No matter what you were doing—if you ran a laundry, your shirts had to be outraged about Vietnam.

Upon release, the movie took off with Jewish audiences in a few Manhattan theaters and slowly became a juggernaut nationally. It was lavishly praised for being the first movie to plumb the depths of the Generation Gap that suddenly everybody was talking about. Nichols admitted later:

> At that particular moment, "the generation gap" was everything. It never even entered our minds! The generation gap? Was it worse than Romeo and Juliet? What're they talking about?

So what was *The Graduate* about?

While Benjamin certainly feels beleaguered by his parents' hearty, talkative friends, they are the only people who will talk to him. He's an odd choice for the spokesman for the rising generation, since he appears to have no friends his own age.

In fact, Benjamin, with his flat affect, appears to be not quite right in the head.

In the Freudian style of the era, the movie briefly implies that Benjamin's affair with Mrs. Robinson is a displacement of his Oedipal urges toward his own mother. But a contemporary viewer would possess a more useful vocabulary to describe Benjamin than was available during Freud's monopoly upon popular psychologizing.

Today, we might call Benjamin an Aspergery nerd, a depressive, and an obsessive-compulsive stalker. In the future, people will no doubt look back and laugh at the crudity of 2013's psychological categories. Still, you have to admit we've at least made progress over the last 46 years by losing interest in Freud's.

In retrospect, Benjamin Braddock seems like Hoffman's beta release of his Oscar-winning portrayal of autistic Raymond Babbitt in 1988's *Rain Man*. Before his unexpected stardom, Hoffman had made ends meet working as an attendant at the New York Psychiatric Institute, so he had some hands-on familiarity with actual mental disabilities rather than the fanciful ones discussed by the patients of expensive Freudian shrinks.

Strikingly, Benjamin's personality is a little like that of Bancroft's real-life son Max Brooks, the very nervous author of *World War Z*. Max's father Mel Brooks was busy filming *The Producers*, a less suave reflection of the same general urge as *The Graduate*.

Nichols has reflected that he originally wanted to make a message movie in which "I said some fairly pretentious things about capitalism and material objects, about the boy drowning in material things and saving himself in the only possible way, which was through madness."[14]

Nichols, however, came to notice that he really liked making money and buying material objects. His total take from *The Graduate* may have made him the first director in history to rake in one million dollars from a single movie. He's since spent fortunes on hobbies such as Arabian horse breeding. Nichols once hired a friend of mine to design some home improvements for the palatial apartment he shares with his fourth wife, newscaster Diane Sawyer (who is so all-American that her father was a Republican judge in

Louisville named...Tom Sawyer). Nichols was the most demanding client my friend ever endured.

Nichols likes to claim that he hadn't realized what *The Graduate* was actually about until he saw it parodied in a juvenile humor magazine in October 1968:

> It took me years before I got what I had been doing all along—that I had been turning Benjamin into a Jew. I didn't get it until I saw this hilarious issue of *MAD* magazine after the movie came out, in which the caricature of Dustin says to the caricature of Elizabeth Wilson, 'Mom, how come I'm Jewish and you and Dad aren't?' And I asked myself the same question, and the answer was fairly embarrassing and fairly obvious: Who was the Jew among the goyim? And who was forever a visitor in a strange land?

This may be a story that has gotten better in Nichols's retelling because the ethnic angle had not been so mysterious to Nichols's underlings. J. W. Whitehead's book *Appraising The Graduate* includes Hoffman's memory of protesting to his self-confident director the implausibility of his casting:

> "I'm not right for this part, sir. This is a Gentile. This is a WASP. This is Robert Redford...."
> Nichols replied, "You mean he's not Jewish?"
> "Yes, this guy is a super-WASP. Boston Brahmin."
> And Mike said, "Maybe he's Jewish inside."

During filming, Hoffman picked up his first groupie: "Beautiful, thin, a real shiksa goddess. I think Nichols took that as a sign—at least somebody found me attractive. And it didn't get past me, either!"

Screenwriter Buck Henry argued for Hoffman's plausibility in the role by appealing to Cesare Lombroso's 1870s theory of racial atavism:

> You know my theory about California genetics? Jews from New York came to the Land of Plenty, and within one generation the Malibu sand had gotten into their genes and turned them into tall, Nordic powerhouses. Walking surfboards. We were thinking about how these Nordic people have Dustin as a son, and it's got to be a genetic throwback to some previous generation.

At whatever point Nichols got the idea, he ran with it:

He couldn't be a blond, blue-eyed person, because then why is he having trouble in the country of the blond, blue-eyed people? It took me a long time to figure that out—it's not in the material at all. And once I figured that out, and found Dustin, it began to form itself around that idea.

Whitehead says, "Nichols wanted Hoffman to project an estrangement that began in the blood."

In 1938 Nichols had arrived in America from Berlin, where his anti-communist Jewish ancestors had found refuge from the Soviet Union. His father quickly became successful again in the US. And the son became even more so, first triumphing at stand-up comedy with Elaine May, then directing Neil Simon blockbusters on Broadway. His first movie, *Who's Afraid of Virginia Woolf?*, earned him an Oscar nomination. He's since completed the coveted EGOT career grand slam, winning four Emmys, one Grammy, one Oscar (for *The Graduate*), and nine Tonys.

But everybody feels a bit estranged and unappreciated, even if (or especially if) he is Mike Nichols.

Ultimately, *The Graduate* is about the pain of being Jewish in a gentile society. This theme had been downplayed by previous generations of Jewish filmmakers, who were grateful for how nice Americans had been to Jews. But as the years went by, Jewish-American artists discovered that there was little danger and much profit in violating this old norm.

Not surprisingly, Nichols's ethnic alienation is reflected throughout *The Graduate*. In the wake of Israel's smashing June 1967 triumph in the Six-Day War, this proved tremendously popular with the American public at large.

For example, in the first scene in the hotel lobby, the unaggressive Benjamin has to step aside while dozens of pushy WASPs in formal attire shove through a revolving door ahead of him. And, of course, there's the memorable last scene in which Benjamin rescues his shiksa goddess from her new husband at the Methodist church by swinging a giant cross at the resentful blond beasts.

It doesn't get much more obvious than that.

The Myth of the Golf Nazi

Taki's
November 19, 2014

F OR most of history, being a hereditary aristocrat was a good job. The only catch was the old concept of *noblesse oblige*, which suggested that people of wealth, power, and influence were honor bound to defend the general public.

Today, however, it's more prestigious to be a victim of the majority. That seems to release you from any nagging worries about aristocratic responsibility.

Being an actual victim, though, is still no fun. So the best thing is to be recognized as a member of a hereditary victimocracy. The president, for example, is a victim-by-blood, as illustrated by *New Yorker* editor David Remnick's bestselling 2010 biography, *The Bridge: The Life and Rise of Barack Obama*. Remnick pleased his intended audience by interspersing thrilling chapters about heroic civil rights protestors in 1965 being beaten on the bridge in Selma, Alabama with admittedly less thrilling chapters about the young Obama building sand castles on Waikiki Beach.

One of the most popular varietals of hereditary victimocracy is to claim to be related to somebody who couldn't get into an exclusive golf club and thus had to found his own country club.

This widespread obsession with WASP country clubs as the locus of evil in America runs throughout a 4,000-word *New York Magazine* article, "Barbarian at the Tee," in which novelist Peter de Jonge recounts the mental terrors he endured sneaking on to play the old-money Maidstone golf course in the Hamptons. Here's a representative sample:

> In Frankfurt in 1938, well after ARYAN ONLY signs went up at the Opera House, my fair-haired Jewish father, then 12, kept attending performances on his own. It wasn't a protest. He did it because he felt like it and thought he could get away with it, and I'm playing Maidstone for about the same reason.

The article ends anticlimactically, with Maidstone's golf Nazis failing to even notice the author's transgressive intrusion.

In his memoir, *The Wolf of Wall Street*, swindler Jordan Belfort—who was portrayed so energetically by Leonardo DiCaprio in Martin Scorsese's movie—reflects upon his motivations. In a prose style he evidently developed from reading *The Bonfire of the Vanities* and *Fear and Loathing in Las Vegas* in prison, Belfort rationalizes:

> The country club was remarkably close to my estate.... But, of course, I never bothered applying for membership, what with my status as a lowly Jew, who had the utter gall to invade WASP heaven. And it wasn't just the Brookville Country Club that restricted Jews. No, no, no! All the surrounding clubs restricted Jews, or, for that matter, anyone who wasn't a blue-blooded WASP bastard.... I came to realize that the WASPs were yesterday's news, a seriously endangered species no different than the dodo bird or spotted owl. And while it was true that they still had their little golf clubs and hunting lodges as last bastions against the invading shtetl hordes, they were nothing more than twentieth-century Little Big Horns on the verge of being overrun by *savage* Jews like myself, who'd made fortunes on Wall Street and were willing to spend whatever it took to live where Gatsby lived.

Rob Eshman, publisher of the *Jewish Journal*, noted in an interesting essay, "'The Wolf' and the Jewish Problem":

> The hole in him wasn't from poverty, but from desire for acceptance. The "blue-blooded WASPs," Belfort writes, "Viewed me as a young Jewish circus attraction." Belfort had a chip on his shoulder the size of a polo pony, and so did everyone he recruited. They were, he writes, "The most *savage* young Jews anywhere on Long Island: the towns of Jericho and Syosset. It was from out of the

very marrow of these two upper-middle-class Jewish ghettos that the bulk of my first hundred Strattonites had come."[15]

Belfort named his pump-and-dump boiler room "Stratton Oakmont" to imply WASP respectability. Oakmont, an elite golf club outside Pittsburgh, has hosted the U.S. Open more often than any other course. Eshman goes on:

> It's not complicated, really. Poor little Jordan wanted to show those WASPs whose country clubs he couldn't join that he was smarter, richer, better. What he failed to understand is that just about every Jew, every minority, shares the same impulses. But only a select few decide the only way to help themselves is to hurt others. Belfort, like Bernie Madoff, is an extreme example.

The surprisingly common Jewish-American preoccupation with vague family legends of a grandfather being blackballed at a country club has led me to study up on the history of private clubs. It turns out that most of what we think we know is a retconning of American social history.

Contrary to mythos, as far as I can tell:

First, as early as 1925, a higher percentage of Jews than gentiles may have belonged to country clubs.

Second, Jewish country clubs were, on average, more luxurious and expensive than gentile clubs.

Third, a 1962 study by the Anti-Defamation League found that Jewish country clubs were more discriminatory than Christian clubs.

Fourth, historically, Jewish applicants were mostly excluded for ethnic reasons by *Jewish country clubs.*

Granted, it's difficult to find hard information about any private golf clubs, since they value privacy, so my surmises aren't always rock solid. In particular, Jewish country clubs are far more obscure on average than comparably big-budget non-Jewish clubs, because Jewish clubs stopped hosting major championships a half-century ago.

I had expected to find that traditionally Jewish country clubs don't hold big tournaments because of residual anti-Semitism from the super-WASPy United States Golf Association and the less upscale Professional Golfers of America. But it turns out that the USGA and PGA had Jewish clubs host their major championships back in the bad old days of the 1920s and 1930s.

For example, Bobby Jones won the U.S. Open at Inwood on Long Island in 1923, and Gene Sarazen triumphed at Fresh Meadow in Queens in 1932.

The PGA Championship also visited Jewish clubs in the Tom Buchanan era: Walter Hagen won at Inwood in 1921, Leo Diegel at Hillcrest (the famous movie industry club in Los Angeles) in 1929, and Tommy Armour at Fresh Meadow in 1930.

Ever since the civil rights movement turned its unwelcome attention upon the all-Jewish (and thus all-white) Brentwood Country Club in Los Angeles for planning to host the 1962 PGA Championship, it's been hard to learn anything about the membership policies of Jewish country clubs.[16] The highest profile tournament hosted since then by a traditionally Jewish club might be the 1997 Walker Cup (an America v. Britain amateur match named for George Herbert Walker, great-grandfather of the previous president), held at Quaker Ridge in Westchester County.

Still, we can piece together some general impressions.

One irony is that, even in the early 20th century, Jews were more likely to belong to county clubs than gentiles. According to *Sports and the American Jew*, in a 1925 article in *American Hebrew* entitled "The Common Ground of Golf," Italian-American champion Gene Sarazen:

> Praised their courses as among the best in the country. Noting that of the estimated five hundred thousand golfers in the United States, more than thirty thousand were Jewish, he argued that this number, "entirely out of proportion with the Jewish proportion of the populations," demonstrates the popularity of the sport among Jews.

Why have a higher proportion of Jews than gentiles belonged to country clubs? Because, with the possible exception of a couple of decades around 1900, Jews in America have always tended to be richer on average than gentiles. For instance, Hillcrest was said to be the most expensive club to join in the country during the Gatsby era.

Jewish clubs tend to have surprisingly dull golf courses relative to the lavishness of their facilities for socializing. The WASP urge to invest in the golf course rather than the clubhouse surprised even the Quaalude-hindered brain of Belfort. In the most memorable of the many scenes of excess essayed by DiCaprio, the self-proclaimed Wolf of Wall Street finds himself in need of an unbugged telephone after taking a Quaalude. He drives his Lamborghini to the nearest pay phone, which is at the Brookville Country Club. Belfort recounted for *New York Magazine* his Tom Wolfe-style thoughts when he collapsed in the clubhouse:

"I'm lying on my back and see the ceiling has cracks in it," Belfort says. "I'm like, Why are the WASPs not paying for their ceiling? What a troubling thought that they don't fix the ceiling in this WASP heaven. Maybe they're running out of money?"

Bradley S. Klein, a *GolfWeek* writer who has done much to publicize Jewish country clubs, recounts an anecdote from 1990 told by an Inwood member:

> The conversation turned to annual fees. I forget the exact numbers, but it was something like $5,000 for Olympic and about $5,500 for Medinah. Our host from Oakmont said that his dues were right in the middle.[17]

Olympic, Medinah, and Oakmont are all world famous courses that regularly host the U.S. Open or PGA Championship.

Inquiring minds naturally turned to Davidson.
"I said, 'We're about where all of you are—combined.'" Back then, Inwood charged a princely sum of $18,000.

Jewish clubs were universally acknowledged to have had much better dining rooms than gentile clubs. Robert H. Boyle reported in *Sports Illustrated* in 1962:

> Members of Jewish clubs habitually eat more and drink less than do Christian club members.... Significantly, of all the clubs surveyed by *Sports Illustrated*, the one most esteemed for its food was the Hillcrest Country Club in Los Angeles, a predominantly Jewish club drawing heavily on show business.... "Hillcrest," Milton Berle, a member, once remarked, "is a dining club with golf."

Hillcrest's golf course, while located on rolling hills close to the superlative North Course of the Los Angeles Country Club (which will host the 2023 U.S. Open), is surprisingly pedestrian. Golf architect Tom Doak rated Hillcrest only a 3 on his 0 to 10 scale in *The Confidential Guide to Golf Courses*. Nothing much has changed since Groucho Marx, Jack Benny, and George Burns had the big table in the Hillcrest dining room. *Sports Illustrated* wrote in 1995:

> Today, in many ways golf is secondary at Hillcrest.... Is there anything different about the predominantly Jewish clubs? Food, it seems, is the only thing. Both Brentwood and Hillcrest are renowned for their chow because their members demand it. "Our

members would rather spend money on upgrading the food than the golf course," says Brentwood V.P. Bennett Wolf with a wry (rye?) smile.[18]

Although it's almost universally claimed that the only reason Jews formed their own clubs was because of discrimination by gentiles, that seems increasingly like a tendentious talking point. After all, they had separate ideas of what was fun: WASPs and Irish Catholics liked golf and drinking, while Jews liked dining and entertainment.

A rare partial dissent from the conventional wisdom that Jews would never have built their own country clubs if not for anti-Semitism appeared in an elegy in *D Magazine* entitled "Goodbye, Columbian." Curt Sampson wrote sadly of the Dallas country club that ran out of money, dropped its Jewish-only policy in 2007, and was now letting in golf-crazy gentiles such as Cowboys quarterback Tony Romo and PGA legend Lee Trevino (who enjoyed finally being allowed to be a member of the club where he once worked on the maintenance crew). Sampson observed:

> Why Jews felt compelled to band together was simple: they enjoyed their own company, and the other clubs were not letting them in.... Not that there aren't abuses in this sliver of society—try joining Dallas Country Club, Mr. Goldstein!—but there is joy in banding together with people who look like you and talk like you and believe what you believe. We get enough melting pot in public schools and at the Cowboys game.

Despite the paucity of public information about Jewish clubs, Hillcrest, which is across the street from 20th Century Fox studios, is an exception because the movie industry has been so well documented. In short, the Hillcrest Jews had a blast being extremely Jewish at Hillcrest. Stephen Birmingham, author of the 1967 bestseller *"Our Crowd:" The Great Jewish Families of New York*, wrote in his follow-up, *The Rest of Us: The Rise of America's Eastern European Jews*:

> But in Los Angeles, as in other cities, the leading Christian club, the Los Angeles Country Club, would not accept Jews.... So the Jews of Hollywood had formed Hillcrest, a country club of their own.... Since it was newer, its facilities were far more modern and luxurious than the Los Angeles Country Club's.... It was just as exclusive as the Los Angeles Club and membership was rigidly closed

to Christians, though many, including Joseph P. Kennedy, tried to join. Its initiation fee of twenty-two thousand dollars was the highest in the country.... Jokes and insults were swapped in Yiddish, a language never used in the office or on the set.

Interestingly, Jews were even more ferocious discriminators than gentiles. "A Study of Religious Discrimination by Social Clubs" was published in 1962 by the Anti-Defamation League of the B'Nai B'rith. The survey reported on 803 country clubs, of which 224 (28%) were open to Christians and Jews alike. (Probably most of these were founded by Christians.) Of the 505 clubs that considered themselves Christian, 89 (18%) let in some number of Jews. In contrast, of the 74 Jewish clubs, only three (4%) let in any non-Jews. *Sports Illustrated* pointed out:

> The ADL report concluded that although "the extent of discrimination against Jews by clubs is far greater than the levels of discrimination against Jews in other areas such as education, employment, housing and public accommodations," the fact that a significant number of clubs "were 'Jewish clubs'" that discriminate against Christians is eloquent testimony to the further institutionalization of religious prejudice. When, as and if Jewish community relations agencies conclude that the problem of the "Christian club" merits their attention, they will inevitably have to cope with the other side of the coin "the 'Jewish club.'"

Hillcrest was one of the more tolerant Jewish clubs, admitting Lebanese-American television star and philanthropist Danny Thomas as its first Gentile member only a few decades after its founding. Jack Benny quipped that if they wanted to get credit for not discriminating, they should have picked somebody who looked less Levantine.

Interestingly, Christian clubs were slightly less discriminatory against Jews in the South, following a pattern of Jews being not rebels and dissidents in the old South (as many Jews assume today) but instead popular members of the local white establishment. For example, Augusta National, now perhaps the most exclusive club in America, is said to have always had local Jewish families as members, even when its Northern national membership of CEOs weren't inviting their Jewish peers to join.

But an even bigger surprise I discovered in my research is that these common memories of grandpapa's application for membership being turned down for ethnic reasons generally didn't involve Jews trying to get into gentile country clubs. Instead, Eastern European Jews were typically shot down by German Jewish country clubs who saw the *nouveau riche* immigrant Jews as pushy and crass Al Czerviks.

Sports Illustrated reported in 1962:

> In larger cities one sometimes finds two or more Jewish clubs, the top one composed principally of German Jews who tend to find eastern European Jews unacceptable.

For example, Birmingham, Alabama long supported two standoffish Jewish country clubs. According to the *Encyclopedia Judaica*:

> Since Jews were frozen out of local country clubs, they established the Hillcrest in 1883 for German Jews, and the Fairmont in 1920, for East European Jews. They merged in 1969, forming the Pine Tree Country Club, which opened its membership to non-Jews in 1991.

Stephen Birmingham writes:

> But now, in nearly every American city of any size, there were at least two Jewish country clubs—the 'good' one (German), and the less good (Russian). In New York, the best Jewish country club was the Germans' Century Country Club in suburban White Plains [now Purchase]. The second-best was the Russians' Sunningdale Golf Club in Scarsdale.

Birmingham observed in *"Our Crowd"*:

> For years the Century was an almost exclusively German club, with an unwritten rule against "Orientals."

The Century Country Club built its first golf course in 1908 (Sunningdale's course opened in 1918), but didn't begin to admit Russian Jews until after World War II. Birmingham notes in *The Rest of Us*:

> Bastions of German-Jewish supremacy were falling on all sides by the 1940s.... At the Century Country Club, which considered itself not only the best Jewish club in New York but the best Jewish country club on earth, and where the anti-Russian bias had been all but written into the bylaws for generations, a few Russians were now being cautiously taken in as members, and one of the first of

these, in 1948, was the Flatbush-born Dr. Herman Tarnower, the son of Russian immigrants.

Presumably, the imperious Dr. Tarnower was expected to never bring scandal to the club. His later publication of the bestselling *The Complete Scarsdale Medical Diet*, however, set him on the road to national celebrity, murder by his jealous mistress Jean Harris, and commemoration in the greatest of all *Seinfeld* episodes, "The Summer of George," in which (among much else) Kramer is handed a Tony Award for a Broadway musical about the Tarnower murder, *Scarsdale Surprise*.

If we go even further back into the past, did German Jews start their own country clubs solely because of golf Nazis? Or did German Jewish financiers build their discriminatory country clubs to strengthen their ties of friendship, business, and marriage?

After all, country clubs existed in the U.S. even before golf arrived in 1887. A major reason was to provide young people with romantic grounds, resembling the country estates in Jane Austen novels, upon which to stroll about and fall in love with suitable marriage partners.

And German Jewish bankers were famously endogamous. The most famous family of all, the Rothschilds, kept business in the family by practicing not just marriage between first cousins, but even uncle-niece marriage.

The 1968 *Commentary* review by Marshall Sklare of Birmingham's *"Our Crowd"* begins with a discussion of how profitable this endogamous clannishness had been to the German Jews of Wall Street:

> Ten years ago, Barry E. Supple, an economic historian then teaching at Harvard, published a scholarly article which demonstrated that in the 19th century a significant share of American investment banking was concentrated in Jewish hands. In reviewing the history of such banking houses as Kuhn, Loeb; J & W Seligman; Goldman, Sachs; and Lehman Brothers, Supple drew attention to the fact that it was not only common for the children and relatives of the partners of a given firm to marry each other, but that marital alliances frequently occurred among, as well as within, the different Jewish banking houses.
>
> Indeed, Supple's careful analysis showed that the role of marriage in business went even further than this. The scions of banking families would marry the offspring of the owners of large German-Jewish companies in a variety of fields, and these companies—some of

them later to become the country's leading department stores and mail-order firms—would then raise capital through the banking houses with whom they had formed family connections....

The Gentile houses, however, lacked the network of kinship ties which Supple uncovered in his patient genealogical probing.... It was his intention to show that the Jewish firms, and not their Gentile counterparts, constituted the "ideal type" of business combination prior to the rise of the mammoth corporation. He was particularly impressed by the tightly knit social network created by the Jewish firms around family, temple, city clubs, and philanthropic organizations; and he viewed their clannishness as "a valid and often necessary means of creating an identity of interests and attitude most conducive to business activity and development."

Under such a system, it makes all the sense in the world to form country clubs with potential in-laws and keep out families you don't want your children to marry into.

The resentments engendered in the first half of the 20th century by German Jews blackballing Russian Jews have been almost forgotten as their descendants have patched over these rifts by coming to an unspoken agreement to blame it all on the gentiles.

Henry Kissinger observed that Israel's foreign policy often seems less intended to advance Israel's interests abroad than to heal domestic divisions among Israeli Jews by giving them somebody foreign to hate. While nearby Levantine countries such as Syria and Lebanon have suffered hideous civil wars, the fractious Israelis have managed to successfully direct their animosities outward. Similarly, the current American Jewish obsession with golf Nazis has less to do with whether Jews in ages past actually wanted to join stuffy WASP clubs than with healing gaps within the Jewish community by castigating Christians.

Indeed, this displacement process may be observed in many aspects of American social history, which has been repeatedly rewritten to foster Jewish solidarity by projecting blame for grievances held by one set of Jews against another onto the majority culture.

CHAPTER TWELVE

The Coalition of
the Fringes

Hate Hoax

The American Conservative
May 10, 2004

I AM perhaps the world's most easily amused person. As an old marketing researcher who enjoys looking for patterns in daily life, I'm almost never bored. Yet, while wandering the flowery campuses of Southern California's Claremont Colleges, I found the soft spring afternoon so placid that I was ready to curl up under a tree for a snooze. The most exciting moment during my exploration came when a Frisbee golf foursome politely waited for me to walk by before playing through.

Perhaps all this genteel serenity explains the psychodramas that a sizable fraction of the staff and students seem compelled to concoct for themselves. Just the month before, a long-festering mass hysteria over white racist student-thugs supposedly infesting the campus had culminated in a huge night rally in which thousands of blackshirted students had chanted their hatred of "hate," while the administration stood by silently, despite knowing that there had been no hate crime, just a leftist professor's hoax.

In 1887, New Englanders founded Pomona College, now ranked fourth among liberal arts colleges in the country by *U.S. News*. With the population of the San Gabriel Valley's posh orange grove belt booming in the 1920s, the trustees chose a clever way to expand. To preserve small college intimacy while exploiting the economies of scale of the mid-sized university, they created a collegiate consortium modeled on Oxford and Cambridge. Eventually, four more undergraduate colleges of about a thousand students each sprang up on adjacent campuses sharing a single massive library.

Claremont fostered institutional diversity while other universities were homogenizing themselves in their attempts to be all things to all people. Claremont's Harvey Mudd is sometimes derided as an imitation Caltech, but, then, Caltech is well worth emulating. In contrast, Pitzer, the least prestigious school, is a Sixties relic stressing social activism.

Opened in 1946, Claremont Men's College taught economics and government from a conservative perspective rare during that era of liberal dominance of intellectual life. Political philosopher Harry V. Jaffa, still energetic today in his mid-80s, made CMC a hub for his idealistic, Lincoln-lionizing interpretation of his mentor Leo Strauss' theories.

In 1976, Claremont Men's College went co-ed, although its neighbor Scripps remains all-female, changing its name in 1982 to Claremont McKenna College to keep its CMC initials. It is quite exclusive today, with an average SAT score around 1380.

In 1999, Pamela Gann became CMC's first president who was a registered Democrat. She didn't seem happy heading a college with a moderately conservative reputation, and tried to use "diversity" to make CMC less diverse and more like every other college. Gann and the conservative professors fought bitter battles over affirmative action hiring.

Gann's frustration with her rightist holdovers seemed to feed into the growing paranoia at some of the other Claremont colleges, where the staffs nurture an obsession among its "diverse" students (i.e., everybody except non-Hispanic heterosexual gentile white males) to navel-gaze over whether or not they feel "comfortable with the climate."

It was 72 degrees with a gentle breeze blowing, so the climate seemed okay to me, but a flier on Pitzer bulletin boards made the local *idée fixe* a little clearer: "Diversity and Campus Climate: You are invited to participate in a discussion about campus climate."

Another advertised: "Queer Dreams and Nightmares: What is it like to be a student at the Claremont Colleges? Student panel discussion addressing the current climate at the 5-Cs, both academically and socially." This was part of a conference entitled, with that profusion of punctuation that is the secret fraternity handshake of post-modern academics, "[Re]Defining a Queer Space at the Claremont Colleges."

The university's main concern appears to be to make students feel "comfortable," a word that reappears constantly in Claremont publications despite the obvious hopelessness of the project. The only way to make 19-year-olds feel comfortable is to wait 30 years while they sag into their well-padded maturities. Right now, they are teenagers and their surging hormones have far more important emotions for them to feel than comfort. Adults, however, who make careers out of encouraging kids to mold permanently self-pitying identities around their transient social discomforts have much to answer for.

A series of semi-nonexistent "racial incidents," such as liberal Scripps students advertising a racial sensitivity seminar with posters featuring the N-word, were parlayed by activists into a mood of dread. Kerri F. Dunn, a 39-year-old academic prole, a visiting professor of social psychology at CMC whose contract was up in June, repeatedly harangued her students about the racists and sexists lurking in the shadows. On March 9th, she gave a fiery speech at a campus event on "Hate Speech Versus Free Speech." She then walked to her 1992 Honda Civic and returned some time later, claiming she had found it spray-painted with anti-black, anti-female, and anti-Semitic slurs. The Irish-American Dunn pointed the finger at her own students, arguing that only they had heard she was considering converting to Judaism: "How else would they believe I was Jewish unless they were in my class?"

Dunn's allegation triggered a frenzy of fear and loathing.

Although faked hate crimes have become routine in the years since the Tawana Brawley hoax, the college presidents immediately canceled the next day's classes (costing parents paying the full $37,000 per year list price for 150 days of education about $250 each, or close to two million dollars in total at list price). At the mass rally the next night, Dunn announced, to rapturous applause: "This was a well planned out act of terrorism. And I don't believe for one second it was one person. I think that there's a group here, a small group, but I do believe that there is a group here that perpetuates this in all different kinds of ways."

Dunn's image of a secret goon squad of marauding junior Straussians was as memorable as it was preposterous, but the administration had already been apprised of the unsurprising truth. Earlier that day, two eyewitnesses had told the Dean of Students that Professor Dunn had slashed her own tires. The FBI and local police quickly found inconsistencies in Dunn's story. A week later, they announced publicly that Dunn had done it. (They also found that during her mid-30s, Dunn had been arrested three times, twice for shoplifting, once for driving with a fake license.)

University officials suspended Dunn, but with pay, and continued to rent her a replacement car. A suddenly indecisive Gann ruminated, "One has to learn to perhaps live with ambiguity here, and never know the answer and reach a closure because the likelihood of actual prosecution … is very small."

One Claremont college president told me that my comparing the reaction to the Reichstag fire was not the "least bit appropriate." He informed me, "The full campus community felt that this was a very positive day for everyone involved. If you had been here you would have felt the positive energy in the student body, as well as a commitment to change that I share."

Apparently, having your entire university jerked around by a criminal professor who tries to frame her white male students for her own hate crime is a "very positive day."

KKK is the New UFO

Taki's
March 6, 2013

T HE current identity-politics hysteria was launched about a year ago (conveniently enough for the Obama reelection campaign) with the news that an angelic black baby named Trayvon Martin had been gunned down by white racist George Zimmerman.

In the latest brouhaha, Oberlin, a (very) liberal arts college outside of Cleveland, immediately shut down all classes Monday to hold a frenzied, Cultural Revolution-style rally against the rising tide of racism because one student claimed to have spied a one-man Ku Klux Klan rally on campus in the wee hours of the morning.[1]

The past year reminds me of a similar frenzy in the early 1990s that Bill Clinton rode to the White House. Do you remember the "Year of the Woman," in which Clinton (of all people) ran as the nemesis of bosses who make passes at the women who work for them? No? Well, since nobody else seems to remember the recent past, it's worth mentioning how these manias seem to start up in conjunction with Democratic presidential campaigns, then sputter on for years.

The Year of the Woman was kicked off 13 months before the 1992 election when the Democrats trotted out Anita Hill to accuse Supreme Court nominee Clarence Thomas of sexually harassing her back when they were bachelor and bachelorette. As far as I could tell, the two well-educated blacks would have made a well-suited couple, and, indeed, Anita remained on friendly terms with Clarence until after he married a white woman.

But to everybody else, Anita Hill's office gossip was apparently the biggest news in world history. Or at least it was long enough to help get Bill and Hill into the White House, at which point the media's interest in sexual harassment evaporated.

I pointed out back then that if sexual harassment consisted of making "unwanted sexual advances" to underlings, the Arkansas governor was surely—by the Law of Large Numbers—guilty and would eventually run into a scandal.[2] Sure enough, he did in the Paula Jones lawsuit, which led to Monica Lewinsky and his impeachment. But by 1998, the press had forgotten all about Anita and the Year of the Woman.

Similarly, Oberlin's ghostly KKKer is reminiscent of scores of campus hate fiascos of recent years. But who can remember anything?

While the college administration's story of the campus Klansman has excited the national media, only two newspapers so far have bothered to call up the local cops to find out what really happened. One is the local *North Coast Chronicle-Telegram* of Lorain County, Ohio, which reported:

> Oberlin College's "Day of Solidarity" on Monday was sparked by a student who reported seeing a person wearing what appeared to be a Ku Klux Klan hood and robe near the college's Afrikan Heritage House while driving through campus between 1 and 2 a.m.
>
> College security officers responded to the area, but weren't able to find a person wearing the infamous KKK garb.

Oberlin police Lt. Mike McCloskey said that authorities did find a pedestrian wrapped in a blanket. He said police interviewed another witness later in the day and that person also saw a female walking with a blanket.

Oddly enough, the other is the leftist *Guardian* of London, which noted:

> Lt. Mike McCloskey of Oberlin police told the Guardian on Monday that officers were still following up the KKK sighting, but suggested that the only witness may have been mistaken.

In other words, KKK is the new UFO.

After the 1950s, the press slowly figured out that it shouldn't get too worked-up over flying-saucer sightings. But Klansmen on the campus of what is perhaps the most frenetically liberal college in America? How couldn't it be true?

Seeing racists under the bed is the latest manifestation of the adolescent hysteria that triggered the Salem witch trials in 1692.

But nobody much cares whether this horrifying hate crime went through the formality of taking place. This non-event has received enormous publicity (for example, Matt Lauer talked it up on Tuesday's *Today Show*), just like all the other campus hate hoaxes and hysterias, because so many people want it to be true.

The racial atmosphere in America is starting to resemble that bizarre 1980s-1990s frenzy over Satan worshippers purportedly molesting preschoolers. We live in an era in which hate-porn movies such as *Django Unchained* and *The Girl with the Dragon Tattoo* win Oscars.

There is such a hunger in 2013 to sniff out racists and punish them that the actual shortage of racists is leading people to imagine that a girl in a blanket is a lone lynch mob.

It's typical for the kind of incidents that create media furors to turn out to be hoaxes perpetrated by minorities. For example, Oberlin already had one of these tumults, complete with an official Two Minutes Hate rally, back in the 1990s. The coed who wrote an anti-Chinese slur on an Oberlin monument turned out to be Chinese.[3]

Every so often, perpetrators of these hoaxes annoy the cops enough to get sent to jail, such as Claremont McKenna professor Kerri Dunn, who tried to frame her white male students after she painted anti-Semitic slogans on her own car.[4]

But is anybody in the press ever held accountable for hyping the hysteria?

The KKKrazy Glue That Holds the Obama Coalition Together

Taki's
March 13, 2013

WE are constantly told that the GOP is doomed because it's the party of straight white men. That may well be true, but few have asked: How can the diverse Democrats hold together? How can special interests as different as blacks and gays be kept in sync?

The answer appears to be: The Obama coalition can stay together only by stoking resentment—and, indeed, hatred—of straight white men. This naked animus is rationalized by projecting the hate felt by the victorious Democrats onto the losers:

> We hate straight white Republican men because...they are so full of...uh...hate. Yes, that's the ticket: We hate them because they are hateful. No, wait, I mean, we hate them because they are hate-filled. They're practically Ku Klux Klanners.

To service this Hunger for Hate, the prestige press assiduously generates the Democratic Party's KKKrazy Glue by whipping up fear and loathing over hate crimes, even when they didn't technically happen.

Last week we were solemnly informed of a one-man KKK rally at Oberlin College. (Apparently it was a lady in a blanket.)[5]

Then the top story on the *Washington Post* last Friday evening was the "mysterious" murder back on February 26th of Marco McMillian. He was a black gay candidate for mayor of Clarksdale in Mississippi, a state with a "dark history of racial brutality," as the *Post* helpfully reminded.[6]

A hate crime, right? It's Mississippi, so what else do you need to know? Clearly, a gang of homophobic redneck Christians had hunted down with their AR-15s the gay black activist bravely challenging Clarksdale's white power structure. No doubt, County Sheriff Bull Connor III then covered it up, which must be why it's still big news in the *Washington Post* a week and a half later.

Thus, a recent Google News search found 1,750 hits for "Marco McMillian" and "hate crime."

Except for...well, except for everything.

First, the sheriff of Coahoma County, Charles Jones, is black.

And McMillian was running against a local black political dynasty. Clarksdale has had a black mayor for 20 of the last 24 years, Henry Espy. You might vaguely recognize the Espy name because Henry is the brother of Mike Espy, who was Bill Clinton's first Secretary of Agriculture. One favorite in the race is the mayor's son Chuck, who just resigned from the Mississippi legislature to run.

As mentioned in countless blues songs—Clarksdale is home to Robert Johnson's "Crossroads," where Highway 49 and Bob Dylan's Highway 61 intersect—the Mississippi Delta is a poor place. Thus, political jobs are sharply contested. The Espy family has spent much time in court on corruption charges but always seems to come out on top.

(The 34-year-old McMillian had himself already figured in a financial scandal when he had been executive assistant to the president of Alabama A&M University. Improprieties in his pay led to the downfall of his boss.)

The *New York Times*, which embarrassed itself in its initial Oberlin assault-blanket story, actually did a reasonable job of hinting back on February 28th that the dead man's family was suspicious of the local black power structure:

> The police said they had no reason to suspect that his death was a hate crime.... "I believe it was political," said one family member.... "Maybe some people didn't want him to run. Maybe he was a threat. They wanted Clarksdale to stay the same."

The *Times* didn't mention the race of who wants things to stay the same in Clarksdale, but it did link to the hereditary leaders' pictures:

351

With the exception of a four-year period during the 1990s, the town has been led since 1989 by Mayor Henry Espy, who has announced that he would not seek another term. Those vying to succeed Mr. Espy include his son, Chuck Espy, a member of the Mississippi House of Representatives.

But how many journalists can be bothered to click on links before hyping their favorite obsession: white hatred and homophobia in Dixie? Very few, apparently.

The bereaved family then issued a press release claiming that the victim had been "beaten, dragged and burned (set afire)."[7] These words triggered a Pavlovian media mania, complete with stock references to the dragging death of James Byrd in Texas and the beating death of Matthew Shepard in Wyoming. (Texas, Wyoming, and Mississippi...why, they all voted for Romney!)

On March 5th, the *Times* tried to quell the hysteria with another surprisingly responsible story:

> A Mississippi mayoral candidate who was found dead last week was not killed by being beaten, burned or dragged, the coroner said on Tuesday, challenging a statement from the victim's family that the official said was misleading.[8]

But that only had a modest dampening effect on the flames of press hatred.

The most striking thing about McMillian's "mysterious" murder is its lack of mystery. There's no need for conspiracy theories because the killer, a poor 22-year-old black man named Lawrence Reed, confessed last month. The cops didn't even know the missing man was dead until Reed crashed the victim's stolen SUV on February 26th, then confessed where he'd stashed the body. The auto accident, which might have been an attempt at suicide, happened moments after Reed, who had become friendly with McMillian at a Clarksdale bar, told female friends that he'd strangled the politician with his wallet chain.

That's about as open-and-shut a case as there is. (The killer's precise motivation will no doubt be argued over at the trial. Carjacking? *Thelma & Louise*-style rape resistance? Gay lovers' quarrel?) But London's *Daily Mail* had the black killer's picture on February 28, more than a week before the *Washington Post* splashed the story.

One of the reasons the national media keeps making ever-stupider mistakes about local police-blotter items is that pragmatic wisdom about human beings is increasingly demonized as stereotyping. For example, there's a two-word phrase that ought to have occurred to journalists when thinking about a case involving an affluent 34-year-old gay and a poor 22-year-old, and it's not "hate crime." Instead, it's "rough trade." But that term seems to have disappeared from public consciousness for being "homophobic" (i.e., not on GLAAD's Approved List).

When my wife and I owned a condo in Chicago two decades ago, we suddenly started running into strung-out young men on our building's interior staircase. Who was buzzing in 19-year-olds in black leather? And why?

We figured out that our upstairs neighbor, a fat, middle-aged, effeminate white corporate comptroller, had developed a taste for rough trade.

That's not extremely rare. Some affluent gay men are fascinated by poor young men of a more masculine demeanor. The *Wikipedia* article explains:

> Often the attraction for the gay male partner is finding a dangerous, even thuggish, partner who may turn violent.

Not surprisingly, bad things sometimes happen to wealthy gays who like to be alone with brutish yobs.

It wouldn't have been terribly startling if my neighbor's hobby of trading drugs for sex with barely legal boys had wound up getting him murdered. (I'm glad one of the hustlers he let into our building didn't break into our condo.) The comptroller's health soon failed, requiring a colostomy, and he sold his apartment to two male flight attendants who proved to be a wealth of stylish decorating tips.

In the Marco McMillian-Lawrence Reed case, the phrase "rough trade" should have gone off like an alarm in reporters' heads back in February.

But the concept of rough trade has largely been prodded down the memory hole for the last 15 years. Thus, a Google News search for "Marco McMillian" "rough trade" brings up zero pages.

What happened to this useful concept? When the well-to-do Matthew Shepard left a bar with two meth-heads who were out looking to rob somebody to get a fix, the media hive-mind immediately decided to turn it into an iconic lesson about hate crimes rather than the felony murder it actually was.[9]

Camille Paglia had the bad taste to point out about the Shepard murder:

> It used to be called "rough trade"—the dangerous, centuries-old practice of gay men picking up grimy, testosterone-packed straight or semi-straight toughs.[10]

She was excoriated for doing so. And most pundits have less courage than Paglia. So say goodbye to the notion of "rough trade." As Orwell pointed out in the appendix to *1984*, reducing our vocabularies benefits those with political power by making us all stupider.

Identity Stalinism

Taki's
January 23, 2019

THE media's latest Days of Rage, in which a white boy drove the national press into a frenzy by smiling at the leftist Person of Color banging a drum in his face, was like a greatest-hits collection of my old observations. So I'm going to take a victory lap to review how ideas I've been offering for years help explain much of the latest elite fury.

Tucker Carlson summed up his eloquent dissection of this outbreak of Hate Hysteria as: "It's not really about race."[11]

Actually…it's really about race.

That's why so many journalists and Hollywood figures explained how they could tell the kid was evil just by looking him. It's written on his face! Sure, he didn't do anything, but did you see that smirk?[12] Anybody who looks like him deserves to be punched.

The least inappropriate way for a white male to respond to being berated by his racial superiors is like that Starbucks barista who got shouted at with a megaphone from three feet away. And even his stoicism seemed suspiciously dignified.[13]

Or, to be precise, the roar of racist rage from the great and good directed at an innocent Kentucky boy is all about implementing the Democrats' grand strategy, which is to assemble a coalition of the margins of American society: immigrants, welfare mothers, tech billionaires, transgenders, hedge-fund

355

guys, black church ladies, gays, Jews, the unmarried, movie stars, felons, and so forth and so on.

In contrast, the more similar you are to a Minuteman of 1776, the more likely you are to vote Republican. The GOP appeals to Core Americans, the Democrats to Fringe Americans.

Mass immigration offers the Democrats good reason to hope to overwhelm their foes in the long run.

But merely listing the Democrats' constituent interest groups points out the main problem with their master plan: Their various fringes can't stand one another.

For example, the once-celebrated Women's March self-destructed last weekend over how high on the totem pole of victimology rank Jews. Most of its Muslim leaders consider Jews to be oppressors of Palestinians, and most of its black leaders see Jews as just white people with even more money. But feminist groups need Jewish donors because…Jews really are richer on average.

Similarly, in this incident at the Lincoln Memorial, Black Hebrew Israelites, a bizarre black cult rather like the Westboro Baptist Church in their repugnant behavior, repeatedly screamed racist insults at both the American Indian leftists and the Catholic schoolboys.

The progressive stack is purposefully kept vague, other than that white Christian males are at rock bottom. But it's clear to Indians these days that they are lower than blacks on the intersectional totem pole.

Standing up to blacks can turn you into another "BBQ Becky" on social media, or get you killed.[14] So eventually the Indians tried to regain some dignity, in a "cheese stands alone" maneuver, by trying to humiliate the even lower-ranking white boys, who were hardly likely to respond violently. Bullying those you aren't afraid of has recently been renamed Punching Up.

As these examples from the weekend suggest, the only way the Democratic Party can hold together is by constantly ginning up excuses for Fringe Americans to hate Core Americans even more than they hate each other.

Because the Democrats' fundamental problem is all the hate roiling their own constituents, they project onto Republicans their own tendency toward hatred. Freud came up with a lot of bad ideas, but one of his better ones is "projection": Human beings defend themselves by attributing their own bad traits to others.

Dennis Dale observes:

These hoaxes pull the veil back, by releasing the demonic resentments of those who think they've suddenly been given free reign to express them. There's a reason the left projects the charge of the "dog whistle".... It's precisely where they're at, itching to give their animus and hatred free reign.

Thus, the Democrats constantly claim that the reason they hate their enemies is not because they are inconveniently in their way, but because they are hateful. And the reason they are hateful is because they are hate-filled. Thus, a high school junior waiting for his bus becomes a Symbol of Hate.

This political logic generates much hate hypochondria in the media. For example, countless trained journalists watched a brief video of the American Indian leftist trying (and failing) to provoke the poor kid and immediately concluded that the reason they felt so much hatred toward the white youth is because he was the hater.

Not surprisingly, the media offer up a constant supply of Two Minutes Hates to serve as the KKKrazy Glue of the Coalition of the Fringes, many of which turn out to be fiascos. Countless battlefields chosen by the Establishment have turned out to be self-defeats.

The Democrats' fundamental problem is that white people, on the whole, just aren't hate-filled enough for their strategy to wholly succeed.

For example, earlier in January, the *New York Times* was in a lather about how a Great White Defendant in Texas had purportedly gunned down a beautiful black child.[15] But when the cops arrested two black criminals, the embarrassing incident was quickly memory-holed.

Our society's fervid "hunt for the Great White Defendant" is the central insight of Tom Wolfe's 1987 novel *The Bonfire of the Vanities*. The supply of white wrongdoing falls short of demand, so our culture offers rich rewards to those who can concoct instances of whites behaving badly.

Upton Sinclair observed, "It is difficult to get a man to understand something when his salary depends upon his not understanding it!" Not surprisingly, many in the Democratic-media complex misunderstood the video of the besieged boy acting classy as yet more evidence of the white wickedness for which they hope to be rewarded for uncovering.

A basic concept that explains much fashionable moral reasoning in the current year is "Who? Whom?" While promoting the collectivization of agriculture in 1929, which led to the Ukrainian Holomodor, Stalin announced:

The fact is, we live according to Lenin's formula: *Kto-Kovo*? [Who-Whom?]: will we knock them, the capitalists, flat and give them (as Lenin expresses it) the final, decisive battle, or will they knock us flat?

Other principles of morality believe in objective standards of behavior, but Stalinism assumed that something was good if the good people (e.g., Stalinists) did it, but bad if the bad people (i.e., those hated by Stalinists) did the same thing.

Similarly, under today's rules of Identity Stalinism, while the aggressor, objectively, was obviously the man banging his drum in the boy's face, that adult was nonwhite and leftist, while the child was white and a Trump supporter. So, by the rules of Who? Whom?, the assailant had to be the victim and the victim the attacker.

And, under the current dispensation, the white boy's manly impassivity under assault just proved he was the bad guy. As Orwell wrote in 1984:

> To wear an improper expression on your face (to look incredulous when a victory was announced, for example) was itself a punishable offense. There was even a word for it in Newspeak: facecrime....

The Emmett Till Effect

Taki's
August 08, 2018

I 'VE figured out a way to quantify how Establishment news organizations manipulate the contents of our minds: just track the use of tendentious phrases over the years.

Since 2016, there has been much talk of "fake news." For example, *The New York Times* used the phrase "fake news" 901 times in 2017. Both sides of the political spectrum believe the other is outright making up events that never happened to promote their worldview.

That does happen...to some extent. For example, many of the most publicized hate crimes blamed on white men in recent decades have been either outright hoaxes or badly misreported.

A subtle but likely more important issue, however, is the question of *which* true news gets emphasized. There is always vastly more news than a person can remember. Thus your picture of reality is inevitably distorted to some extent by the power of the media, what I call the Megaphone, to pound over and over into your head certain true news, but not other true news.

Moreover, the press furnishes us with convenient concepts, such as "white privilege," that make it easier to remember the facts they prefer you to know and harder to remember the facts that undermine the concepts.

For example, consider two black teens who once were true news.

In 1955, Emmett Till was murdered by two white men who were quickly acquitted, making his story memorable for being one of the last examples from a long era of state-excused white-on-black civilian violence over black males hitting on white females.

In 1987, Tawana Brawley launched our present era of making up hate hoaxes against whites by claiming that the reason she got home late was because she was being gang-raped by six white policemen.

Which incident is more rationally relevant to 2018? But which does the prestige media consider more *au courant*?

Tracking the numbers isn't as easy as it ought to be.

In 2012, *The New York Times* graciously offered a tool called Chronicle for graphing its frequency of use of words since 1851. But as I pointed out in 2016, that made it almost too easy to document the *Times'* increasing obsession during the Late Obama Age Collapse with words such as "racism," "sexism," and "transgender."[16] By 2015, in the sound of the Establishment suffering a nervous breakdown, the *NYT* was treating "racism" as five times more newsworthy than it had in 2011.

Not long after, the Chronicle web page was disabled.

Google offers its Trends to track search requests over time, but I'm less interested in measuring what the public asks for than what the media offers it.

Google's Ngram helpfully graphs word usage in books, but its last full year of data remains 2007. The striking differences in elite fixations before and after Obama's reelection are invisible to it.

So, I wound up using Google to do a brute-force search of each year in this century, plus 1980 and 1990, restricting the site to nytimes.com. (Bing and the *New York Times* search system give similar results, while DuckDuckGo doesn't offer an obvious way to search one year at a time.)

What did I find? In 1980, the name "Emmett Till" did not appear in the pages of the *NYT*. In 1990 it showed up twice, and in 2000 four times.

From 2004 through 2012, the *Times* mentioned this old incident an average of nine times per year, and from 2013 to 2016 almost two dozen times per year.

Last year, "Emmett Till" appeared in 72 different *Times* articles. And this year is on track for 92 stories about the 63-year-old tragedy.

In contrast, the name "Tawana Brawley" might seem of slightly less antiquarian interest. The New York teen launched the modern era of antiwhite hate hoaxes in 1987, a few weeks after the publication of the late Tom Wolfe's *Bonfire of the Vanities* best-seller about the "hunt for the Great White Defendant."

The talented young race-racket activist Al Sharpton, the basis for Reverend Bacon in *Bonfire*, latched on to Tawana's tall tale and turned it into a huge national brouhaha before it was utterly debunked and her half-dozen victims exonerated.

For a couple of decades, this instructive New York-area story was mentioned in the *NYT* (often in profiles explaining how Reverend Al had matured since his Tawana Brawley days, or occasionally in references to Wolfe's *magnum opus*) about half as often as Emmett Till.

But in the 2010s, Tawana Brawley has come up in only 15 articles versus 249 mentioning Emmett Till.

Now, *The New York Times* would no doubt answer that it is merely responding to the great surfeit of events related to the Emmett Till case, such as a spat over whether a white artist should be allowed to display a painting of Emmett or whether only black painters should make money off the sacred subject.

On the other hand, the *Times* takes pride that it traditionally sets the agenda for the rest of the news business. So if the *Times* says that in 2018 Emmett Till is breaking news while Tawana Brawley is ancient history, lots of other influential media folks will follow its lead.

Moreover, whether you find Emmett Till or Tawana Brawley germane today can depend upon what concepts you have in your head for organizing the blooming, buzzing confusion of the world.

Why has the frequency of "Emmett Till" in the *Times* risen from a name referenced annually in the late 20th century to one mentioned monthly in the early 21st century to the name's remarkable 2018 status as being as omnipresent in the news (55 mentions so far) as Chief Justice John Roberts (57 mentions)?

The growth of "Emmett Till" has correlated closely ($r = 0.88$) with the similarly increasing ubiquity of the phrase "white privilege."

The term "white privilege" has been around for a long time, but the *NYT* didn't obsess over it until recently, using it only once in 2000 and three times in 2010. Then it exploded in popularity with *Times* writers and editors in 2013 and is headed for about 60 usages this year.

If your head is stuffed full of the notion of "white privilege," it's only natural to remember "Emmett Till," and vice versa.

"Emmett Till" and "white privilege" are mutually reinforcing pieces of the mental architecture of the average *NYT* reader. If you ever feel twinges of skepticism about the current stress on "white privilege," just remember how Emmett Till's murderers got off due to their white privilege and your doubts will recede.

Or if you start to wonder whether the reason we keep hearing over and over about this Eisenhower-era case is that it's increasingly a man-bites-dog story, just remember how much everybody talks about "white privilege" all the time. So there must be many examples more recent than 1955, but the white male power structure is keeping them a secret. Or something.

On the other hand, if you are one of the few bad people who are familiar with Tom Wolfe's theme of the "hunt for the Great White Defendant"—the observation that everybody is so bored with the endless supply of nonwhite criminals that they would love to boost their careers by reeling in a high-status white villain, like you see on all the TV shows—then it's easier to remember Tawana Brawley.

In the history of *The New York Times*, the phrase "Great White Defendant" has appeared about five times, including one online comment from me. Thus, it's not a concept that exists in the mental toolbox of the average *Times* reader, or even *Times* writer.

The absence of this idea makes it much harder to notice how often the press goes crazy hunting for Great White Defendants who turn out to be not guilty, such as Ferguson policeman Darren Wilson, or nonwhite, such as George Zimmerman, or nonexistent, such as cruelly handsome UVA frat-boy rapist Haven Monahan.

Not surprisingly, the name "Haven Monahan" has never appeared in the *Times*.[17] Nor has the last name of the coed who catfished him up, Jackie Coakley. The full story is hilariously memorable, so the *NYT* has suppressed it to make *Rolling Stone*'s shame seem like a dull tale of methodological shortcuts.

Amusingly, the newest member of the *Times*' editorial board, Sarah Jeong, was a true believer in the *Rolling Stone* campus rape hoax, even after *Rolling Stone* walked it back. Jeong blogged:

> The more I see these "inconsistencies" and "discrepancies" touted as evidence of falsehood, the more convinced I am that Jackie is not lying.

Jeong even continued to have faith in the 2006 Duke lacrosse rape hoax years after the local district attorney had been disbarred for his misconduct in framing those Great White Defendants. (The phrase "Duke lacrosse" has been mentioned in the *Times* 25 times in the current decade, which isn't too shabby, but is hardly "Emmett Till.")

But Jeong's credulity at falling for hate hoaxes is hardly surprising when you notice that the *Times* has never printed the phrase "hate hoax." It has used "hate crime hoax" only once (in reference to last year's Air Force Academy fiasco).[18]

Now, you know and I know that hate hoaxes have been common in the newspapers at least since Tawana Brawley. But we possess the phrase "hate hoax" for this recurrent phenomenon so it's easy for us to recognize the many new hate hoaxes that come along.

But many people are cognitively unarmed for noticing this pattern. How would an intellectual conformist like Sarah Jeong learn that hate hoaxes are even a thing? Would any of her tenured Harvard Law School professors have dared mention their existence in a lecture? And she's definitely never read the phrase in *The New York Times*.

No, for poor Sarah these are just random but fascinating news stories about hateful yet sexy white male rapists who can't control their vile but arousing lusts.

Granted, Sarah's favorite kind of news story/rape fantasy often proves disappointingly ill-founded in fact. But she has no conceptual category labeling why she is so often fooled.

Would it help her to have a better-equipped mind?

Personally, I subscribe to the motto of Faber College in *Animal House*: Knowledge Is Good.

Yet considering how successful young Sarah's career at *The New York Times* has been without her knowing much that could cause her trouble, perhaps she knows best: Ignorance is bliss for today's careerists.

CHAPTER THIRTEEN

Sailer's Law of Mass Shootings

If there are more wounded than killed, then the shooter is likely black. If there are more killed than wounded, then the shooter is likely not black.

Does Abortion Prevent Crime?

Slate
August 24, 1999

> *The following is from a 1999 debate in* Slate *between U. of Chicago economist Steven D. Levitt, the future author of the bestseller* Freakonomics, *and myself over his popular theory that legalizing abortion in 1969-1973 cut crime later by culling unwanted children. Last I checked, the debate is still up at* Slate, *but they've take our names off it and now just attribute it to "By Authors."*

YOUR open-minded search for the truth, no matter how disturbing it may turn out to be, epitomizes the scientific ideal. Your study of abortion and crime is exactly what the social sciences need more of: courageous, hard-headed inquiries into the big topics that everybody else is afraid to touch. Even more impressive is your behavior since the controversy started. (Some background for readers: On Aug. 15, I circulated a critique of Steven Levitt and John Donohue's theory that legalized abortion reduced crime to the Human Biodiversity Discussion Group. A member passed it on to Steven, and despite his being deluged with media requests, he wrote to thank me for my criticisms. We then started up an e-mail exchange; this *Slate* "Dialogue" is its public continuation.)

With luck, I'll have room in my next message to respond to your important questions about how to make public and academic discourse less moralistic and more realistic. (Short answer: Junk political correctness.) Today I'll stick to the empirical issues. The problem with your abortion/reduced-crime theory is not that it encourages abortion or eugenic reasoning or whatever, but that it's largely untrue. Your biggest methodological mistake was to focus on the crime rates only in 1985 and 1997. Thus, you missed the 800-pound gorilla of crime trends: the rise and fall of the crack epidemic during the intervening years.

Here's the acid test. Your logic implies that the babies who managed to get born in the 1970s after the legalization of abortion should have grown up to be especially law-abiding teens in the early 1990s. Did they?

Not exactly. In reality, they went on the worst youth murder spree in American history. According to FBI statistics, the murder rate for 1993's crop of 14- to 17-year-olds (who were born in the high-abortion years of 1975 to 1979) was a horrifying 3.6 times that of the kids who were 14 to 17 years old in 1984 (who were born in the pre-legalization years of 1966 to 1970). In dramatic contrast, over the same time span the murder rate for those 25 and over (all born before legalization) dropped 6%.

Your model would also predict that the recent decline in crime should have shown up first among the youngest, but the opposite was true. The murder rate for 35- to 49-year-olds has been falling since the early 1980s, and for 25- to 34-year-olds since 1991, but the two most homicidal years for 14- to 17-year-olds were 1993 and 1994.

The dubiousness of your theory becomes even more obvious when we break down this post-*Roe vs. Wade* generation by race.

Now, you say that your theory isn't "about race," but simply about the greater likelihood that "unwanted" babies will grow up to be bad guys. That correlation sounds plausible. Still any realistic theory about abortion and crime must deal with the massive correlation between violence and race. As you note, African-Americans have three times the abortion rate of whites. You don't mention, however, that, as Janet Reno's Justice Department flatly states that "blacks are 8 times more likely than whites to commit homicide." Therefore, blacks commit more murders than whites in total as well as per capita.

So, let's look at just black males born in 1975 to 1979. Since their mothers were having abortions at three times the white rate, that should have driven down their youth murder rate. Instead, from 1984 to 1993 the black male youth homicide rate grew an apocalyptic 5.1 times. This black juvenile rate also grew relative to the white juvenile murder rate, from five times worse in 1984 to 11 times worse in 1993.

Why, then, is this generation born in 1975 to 1979 now committing relatively fewer crimes as it ages? It makes no sense to give the credit to abortion, which so catastrophically failed to keep them on the straight and narrow when they were juveniles. Instead, the most obvious explanation is the ups and downs of the crack business, which first drove violent crime up in the late 1980s and early 1990s, then drove it down in the mid and late 1990s. That's why the crime rate has fallen fastest exactly where it had previously grown fastest as a result of crack—in the biggest cities (e.g., New York) and among young black males. This generation born right after legalization is better behaved today in part because so many of its bad apples are now confined to prisons, wheelchairs, and coffins. For example, over the last two decades the U.S. has doubled the number of black males in prison, to nearly 1 million.

More encouragingly, the biggest decline in murder from 1993 to 1997 was among the newest generation of black males aged 14 to 17. These kids born mostly in the early 1980s survived abortion levels similar to those faced by the crime-ridden 1975-to-1979 generation. Yet, their murder rate in 1997 was less than half that of the 14- to 17-year-olds of 1993. Seeing their big brothers gunned down in drive-by shootings and their big sisters becoming crack whores may have scared them straight.

Admittedly, it's still theoretically possible that without abortion the black youth murder rate would have, say, sextupled instead of merely quintupling. Still, there's a more interesting question: Why did the places with the highest abortion rates in the 1970s (e.g., NYC and Washington D.C.) tend to suffer the worst crack-driven crime waves in the early 1990s?

The Racial Reckoning on the Roads

Taki's
June 8, 2021

A S I may have mentioned once or twice over the past year, the media-declared "racial reckoning" following the death of George Floyd on May 25, 2020, has been getting a lot of blacks murdered by other blacks.[1] But I am not being ironic in saying that I am now stunned to find out that motor vehicle fatalities among blacks similarly soared 36% in June-December 2020 versus the same period in 2019, compared with a 9% increase among the rest of the population.

Whenever I uncover data that suggests that the reigning mental models of the great and the good have blood on their hands, I'm accusingly asked: Why do I care? What kind of disreputable weirdo am I to speak out just because more of my fellow Americans are dying violently?

Okay, okay, I'll confess: Not only am I a notorious anti-murderist, I'm an anti-crashite as well.

The federal National Highway Traffic Safety Administration recently issued a report entitled "Early Estimates of Motor Vehicle Traffic Fatalities and Fatality Rate by Sub-Categories in 2020" showing that total road deaths among all races were up 7% from 36,096 in 2019 to 38,680 in 2020.

That's despite miles driven by the American public falling 13% last year due to the pandemic. Put them together, and that's a ridiculous increase in the death rate of over 23% per mile.[2]

Among those still on the road, spectacularly bad driving grew. For example, ejections (being thrown out of the vehicle) roughly doubled between February and April and remained consistently above 2019 levels for the rest of 2020.

Impairment due to alcohol among crashing drivers was up moderately in 2020 over 2019, but not as much as marijuana and opioids.

Average speed was up about 5% on urban roads (where traffic was less of a hindrance in 2020) but was no different on rural roads.

Traffic deaths were up 7% overall comparing 2020 with 2019, and some crash factors and demographics grew even more:

Alcohol-impaired crashes killed 9% more;
Single-vehicle crashes (+9);
Rollovers (+9);
Weekends (+9);
Nighttime (+11);
Rural local/collector roads (+11);
Speeding-related crashes (+11);
Urban local/collector roads (+12);
Urban interstates (+15);
No seatbelt (+15);
Occupant ejection (up 20%)

But the worst single increase in deaths from 2019 to 2020 is 23% more black people being killed. The NHTSA writes:

Non-Hispanic Black fatalities, as a proportion of all fatalities, increased in most months from March to December. The greatest increase occurred in June (20% [black share in 2020] versus 15% [in 2019]). Total estimated Non-Hispanic Black fatalities increased by 23% from 2019 to 2020.

In contrast, among everybody else, road deaths were up less than 4% in 2020.

As I mentioned, in the last seven months of 2020, the era of the racial reckoning, black deaths increased 36% over 2019, while nonblack deaths rose 9%.

The graph above shows the percent change in 2020 over 2019 in raw fatalities (not the death rate per mile driven—while we now have a count of traffic

SAILER'S LAW OF MASS SHOOTINGS

Traffic Fatalities in 2020

■ Blacks: % Change from 2019 to 2020
■ Nonblacks: % Change from 2019 to 2020

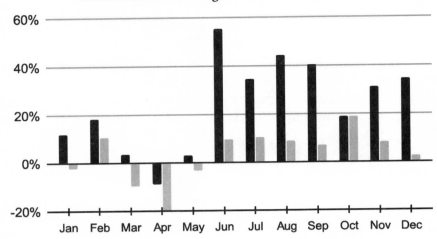

deaths by race, we don't have miles driven by race, so we can't break down traffic fatalities per mile driven by race).

While black fatalities were up more than those of nonblacks in each of the first five months of 2020, black road deaths exploded in June along with riots and murders. In the tumultuous first month of the racial reckoning, 743 black people were killed in traffic fatalities, up from 478 in June 2019, a 55% increase.

Over the last seven months of 2020, 4,995 blacks died in traffic accidents compared with 3,660 during the same period in 2019, a worsening of 36%.

In the social sciences, that's an enormous increase.

Traffic deaths should be going down, constantly. Indeed, deaths per mile driven steadily fell through 2014 (after a bump up in the party-hearty late 1970s). After all, vehicles ought to be getting safer due to technological progress. And we now have the big data artificial intelligence capability to figure out which roadways are most hazardous and why, and fix them.

But then, like the number of murders going up 23% in the last two years of the Obama Administration when the White House turned anti-cop, road deaths grew 15% from 2014 to 2016.

Did the same factors that exacerbated the murder rate during the first and second BLM eras—cops withdrawing and black lowlifes feeling validated— also worsen the carnage on the blacktop?

372

I don't know. The NHTSA only began breaking out fatalities by race in 2019, so I'd barely looked into these trends before.

Note that blacks are not terrible drivers. While blacks were 55.9% of known murder offenders in 2019's FBI crime statistics and 53.2 of homicide victims, they were a much more reasonable 16.9% of traffic deaths in 2019.[3] So, blacks are somewhat more likely to be killed in car crashes, but the proportion is nowhere near as absurd as with murder. If blacks could get their share of America's murders down to 16.9%, this country would be a racial utopia.

(Two methodological asides: While we can usually distinguish between perpetrator and victim in homicides, although they don't differ much racially, guilt is murkier in traffic statistics. Also, like most police reports, the car-crash statistics don't do a good job of distinguishing between whites and Hispanics, so in my graph I simply lumped the rest of the U.S. population together into "nonblacks.")

But then the black share of road fatalities rose to 19.7%t during the racial reckoning of June-December 2020: still not as awful as black gun violence, but moving in the wrong direction.

I had speculated in 2016 "Is There a 'Ferguson Effect' Behind Rising Highway Deaths?":

> Presumably, much of what's going on is a belated rebound from the rise in gasoline prices in the later 2000s and the ensuing Great Recession, which cut miles driven and drove a lot of marginal drivers (e.g., teens, illegal aliens, etc.) out of owning a car.... As commenters have suggested, maybe the spread of smartphones is making us more distracted drivers?
>
> But still...is this related to the Ferguson Effect that has been driving up homicides over almost precisely the same time period? Are cops policing the streets and highways less proactively, spending more time in the donut shop, because they don't want to wind up on YouTube as the face of Implicit Bias and Systemic Racism Against Black Bodies?

But we didn't have data broken out by race back then so I couldn't pursue the question.

During the first three years of the pro-cop Trump administration, traffic fatalities per miles driven, like murders, drifted downward.

But then came the pandemic and the racial reckoning. Police stops declined in March 2020 as cops socially distanced, and then went lower in the summer as The Establishment indulged in an anti-police hissy fit.

For example, the *Associated Press* articulated this month:

> Traffic stops and arrests resulting from those stops declined sharply in Missouri last year due in large part to the COVID-19 pandemic, but Black motorists were still far more likely to be pulled over and arrested, according to a report released Tuesday.... For arrests, 3.7% of white motorists who were pulled over were arrested, compared to 4.61% of Black drivers who were pulled over. Those percentages were actually an improvement. In 2019, Black drivers were 95% more likely to be pulled over by police in Missouri, and 36% more likely to be arrested.[4]

In other words, according to the *AP*, the law arresting fewer criminals is an "improvement," so long as they are black criminals. Not surprisingly, the murder rate in St. Louis was the worst in the country in 2020.

About the time last summer that the *Associated Press* started reverentially referring to blacks as "Blacks" (but continued to spell whites as "whites"), evidence began piling up that blacks had become a little too thrilled by their new image as morally deserving to be above the law. Mass shootings at black parties exploded as the thought of a black man being dissed (by another black) became increasingly intolerable in an American culture that now values black self-esteem above all.[5]

Could it be that between the declining fear of being pulled over, the explosion in black feelings of exuberance and entitlement, not to mention the stimulus checks, blacks just started driving more recklessly?

Back in 2005, I was intensely denounced by ethical paragons such as John Podhoretz for observing that blacks "need stricter moral guidance from society."[6]

Well, we've since tried telling blacks that they are morally better than whites. How's that working out for all concerned?

The Geography of Homicide

Taki's
August 24, 2022

EVERYBODY has an opinion on matters of crime and race, but not that many people are familiar with the facts. So I'm going to devote this column to furnishing basic data about the best documented and most important crime, homicide.

The single most important fact about crime in the United States is the extraordinarily high rate at which African Americans die violently: almost ten times the rate of white Americans. That's one of the most gigantic racial ratios in all the social sciences.

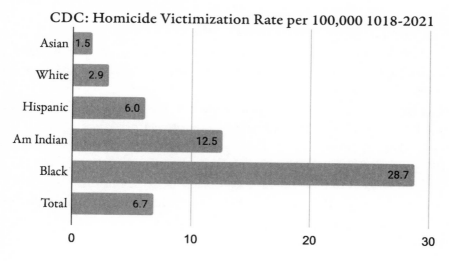

CDC: Homicide Victimization Rate per 100,000 1018-2021

Group	Rate
Asian	1.5
White	2.9
Hispanic	6.0
Am Indian	12.5
Black	28.7
Total	6.7

In contrast, Hispanics, who are roughly comparable to blacks in average income, education, and age, die by homicide just over twice as often as whites. The black homicide death rate is thus 4.8 times the Hispanic rate, a gap that is hard to explain in any politically correct fashion, so almost nobody ever mentions it.

The second-highest homicide rate is among American Indians, who die violently over four times as often as whites. Asians get killed only half as much as whites.

Despite making up only about one-eighth of the population, over half of homicide victims in the U.S. are black, with a little over a quarter being white. In all likelihood, a pie chart of perps would be even more lopsided.

CDC: Homicide Victimization by Race 2018-2021

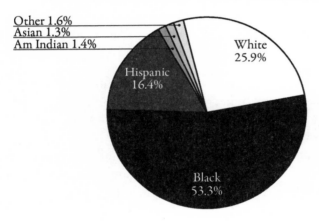

My source is the CDC's WONDER database for mortality statistics from 2018 to 2021, which tracks deaths by homicide. (Homicides are a superset of murders and manslaughters, including both crimes and justifiable killings. But homicides tend to be an informative proxy for murders.)

Note that the CDC tracks the race of victims, but not the race of perpetrators. Presumably, the offending rate of groups that get killed a lot, such as blacks, tend to be even somewhat higher than their victimization rate—the FBI counts blacks as 56.5% of known murder offenders in 2020—while those with low rates of dying by homicide, such as Asians, probably do unto others even less often than they are done unto.[7] But most killings are intraracial, so counting victims can help us get a general sense of the number of perpetrators.

Crime shot upward in 2020, whether due to Black Lives Matter declaring the "racial reckoning," the pandemic, increased gun purchases, stimulus checks, sunspots, or whatever. A simple way of measuring the change is to compare total homicides in the two years 2020-2021 with the previous pair of years, 2018-2019. It might not have seemed like it at the time, but in hindsight, 2018-2019 were the Good Old Days.

Over the past two years, black homicide deaths shot up 45%, Hispanics 37%, whites 17%, American Indians 16%, and Asians (whose victimizations have probably gotten the most publicity per capita) 9%.

More concern should be paid to the fact that Hispanics, after becoming notably better behaved since the 1990s, have regressed considerably over the past two years. More than anybody else during America's tough-on-crime decades, Latinos seemed to get the message. Their murder rate declined relative to blacks and whites (and my vague impression is that they also drive drunk less often than in the 20th century).

But, as The Establishment signaled over the past two years that they were just kidding about rule of law, more Hispanics seemed to have decided that the *gringos* weren't serious anymore about law and order.

There's much discussion in the respectable press about legal gun purchases as being the cause (rather than, more likely, the effect) of the historic increase in shootings. It's difficult to find statistics on what percentage of murders are committed with legally owned guns, but the CDC data lets you calculate the share of homicides due to gunfire rather than knives, blunt objects, fists, poison, or whatever. Among black homicide victims, 87% died by firearms compared with only 56% of American Indians, 62% of Asians, 63% of whites, and 75% of Latinos.

As you might guess from rap lyrics, African American culture tends to encourage knuckleheads to use guns to settle beefs. Native Americans are also quite violent, but they aren't as quick to resort to guns.

America has a high homicide rate for a first-world country, although over half of that number is due to African Americans.

The African American homicide rate is similar to that of cartel-plagued Mexico, and lags Nigeria, South Africa, and Jamaica. According to a U.N. list, the highest-known homicide rate is in the U.S. Virgin Islands, Jeffrey Epstein's favorite place to relax.[8]

Not surprisingly, within the U.S., a state's total homicide rate tends to correlate closely with how black its population is:

SAILER'S LAW OF MASS SHOOTINGS

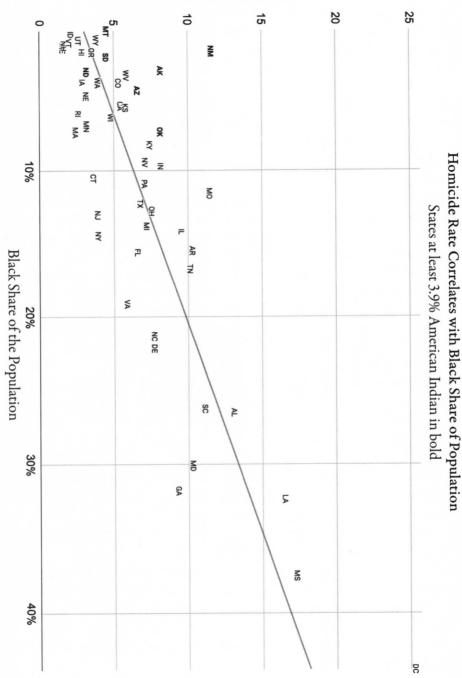

Total Homicide Rate

Black Share of the Population

Homicide Rate Correlates with Black Share of Population
States at least 3.9% American Indian in bold

If you count Washington, D.C., as a state, the correlation coefficient is a very high $r = 0.82$.

New Mexico stands out as a state with a high murder rate despite very few blacks. Georgia, which increasingly attracts middle-class black migrants, is an outlier in the opposite direction, with a relatively low murder rate for its high proportion of African Americans.

Following the general pattern laid out in historian David Hackett Fischer's *Albion's Seed*, Northeastern, North Central, and Mormon West whites have a homicide victimization rate similar to one of the more violent Western European countries such as gangster-ridden Belgium, remote Finland, or hard-drinking Britain:

Southern, hillbilly, and Wild West whites tend to get killed at rates more like Eastern Europeans.

White Homicide Rate

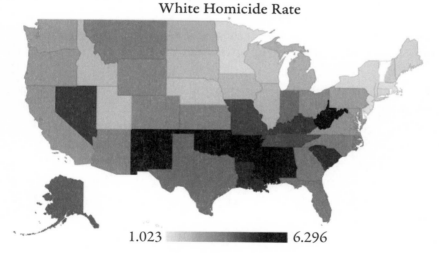

1.023 ▬▬▬▬▬ 6.296

The black homicide rate is twice as high in the safest state (Massachusetts) as the white rate in the most dangerous state (Mississippi). States in white have missing data.

Still, there are major differences among states in the black rate. The pattern, though, is perhaps unexpected: As far as I can tell, blacks tend to get themselves killed the most in states, north or south, near the Mississippi, Ohio, and Missouri Rivers.

In recent years, due to the Ferguson Effect, the black rate has been the worst in the state of Missouri, followed by Illinois, Indiana, and Wisconsin. I don't have a good sense of whether this is a recent development due to the

Black Homicide Rate

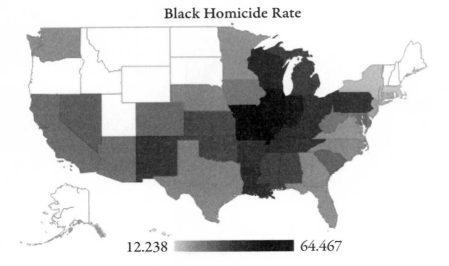

12.238 ▦ 64.467

Ferguson and Floyd Effects, a medium-term reality (possibly due to the hollowing out of American industry), or whether the Mississippi watershed has always had a higher black murder rate. Fischer talked about Louisiana being highly violent ever since its founding by the French, but what about blacks farther north?

One bit of good news is that the black homicide rate tends to be below the national black average in the warmer states that have been attracting black migrants in recent years, such as Georgia, Florida, and Texas. On the other hand, as blacks and immigrants pour into these traditionally business-friendly Republican states, will the new Democratic voters kill the goose that laid the golden egg?

If you divide the black homicide rate by the white rate to get the racial ratio, you'll find that the races are somewhat less unequal in the South. The lowest black-white ratio at 4.8 to 1 is in West Virginia, where the whites tend to be ornery and the blacks relatively well-behaved.

The biggest racial gaps are found in the North Central states with their well-behaved whites, especially Wisconsin and Illinois, where blacks are 25 times more likely than whites to die by homicide. One theory for this is that the Illinois Central railway brought welfare-seeking Deep South blacks to Illinois in the 1960s and then to naive Wisconsin in the 1970s.[9]

The black homicide rate grew from 2018-19 to 2020-21 in all states with enough sample size to measure:

Black/White Homicide Rate Ratio

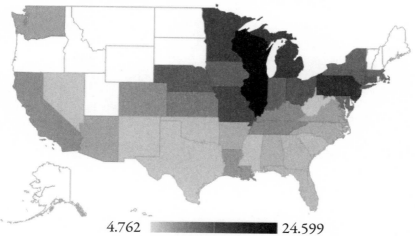

4.762 ▬▬▬▬▬ 24.599

The worst increase was near the epicenter of the Floyd Effect in Minneapolis. Black homicides in Iowa were up 119%, in Minnesota 113%, Nebraska 93%, and Wisconsin (home of the Jacob Blake riots in Kenosha) 92%. Kentucky, where BLM had a martyr in Breonna Taylor, also stands out, as do Connecticut and New York.

For a big state, Florida had a relatively small increase of only 23%.

Way back in 1760, Ben Franklin wrote a pamphlet attempting to explain to the British government the future world-historical importance of the Mississippi watershed: Whoever ruled it would dominate the 20th century.

That came true.

But in the 21st century, we seem to be letting the middle of the country fall apart.

America's Black Male Problem

Taki's
February 15, 2023

S INCE May 25, 2020, America has crucified itself over a single statistic: Blacks are two to three times more likely to die at the hands of the police than are whites, making up 25% to 35% of police killings.

In contrast, other data points that could add nuance to the conversation are considered by the prestige press to be extremely inappropriate to mention.

For example, the most careful estimate yet of what percentage of murders in America blacks committed in 2021 comes up with a best guess of 64% of all cases, cleared and uncleared. This suggests that blacks are recently an order of magnitude more homicidal than the entire rest of the population (including Hispanics).[10]

This is an astonishing ratio. Without being aware of it, it's practically impossible to think intelligently about many of the most pressing public issues of the 2020s.

My impression is that most Americans are only aware of this datum in their private lives but not when it comes to public debate. Only the growing ranks of the consciously anti-woke (the type of ornery individual who responds to the usual clueless mainstream media articles with quantitative comments citing government crime statistics) understand the magnitude and importance of this statistic.

I've noticed that when true believers in the conventional wisdom are confronted with the official numbers, they often respond with arguments that clearly haven't been battle-tested.

For example, a common rejoinder is that blacks have higher homicide rates only because the police are keeping an eye on them more closely. This might sound plausible for, say, jaywalking tickets, but it makes no sense to postulate that tens of thousands of additional whites must be getting murdered each year by other whites without anybody noticing or talking about it. In reality, unsolved murders of young white women tend to become national obsessions.

Other retorts focus on moral culpability: e.g., blacks shouldn't be blamed for committing more murders because of the lingering effects of 1619, Jim Crow, and/or New Deal redlining.

First, whether or not blacks have a good excuse for their murder rate is irrelevant to the fact that their murder rate is what it is. We could have avoided public policy disasters like the current boom in homicides and traffic fatalities during the "racial reckoning" if we hadn't been so willfully ignorant of this fundamental fact of American life.

Second, it's hard to see how putative causes in the increasingly distant past, such as the white murder of black Emmett Till 68 years ago, can explain why black shootings and car crashes exploded immediately after George Floyd.

Third, the most scientific-sounding excuse is that blacks commit more killings because they were raised in lower-income households (which can in turn be blamed on slavery or whatever).

After all, it is true that the poor do shoot each other more than the rich do, and blacks are, indeed, less well-paid than are whites.

So, do differences in income explain all of the black-white gap in serious crime?

No.

The conclusive data was assembled by the remarkably industrious Harvard economist Raj Chetty in his 2019 paper "Race and Economic Opportunity in the United States: An Intergenerational Perspective."[11]

Chetty has strenuously positioned himself as an anti-racist good guy, so the fact that his data has repeatedly vindicated bad guy Steve Sailer's perceptions has yet to register on the less bright members of the media (e.g., not Matt Yglesias).

Over a decade ago, Chetty set out to find where in America was the Magic Dirt upon which poor kids most often rose to the middle class. And where was the Tragic Dirt that condemned them to another generation of poverty? Then, all we'd have to do is learn the lessons of what they are doing right in the good places and doing wrong in the bad places.

But when Chetty published his first map of high and low social mobility in *The New York Times* in 2013, I immediately pointed out that his findings of regions with strong upward mobility were simply white places, like the upper Great Plains and Utah.[12] And his low upward mobility spots were black regions like the Cotton Belt or American Indian reservations. This is because blacks and Native Americans regress toward lower mean incomes than whites.

Ever since, I've probably developed more insights from Chetty's data than he has. The Indian-born savant is not a particularly acute analyst of this country. But he *is* a prodigious compiler of data that previously had been thought off-limits due to privacy rights.

Chetty's methodological brainstorm was to forge relationships with federal agencies like the Internal Revenue Service and the Census Bureau so that they would provide him with individual data, such as your tax returns, but in "anonymized" form.

So far, I haven't heard of any scandals about leaks of personal information from Chetty's operation, so the feds appear right to have trusted him.

Chetty then linked information from different bureaus using an anonymized version of your Social Security number, so he knows what your income is from your 1040 and what your race is from your Census form. He knows who your kids are from whom you claimed as a dependent in the 1990s, what college they went to, if they were involuntary guests of correctional facilities on the day of the 2010 Census, and how much income they earned up through 2015.

He's built a database of 21 million Americans born between 1978 and 1983. He knows their parents' incomes for 1994–2000 (when the kids were between 11 and 22 years old), if they were in jail on April 1, 2010, when they were about 30, and how much income they reported in 2014–2015 when they were in their mid-30s.

Here's my graph of Chetty's crucial findings:

If you don't believe my graph, *The New York Times* published a fairly similar graph[13] of the same data in 2018, and Chetty created his own graph.[14] My graph is more self-evident, but it's the same shape as the other two.

Raj Chetty's Data:
% of Incarcerated Men vs. Their Parents' Income Percentile

▬▬▬ % of Black Sons Incarcerated
▪ ▪ ▪ ▪ % of White Sons Incarcerated   ▬▬▬ Ratio of Black Sons/White Sons Incarcerated

Left axis: % of men born 1978-1983 locked up on 4/1/2010. Right axis: black/white ratio.

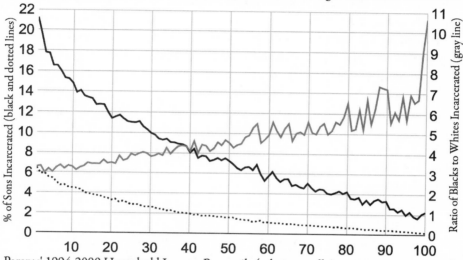

Parents' 1994-2000 Household Income Percentile (relative to all Americans, not own race)

By the way, I don't know why Chetty didn't make available to the public the Hispanic imprisonment rate. Perhaps framing his data solely as black vs. white makes more plausible-sounding racist, antiwhite interpretations such as the *NYT*'s hilarious headline on Chetty's findings: "Extensive Data Shows Punishing Reach of Racism for Black Boys."

The fact that Hispanics have improved their relative law-abidingness while blacks have not is an unwelcome distraction for Chetty's career prospects.

The horizontal axis represents their parents' income in 1994 to 2000 by percentile of the entire population. Each single percentile represents 213,000 Americans born around 1980.

In case you are wondering, Chetty is using the same income scale for both blacks and whites. Thus, in the highest percentile, the "One Percent" of Occupy Wall Street demonology, there are 186,600 whites and only 1,800 blacks.

The left vertical axis is the percentage of the parents' sons who were incarcerated on April 1, 2010, when they were 26 to 32 years old. Among black men (black line) raised in the lowest percentile of parental household income, over 21% were locked up vs. over 6% of white men (blue line) raised in the same extreme poverty.

For both races, incarceration rates fall steadily with increasing affluence of upbringing. Among whites, only 0.2% of sons of the One Percent were in the slammer. Among blacks, the lowest percentage (1.6%) is found in the 98th percentile, before the incarceration rate rises in the two highest-income percentiles.

This curious anomaly could just be due to statistical noise. In the top two percentiles of upbringing reckoned across all races, there were only about 2,100 youngish black men altogether and roughly 45 of them were under lock and key.

Or it could be that this third-highest percentile is the most bourgeois among blacks, featuring, say, partners in law and CPA firms, while the top two percentiles are more loaded with black jocks and entertainers, whose sons tend to be more of a handful.

With that minor exception, why do richer kids wind up in jail less often? There are no doubt numerous reasons of nurture and nature, ranging from the wealthy being able to afford better defense attorneys, to neighborhoods without youth gangs to ensnare your son into a life of crime being more expensive, and on to genetics. In general, being wealthy is good, and you should strive for it for the sake of your kids.

The right vertical axis denotes the ratio (red line) of the black percentage incarcerated divided by the white. Unexpectedly, it rises steadily with childhood affluence.

Among men raised in the dirt-poor first percentile, blacks are 3.3 times as likely to be imprisoned.

At the 25th percentile, blacks are confined 3.9 times as often.

At the 50th percentile, the ratio is 4.5 to one and at the 75th percentile it's 5.0.

At the 98th percentile, the ratio is 6.7, before exploding to 10.7 at the 100th.

The median black household income falls around the 27th to 28th percentile nationally, where black men are locked up 4.0 times as often as white men. So that's probably the best summary statistic: All else being equal in terms of household income during adolescence, black men are four times as likely to find themselves behind bars as white men.

That's a huge disparity.

For instance, black men at the 98th percentile of upbringing, the best-behaved black cohort, are jailed as often as white men at the 50th percentile. Similarly, the black rate at the national median of income is 7.2 percent, a little higher than the white rate at the single lowest percentile.

That suggests that there is approximately a two standard deviation difference in racial propensity to be prison-bound even when controlling for affluence when young.

In the social sciences, a one standard deviation difference, such as in IQ, is very large. Two is almost unheard of. Two standard deviations after adjusting for childhood income is off the charts.

Why does the black-to-white ratio get steadily worse with higher income? I don't know. Before seeing Chetty's data, I might have guessed it shrank. Is the cause racism?

Well, if it is, racism doesn't much hinder black women. They appear to be incarcerated only about 30% more often than white women raised with the same family income, not 300% more often as with black men.

In general, racism provides a boring and obtuse all-purpose faith-based rationalization for everything otherwise interesting about American life. But can racism create a rock too heavy to lift off the backs of African-Americans?

More interestingly, I've been arguing since the 1990s that blacks average more masculinity than other races. This has its upsides where maleness is a plus, such as blacks playing more on Super Bowl-winning teams. But it also has its downsides, such as blacks committing more felonies.

Every culture has to deal with the inevitable problems caused by rampant masculinity. For example, Europe spent over a thousand years nagging and cajoling its hereditary warlords into behaving a little more like Christian gentlemen.

What has never worked is giving up the struggle, as American culture has more or less done in this decade. Lately, we've declared that all empirical evidence of bad behavior by blacks *must* be proof of white malevolence.

Not surprisingly, this cultural collapse is inducing blacks to behave even worse.

CHAPTER FOURTEEN

The Great Awokening

The Basic Logic of Wokeness

The Unz Review
December 8, 2021

THE BASIC LOGIC OF WOKENESS:

- Whites own more nice things (such as real estate, stocks and bonds, credentials, credit-ratings, lack of criminal records, and so forth) than do blacks;
- And that can't possibly be any fault of blacks;
- So, therefore, whites stole their wealth from blacks;
- And therefore whites must give their wealth to blacks.

The First Rule of White Club

Taki's
July 29, 2015

> I have found that, in the African-American oral tradition, if the words are enunciated eloquently enough, no one examines the meaning for definitive truth.
> —Biracial novelist Mat Johnson, *Loving Day*, 2015

AMERICA'S foremost public intellectual, Ta-Nehisi Coates, has published a new best-selling minibook, *Between the World and Me*, that's interesting for what it reveals about a forbidden subject: the psychological damage done by pervasive black violence to soft, sensitive, bookish souls such as Coates. The *Atlantic* writer's black radical parents forced the frightened child to grow up in Baltimore's black community, where he lived in constant terror of the other boys. Any white person who wrote as intensely about how blacks scared him would be career-crucified out of his job, so it's striking to read Coates recounting at length how horrible it is to live around poor blacks if you are a timid, retiring sort.

Coates' lack of physical courage is a common and perfectly reasonable trait, although writers typically cover it up. For example, Hunter S. Thompson transmuted his recurrent paranoia about impending carnage (which beset him even in venues as family-friendly as the Circus-Circus casino) into hallucinatory comedy in *Fear and Loathing in Las Vegas*.

Coates, however, is humorless. Worse, his fans have encouraged him to believe he is the second coming of James Baldwin, egging him on to indulge in a prophetic-hysteric-postmodern style that is easier to parody (e.g., just repeat endlessly the phrase "black bodies" and the distractingly stupid formulation "people who believe they are white") than it is to endure over even the course of Coates' very short second autobiography. (As with the president, both of Coates' books are memoirs.)

White writers have seldom had the courage to confess their fear of black violence so fully, at least not since 1963, when Norman Podhoretz responded to the hullabaloo over James Baldwin with an essay about growing up in Brooklyn in the 1930s and 1940s:

> And so for a long time I was puzzled to think that.... Negroes were supposed to be persecuted when it was the Negroes who were doing the only persecuting I knew about—and doing it, moreover, to me.... A city boy's world is contained within three or four square blocks, and in my world it was the whites, the Italians and Jews, who feared the Negroes, not the other way around. The Negroes were tougher than we were, more ruthless, and on the whole they were better athletes.... Yet my sister's opinions, like print, were sacred, and when she told me about exploitation and economic forces I believed her. I believed her, but I was still afraid of Negroes.[1]

In the 52 years since Podhoretz's "My Negro Problem—And Ours," overwhelming evidence has piled up validating the prescience of his boyhood traumas at the hands of black juvenile delinquents. But it's precisely because the scale of black violence over the past half century is so blatantly obvious that white intellectuals have been largely self-silenced on the topic—even as the most cunning minds among today's liberal whites plot to reverse the mistake their grandparents made in fearfully ceding much of the best urban turf to black criminality.

The central real estate question of this century has become: How can big cities drop their hot potato of poor urban blacks in the laps of naive suburbs and small towns? That helps explain the unhinged reaction among elites to Donald Trump publicly pointing out that Mexico isn't sending us its highest-quality citizens to be our illegal aliens. The unspoken plan is to continue to use the more docile Hispanics newcomers to shove the more dangerous African-American citizens out of desirable cities; thus, only a class traitor like

Trump would dare allude to the unfortunate side effects suffered by the rest of the country.

Despite all the violence Coates has suffered at the hands of other blacks, his racial loyalty remains admirably adamantine. Thus, his ploy, as psychologically transparent as it is popular with liberal whites, is to blame his lifelong petrified unhappiness on the white suburbanites he envied for being able to live far from black thugs.

Unfortunately for Coates' persuasiveness, white people, unlike blacks, have never actually done anything terribly bad to him. The worst memory he can dredge up is the time an Upper West Side white woman pushed his 4-year-old son to get the dawdling kid to stop clogging an escalator exit. She even had the racist nerve to say, "Come on!"

Coates reacted as unreasonably as a guest star on *Seinfeld* would. Ever since this Escalator Incident, he's been dwelling on how, while it might have looked like yet another example of blacks behaving badly, it was, when you stop to think about slavery and Jim Crow (not to mention redlining), really all the fault of whites.

The central event in *Between the World and Me* is the fatal shooting in 2000 of an acquaintance from Howard U. by an undercover deputy from Prince George's County, the country's most affluent black-majority county. Coates refers to this tragedy repeatedly as proof of America's demonic drive to destroy black bodies. (The dead man's family, I found, was eventually awarded $3.7 million in their wrongful-death suit, much like the $3 million awarded to the parents of a teen gunned down by an undercover Obama Administration agent in a shooting that I investigated in 2010. You have never heard of my local police blotter item, though, because the victim was white.)[2]

Since I'm a horrible person, my immediate response to Coates' tale was... okay...black-run county, affirmative-action hiring, and poor police decision-making...you know, I bet the shooter cop was black.

And sure enough, the Carlton Jones who shot Prince Jones turned out to be black.[3] Coates eventually gets around to briefly admitting that awkward fact, but only after seven pages of purple prose about people who believe they are white destroying black bodies.

In fact, I discovered Coates himself had written about this tragedy before. Seven years ago he explained in *The Atlantic* in a poorly proofread but less pompous prose style:

> I am going to try to be fair about this. The cop was in an unmarked
> car, and wasn't wearing a uniform. According to his own testimony,
> he basically cornered Prince's car pulled out a gun "but no badge"
> and IDed himself as an officer. Prince. whose vehicle was hemmed
> in, rammed the cops car. The cop shot him Prince and he died. The
> officer was presumably in pursuit of a "suspect." But the suspect
> looked nothing like Prince, except that they were both black. All
> I could think when that happened was about what I would have
> done. The way we come up, if a black dude with dreads (which is
> how officer Carlton Jones looked) is following you and then he
> corners you, pulls a gun, but doesn't have a badge, you don't assume
> he's cop. You assume he's trying to rob you.[4]

In other words, the two black men racially profiled each other as dangerous criminals and then violently attacked each other.

Why did the two blacks profile each other?

Oh, sorry, I forgot: because white people.

Wait, my mistake: because people who believe they are white.

Occam's razor suggests that the reason blacks tend to fear violence from
one another is because they tend to be violent.

But you are forgetting something: The first rule of White Club is: You
do blame White Club. The second rule of White Club is: You *do* blame
White Club.

Coates has thus elaborated a theory of history in which everything bad
ever done by blacks is the fault of American whites (whom he describes—
metaphorically, I hope—as "cannibals").

Unfortunately, Coates, a 39-year-old Howard U. dropout, doesn't actually
know much about history because, even though he frequently reads history
books, he lacks a retentive mind. He reminds me of another autodidact who
is always amazed by whatever he is currently reading: Glenn Beck.

Coates is unable to keep in his head a coherent timeline of the past, which
means he is frequently clueless about what could possibly have caused what.
For example, when recounting his arrival at Howard U. around 1993, he com-
plains that outside his HBCU "black beauty was never celebrated in movies,
in television...." Personally, I watched a lot of television in 1993, and my recollection is that the beauty of Michael Jordan's black body was rather often
celebrated. But who can expect the New James Baldwin to remember 1993?

The intellectual limitations that have helped Coates achieve his level of conventional wisdomhood include his lack of interest in races other than blacks and whites. The country has 55 million Hispanics, 17 million Asians, and 4 million American Indians, yet Coates has barely deigned to notice their existence, much less ask himself why they have their own problems, which are on average quite different from black problems.

History, for Coates, began in 1619 with the first blacks to arrive in America. He has no interest in what blacks brought with them from their tens of thousands of years of evolution in Africa. (He appears wholly ignorant of science.)

And history sort of peters out for Coates and his admirers about 50 years ago, when liberals took charge of race in America. For instance, Coates is convinced that redlining by the FDR Administration explains why the West Side of Chicago is like it is. But he had no interest in learning from, say, Alyssa Katz's 2009 book *Our Lot,* which documents how Chicago's once crime-free Austin neighborhood (from which my wife's family was driven in 1970 after the third felony committed against the children by blacks) was destroyed by the liberal 1968 Fair Housing Act.

There are tens of millions of Americans who remember being shoved out of formerly functioning urban communities by black criminality. But who speaks for them? Will they ever be allowed to publicly commemorate the injustice that was done to them?

The Grateful Deaf

Taki's
October 20, 2021

THE FDA's approval in 1990 of cochlear implants that enable some of the deaf to hear set off a political struggle. On one side were the hearing parents of deaf children, who tend to assume that five senses are better than four. On the other were deaf civil rights activists who saw technological fixes for an identity they didn't view as needing repair as stigmatizing and even genocidal toward "Deaf culture."[5]

Curiously, this clear predecessor of the Great Awokening, the promotion of deafness as equal to hearing, has never quite taken off the way crazier manias such as transgenderism have. Sympathy for the deaf would seem natural, but other identity groups attract more allies these days.

The high points of deaf activism were the 1988 and 2006 student strikes at federally funded Gallaudet University for the deaf in Washington, D.C., over plans to appoint as president persons not fully fluent in American Sign Language.

In contrast to residential schools for Canadian Indians, which are now the worst thing ever, boarding schools for the deaf are prized by activists as the font of deaf culture because it's where deaf children can talk to each other in sign language. Yet, deaf militance over the cochlear menace appears to have faded somewhat in recent years even at residential schools. (By the way, in this article when I use "deaf," I'm referring only to those who were deaf as children, like Helen Keller, not adult-onset deaf people like Beethoven.)

I hadn't thought about deaf demands for a while until reading geneticist Kathryn Paige Harden's new book *The Genetic Lottery* in which she enthusiastically cites, perhaps to show that eugenics can be Woke, two deaf lesbians who are trying to find a congenitally deaf sperm donor to help one of them conceive a deaf child for, as they say, the culture.

Then I was reminded again by a *New York Times* op-ed "Fear of a Deaf Planet" complaining that hearing people don't learn sign language. But even that was phrased in less abrasive language than the typical identity-politics manifesto:

> Rather than a purely curative focus, we should be attempting to eradicate the stigma that surrounds hearing loss.[6]

Much of the argument for spreading sign language would seemingly fit in well with current obsessions such as remodeling American society, the Spanish language, and human nature in general to suit the whims of the differently gendered.

And yet, I was struck by how seldom lately we hear about the deaf community and their fears of eradication by technological progress. Not long ago, Deaf Replacement Theory was a big deal among the deaf, but it has gotten drowned out by more fashionable identities.

Indeed, the *Times*' commenters were largely dismissive, brusquely pointing out that learning sign language is time-consuming, and that the deaf are a small minority so why should they get special consideration when there are more practical projects to undertake? Empathy for the deaf is not a high priority these days, evidently.

It's useful to think about why there is deaf culture but not blind culture. *Wikipedia*'s article on the former is vastly longer than its short squib on the latter, which sums up, "...blind people integrate with the broader community and culture, and often do not identify blindness as a defining part of their culture."

That's because language can be essential to identity. Just as nationalism in Europe was an offshoot of the consolidation of local spoken dialects into a standardized national written language (such as the French government's imposition of the Parisian dialect on its sprawling domain), deaf culture exists due to the consolidation of sign languages.

Language is fundamental to communication, of course, and perhaps even to thought. So life tended to be extremely difficult for those born deaf, especially if they didn't work out an idiosyncratic sign language with their families.

The term "dumb," as in "deaf and dumb," referred to an inability to speak, but it has the connotation of stupidity as well. In some cases, this was the bigotry of the times, but it also connoted an unfortunate tendency: Children who miss the language development window can wind up cognitively impaired for life. How do you carry on a monologue in your head without words? Granted, some people get by fine in life without talking to themselves silently. But, in general, it's a necessary useful skill.

Fortunately, there exist sign languages. According to neurologist Oliver Sacks, many signers conduct their internal monologues by picturing fingers moving in their mind's eye.[7]

Fairly sophisticated sign languages can more or less spontaneously arise in communities with a high percentage of congenitally deaf children due to inbreeding, such as on 18th-century Martha's Vineyard (which the deaf movement sees as its utopia because deafness was so common that the hearing learned the local sign language too), or in the Al-Sayyid Bedouin village in modern Israel. But for most rural deaf children without a critical mass of neighboring signers to interact with, lack of language development could be a lifelong impediment.

Europeans began formally documenting sign languages over the last few centuries, and in the West, most deaf children now have access to a well-developed system of signs.

Strikingly, a sign language can be orthogonal to the local spoken language. For example, American Sign Language is not speaking English with your fingers. It's not English at all. Thus, when in England, ASL signers are as linguistically isolated from British signers as English-only speakers are when trying to talk to the French. Instead, ASL is an offshoot of French Sign Language, so American signers can communicate with the local deaf when visiting France.

Indeed, deaf activism is rather reminiscent of the successful effort by French *Canadiens* in the late 1960s to protect their language identity by wringing major concessions from the Canadian government. Was that progressive or defensive?

Likewise, ASL-only speakers can be highly protective of their culture, and some fear its eradication by cochlear implants, somewhat as many lesbians fear that the current popularization of sex change therapies among butch girls threatens the long-term existence of their sexual orientation.

It remains puzzling why deaf identity, like lesbianism, is not in fashion in a time of fervent identity politics.

One possibility is that the deaf, due to their speech difficulties (not to mention their lack of musical ability), are not cool in the age of TikTok.

Moreover, the deaf are perhaps not as articulate in writing on average. IQ studies tend to find that the deaf have some advantages in visuo-spatial reasoning, rather like the blind are more likely to have perfect pitch. But the deaf tend to lag in memory-related skills. Sign languages are a blessing, but they are perhaps not as efficient for some mental purposes as speech languages.

Much of the current transgender fad is enabled and even inflated by parents who think they are doing their children a favor. But, outside of a few hardcore deaf culture fanatics like Harden's lesbians (and they are rare because a large majority of deaf children have hearing parents), most parents see deafness as a misfortune they wish to alleviate. And doctors can make honest money doing cochlear implants.

Hence, over time, there are fewer deaf children.

On the other hand, who knows what bad ideas might get spread next on social media? For example, beside deciding they are boys, moody teenage girls have lately been coming down with fake Tourette's syndrome ever since a YouTube influencer in Germany got big on the internet in 2019 by exaggerating his affliction.[8]

Deafness is not in style at the moment, but never say never these days.

The Bonfire of the Insanities

Taki's
June 03, 2020

WHITE elites are currently fantasizing that they can use the People of Color mob of young looters to overthrow Trump, somewhat like in Georgia in 2003 and Ukraine in 2014.

Serious people in Washington and New York take seriously warnings from abroad that the American Empire can endure four years of Trump, but not eight. Granted, the traditional, Constitutional way of bringing about regime change is to wait for the November election.

And, Trump has never been a terribly popular president, even during his three years of peace and prosperity before 2020's series of unfortunate events. So the notion that he would lose in November seemed pretty plausible.

The Democratic Party, though, saw itself as so morally beholden to blacks that it wound up outsourcing the job of picking its nominee to the church ladies of South Carolina. And they went for that nice Joe Biden, because he was such a properly deferential flunky to America's first black president.

Joe, however, is not getting any younger. For example, on Monday he unveiled to a black audience his breakthrough innovation for how to cut down on police shootings of "unarmed" blacks:

> "There is the idea that instead of standing there and teaching an agent when an unarmed person comes at him with a knife or something, shoot him in the leg instead of the heart."[9]

Is Joe's cognitive level going to bounce back by the fall?

Who knows?

So, perhaps as Plan B, the Deep State could use the latest Twitter brouhaha over some knuckleheaded black criminal who got himself killed while resisting arrest to gin up a medium-size race war and then...something...something...something...and Trump flees to exile in Dubai!

But, as you may have noticed over the past week, America's People of Color aren't really up to the organizational demands of pulling off a Ukraine/Georgia-style Color Revolution. They're less suited for engineering a coup than for boosting Air Jordans and Yeezys. So, ironically, the blue-state elites' favorite pets are now smashing up Santa Monica and SoHo, because blue cities have cooler shoe stores than Trump's Flyover Country.

Indeed, the main strategic innovation of this latest set of riots has been that instead of just robbing the Korean- or Arab-owned liquor store in your own slummy neighborhood, you drive to a nice part of town and steal stuff you saw a Kardashian wear on TV.

So far, the master strategist of the new riots has been Sherelle Smith, the sister of the black criminal whose killing set off the 2016 Milwaukee riot. She then famously explained to her rioting neighbors:

> Y'all burnin' down shit we need in our community. Take that shit to the suburbs. Burn that shit down! We need our shit! We need our weaves. I don't wear it. But we need it.[10]

The George Floyd Riots, such as Monday night's Sack of Manhattan, are the culmination of the Great Awokening that got going with Trayvon Martin in 2012 and came to monopolize the media's mindset with Ferguson in 2014. What we are seeing played out in the unfortunate shoe and handbag stores of our big cities is the logic of mainstream anti-racism in action.

As Frank DeScushin observed on Twitter:

> It's bizarre to see people Tweet "A riot is the voice of the unheard!" when the black voice on race issues is the one promoted by The Establishment (media, academia, politicians & corporations) with all those same parties censoring or demonizing any dissent.

White Americans have made vast efforts over the past sixty years to exterminate all manifestations of white racism. And yet, each new generation of black youths still likes to loot shoe stores.

It's a puzzlement.

The now-dominant view is not, exactly, that all men are equal. Instead, it's that all races are equal, but some are *much* more equal than others. In particular, African-Americans are the equalest people on earth.

Blacks are so equal that they are just racially superior to everybody else at sports, music, dance, acting, and comedy. (Which they might be.)

And blacks are, obviously, no worse than equal to everybody else at theoretical physics, contract law, and mechanical engineering.

Obviously.

Not to mention, their hair is at least as touchable as anybody else's during World War Hair, if not more so.

Only a vile racist might have any doubts.

The highest priority of our culture in recent years has become to prevent blacks from suffering from any inferiority complexes. In fact, we should stoke their superiority complex. Indeed, inculcating black megalomania is the least we can do.

(Whites find blacks vastly more entertaining than Mexicans, so white elites are much more attracted to harebrained plans to recruit blacks to help them beat the Real Enemy: other whites.)

As we are witnessing in countless videos this week of robbery and assault, this orthodoxy, not surprisingly, doesn't improve the behavior of blacks. Granted, as a critic I'm biased, but, having been subjected to a lot of criticism myself, I believe that being criticized tends to make us behave better, if only to not give our critics an easy target.

But blacks are increasingly excused from all critique, so their conduct is not improving, as we've seen nightly on the local news this week.

What America needs to do is treat blacks as human beings with free will who when they make good choices should enjoy the benefits and when they make bad choices should experience the consequences. Instead, The Establishment views blacks as our Sacred Cows, above criticism, but beneath agency.

The Only Polemicists Left

Taki's
October 21, 2020

"WHY Is Wokeness Winning?" asks veteran pundit Andrew Sullivan, recently fired by *New York* magazine for distressing its more fragile younger staffers by thinking for himself. Sullivan sums up the idiotic but undeniable reasons for the real-world success of Critical Race Theory:

> It gives you the simplest template for understanding the world, it assigns you virtue if you assent, it gives you instant power over others purely because of your and their identity, and it requires nothing more than tribal instinct to thrive. That's why it is here to stay.[11]

I would add some additional considerations to Sullivan's list.

First, we should admit that Wokeness is *not* Marxism, which is a theory about class rather than race. White people condemn Wokeness as Marxism because they aren't brave enough to call it what it really is: antiwhite racism.

Second, a huge reason for Woke Capital is that firms can be sued for discrimination if employees speak the truth about racial realities. But is employers browbeating white workers into lying about race creating a "hostile work environment"?

Importantly, the Trump Administration's Sept. 22 executive order against critical race theory training at federal contractors instructed the Attorney General to assess whether these indoctrination struggle sessions contribute to a "hostile work environment," which, of course, they do. Crushing white dissenters is the point of diversity training.

But Trump didn't dare point out that critical race theory is hostile to whites, but instead the president felt forced to say it was anti-American (which it is, too).

A fundamental Constitutional question is whether the 14th Amendment's guarantee of "the equal protection of the laws" applies to whites, as you might imagine from the Constitution's wording, or just to protected races, as the conventional wisdom decrees. Many today seem to believe that while all men are created equal, some are to be protected and others are to be prey.

Third, it's important to understand the Overton Window of which arguments are allowed to be made in polite society explains a lot about why Ibram X. Kendi, who is a lauded public intellectual despite barely scoring over 1000 on the SAT, keeps winning arguments, with his ideas, dim-witted as they obviously are, constantly inspiring moronic new policies.[12]

The central question of 2020 is: Why after all these years do African-Americans continue to underperform badly on average?

For example, in 2019 blacks were murder offenders at 8.2 times the rate at which nonblacks were murder offenders.[13]

Similarly, in 2019-2020, only 1% of blacks scored 1400 or higher on the SAT, compared to 7% of whites and 24% of Asians.[14]

To Kendi, there is only one possible explanation for the existence of racial disparities in behavior like these: white evilness. As Kendi told *Vox*:

> And there's only two causes of, you know, racial disparities. Either certain groups are better or worse than others and that's why they have more, or racist policy. Those are the only two options, and antiracists believe that the racial groups are equal, and so they're trying to change policy.[15]

Granted, that sounds about as silly as Kendi is, but who dares dispute him in 2020?

Kendi's buzzword "antiracist" is inspiring institutions across America to make futile and stupid gestures. For example, the school board in normally sensible San Diego just announced that to antiracistly fight the racial gap in class grades, teachers will no longer be allowed to mark down the grades of students for failing to turn in homework or for disrupting classes with their bad conduct.[16]

Instead, grades will depend solely upon performance on an end-of-year test of the students' "mastery" of the material.

That kind of one-giant-test system works fine at Yale Law School or Oxford. But will telling typical black public schoolchildren to, in effect, procrastinate actually help them compared with a system where they are encouraged to work steadily?

Do basketball and football coaches tell their athletes they don't need to practice as long as they win the championship in the end?

Of course not.

On average, what blacks need is not indulgence of their bad habits, but discipline administered as a matter of course.

There are two fundamental schools of thought about why blacks behave worse on the whole than other races in America: the Realists and the Moralists. The Realists, who include such marginalized figures as Charles Murray, Andrew Sullivan, and myself, assume that complex webs of both nature and nurture influence most social phenomena, including racial ones.

Not surprisingly, we Realists tend to be able to come up with more interesting insights and make more accurate predictions because we don't rule out either nature or nurture.

Indeed, large amounts of reality are increasingly off-limits to all but Realists, because the implications of the data are too flagrant to be allowed to be known. For example, nobody except unmentionable Realists like myself has called attention to the stunning numbers in the most recent data releases by the FBI and College Board.

Realism has long been an unpopular and often persecuted position—e.g., after Berkeley psychologist Arthur Jensen published in 1969 a landmark meta-analysis in the *Harvard Education Review* showing that vaunted Great Society programs like Head Start weren't raising black IQs, death threats forced him to move to an undisclosed location far from campus.

Likewise, when Sullivan, as editor of *The New Republic*, published an excerpt from Murray and Richard Herrnstein's *The Bell Curve* in 1994, Sullivan's underlings rebelled, in a prefiguration of today's Woke mutinies by junior staffers. So Andrew simply published 15 (mostly poorly informed) negative commentaries.[17]

But here we are, 26 years later, and 51 years after Jensen's article, and very little has changed.

In contrast, the mainstream Moralists are adamant that *only* nurture can explain racial disparities: Bad decisions must explain bad outcomes.

The Moralists used to be divided into a Right and Left wing, with the rightists blaming poor black decision-making (e.g., their high rate of illegitimacy) and leftists blaming white decision-making (e.g., racial prejudice).

In an intellectual sphere where the Realists occupied the right flank of allowed discourse, that left the Right Moralists in the center of the Overton Window. You might think that would be a nice place to be, but instead the Right Moralists allowed the Realists to be shoved out of the allowable "opinion corridor."

Yet, the exclusion of the Realists didn't make the Left Moralists grateful to the Right Moralists. Instead, the cancellation of the Realists made the Right Moralists no longer the moderates, but instead the New Nazis next on the list to be canceled.

The Right Moralists inevitably got canceled in turn, leaving Ibram X. Kendi and his lowbrow true believers the only polemicists currently entitled to express an opinion on the dominant question of the day.

Good luck, America.

AFTERWORD

What If I'm Right?

What If I'm Right?

Adapted and expanded from two Taki's *articles of the same title, published June 2, 2021 and November 23, 2022*
August 21, 2023

WHAT if I'm more or less right about how the world works?
What if my way of thinking is, in general, more realistic, insightful, and reasonable than the conventional wisdom?
What would that imply?

Note that I dislike thinking of my system of noticing as an ideology that demands certain policies. I don't propound "Sailerism." I lack the ambition and the ego. I am by nature an extreme staff guy rather than a line boss. I've never especially wanted to be a George W. Bush-like "decider." Instead, I like being a noticer. I'd rather explain to you the tradeoffs. Indeed, I most of all want to show you how you can make use of my techniques for figuring out things for yourself.

My basic insight is that noticing isn't all that hard to do if only you let yourself: the world actually is pretty much what it looks like, loath though we may be to admit it.

My main trick for coming up with enough insights to make a living as an unfashionable pundit for 23 years has been to assume that private life facts—what we see with our lying eyes—and public life facts—what the scientific data tell us—are essentially one and the same. There is only one reality out there. We don't live in a gnostic universe in which there is a false reality of mundane cause-and-effect and a horrifying true reality in which unnoticeable racism determines all fates.

In contrast, most commentators assume that issues of daily life, such as deciding where to live, are of a lesser, more sublunary realm than the high public issues, such as the rightness, sanctity, and effectiveness of the demands of Black Lives Matter. So, the unfortunate facts that they prudently observe when making real estate choices for their families about "safe neighborhoods" and "good schools" couldn't possibly have any relevance to the great topics of the day they discuss in the media; only vulgar lowbrows would confuse these two vastly different domains of being.

It's rather like Platonism, except that while Plato believed that there were many "tables" he had sat at and also a "Table" in the Platonic realm of perfection, white progressives assume there is a "crime" problem that they try to sidestep with their money and a "Social Justice" problem that try to solve with other people's money by imposing upon the rest of society the opposite of what they do in their own lives.

In truth, you don't need unfalsifiable gnostic dogmas like "systemic racism" to explain why, say, blacks on average are relatively better at playing cornerback than center in the NFL. Biological and cultural differences explain these and countless other patterns. Indeed, trying to figure out how nature and nurture intertwine in modern America is one of the great challenges of the examined life.

Public intellectuals should try it. It's fun.

When it comes to human behavior, there mostly aren't systematic differences between what your lying eyes tell you and what The Science says.

Instead, there's a continuum between anecdote, anecdata, and data. For instance, if you can recall several examples suggesting a pattern, you might well be able to find large-scale data against which to test your supposition.

Conversely, if there's a strong statistical pattern in the numbers, you should be able to come up with vivid real-life examples of it. If you can't think of any, maybe there is something wrong with the statistically esoteric analysis.

That I assume all truths are connected to all other truths helps explain why my columns often seem to end somewhat abruptly and arbitrarily: I don't act as if I've reached the conclusive end of a topic because, from my perspective, there is no conclusion, just an endless network of cause and effect. So, instead, I merely tend to knock off around dawn when it's long past time to go to bed.

Quite possibly naively, I like to think that my approach to noticing the realities of human societies will eventually seem obvious. So I shouldn't claim too much credit now for what is simply solid empirical thinking applied to the more contentious subjects. I've observed far more ingenuity from base-ball statistics analysts than I've managed to bring to the great issues of society and state. Yet, still, I seem to be able to notice what others cannot.

I like to tell myself I should just keep coming up with more ideas that are (in declining order of importance to me) true, interesting, new, and funny. Eventually, people will notice how much better my approach to reality has been than that of the famous folks winning MacArthur genius grants and try to figure out for themselves how I do it so that they can too.

Or at least that's what I hope.

On the other hand, it's now 2023 and public discourse has just gotten stupider and more socially self-destructive over the course of my career.

Maybe that's partly my fault?

What if I had just kept my mouth shut and, instead of challenging popular pundits to be honest and intelligent, I'd let them work it out for themselves?

After all, while people who know me tend to find I'm an okay guy, people who don't know me tend to hate me. Many opinionators seem enraged over the idea that I might prove right. This tendency to personalize social science disputes has always struck me as dim-witted, but, apparently, the fear "What if Sailer is right?" is infuriating and/or terrifying to many. It's almost as if what gets people mad is my being correct so often.

Thus, when I point out the facts, I'm often greeted with incoherent anger centering on the allegation that I must be a bad person for being so well-informed.

Actually, while I'm of course highly biased, my impression is that I am rather a good person, more Orwell than Waugh.

When I started writing in the 1990s, my views were edgy but not un-known. Intellectually, I'm basically an heir to the debates in the early 1970s among data-driven social scientists, with me being closer to the domestic neoconservatives like James Q. Wilson and Richard Herrnstein. But I also admired liberals like Daniel Patrick Moynihan and James Coleman, as well as socialists like Christopher Jencks.

What's changed since the 1970s?

Basically, all that has happened is that the data has piled up against the Establishment view. I find it's an exaggeration to say that the left totally dominates the social sciences today. I have been a human sciences *aficionado* for the past half century, and I haven't seen much decline in social science findings supporting my general worldview, in part because I constantly adapt to new findings, but also because new advances have typically validated the best old research. For example, the genetic revolution of the 21st century has mostly vindicated the best human scientists of the second half of the 20th century.

Granted, journalists tend to not grasp that current dogmas like "Race does not exist" are obfuscations to keep geneticists from getting persecuted by know-nothings. But if you read the scientific journals carefully, you will know what's what.

Yet, instead of changing minds, the passing of the years has only made the dominant discourse ever more absurdly antiquarian. For example, the failure of property values to boom in black neighborhoods in the 55 years since redlining was abolished in 1968 has not made it more acceptable to point out that if blacks want higher home values (which it's not clear they do), they should work harder on being better neighbors. Instead, we hear ever more often about FDR's redlining as if that's what is really driving the real estate market in 2023.

My approach in explaining human society has been to follow the general line of Occam's Razor that "It is vain to do with more what can be done with fewer," or that the simplest feasible explanation is less likely to be contrived for political purposes than a more complicated Occam's Butterknife rationalization. For example, home values today tend to be determined by current crime rates and school test scores, not by what FDR did 85 years ago.

And as more data continues to accumulate over the decades, my depiction of the way the world works seems to have a better track record than more fashionable theories. Now, it's not that I'm infallible. Still, (a) I like to argue, and (b) I don't like to lose. So, I look hard for the strongest evidence so that I can make winning arguments.

And when I lose, rather than double down, I usually change my mind.

Sure, I have the usual human reluctance to admit I was wrong. But I try to deploy that in a constructive direction.

If I find, for example, that some sophomoric policy I advocated as a sophomore in 1978 can't be justified today, I tend to assert that that may not be because I was wrong then; instead, times have changed since then. For example, many of the Reagan-Thatcher ideas I liked in the late 1970s were successful in the 1980s-1990s, leaving us today with new problems needing new solutions.

Perhaps I should admit that my callow views in 1978 were utterly wrong, but my approach seems more pragmatic and replicable.

Moreover, I would encourage intellectuals to try to subscribe to a form of vulgar Hegelianism in their thinking that I've found very useful: If you hold a thesis for what seem like good reasons, and somebody counters with a well-argued antithesis, you have three options:

- Reject the antithesis (the most common).
- Convert to the antithesis (the most dramatic).
- Look for a synthesis that makes sense of both your thesis and the other guy's antithesis (usually, the hardest but most productive).

For example:

- Thesis: A racial group is a taxonomical subspecies.
- Antithesis: A racial group is a biologically nonexistent social construct!
- Synthesis: A racial group is a partly inbred extended family.

So, what if I'm right? How would the world look different?

Well, it wouldn't. I've taken pains to make my worldview correspond with how the world actually is.

What policies are implied by my realistic view of humanity?

To my mind, nothing terribly new (although out of fashion): In general, we need rule of law, equal protection of the laws, and other old-time principles.

For instance, the fact that African-Americans seem to have a particular tendency toward criminal violence, for whatever combinations of reasons of nature and nurture, suggests that they need law and order even more, not less, than do the rest of us. As you may recall, we tried in 2020 reducing the rule of law over blacks during Black Lives Matter's "racial reckoning." The result of less policing was that in 2021 44% more blacks died by homicide than in 2019 and 39% more died in traffic fatalities.

On the other hand, the one thing that really scares me is that progressive intellectuals seem to assume that if modern science demonstrates that the races often differ genetically, well, that just proves Hitler was right and therefore genocide is the only alternative. This malevolent insanity on the part of orthodox liberal thinkers alarms me.

Fortunately, I don't think they are serious about their genocidal logic.

My best guess is that what white liberal intellectuals really believe at the core of their being is that their having a high IQ makes them better than other whites. After all, it's natural for each human to assume that his best traits make him superior to other people. But it also sounds kind of racist: if being smarter makes liberal pundits better than other whites, then if whites average a higher IQ than blacks, does that make whites better than blacks?

So they bellow that The Science has *proven* beyond a shadow of a doubt that all races (which don't exist) have equal IQs (which aren't scientific). Or something. And anybody who giggles is a horrible person and probably Hitler.

My suggestion: The dominant intellectuals should do some soul-searching and stop projecting their own complexes onto others.

Despite the success my methods have demonstrated over the years at explicating some of the major public affairs conundrums of this century, the answers I come up with are widely considered unmentionable.

Why?

The usual responses I'm given by my critics are either:

- My findings are rejected by all experts as completely untrue, or:
- Everybody already knows that what you are saying is true, they just don't want to talk about it.

Among those who assert the latter, I am told that we shouldn't mention the truth because either:

- The facts have no possible policy implications, or:
- The facts have overwhelmingly horrible policy implications, such as the logical necessity of reimposing slavery or instituting genocide.

The former strikes me as obtuse and the latter as insane and/or evil.

When I try to think through the policy implications that would flow from honest public discussion of American realities, it strikes me that it could be useful if more people knew more about what they are discussing.

Knowing the facts doesn't prove one set of values is better than another—that's what politics is for deciding—but it can help you avoid making things worse than they have to be.

For example, consider affirmative action. Except when the Supreme Court considers it, the mainstream media has tried to cover up the existence of racial preferences since 1969, so the sophistication of our debate on the implications has not much progressed...including at the Supreme Court.

When surveyed, thumping majorities of the public incoherently endorse contradictory policies. In a recent *Washington Post* poll, American voted 63-36 in support of:

Q: Would you support or oppose the Supreme Court banning colleges and universities from considering a student's race and ethnicity when making decisions about student admissions?

But then the same respondents turned around and went 64-36 for:

Q: In general, do you think programs designed to increase the racial diversity of students on college campuses are a good thing or a bad thing?

It's hard to be sure what people are imagining about affirmative action.

Most likely, they are largely ignorant of how large the racial gaps are at the high end and how hard colleges have been toiling to squeeze in more underqualified blacks for the past half century, with little efficacy other than by simply putting a massive thumb on the scale for blacks.

For instance, the previous really important Supreme Court decision on affirmative action, Sandra Day O'Connor's controlling opinion in the 2003 *Grutter* case, blithely assumed that racial gaps would become too trivial to worry about anymore by 2028:

It has been 25 years since Justice Powell first approved the use of race to further an interest in student body diversity in the context of public higher education.... We expect that 25 years from now, the use of racial preferences will no longer be necessary to further the interest approved today.

Today, 20 of those 25 years have elapsed, and Justice O'Connor's hoped-for happy ending is more chimerical than ever. But how many are aware of the real numbers and their implications?

In particular, almost nobody is cognizant of how the extraordinary rise in college admission test scores among Asians in this century has worsened the chances of blacks to be admitted under any colorblind system. While whites are seven times more likely than blacks to score 1400 (out of 1600) or higher on the SAT, Asians are 24 times more likely.

You aren't supposed to talk about these realities, so virtually nobody knows about them other than college presidents, who all appear to support quotas. I like to joke that just as in the old Nicolas Cage movie in which the new president of the United States gets the key to the *President's Book of Secrets* that divulges what really happened at Roswell and Dealey Plaza, there's a *Harvard President's Book of Secrets* that turns out to be a well-thumbed, dog-eared copy of *The Bell Curve*.

AFTERWORD

If more people knew the facts, what could be done?

One possibility is that the SAT and ACT have broken down under the extreme test prepping paid for by so many Tiger Mothers, but that the tests could be fixed. Unfortunately, rather than attempt reform we are far more likely in the current climate to ban tests as racist than to seriously investigate how to improve them under the Asian onslaught.

Other improvements to college admissions could be undertaken. For example, Asians have been disproportionately exploiting the simplistic custom of college admission departments to grant one extra point of high school grade point average to students taking Advanced Placement classes. A study of University of California students found that a half-point boost generates more accurate predictions of student performance in college than the current system.

More broadly, we should reconsider the quantity of legal immigration in light of how much harder it is making it for African-Americans to earn elite status for themselves without race preferences. American blacks had a hard enough time competing with American whites. Putting them up against ever more of the cleverest and most ambitious of four billion Asians is increasingly a wipe-out.

To the extent that we decide we need preferences to admit enough blacks to elite colleges, we should use strict racial quotas that let in only the best of each race rather than the current trend toward wrecking the admission system to make evidence of race preferences fuzzier.

And let's stop the pretending that has been rampant ever since the 1978 *Bakke* decision exalted "diversity" as the excuse for violating the 14th Amendment's requirement of equal protection of the laws that affirmative action makes colleges more intellectually stimulating, when obviously the opposite has proven true. Quotas have helped make colleges minefields of cancel culture by dragooning onto campus insecure and resentful masses of racially preferred students out to punish anyone who alludes to the race gaps that are American society's central fact. Instead, if we are going to have quotas, under-qualified preference beneficiaries should be frankly instructed to be thankful for their privileges.

Similarly, American institutions currently waste huge amounts of effort interrogating themselves for racism whenever their objective systems find that blacks behave worse on the whole than other races. For example, New York City's Administration for Children's Services is currently torturing itself to discover the source of the racism that must be behind why "Black families are seven times as likely as white families to be accused of child maltreatment," according to a breathless *New York Times* article.

But if you read deep enough into the investigation about racism at this office, you find:

> Most A.C.S. caseworkers are Black, as is most leadership in the agency's Division of Child Protection, the agency said.

And

> A *New York Times* analysis of 83 child homicides from 2016 to 2022 found that Black children in the city were killed by family members at about seven times the rate for white and Asian children and three times the rate for Hispanic children.

So what's the worst that can happen when Child Protective Services guts itself over its own charges of racial inequity?

I mean, besides more murdered children?

But what if noticing became widespread?

Are liberals correct that awareness of reality would inevitably lead Americans to conclude that Hitler was right?

First, the Holocaust targeted Ashkenazis, the most intelligent ethnicity known to world history.

Second, as usual, my mind wanders to baseball statistics analogies. In September 1998, Harvard professor Stephen Jay Gould, author of the 1981 *The Mismeasure of Man* that many assume debunked 1994's *The Bell Curve*, published an op-ed in the *Wall Street Journal* celebrating Mark McGwire breaking Roger Maris's single-season home run record. Gould eloquently opined of McGwire's feat:

> When faced with such an exceptional accomplishment, we long to discover particular reasons. But no special cause need be sought beyond the good fortune of many effectively random moments grafted upon the guaranteed achievements of the greatest home-run hitter in the history of baseball.

I immediately sent Gould a fax to the effect of, "Nah, McGwire's on the juice."

He did not reply.

Today, of course, all baseball fans know that was the Steroid Era.

What were the effects of the public discovering this unwelcome truth?

Well, some naive children had their hero-worshiping hearts broken, a number of prominent individuals and institutions were publicly embarrassed, and the game had to adjust some of its rules. But, mostly, life went on.

What if Gould's *Mismeasure of Man* became, in the fullness of time, as disproved and as discredited as his McGwire worship? Would it be the end of the world to discover that Herrnstein and Murray were more correct than Gould about race and IQ?

To explore this question, let's focus in on one small subsection of the PED years in which, to my surprise, I wound up largely winning the debate and changing highbrow opinion: the gender gap in Olympics track. In my 1997 article "Track and Battlefield," I pointed out that the then-celebrated convergence of times between men and women runners ended when stricter steroid testing was instituted after Ben Johnson was caught loaded with steroids while setting a world record in the 1988 Seoul Olympics 100 meter dash and the East German women's team collapsed along with the Berlin Wall. Why? Because women got a bigger bang for the buck from these synthetic variants of masculine hormones, so they'd been improving more than men had.

For a number of years after that I would see articles repeating the 1990s nostrum that science had shown that male and female athletic performance would continue to equalize. I'd send them my article and occasionally I'd even get a response that, yes, I was probably right.

Over time, I stopped seeing prognostications of convergence among all but the most ill-informed in the media.

What were the dire side effects of people learning the truth?

Did high school girls stop running in despair? Were women's sports banned? No.

The main effect, so far as I can tell, has been a beneficial one for women's sports: when the transgender push in the press started around 2013 and ex-men like MMA fighter Fallon Fox, whom the *New York Times* championed to be allowed to beat up women for money, and Penn swimmer Lia Thomas began intruding themselves into women's sports, the autogynephilia fetishists found themselves disarmed of the old feminist talking point that women would soon equal men on the playing fields. Only the silliest social constructionists still believed that. Therefore, the trans dudes couldn't persuasively argue that it was only a matter of time before women were as good as men, so what did it matter if female impersonators jumped the gun a little?

Fortunately, defenders of women's sports were able to persuasively argue that letting biological men crush women would be a permanent disaster. And, as of 2023, they've won most of these debates and appear to be making steady progress on banning fetishists from making a farce out of women's athletics.

That strikes me as the most likely model for what would be the result of more of my ideas coming to be accepted as sensible: neither utopia nor apocalypse, but some improvement in the rules and discourse. And, perhaps most valuably, various even worse new ideas that we haven't yet imagined would be headed off at the pass.

That may not be the most decisive way to conclude this book. Perhaps I'm merely knocking off around dawn because it's time for bed.

Yet, ultimately, I believe that the truth is better for us than ignorance, lies, or wishful thinking.

Notes and References

Editor's note: Below citations and references were culled from the original articles and still extant hyperlinks where possible. However, some of the articles were written before the use of links became commonplace and the source material has been lost to time.

Chapter 1: Citizenism

1. Margaret Blakely Alverson. *Sixty Years of California Song.* (1913)
2. Emilio Parrado. "Hispanic fertility, immigration, and race in the twenty-first century." *Race and social problems,* Vol. 4-1, 25 Feb. 2012.
3. Pat Buchanan. "Buchanan on the Stump in Arizona." Phoenix, 19 Jan. 2000.
4. Charles Murray. *Income Inequality and IQ.* (AEI Press, 1997)
5. Linda Gottfredson. "Equal potential: A collective fraud." *Society,* Vol. 37-5 (2000).
6. Charles Murray. "IQ Will Put You in Your Place." *Sunday Times,* UK, 25 May 1997.
7. Christine Kennealy. "'The Making of Intelligence' by Ken Richardson." *Salon,* 9 Aug. 2000.
8. Alicia Montgomery. "Too Slow for Death Row." *Salon,* 9 Aug. 2000.
9. Ibid, Murray, "IQ Will..."

Chapter 2: Invade the World, Invite the World

1. Andrea Elliott. "More Muslims Arrive in U.S., After 9/11 Dip." *New York Times,* 10 Sep. 2006.
2. Daniel Larison. "Barnes: GOP Should Be the Party of Immigration, Imperialism and Insolvency." *Eunomia,* 13 Mar. 2006.
3. Daniel Benjamin. "President Cheney." *Slate,* 7 Nov. 2005.
4. "Dahoum." PBS, Lawrence of Arabia, The Players. http://www.pbs.org/lawrenceofarabia/players/dahoum.html
5. Paul Blustein and Richard Leiby. "Europeans Resist Wolfowitz for World Bank." *Washington Post,* 18 Mar. 2005
6. Eric Kaufmann. "Is tribalism racist? Antiracism norms and immigration." *London School of Economics, British Politics and Policy,* 9 Jul. 2017.
7. Ezra Klein. "The Vox Conversation: Bernie Sanders." *Vox,* 28 Jul. 2015.
8. Megan Garber. "In Switzerland, You Can Be Denied Citizenship for Being Too Annoying." *The Atlantic,* 14 Jan. 2017.
9. "Label drops Austin band Dream Machine over comments on immigration, feminism." *Austin-American Statesman,* 23 Jun. 2017.
10. Steve Sailer. "CIA ex-in-law of Bomb Brothers confirms one of my theories." *iSteve,* 27 Apr. 2013.
11. Seda Sezer and Dan Williams. "Erdogan vows graft scandal in Turkey won't topple him." *Washington Post,* 29 Dec. 2013.
12. Embassy Turkey. "Gulen - Turkey's Invisible Man Casts Long Shadow." *Wikileaks Cable,* 09ANKARA1722_a, 4 Dec. 2009.

13. Charlotte Oberti. "Turkey's Gülen: Opposition movement or cult?" *France24*, 28 Dec. 2013.

14. Tom Wolfe. "The 'Me' Decade and the Third Great Awakening." *New York Magazine*, 23 Aug. 1976.

15. *WernerErhard.com*, Work and Ideas. 2007. http://www.wernererhard.com/work.html

16. Hakan Yeşilova. "'Gray domination' and Turkey's civil rights challenge." *Today's Zaman*, 25 Dec. 2013.

17. Martha Woodall and Claudio Gatti. "U.S. charter-school network with Turkish link draws federal attention." *Philadelphia Inquirer*, 20 Mar. 2011.

18. Sibel Edmonds. "Additional Omitted Points in CIA-Gulen coverage & A Note from 'The Insider'." *Newsbud*, 11 Jan. 2011.

19. Steve Sailer. "Did Tsarnaevs get asylum through Deep State nepotism and string-pulling?" *iSteve*, 27 Apr. 2013.

20. "World Population Prospects 2020" *United Nations*, Population Division. https://population.un.org/wpp/

21. Steve Sailer. "Rep. Omar: 'This Is Not Going to be the Country of White People.'" *Unz*, 1 May 2019.

22. Steve Sailer. "758 Million People Want to Migrate." *Unz*, 10 Dec. 2018.

23. Mark. J. Perry. "Tucker Carlson on Ilhan Omar vs. Ayaan Hirsi Ali." *AEI*, 11 Jul. 2019.

24. Steve Sailer. "Immigration and the Deep State." *Taki's*, 17 Jan. 2018.

25. Steve Sailer. "Somali Immigrant Goes Back to Somalia to Make It a Better Place by Changing the Racist Media Narrative About Somalia, Gets Blown Up by Terrorists." *Unz*, 15 Jul. 2019.

26. "By 2100, half of babies born worldwide are expected to be born in Africa." *Pew Research Center*, 17 Jun. 2019.

27. Fumbuka Ng'wanakilala. "President urges Tanzania's women to 'set ovaries free', have more babies to boost economy." *Reuters*, 10 Jul. 2019.

Chapter 3: The Sailer Strategy

1. Nancy Cleeland. "AFL-CIO Calls for Amnesty for Illegal U.S. Workers." *LA Times*, 17 Feb. 2000.

2. Paul Caron. "Median Income Data Mirrors Red State-Blue State Divide." *TaxProf Blog*, 3 May 2005.

3. Steve Sailer. *iSteve*, May 2004 archive, based on an analysis of the 2003 "National Assessment of Educational Progress" report.

4. Steve Sailer. "Democrats Recoil From GOP's Electoral Secret: Marriage Plus Children." *VDARE*, 12 Dec. 2004.

5. Ibid

6. Steve Sailer. "Hu's Rule in Action—Why The GOP Won't Be Getting The Asian Vote, Either." *VDARE*, 21 Dec. 2007.

7. John Derbyshire. "The Asian Vote 2000." *VDARE*, 15 Nov. 2000.

8. Steve Sailer. "GOP Future Depends on Winning Larger Share of the White Vote." *VDARE*, 28 Nov. 2000.

9. Steve Sailer. "Stomping On The 2004 Exit Poll's Grave (And Some Other Myths)." *VDARE*, 25 Jan. 2005.

10. Nate Silver. "Will The Electoral College Doom The Democrats Again?" *FiveThirtyEight*, 14 Nov. 2016.

Chapter 4: Villains & Heroes

1. Ta-Nehisi Coates. "My Heroes. Your Stamps." *The Atlantic*, 27 Dec. 2012.

2. Roger Kimball. "The Perversions of M. Foucault." *New Criterion*, Mar. 1993.

3. Noam Chomsky and Michel Foucalt. "Human Nature: Justice versus Power." Eindhoven University of Technology, Netherlands, 28 Nov. 1971.

4. Gregory Cochran. "Gay Genes." *West Hunter*, 23 Sep. 2019.

5. Daniel Zamora and Kévin Boucaud-Victoire. " How Michel Foucault Got Neoliberalism So Wrong." *Jacobin*, 6 Sep. 2019.

6. "Sexuality Morality and the Law." *Michel Foucault: politics, philosophy, culture: interviews and other writings*. Ed. by Lawrence D. Kritzman. (Routledge, 1988)

7. James Miller. *The Passion of Michel Foucault*. (Simon & Schuster, 1993).

8. Justus Reid Weiner. "'My Beautiful Old House' and other Fabrications by Edward Said." *Commentary*, Sep. 1999.

9. Sunnie Kim. "Edward Said Accused of Stoning in South Lebanon." *Columbia Spectator*, 19 Jul. 2000.

10. Ethan Trex. "Five Things You Didn't Know about Billy Wilder." *Mental Floss*, 24 Jul. 2009.

Chapter 5: Human Biodiversity

1. Steve Sailer. "Commentary: Oscar observations." *UPI National*, 25 Mar. 2002.

2. Karen Wickersham. "Studying Species by Examining the Evolution of the Canidae Family." *Woodrow Wilson Biology Institute*, 1995.

3. Jon Entine. "The Straw Man of 'Race'." *The World & I* Vol. 16-9, 1 Sep. 2001.

4. R.A. Kittles et al. "Extent of linkage disequilibrium between the androgen receptor gene CAG and GGC repeats in human populations: implications for prostate cancer risk." *Human Genetics* Vol. 109-3, 2001.

5. Kevin G. Hall. "Brazil to start affirmative action program on race bias." *Miami Herald*, 6 Jun. 2002.

6. M.B. Petersen, Daniel Sznycer, et al. "The Ancestral Logic of Politics: Upper-Body Strength Regulates Men's Assertion of Self-Interest Over Economic Redistribution." *Psychological Science*, Vol. 24-7, 13 May 2013.

Chapter 6: The Level Playing Field

1. Komar and Melamid. "America's Most Wanted Paintings." *Alternative Museum*, New York, 1994.

2. Jay Appleton. *The Experience of Landscape*. (John Wiley & Sons, 1975)

3. Celia Woolfrey. "One man went to mow." *The Guardian*, 15 Sep. 2000.

NOTES AND REFERENCES

4. Edmund Burke. *Philosophical Enquiry into the Origin of our Ideas of the Sublime and Beautiful.* 1757.

5. Steve Sailer. "Up the Amazon–Vamps & Tramps: New Essays, by Camille Paglia." *National Review*, 31 Dec. 1994.

6. Malcolm Gladwell. "Complexity and the Ten-Thousand-Hour Rule." *The New Yorker,* 21 Aug. 2013.

7. Dan Mclaughlin. *TheDanPlan.com.*

Chapter 7: Half Full Glass

1. Steve Sailer. "Race Relations: The Myth Of The Military Model." *VDARE*, 26 Jan. 2003.

2. P.L. Roth, C.A Bevier, et al. "Ethnic group differences in cognitive ability in employment and educational settings: A meta-analysis." *Personnel Psychology*, Vol. 54-2, Jun. 2001.

3. Paul Gross, "The apotheosis of Stephen Jay Gould." *New Criterion*, Oct. 2002.

4. At the time this article was originally published in 2007 the data was still somewhat unclear. In 2017, a study published in *Nature* identified 22 genes responsible for human intelligence. Sniekers, Stringer, Watanabe, et al. "Genome-wide association meta-analysis of 78,308 individuals identifies new loci and genes influencing human intelligence." *Nat Genet* 49, 22 May, 2017.

5. Steve Sailer. "Pioneer Fundophobia." *VDARE*, 12 Dec. 2001.

6. International data is drawn from "Lynn and Vanhanen's *IQ and the Wealth of Nations* (2002). Other major data sources include Roth and Bevier, Ibid.

7. See later in this chapter, "A Few Thoughts on IQ and the Wealth of Nations"

8. See Chapter 7, "It's All Relative: Putting Race in It's Proper Perspective."

9. Steve Sailer. "The Case Of The Truth-Telling (But Racially-Incorrect) Teacher." *VDARE*, 27. Oct. 2002.

10. Nanette Asimov. "Summit called to address racial disparities in academic performance." *SF Chronicle*, 12 Nov. 2007.

11. Joseph Kahn. "Losing Faith: Globalization Proves Disappointing." *New York Times*, 21 Mar. 2002.

12. Steve Sailer. "Igbo Supremacy." *Unz*, 21 May 2019.

13. Alfred W. Crosby. *The Measure of Reality: Quantification and Western Society, 1250-1600*. Cambridge University Press, 1997.

14. See Chapter 13, "The Racial Reckoning on the Roads."

15. Steve Sailer. "New Racial Admixture and Cognitive Performance Study." *Unz*, 1 Jul. 2021.

16. Jordan Lasker, Bryan Pesta, John Fuerst, and Emil O.W. Kirkegaard. "Global Ancestry and Cognitive Ability." *Psych*, Vol. 1-1, Aug. 2019.

Chapter 8: The Blank Screen

1. David Maraniss. *Barack Obama: The Story.* (Simon & Schuster, 1992)
2. Ibid.

425

3. Steve Sailer. "David Willetts' The Pinch: U.K. Cabinet Minister's Discreet But Devastating Dissent On Immigration." *VDARE*, 23 May 2010.

Chapter 9: World War T

1. Nathaniel Frank. "Note to Mary Matalin's Gay Friends: She Won't Hide You in a Gay Holocaust." *Slate*, 20 Jan. 2014.
2. Greg Bishop. "A Pioneer, Reluctantly." *New York Times*, 10 May 2013.
3. Lynn Conway. "Introducing Lynn Conway, Prof. of Electrical Engineering & Computer Science, Emerita, University of Michigan, Ann Arbor." *University of Michigan*. http://ai.eecs.umich.edu/people/conway/BioSketch.html
4. Bill Simmons. "The Dr. V Story: A Letter From the Editor." *Grantland*, 10 Jan. 2014.
5. Christina Kahrl. "What Grantland Got Wrong." *Grantland*, 20 Jan. 2014.
6. Mencius Moldbug. "Technology, communism and the Brown Scare." *Unqualified Reservations*, 13 Sep. 2013.
7. Greg Bishop. "A Pioneer, Reluctantly." *New York Times*, 10 May 2013.
8. Warren Throckmorton. "What Kind of Woman is Caitlyn Jenner? Part One of a Q&A on Autogynephilia with Michael Bailey." *Patheos*, 11 Jun. 2015.
9. Philip Roth. "An Open Letter to Wikipedia." *The New Yorker*, 6 Sep. 2012.
10. Gregory Cochran. "The Fluidity of Race." *West Hunt*, 6 Jan. 2015.
11. Jenée Desmond-Harris. "Malcolm Gladwell Reflects on His Afro and Snap Judgments." *The Root*, 24 Jan. 2011.
12. Steve Sailer. "Jeb Bush Registered to Vote as 'Hispanic' in 2009." *Unz*, 6 Apr. 2015.
13. See Steve Sailer. "Nobody Knows Nothing." *Unz*, 29 May 2011.

Chapter 10: Sailer's Law of Female Journalism

1. Hanna Rosin. "Hello, My Name Is Stephen Glass, and I'm Sorry." *The New Republic*, 10 Nov. 2014.
2. Richard Bradley. "Is the Rolling Stone Story True?" *Shots in the Dark*, 24 Nov. 2014.
3. Samuel Hughes. "Through a Glass Darkly." *Pennsylvania Gazette*, 1 Nov. 1998.
4. T. Rees Shapiro and Justin Jouvenal. "Jesse Matthew pleads guilty in slayings of college students." *Washington Post*, 2 Mar. 2016.
5. Steve Sailer. "Breaking National News from NYT: 12-Year-Old Black Girl Arrives Home with New Hairdo But When Her Grandma Objects, Girl Blames Haircut on 'Nappy' Hair-Hating White Male Racists." *Unz*, 27 Sep. 2019.
6. Christine Hauser and Neil Vigdor. "Black Virginia Girl Says White Classmates Cut Her Dreadlocks on Playground." *New York Times*, 27 Sep. 2019.
7. Steve Sailer. "World War Hair." "The Finnish Front Opens in World War H." "English Front Opens in World War H." "Bimbx Who Took Down Richard Stallman: Let's Talk About My Hair." *Unz*, Aug.-Sep. 2019.

Chapter 11: Jews and Gentiles

1. See Chapter 9, "A Few thoughts on IQ and the Wealth of Nations."
2. "Jewish Nobel Prize Laureates." *Israel Science and Technology Directory*. https://www.science.co.il/nobel-prizes/

NOTES AND REFERENCES

3. "Jewish Nobel Prize Winners." *Jinfo.org*. http://www.jinfo.org/Nobel_Prizes.html
4. "Lou Boudreau." *Jew or Not Jew*, 16 Oct. 2009.
5. Steve Sailer. "Charles Murray's Jewish Genius." *VDARE*, 8 Apr. 2007.
6. David Samuels. "Assimilation and Its Discontents: How success ruined the New York Jew." *New York Magazine*, 29 Sep. 2008.
7. Noah Millman. "Monday, March 13, 2006." *Gideon's Blog*, 13 Mar. 2006.
8. Steve Sailer. "Questioning Ricci: Time To Abandon The EEOC's Four-Fifths Rule." *VDARE*, 26 Apr. 2009.
9. Steve Sailer. "UPDATED: 'The Atlantic 50:' Pundit demographics." *iSteve*, 24 Sep. 2009.
10. John Derbyshire. "Kings of the Deal." *JohnDerbyshire.com*, Jun. 2012.
11. Joel Stein. "Who Runs Hollywood? C'mon." *LA Times*, 19 Dec. 2008.
12. Kevin McDonald. "Heidi Does Long Beach: The SPLC vs. Academic Freedom." *VDARE*, 14 Nov. 2006.
13. Steve Sailer. "Prohibition: Twin Sister of Women's Suffrage." *Taki's*, 18 Sep. 2013, and "The Original Nature Boys." Taki's, 27 Jun. 2012.
14. Mark Harris. "Excerpt: Inside 'The Graduate.'" *Entertainment Weekly*, 10 Feb. 2008.
15. Rob Eshman. "'The Wolf' and the Jewish problem." *Jewish Journal*, 31 Dec. 2013.
16. Jim Murray. "Color of Money Will Get PGA's Attention." *LA Times*, 29 Jul. 1990.
17. Bradley S. Klein. "Demise of the Jewish club." *GolfWeek*, USA Today Sports, 22 Jun. 2009.
18. Alan Shipnuck. "The Westside Six In Los Angeles There Are Only A Half Dozen Oases Where The Rich And Famous Do Golf." *Sports Illustrated*, 21 Aug. 1995.

Chapter 12: Coalition of the Fringes

1. Laura Ly. "Oberlin College cancels classes to address racial incidents." *CNN*, 5 Mar. 2013.
2. See Chapter 11, "A Specter is Haunting the Clinton Administration"
3. Richard Pérez-Peña and Trip Gabriel. "Racist Incidents Stun Campus and Halt Classes at Oberlin." *New York Times,* 4 Mar. 2013.
4. Wendy Thermos. "Teacher Gets Prison in Hate Crime Hoax." *LA Times*, 16 Dec. 2004.
5. Ibid, Richard Pérez-Peña and Trip Gabriel.
6. Anne Hull. "In Mississippi, death of politician Marco McMillian stirs old civil-rights fears." *Washington Post*, 8 Mar. 2013.
7. Gabrielle Levy. "Mayoral candidate beaten, burned." *UPI*, 5 Mar. 2013.
8. Campbell Robertson and Robbie Brown. "Coroner Disputes Family's Account of Mississippi Mayoral Candidate's Death." *New York Times*, 5 Mar. 2013.
9. "New Details Emerge in Matthew Shepard Murder." *ABC News*, 26 Nov. 2004.
10. Dan Savage. "The Thrill of Living Dangerously." *Out*, Mar. 1999.
11. Tucker Carlson. "Tucker: MAGA hat-wearing students smeared by media." *Fox News, Tucker Carlson Tonight*, 21 Jan. 2019. Youtube.com.
12. Goldie Taylor. "Boys Will Be Boys. Covington's Showed Yet Again Why Only White Boys Can Smirk Through That." *Daily Beast*, 20 Jan. 2019.

13. Steve Sailer. "Today's America in One Picture." *Unz*, 17 Apr. 2018.

14. Laura M. Holson. "Hundreds in Oakland Turn Out to BBQ While Black." *New York Times*, 21 May 2018.

15. Steve Sailer. "NYT's Hunt for a Great White Defendant in Texas Hits a Snag." *Unz*, 5 Jan. 2019.

16. Steve Sailer. "The Megaphone in One Graph." *Unz*, 13 May 2016.

17. Reference to the 2014 UVA Rape Hoax. See Chapter 11, "A Rape Hoax for Book Lovers."

18. Steve Sailer. "Different Hoax for Different Folks." *Taki's*, 15 Nov. 2017.

Chapter 13: Sailer's Law of Mass Shootings

1. Steve Sailer. "The Racial Reckoning's New Normal: 50 Murders Per Day." *Taki's*, 31 Mar. 2021.

2. National Center for Statistics and Analysis. (May, 2018). "Early estimate of motor vehicle traffic fatalities for 2017 (Crash Stats Brief Statistical Summary. Report No. DOT HS 812 542)." Washington, DC: National Highway Traffic Safety Administration.

3. Steve Sailer. "FBI: Blacks Made Up 55.9% of Known Murder Offenders in 2019." *Unz*, 29 Sep. 2020.

4. Jim Salter. "Fewer 2020 traffic stops in Missouri, but disparity remains." *Associated Press*, 1 Jun. 2021.

5. Steve Sailer. "Black Lives Murdered." *Taki's*, 3 Mar. 2021.

6. John Podhoretz. "The Most Disgusting Sentence Yet Written About Katrina..." *National Review*, 5 Sep. 2005.

7. Steve Sailer. "FBI: Murders Up 4,901 in 2020, Black Share of Known Murder Offenders Reaches Record 56.5%." *Unz*, 27 Sep. 2021.

8. UNODC, Global Study on Homicide 2019 (Vienna, 2019).

9. Steve Sailer. "What's the Matter With Wisconsin?" *Taki's*, 17 Aug. 2016.

10. Steve Sailer. "Black Share of Homicide Offenders Grew from 46% in Early 1980s to 64% in 2020." *Unz*, 6 Feb. 2023.

11. Raj Chetty, Nathaniel Hendren, Maggie R. Jones, and Sonya Porter. "Race and Economic Opportunity in the United States: An Intergenerational Perspective." *Quarterly Journal of Economics*, 135-2, 2020.

12. Steve Sailer. "Breakthrough study: Poor blacks tend to stay poor, black." *iSteve*, 24 Jul. 2013.

13. Emily Badger, Claire Cain Miller, Adam Pearce and Kevin Quealy. "Extensive Data Shows Punishing Reach of Racism for Black Boys." *New York Times*, Upshot, 19 Mar. 2018.

14. Dylan Matthews. "The massive new study on race and economic mobility in America, explained." *Vox*, 21 Mar. 2018.

Chapter 14: The Great Awokening

1. Norman Podhoretz. "My Negro Problem—And Ours." *Commentary*, Feb. 1963.

NOTES AND REFERENCES

2. Ruben Castaneda. "Officer Liable in Student's Killing." *Washington Post*, 20 Jan. 2006.

3. Ruben Castaneda. "Washington's Ferguson Next Door." *Politico Magazine*, 8 Sep. 2014.

4. Ta-Nehisi Coates. "The problem of police brutality." *The Atlantic*, 2 Jul. 2008.

5. Joanna Cripps. "What is Deaf Culture?" *Deaf Culture Centre*.

6. Sara Novic. "Don't Fear a Deafer Planet." *New York Times*, 10 Oct. 2021.

7. Oliver Sacks. *Seeing Voices*. University of California Press, 1989.

8. Robert Bartholomew. "The Girls Who Caught Tourette's from TikTok." *Psychology Today*, 6 Oct. 2021.

9. instead of the heart - Steve Sailer. "Biden Suggests Cops Shoot Unarmed Persons Coming at Them with a Knife in the Leg Instead of the Heart." *Unz*, 2 Jun. 2020.

10. But we need it - Steve Sailer. "The General Giap-Style Master Strategist of These Riots Was the 'We Need Our Weaves' Lady." *Unz*, 31 May 2020.

11. Andrew Sullivan. "Why Is Wokeness Winning?" *The Weekly Dish*, 16 Oct. 2020.

12. David Montgomery. "The Anti-Racist Revelations of Ibram X. Kendi." *Washington Post*, 14 Oct. 2019.

13. Steve Sailer. "FBI: Blacks Made Up 55.9% of Known Murder Offenders in 2019." *Unz*, 29 Sep. 2020.

14. Steve Sailer. "Asian Supremacy." *Taki's*, 7 Oct. 2020.

15. Sean Rameswaram and Lauren Katz. "Professor Ibram X. Kendi on why it's not enough to admit when you're being racist: 'Challenge those racist ideas.'" *Vox*, 1 Jun. 2020.

16. Steve Sailer. "San Diego Goes Anti-Racist, Kendi-Style." *Unz*, 17 Oct. 2020.

17. "In Response to 'Race, Genes and I.Q.'" *The New Republic*, 31 Oct. 1994.

Index

INDEX

INDEX

About the Author

STEVE SAILER is an opinion journalist focusing on the major controversies of the age, such as crime, immigration, feminism, transgenderism, the Great Awokening, the Racial Reckoning, and human biodiversity. His willingness to follow the findings of both the human sciences and his lying eyes to their inconvenient implications has made him one of the more influential social and political commentators of his generation. Sailer is a true pundit's pundit, whose ideas, while seldom explicitly cited, are read and pondered by America's leading public intellectuals on both the right and the left. Known both for the notoriety of his trenchant insights and the normality of his personality, he lives in his native suburban Southern California, where he enjoys golf and lawn care.